W9-AQI-051

CONTRABAND

SMUGGLING AND THE BIRTH OF
THE AMERICAN CENTURY

ANDREW WENDER COHEN

W. W. NORTON & COMPANY

New York | London

For information about permission to reproduce selections from this book,
write to Permissions, W. W. Norton & Company, Inc.,
500 Fifth Avenue, New York, NY 10110

For information about special discounts for bulk purchases, please contact
W. W. Norton Special Sales at specialsales@wwnorton.com or 800-233-4830

Manufacturing by Courier Westford
Book design by Chris Welch
Production manager: Louise Mattarelliano

Library of Congress Cataloging-in-Publication Data

Cohen, Andrew Wender, 1968–
Contraband : smuggling and the birth of the American century / Andrew Wender Cohen.
pages cm
Includes bibliographical references and index.
ISBN 978-0-393-06533-6 (hardcover)
1. Smuggling—United States—History. 2. United States—Commerce—History. I. Title.
HJ6690.C56 2015
364.1'3360973—dc23
2015009530

W. W. Norton & Company, Inc.
500 Fifth Avenue, New York, N.Y. 10110
www.wwnorton.com

W. W. Norton & Company Ltd.
Castle House, 75/76 Wells Street, London W1T 3QT

1 2 3 4 5 6 7 8 9 0

TO CAROL

CONTENTS

CONTRABAND

THE PRINCE

On February 10, 1875, wanted smuggler Charles L. Lawrence slipped into the frigid Montreal night, allegedly forty degrees below zero, seeking to outwit the American detectives on his trail. Since he had fled New York City a month before, Lawrence had lodged in the first-class Ottawa Hotel, a limestone neoclassical auberge whose barroom had entertained both Confederate spies and Union Army officers during the U.S. Civil War. Leaving his baggage behind, Charley headed up the St. Lawrence to the town of Rivière du Loup—Wolf River—where he boarded a two-horse sleigh gliding across New Brunswick. Protected from the cold by a Russian astrakhan fleece coat, he rode two hundred miles to St. John and then to Halifax where he bought a ticket for the S. S. *Caspian*, steaming on February 25 to Queenstown, Ireland, and then to Liverpool, England.

Lawrence looked less like a fugitive from justice than an artiste or a foreign grandee. His passport described him as olive-skinned, having black hair above a high forehead, small, gray eyes bordering a Roman nose, and full moustaches framing a broad mouth. What made Charley attractive, according to newspapers, was his "bright, vivacious, and fresh looking" expression. A "liberal, whole-souled fellow," Lawrence had worked as a photographer, inventor, publisher, and impresario. His linguistic skills allowed him to be comfortable anywhere from his native land of England to Cuba, France, and Brazil, where he had once served as an American diplomat. Tammany Hall boss

William M. Tweed found Lawrence so charming that he gave him the singular honor of asking him to bribe a jury on his behalf.[1]

Charley stood accused of what was then the largest customs fraud in U. S. history. Between 1873 and 1875, his clique smuggled over eighty shipments of French silk, lace, and velvet worth $3 million ($60 million today) into the Port of New York, evading $1 million in duties. At the time, this was an awesome figure. Only eight years before, in 1867, the United States had purchased Alaska from Russia for $7.2 million, a price many felt excessive.

The chase had begun in mid-1874, when dry goods importers complained to the collector of customs for New York, Chester A. Arthur, that someone was flooding the market with cheap silk. Agents deduced that the shipments of illicit fabric had been passed by deputy collector Robert W. Des Anges, a well-regarded Union Army veteran. With the detectives closing in, Des Anges dashed a note to Lawrence. "No further communication, verbally or in writing," he scrawled. "You are followed, and so am I. Let everything go to the devil. Export all you can, but let me alone to try and save myself for the future."[2]

Lawrence remained cool. He could not leave New York until he had signed for a shipment worth $50,000 (about $1,000,000 today) arriving from Hamburg on the S.S. *Pommerania*. When the vessel arrived on January 7, 1875, Lawrence left his home and headed to the port. He tried to lose his pursuer by hopping on and off a streetcar, entering a hotel, exiting through another door, then hiding in the custom house amid the swarms of clerks, brokers, merchants, and messengers. But Lawrence was a middle-aged businessman, not the Artful Dodger, and the detective knew where he was headed anyway. When the investigator saw Lawrence inscribe the paperwork, he reported to his superiors that he had found the author of the scheme.

With a New York grand jury considering his indictment, Charley absconded to Montreal, just forty miles from the United States border, where contrabandists had operated since the American Revolution. When detectives followed him there, he embarked on his frigid sleigh ride to Halifax, where he could catch a steamer to England. Lawrence signed the S.S. *Caspian* manifest "George G. Gordon," a name connected with several notorious men. One was an eighteenth-century Scottish aristocrat who shocked his family by converting to Judaism. Another was the dashing poet Lord Byron, who wrote the best-selling verse tale *The Corsair*. Most recently, police had arrested a confidence man pretending to be Lord George Gordon Gordon, the long lost Earl of Aberdeen.

Lawrence probably identified with all three Gordons, for he himself was a Jewish romantic, a modern buccaneer, born in another country and raised under another name: Charles Lewis Lazarus. At fourteen years old, he had moved from England, his native country, to New York City, adopting U.S. citizenship in 1854. Two years later, he married Zipporah Noah, the lively daughter of patriotic newspaper editor Mordecai Manuel Noah. In 1864, Lazarus began using the surname Lawrence, a moniker his British relatives had taken several years before.

Charley's in-laws thwarted his escape. It was a vulnerable moment for his wife's brother, Robert P. Noah, an attorney in the New York City corporation counsel's office. His incoming boss was a reformer, eager to sue Charley's friend Tweed for the $40 million his "ring" had allegedly stolen from the city. Noah distanced himself from his brother-in-law by informing federal officials that he was on the *Caspian*. On March 3, the U.S. ambassador requested the British arrest Lawrence. The diplomat emphasized charges of forgery, which was an extraditable offense under international law, rather than smuggling, which was not.

When Lawrence and the *Caspian* arrived at Queenstown on March 7, representatives of Scotland Yard and the Irish police were waiting. They confiscated his possessions, including 250 gold sovereigns and diamond jewelry given to him by Boss Tweed. Police also seized incriminating telegrams, reassuring letters, and a code book used by the conspirators. Transported to London, Lawrence awaited trial in the Clerkenwell, a holding facility bombed by Irish Fenians eight years earlier. Though the jail eschewed punishments like whipping, Lawrence was terrified. Each inmate had his own cell, but the men took their exercise together, pushing a wheel in circles. A friend secretly passed Lawrence a "dirk," either to defend himself against other prisoners, to abet his escape, or to end his own life. Discovering the dagger, officials put him in solitary confinement, restricted his diet to bread and water, and limited visitors to one hour each day.

The scandal now threatened Abraham Hoffnung, the Liverpudlian backer of Charley's scheme. Born in Poland but raised in England, Hoffnung possessed the confidence of a man who had made a fortune peddling watches in St. Louis, selling jewelry in Montreal, and running guns to the Confederacy. He assured Lawrence that the courts of free-trade Great Britain were "not going to aid in the punishment" of "a breach of the revenue laws of the United States." The scandal would quickly fade and "business" would "be resumed later on." "The fire seems very hot in New York," Hoffnung wrote, "but, like all fires, will the sooner burn out. The affair will be the usual 'nine days' wonder' and then will be forgotten."[3]

Hoffnung was wrong. The scandal remained on the front page, and U.S. officials insisted the British extradite Lawrence. Charley fought his return by hiring George H. Lewis Jr., a solicitor known for defending England's scandal-plagued elite. He also engaged Judah Benjamin, the exiled Confederate secretary of state, who lived in London. Before the end of his trials, Lawrence would employ other powerful lawyers, including a congressman, an attorney general, a secretary of war, and an ambassador to Russia. Thwarted in court, Hoffnung and his associates offered bribes of $10,000 in gold to free Lawrence. Their efforts failed. Lawrence was escorted onto the steamship *Scythia* on May 1, 1875, arriving in New York City twelve days later.

The ordeal had aged Charley, his hair turning "from a glossy black to almost white," his appearance becoming "haggard, prematurely-old, and shabby." His spirits improved slightly when the judge sent him to Ludlow Street Jail. There he found his friend Boss Tweed, being held pending a $6 million civil suit. The two men lived not in steel and concrete cells, but in adjoining rooms that were part of the warden's quarters. The defendants could import their own food, and Tweed even had an African-American waiter. Ever the bon vivant, Lawrence entertained friends and young women, while Tweed met with his family and attorneys. Given the relative comfort of their surroundings, Tweed and Lawrence might have occasionally forgotten they were both prisoners, accused of betraying the public trust, debasing the government, and defrauding the American people.[4]

THE FLIGHT, ARREST, and trial of Lawrence made headlines internationally. As the United States approached its centennial, it seemed that the nation itself was in crisis, beset by terrorism in the South, corruption in Washington, criminality in corporate boardrooms, and seduction in elite bedrooms. Yet, in its time, the silk smuggling ring was in bold type alongside much-better-remembered controversies. Papers offered regular updates, the last calling Charley "The Prince of Smugglers." On its cover, the New York *Daily Graphic* prominently featured the silk-smuggling cabal, anthropomorphizing it as a short bald pirate with long *payot*, curls of hair worn in front of the ears by Orthodox Jews. The cartoon showed him next to a bewhiskered backwoods farmer shaped like a bottle marked "the Whiskey Ring," a major scandal implicating corrupt federal liquor inspectors.[5]

The scandal resonated because it threatened to disrupt U.S. politics. Fearing what new secrets Charley might reveal, businessmen deluged the port with telegrams asking when he would arrive in New York. The ensuing investigation snared several of the city's most eminent merchants. Through Lawrence's good friend Tweed, it implicated New York State's Democratic Party. It tainted Republican president Ulysses S. Grant, whose custom-house collector, future

No portraits of Charles L. Lawrence remain, but cartoonists in 1875 personified his scandal as a pirate wearing traditional Jewish ear locks. Courtesy The American Antiquarian Society, Worcester, Massachusetts

president Chester Arthur, had failed to stop the smuggling. It had a profound impact on the pivotal, contested election of 1876.[6]

Lawrence's arrest upset the delicate relationship between the United States and Great Britain. When Charley arrived in New York, he contended that the U.S. had lied to British officials to secure his extradition. Three years before, the two nations had signed a treaty healing the breach created during the Civil War, when England had surreptitiously aided the Confederacy in violation of their stated neutrality. While Americans viewed the $15.5 million settlement as a disappointment—some had hoped to obtain a slice of Canada—many Britons viewed it as a capitulation. In Lawrence's prosecution, Englishmen found a reason for new negotiations and perhaps for war.

Charley's smuggling intrigued the public because it threatened the bonds of nationalism. Silk was not illegal in the United States. During the prior year, over $23 million worth had passed lawfully into the country through the custom house. Charley's crime was not importing something deemed dangerous, such as drugs or pornography, but rather lying to the government, depriving it of revenue, and injuring the nation's workers. In a period when Americans demanded tariffs to shield them from global competition, but also craved foreign goods, the prosecution of the silk smugglers raised questions. What do citizens owe one another? Does the consumption of items manufactured in undemocratic countries undermine equality at home? How should the federal government assist the men, women, and children toiling in the nation's factories?

Smuggling's implications for the nation's future were no less weighty. Having reached its limits at the Pacific edge of North America, the United States considered expanding to new territories. Many wondered what form this growth should take. Would the nation enlarge its global presence through trade? Or would the U.S. military conquer new territories in the Caribbean, the Pacific, and beyond? If the latter, then would America grant the racially diverse inhabitants of those lands democracy and full citizenship? As the United States donned an imperial mantle, smugglers tested attempts to create new borders and establish new forms of sovereignty.

The answers to these questions mattered more only a decade removed from the end of the Civil War, when Northerners still recalled how the slaveholders' mix of localism and internationalism had killed nearly one million people and almost destroyed the Union. This was a time when the United States was one of the world's few democracies (however flawed). This America was becoming wealthy, but still gripped by regular depressions. Immigration had diversified the nation but not quelled its ambivalence towards the world. The United States had a military, but not one competitive with the Great Powers of Europe. Lawrence's sin was not trafficking in textiles per se but, rather, challenging the authority of an insecure national government, exposing American industry to global competition, and tempting consumers with foreign luxuries. To truly appreciate the cleavages Lawrence exposed, one must look at the prior century, returning to the founding of the Republic itself.

REPUBLIC

The Prince of Smugglers had his defenders. When the scandal broke in 1875, economist David A. Wells compared Charley Lawrence to John Hancock, the Revolutionary War patriot arrested by the British crown a century before for flouting its mercantile laws. In Wells's view, Charley's smuggling was a protest against unfair tariffs in tune with the Founders' principles. Painting the United States as a nation established by tax resisters, Wells saw Lawrence as reviving the country's lost commitment to free trade.[1]

American culture today embraces this notion of the "patriotic smuggler," who somehow defends the nation by defying its laws. In the 1970s, the United States dedicated one bit of Louisiana bayou, a national park, to Jean Lafitte, a Franco-American smuggler, pirate, and slave trader who fought for the U.S. against England in the War of 1812. Novels and films likewise glorify contrabandists such as Rhett Butler, Rick Blaine, and Han Solo. These men are presented as individualists who become altruists when the community is in peril, rallying in defense of their friends, homes, and freedom.

But contrary to this mythology, the majority of early Americans were nationalists who opposed smuggling. The Founders had defied Britain's King George III, but they believed that citizens needed to obey the popularly enacted laws of the new Republic. At its very first meeting, the U.S. Congress passed tariffs on foreign goods, and these regulations only grew as the society became more democratic and industrial. Contrabandists were popular on the periphery, but the majority deprecated smuggling as treason in miniature, a threat to domestic industry, and a challenge to American identity. It was only in the 1830s that the notion of the "patriotic smuggler" became conspicuous, and even then it prevailed among the anxious slaveholders of the South.

THE ROLE OF CONTRABAND in the nation's founding is well known. America's fight for independence from England began, by many accounts, on June 10, 1768, when British customs commissioners seized John Hancock's sloop *Liberty* for smuggling wine into Boston harbor. Hancock and the king's tidesmen, the officials responsible for collecting import duties, had clashed repeatedly during the previous months. On April 9, Hancock's employees had forcibly expelled inspectors from the hold of his brig *Lydia* for lack of a warrant. When agents examined the *Liberty*, they found only 3,150 gallons of Madeira, less than one quarter of the ship's capacity. Accusing Hancock of passing wine ashore prior to inspection, they confiscated his ship and prosecuted him in an imperial vice-admiralty court.

British officials viewed Hancock's "free trading" as a dangerous form of rebellion. Smuggling had been a capital crime in the British Empire since 1746. The crown needed tariff revenue to field armies against absolutist France. It did not help that contrabandists often hailed from regions hostile to the authority of London, such as Scotland. And worst of all, smuggling was common among Jacobites who demanded the restoration of the Stuart family to the English throne. From 1735 to 1749, a gang of five hundred Jacobite smugglers terrorized the town of Hawkhurst, Kent, until officials hanged thirty-five of their members.[2]

If it is hard to imagine Hancock as a swashbuckling sea dog, that is because he was nothing of the sort. Hancock, whose very name suggests unadventurous topics such as penmanship and life insurance, was raised on Beacon Hill and educated at Harvard. His jutting chin was clean-shaven, and he wore a powdered wig rather than a seafarer's queue. If he depended upon the ocean for his living, it was only because he inherited his uncle's importing business. Though born in Braintree, he had lived in London and had close relations with several royal governors.

Hancock nonetheless threatened the crown. On the surface, smuggling was the kind of lucrative sharp trading that required no intellectual justification. But interest and ideology worked in tandem for Hancock, a Whig hostile to Britain's Tory government. In 1766, the mother country levied new taxes and gave officials authority to search ships, businesses, and homes in pursuit of contraband. Colonial merchants like Hancock protested this law by boycotting British luxuries and smuggling illegal goods, such as Dutch tea.

The seizure of Hancock's *Liberty* inspired a more aggressive phase of the opposition. Boston was restless in the spring of 1768. Port denizens were furious that the recently arrived HMS *Romney*, a fifty-gun warship requiring a crew of three hundred men, had kidnapped residents for service in the Royal Navy. The customs officers also harassed Hancock's fellow merchants. Upon hearing that British sailors were towing the *Liberty* out to the *Romney*, a mob of over three hundred sailors, smugglers, and Whigs threw rocks at customs officials. The tidesmen sought refuge on the *Romney*. To guarantee the safety of their representatives, the British sent four thousand soldiers to Boston. And the presence of these redcoats arguably instigated the American Revolution.[3]

But most Americans ceased identifying with smugglers after declaring independence in 1776. War made trade with the British both illegal and unpatriotic. And after the Revolutionary War's end, the new nation asserted sovereignty over foreign trade. On March 4, 1789, when the Congress met for the first time since the Constitution, incoming Treasury Secretary Alexander Hamilton proposed a tariff to generate revenue and facilitate independence from Britain. Recalling the successful Stamp Act boycott of 1765, Congressman James Madison endorsed the tax, believing it could give the Republic economic leverage to compensate for its lack of military might. Impressed, the House of Representatives imposed duties of 5 to 10 percent on imported goods.

The custom house thus became the core of the new American state. The tariff provided the United States with the income to hire soldiers, build ships, and borrow money against future earnings. It also gave Congress some power to elevate industries and regions, as well as some control over labor standards. The tariff rewarded nationalism, and thus created it. If the U.S. Postal Service forged common identity by fostering communication among a widely dispersed population, then the custom house did the obverse, molding an American consciousness by impeding transactions with a broader world. By suppressing traffic in foreign goods, the tariff forced the development of internal networks that were essential to national identity. New England mills wove flax not from Irish farmers, but from protected Kentucky growers. Through interdependency many politicians believed America could retain its allegedly masculine, egalitarian, frontier values against the supposedly effete sensibilities of monarchical Europe.[4]

From the beginning, protection divided voters. Industrial workers loved it. In 1790, the Providence Association of Mechanics and Manufacturers celebrated Rhode Island's ratification of the Constitution by praying for a protective tariff, which the group promised to support by "discouraging smuggling." But others resented interference with traditional trade between friends and relations living on different sides of the Canadian border. And rural revolutionaries cried betrayal. Albany's Abraham Yates Jr. predicted that Congress would anoint an army of "collectors, deputy collectors, comptrollers, clerks, tide-waiters, and searchers" to enforce the tariff, expanding federal power until the national government "swallowed entirely the sovereignty of the particular states." Yates believed the new nation was swiftly coming to resemble imperial Britain.⁵

Fearing dissent might become disobedience, Hamilton requested that Congress allow the customs to pursue contraband to the warehouses, stores, and streets of the nation's ports. But to allay his enemies' suspicions, he promised to take "the most scrupulous care" to secure citizens against "abuses of authority" by making customs officials both civilly and criminally liable. By taking "precautions," Hamilton suggested, the government could convince the "enlightened class of citizens" to "cooperate in whatever will restrain the spirit of illicit traffic."⁶

Congress responded by extending the Treasury's authority, by creating the Revenue Marine Service, the ancestor of the Coast Guard, and by funding the construction of ten cutters. The largest was the U.S.R.S *Massachusetts*, a sixty-foot, seventy-ton, two-masted schooner armed with six swivel guns. Though the *Massachusetts* was soon sold, other vessels patrolled the nation's shores in search of smugglers and their contraband. For the first decade after the enactment of the Constitution, the Revenue Marine Service represented America's lone sea defense.

Untaxed trade in Caribbean rum and Canadian lumber seems fairly innocent, but one must recall the context: a fragile new republic, the first of its kind, still in debt, fearful of British domination. This was the era of the 1794 Whiskey Rebellion, when President George Washington led a thirteen-thousand-man militia to Monongahela, near Pittsburgh, and then jailed twenty distillers for failing to pay excise taxes. Smugglers never staged a "Rum and Lumber Mutiny" in part because Hamilton did not want lawlessness to become an argument against tariffs themselves. He asked customs agents to behave with "a cool and temperate perseverance in their duty, by address & moderation rather than by vehemence or violence." Likewise, Hamilton wanted judges to "guard against all artifices and contrivances to elude them," but cautioned them against "a disposition unduly rigor-

ous."[7] The last thing Hamilton wanted to do was make the smugglers
into heroes.

THE 1800 ELECTION of President Thomas Jefferson led to a new expansion of federal power, which strengthened smuggling's association
with disunion. Once opposed to tariffs, Jefferson embraced economic
nationalism in response to the Napoleonic Wars that had engulfed
Europe, pitting France against an alliance led by Great Britain. Eager
to keep the United States out of the conflict, Jefferson initiated an
embargo of international trade in 1807. Though Congress narrowed
the prohibition to England and France in 1809 and to Britain alone
in 1810, the federal government imposed significant new barriers to
trade with the United States.

The embargo era's best-known smuggler was Jean Lafitte of Louisiana. Though one well-known portrait shows him as the stereotypi-
cal pirate, with skinny moustache, devil's beard, and wide-brimmed
feathered hat, his former associates recalled his white teeth, apparently rare at the time. They depicted him as a tall, pale man, with
black eyes and dark hair, but a refined expression, an open face,
a square jaw, and side-whiskers. His polite manners reportedly
matched his appearance. A colleague noted "in his pleasant moods,
one who did not know him would have suspected him for being anything but a pirate." For Lafitte's defenders, this countenance marked
him as a noble sort of villain. To his critics, it masked the reality of a
brutal murderer.[8]

In the popular imagination, the smuggler and the pirate were
fraternal twins, bound by their seafaring delinquency. In fact, the
contrabandist and the corsair were different. Even the most daring
smugglers were essentially traders, who dealt not in illicit drugs but
in lawful goods like silk. Relying on stealth rather than force, these
contrabandists sought to profit by avoiding taxes. By contrast, pirates
violently disrupted the trade that smugglers facilitated, diverting it
to themselves. For several centuries, corsairs operating out of North

Africa's "Barbary Coast" had captured ships and raided European towns, taking slaves and booty. In the New World, English pirates terrorized settlements stretching from the Caribbean to Rhode Island.

During the eighteenth century, true piracy declined, and the raiders increasingly fell into line behind governments that defined the control of commerce as the essence of sovereignty. Countries fought not only for territory, but also for markets. Moreover, military tactics emphasized the harassment of merchant shipping. Nations at war offered private seamen "letters of marque and reprisal," permitting them to capture enemy ships. As countries marshaled buccaneers behind their flags, they instilled the pirate ethic into their own navies. British law rewarded members of the Royal Navy for risking their lives by giving them shares of any "prizes" taken. France and Spain adopted similar policies distributing the proceeds from seized vessels.

To fight this legalized piracy, the United States built a navy of its own. Revenue cutters could catch smugglers, but they could not deter Barbary pirates or European men-of-war. When the Washington administration signed a peace treaty with Great Britain in 1794, a jealous France severed relations with the U.S. and began seizing American merchant ships. In response, Congress commissioned six new twenty-gun frigates. But by the time the shipyards had completed the first three, France had already taken over three hundred American merchantmen. Fighting back, the U.S. forced a settlement with Napoleon in 1800, but continued to suffer the harassment of privateers in the Caribbean, North Atlantic, and Mediterranean.[9]

This was the world of Jean Lafitte. Born in Pauillac, France, not far from the port city of Bordeaux, Jean and his older brother Pierre had allegedly traded in Spanish goods since childhood. When the French Revolution of 1787 ruined the family business, Pierre left Europe for the Caribbean island of Saint-Domingue. In 1803, he moved again, escaping the Haitian revolution by moving to New Orleans. Jean followed Pierre to Louisiana, becoming a ship's captain. Off the Gulf

Coast, the brothers raided shipping and smuggled slaves, provisions, and luxuries into the newly American territories west of the Mississippi River.

Louisiana was already known for contraband. Its diverse community of Spaniards, Frenchmen, Cajuns, Indians, slaves, free blacks, and Creoles had weak ties to the United States, having become Americans only in 1803, with President Jefferson's purchase of the territory from France. Before that, Louisianans had paid little fealty to Napoleon, who had secretly taken possession of the region only three years earlier. And the prior sovereign, Spain, had hardly encouraged devotion, imposing high taxes in return for minimal protections. The first American governor of the territory, William C. C. Claiborne, complained that "I have been at great pains to convince the people of the state that smuggling is a moral offense." Blaming "bad example," Claiborne continued, "Formerly, under the government of Spain, smuggling in Louisiana was universally practiced, from the highest to the lowest member of society." Seeing government as transient, distant, and rapacious, inhabitants ignored laws enacted in Washington, D.C.[10]

The Lafittes began as vicious slave smugglers, violating the ban on the importation of foreign bondsmen into the Louisiana territory. In 1803, Governor Claiborne ordered customs officials to hold a French ship named *La Soeur Cherie*, commanded by a "Captain La fette," on suspicion of slipping slaves from Saint-Domingue into Louisiana. In 1806, Pierre moved his family to the Spanish city Pensacola, a four-day trip to New Orleans by inland waterway. For three years, he sent slaves to Louisiana, before taking his business back to New Orleans in 1809. By this time, the federal government had abolished the African trade altogether, but this only increased the kidnappers' profits. In the summer of 1810, selling human chattels from Cuba, Saint-Domingue, and Africa, the brothers accrued $7,903 (about $140,000 today).

Soon the Lafittes were trading in every sort of contraband. By 1810,

New Orleans's population had doubled, creating demand for goods from embargoed colonies. Jean based his operation on Grand Isle, in the bay called Barataria ("Cheap Lands") after the fiefdom given to Sancho Panza in the novel *Don Quixote*. The bay boasted of "a safe and commodious harbour for merchant vessels and small ships of war." There the Lafittes created an open-air market for illegal merchandise. But they also engaged pirogues—small paddleboats, flat-bottomed for shallow water, and light enough to be carried on land—to ferry goods into New Orleans via Bayou Lafourche, a long waterway stretching far inland, meeting the Mississippi River at Donaldsonville.[11]

From Grand Isle, Lafitte also raided merchantmen off the Louisiana coast. Jean initially obtained letters of marque from Napoleon, but later bought the right to fly the flag of Cartagena, a South American city that had declared independence from Spain. This gave the Lafittes the right to seize any Spanish vessel they could catch. Still better, amid the revolutionary chaos, Cartagenians declined to ensure that the brothers brought their prizes south for lawful condemnation. Using water routes, the Lafittes slipped these stolen goods past the custom house and into the city.

U.S. officials disapproved of this smuggling, but Louisiana politicians impeded enforcement of the embargo. In 1808, President Jefferson sent U.S. Navy Master Commandant David Porter to the Gulf. Though only twenty-eight years old, Porter was a seasoned officer, having engaged the French in the 1790s and North African pirates in the 1800s. In the spring of 1810, Porter captured three ships in the Mississippi, but the U.S. attorney ordered him to release the vessels. Porter refused, threatening to sail the libeled prizes to another jurisdiction. The captain's victory made him a pariah in New Orleans, causing him to resign.

The situation barely improved after Porter's departure. In 1810, the acting territorial governor raged at the "brigands who infest our coast," but the government did little to remove them from Grand Isle.

Then in 1811, a navy gunboat attacked Lafitte's Barataria base itself, prompting the privateers to set their prize, the *Divina Pastora*, aflame and flee in their pirogues. The sailors saved the vessel, but the raid failed to stop smuggling on the island. Early the next year, a local grand jury complained that "characters considered respectable in this Community" had rendered assistance to the smugglers, making their prosecution impossible.[12]

Immune from punishment, the Lafittes essentially ruled their own imagined nation of smugglers based on the American soil of Grand Isle. In his 1815 memoir, Major Arsène Lacarrière Latour recalled the island as a principality where the brothers were sovereigns and government officials dared not go. Its inhabitants were "Baratarians," whom Latour described as "mostly aliens, cruising under a foreign flag," who "audaciously infringed our laws."[13] Latour did not note that the respectable residents of Louisiana were scarcely more American than the Baratarians; he himself was a Frenchman, who died in his homeland in the 1830s.

THOUGH THE LAFITTES were the era's most vicious smugglers, U.S. officials worried more about illicit trade on the Republic's northern border. In 1810, over one million Americans lived near Canada, compared to fewer than seventy-seven thousand in Louisiana. Moreover, border inhabitants were primarily Federalists who viewed Jefferson as a tyrant and his embargo as disastrous. In 1810, Federalist John Lowell Jr. wondered when the northeastern states would "feel compelled to seek by the law of self-preservation, their safety by a separate peace, and to leave the southern states to prosecute a war which they had most wantonly brought upon the country?" Disunion was in the air.[14]

Defiance was more common than secessionism among New Englanders. Dry goods merchant Nathan Appleton seemed the antithesis of Jean Lafitte. Lafitte was tall, Appleton unimposing. While the pirate was sharply handsome, the Yankee trader's face was soft, his chin round, his hair reddish, and his eyes kindly and blue. Appleton's roots in the nation were as deep as Lafitte's were shallow. He was born during the American Revolution to a family of New Hampshire farmers who had migrated from England five generations before. A religious Unitarian, he maintained a lifelong commitment to reform. While Lafitte possessed no scruples about kidnapping African slaves, Appleton prayed for an end to southern bondage.

Yet despite these differences, Appleton was also called a smuggler. In 1810, he began selling English textiles in the United States, just in time for the new restrictions on British trade. But unlike other northeastern merchants, Appleton shrewdly turned the regulations to his advantage. Just before hostilities were declared, he delivered British manufactures to the United States. Customs officials seized the goods, forcing Appleton to pay bonds for their release. But by the time he sold his merchandise, scarcity had increased its price. Flush with wealth, Appleton then went to the capital and somehow convinced Congress to void the bonds.

Appleton was hardly unique among Federalist merchants. In 1808, Congressman William Cooper tried to save his struggling DeKalb, New York, community by making it an entrepôt for illicit traffic with Canada. Future abolitionists Arthur and Lewis Tappan left Boston for Quebec and Maine, where they traded in British dry goods. James Colles, the nineteen-year-old son of a prominent New York City wallpaper manufacturer, took a position arranging the illicit importation of British goods from St. John, New Brunswick, to Passamaquoddy, Maine.[15]

In response, the Jefferson and Madison administrations stationed the navy on border lakes and rivers, and at sea. While William Cooper was sneaking goods across the St. Lawrence, his eighteen-year-old son, James Fenimore Cooper, was serving as a midshipman on a Lake Ontario brig charged with intercepting British smugglers. The future author's service was uneventful. In 1809, the Oswego customs collector sought Cooper's aid in handling a contrabandist, but most of his time was spent recruiting sailors to serve on various vessels patrolling the border. But he mentioned smuggling in several works, particularly the novella *The Water-witch* (1826).

The boundary between New England and Quebec grew violent. In 1808, the commander of the twelve-oared U.S. Revenue Cutter *Fly*, stationed in Vermont, learned that a forty-foot, seven-oared, tar-coated sailboat called the *Black Snake* was stealing down to St. Albans Bay to pick up potash for shipment to Quebec. When the patrol met the smugglers, they exchanged fire, killing three men before the *Black Snake* crew could be arrested. The leading contrabandist, Cyrus Dean, was sentenced to death and hanged before ten thousand spectators. The following election, Vermonters demonstrated their sympathies by sending Federalists to Congress and the governor's mansion.[16]

Frustrated by the defiance of northeastern border residents, President Jefferson's successor, James Madison, asked Congress for "further guards against evasions and infractions of our commercial laws" to stem the "odious" practice of smuggling. Madison saw illicit trade as unforgivable in a democracy, where contrabandists stole from the people's treasury rather than from the sovereign's treasure. Judging it "a treacherous subserviency" to other nations, he called for Congress to express "the virtuous indignation of the public" by passing "competent laws." The result was the Enforcement Act of 1809, which gave the Customs the right to search vessels, seize contraband, and request military action against smugglers.[17]

Federalists defended the smugglers, but only to a point. Following Madison's 1811 speech demanding new powers, the editor of a Vermont newspaper reasoned that the average offender "has no idea of treason; . . . he thinks of nothing worse than putting a few cents in his pocket or a little salt into his children's porridge." The editor was careful, however, not to valorize the smuggler. The next year, he published a widely disseminated piece urging his readers to criticize the administration's policies, but not to disobey the law and the Constitution.[18]

In June 1812, tensions with England became open warfare. At sea, the nations struggled for control over shipping. The United States restricted trade with the English, the British sought to blockade American ports, and both nations sought to capture the other side's merchantmen. In August 1812, having recovered from his bitter time fighting smugglers in New Orleans and having won promotion to commander, David Porter became the war's first hero, when his thirty-two-gun frigate U.S.S. *Essex* captured the HMS *Alert*. Porter then sailed the *Essex* round the horn of South America to sow chaos in the Pacific. Within a month, he had taken eight British prizes, worth an estimated $300,000 (over $5 million today).[19]

Opposed to the war, Federalists spoke openly about dissolving the Union. But a larger number protested by smuggling. One general grumbled that "from the Judges on the bench to the drayman in the street you find persons either directly or indirectly engaged in trading with the enemy." One treasury officer stationed on Cape Cod complained that "his inspectors dare not now attempt to search stores or houses there" because "the mass of the population . . . threaten such opposition as renders the attempt . . . futile." In 1813, the U.S. Army ambushed a New Brunswick crew attempting to land $40,000 in British goods on Moose Island, Maine. But customs agents protested that the military had invaded their jurisdiction, sued for the contraband, and then split the proceeds with the smugglers themselves.[20]

Jeffersonians used this smuggling to demonstrate Federalist disloyalty. In 1813, the *Boston Patriot* accused its rival, the *Daily Advertiser,* of "treasonable practices, open oppositions to the laws, constantly reviling the officers of government, preaching up sedition, and a dissolution of the Union; and smuggling, and comforting and feeding the enemy, for the sake of gain." William Charles Jr. published his cartoon "Leap or No Leap," which portrayed King George III luring states back into the empire with an offer of "plenty molasses and Codfish; plenty of goods to Smuggle; Honours, titles and Nobility into the

IN THIS 1814 CARTOON, KING GEORGE III ENCOURAGES STATES TO REJOIN
THE BRITISH EMPIRE, PROMISING "GOODS TO SMUGGLE; HONOURS, TITLES
AND NOBILITY INTO THE BARGAIN. Courtesy Library of Congress Prints and Photo-
graphs Division

bargain." Here, smuggling implied not only disunion and treachery,
but also aristocracy, an association that remained potent for over a
century.[21]

Federalists complained that the Jeffersonians were hypocrites,
who smuggled themselves. After all, northern contrabandists only
operated by the leave of pliable Madison appointees. In the south,
the president's strongest supporters traded illegally with British mill
owners, desperate for cotton. In 1810, the year before the embargo's
repeal, fifty-four vessels illicitly left southern ports, carrying 21,000
bales of cotton, or 12 percent of the year's yield. After the war began,
Georgia residents traded with the British through Spanish-controlled
Amelia Island.

But the countercharges failed to stick. After the war's end, Jeffersonians reminded voters of the Federalists' embrace of the enemy. In August 1815, a song published in Bennington, Vermont's *Green Mountain Farmer* observed:

> *And soon the rich sentiment spreads through the land,*
>   *Divided we fall but united we stand—*
> *But faction arose,*
> *To strengthen our foes,*
>   *And smuggling and treason prevailed in some quarters;*
> *Strange doctrines too 'rose,*
> *To comfort our foes,*
>   *And strengthen the faction dispurs'd thro' our borders . . .*[22]

Here was the old revolutionary republicanism, in all the fullness of its language. The Federalist Party was a "faction," bent on betraying the nation by fomenting the "strange doctrines" of disunion. Smuggling had become secession in miniature.

JEAN LAFITTE'S LEGEND emerged as the war finally came to Louisiana. By 1815, the British had repulsed America's invasion of Ontario and burned Washington, D.C., but the U.S. Navy was victorious in the Great Lakes and Baltimore. Eager to make some gains in the irritating conflict, the British sent ten thousand troops to New Orleans. President Madison charged General Andrew Jackson with leading the defense of the city.

By this time, Gulf residents had become more ambivalent toward the Lafitte brothers. The embargo of France was over, reducing the demand for contraband. Louisiana statehood made it harder for residents to rationalize smuggling as defrauding a distant sovereign. Law-abiding New Orleans merchants complained that they could not compete with Lafitte. Emboldened by popular support, customs inspector Walker Gilbert raided Lafitte's men, seizing a valuable ship-

JEAN LAFITTE, AS IDEALIZED BY SOUTHERNERS IN 1879. Courtesy The Portal to Texas History

ment of contraband. As Gilbert floated the goods downriver to New Orleans, the smugglers struck back, shooting one of his deputies and retaking "Mr Lafite's" merchandise. Searching Bayou St. Denis for smugglers, a navy longboat stumbled upon Pierre Lafitte leading a gang of ninety men and a flotilla of heavy-laden pirogues. A firefight erupted, leaving three sailors wounded.

Politicians finally decided to crush the Baratarians. Pierre DuBourg, the collector of the Port of New Orleans, begged the secretary of the treasury for assistance. The administration put the New Orleans naval command in the hands of Master Commandant David Todd Patterson, an enemy of the Lafittes. Next, Governor William Claiborne offered a $500 reward for Jean's arrest. Donaldsville collector Gilbert mocked Claiborne's bounty as insufficient to stop "banditti, the most base and daring ever known in any country on Earth," but only as a way of pressing for greater assistance in stopping the brothers. Finally, officials arrested Pierre Lafitte on charges of piracy and smuggling, holding him in a New Orleans jail.[23]

Jean continued privateering and smuggling, but he found his business increasingly constrained. The new rigor of revenue officials was less troubling than the growing presence of the British Navy, which had just liberated Spain from Napoleon's armies and thus disapproved of Lafitte's raids on Spanish ships. In the smuggler Lafitte the English saw a potential ally who commanded nine hundred men skilled with sail, shot, and cutlass. After a sortie with one of Lafitte's ships in September 1814, a British commander made overtures to Jean, promising him $30,000 and a captaincy in return for his support in a coming attack upon the port of Mobile.

Lafitte brought this offer to Claiborne and Jackson. His decision implied no patriotic devotion. The United States held his brother. Likewise, he knew that his methods depended upon American victory, since Royal Navy commanders had to share their prizes with their superiors. If he resigned his commission, his enterprise could not survive British dominance of the Gulf. Like all smugglers, Lafitte wanted a government strong enough to enforce the law, but not potent enough to arrest him. The scattered American gunboats seemed less threatening than the awesome Royal Navy.

General Jackson initially rebuffed Lafitte's proposal, favoring the arrest of the "hellish banditti." But Jackson needed naval support, as well as flint and shot for his men's muskets. Concluding that British frigates threatened the territory more than "South American" privateers, Jackson agreed to ask President Madison to pardon any Baratarian who resisted the redcoat invasion of Louisiana, Alabama, and West Florida. Within days, Pierre was free from jail, and the Lafittes had begun encouraging their men to join the militia.[24]

On January 8, 1815, the Battle of New Orleans was joined. As promised, the Lafittes and their men performed with special distinction. Jackson's forces repulsed the British Army, exacting heavy casualties while suffering few losses; after a subsequent naval defeat, the English fled to Mississippi. In victory, Old Hickory was generous to the Baratarians, lauding Jean and Pierre for demonstrating "courage and fidelity." For their heroism, the contrabandists received pardons from President Madison on February 6, 1815.

After receiving their absolution, the brothers crossed the border to the Spanish port of Galveston, where they returned to trading in kidnapped Africans. That summer, a customs official described seizing illegal slaves and a felucca carrying coffee, cocoa, wax, clothing, and "about 10,000 pounds of quicksilver" from one of the Lafittes' men.[25]

IN ENSUING DECADES, other former smugglers became manufacturing titans. Massachusetts governor John Hancock, once wanted for landing wine in defiance of the king's customs officers, pushed for the construction of canals providing transportation and water power. In 1813, accused contrabandist Nathan Appleton joined with merchant Francis Cabot Lowell, the brother of Federalist secessionist John Lowell Jr., and ten other investors to build the nation's first major textile mill in Waltham.

These former contrabandists also pushed the government to protect their industrial experiments. Appleton and Lowell approached Henry Clay of Kentucky, the Speaker of the House of Representatives, seeking higher taxes on foreign cloth. The result was the Tariff of 1816, which increased rates on raw fiber and textiles. Clay argued that the law could shield American manufactures against British goods, which had dropped in price. Moreover, like his predecessor Hamilton, he believed that America's infant industries, like the New England mills, required protection to survive. Finally, the law claimed to ensure that workers were protected from what he would later call "the pauper labor of Europe." Clay believed that competition with European workers, toiling without basic political rights, undermined the freedom and high wages enjoyed by white American workingmen.

Under conditions of protection, the mills of Massachusetts thrived, creating a powerful political interest dedicated to supporting the tariff. In 1822, Appleton and his partners expanded the area's canal system and built a new mill in nearby East Chelmsford. The facility employed young, unmarried women to operate the textile machines, but the city attracted thousands of men as well to perform traditional masculine labor: dig canals, build homes and factories, forge tools, and fix equipment. In 1826, after Francis Cabot Lowell's premature death, the proprietors incorporated the town, which now had 2,500 residents. Grateful for what their dead partner had bequeathed them, Appleton and the other grieving stockholders renamed the new town "Lowell" in his honor. By 1840, Lowell had become a major city with over twenty thousand residents.[26]

Lowell residents demonstrated their faith in their employer by electing former smuggler Nathan Appleton to Congress in 1830. Now fifty-one years old, Appleton was the nation's foremost industrialist, as well as a philanthropist and state legislator. He still possessed kind eyes, but his "round chin" had become jowly and his "middling nose," long and curved. Appleton won office in "one of the most exciting and closely contested political struggles Boston has ever witnessed," an election pitting the district's protectionist manufacturers against its free-trade merchants.

Appleton was assigned the job of redesigning the tariff before the 1832 election. The calico magnate was predisposed to keep rates high but also well positioned to deflect the northeastern hostility to the tariff reductions demanded by the South. Appleton devised a compromise bill that retained taxes on iron and cotton textiles, but reduced rates on nearly every other imported item. By nearly a two-thirds majority, the bill passed Congress. In principle, President Andrew Jackson opposed the tariff. But in practice, he needed the support of working voters in states like Massachusetts. Thus, in July 1832, he signed Appleton's bill.[27]

By this time, however, planters who had supported Jefferson, Madison, and Jackson had soured on trade restrictions, which raised the price of imported goods, but offered no protection to their products. The new canals and roads opened new lands to cultivation, increasing competition. The federal ban on the African slave trade increased the cost of labor, leading planters to purchase as many as five thousand African slaves each year illegally from smugglers like Lafitte. Global demand for cotton connected slaveholders to foreign markets. Planters became more transnational and disconnected from the Pennsylvania ironmonger and the Massachusetts mill hand.

Resentment peaked in late 1832, when South Carolina challenged federal supremacy itself. Arguing that states possessed the right to determine which national laws were constitutional, its legislature declared the tariff void and forbade its enforcement in local ports. Most disturbing, the state threatened to secede if the federal government collected the duties prescribed by Congress. If nullification was the most potent challenge to the authority of the national government since 1790s, many Southerners did not see it as such. The *Baltimore Republican* predicted that South Carolina's assertion of supremacy would neither impede "the regular operation of the laws of Congress," nor produce disobedience greater than "an attempt to smuggle goods contrary to law."[28]

Jackson responded to South Carolina's mutiny with his characteristic mixture of truculence and hypernationalism. On January 16, 1833, the president asked Congress for the power to close existing custom houses at Beaufort and Georgetown, and employ the military to collect duties at a federal fort in Charleston harbor. On February 25, Congress gave Jackson the authority he sought, but also enacted a compromise tariff, promising reductions over the ensuing decade. In return, South Carolina withdrew the nullification resolution, and the crisis subsided.

THE NULLIFICATION CRISIS made Jean Lafitte a southern legend. Before that, few Americans knew of the pirate's gallantry at the Battle of New Orleans. Few newspapers described his heroics, and the reports were often negative. In 1816, one disparaged the deal with the Baratarians, arguing that "holding out such lures and temptations to desperate men" was a "dangerous game." After Lafitte's death in 1823 near Honduras, no U.S. newspaper published an obituary for him. Only in 1826 did Jacksonian editor Richard Penn Smith write a fictional pamphlet entitled, *Lafitte, or the Baratarian Chief*, which painted the slave smuggler as a romantic figure.[29]

This changed in 1836, when Gulf Coast author Joseph Holt Ingraham published *Lafitte: Pirate of the Gulf*, a novel with Lafitte as the protagonist. In the 1850s, as southern nationalism peaked, several more articles appeared in *DeBow's Review*, a hotbed of proslavery sentiment. Lafitte's "commanding mien, his firmness, his courage, his magnanimity, and his professional skill" all made him "universally respected by his crew." Authors proposed to show that Lafitte "was more of a patriot than a pirate, that he rendered services of immense benefit to his adopted country, and should be held in respect and heard, rather than defamed and calumniated." Such accounts painted Lafitte as an authentic slaveholder-hero, a man whose loyalty to the flag superseded his hostility to the nation's laws.[30]

By contrast, nationalists and Northerners increasingly deprecated Lafitte. In 1836, Edgar Allan Poe critiqued Ingraham's novel for portraying Lafitte as both a "vacillating villain, a fratricide, a cowardly cut-throat" and an "elegant," "noble," and "resolute" hero. In 1837, Bostonian Charles Ellms concluded that Lafitte's "reckless career was marked with crimes of the darkest dye." Newspapers charged that the pirate was a mere "blacksmith from Marseilles, who could scarcely manage a jolly boat." In 1852, a Boston magazine debunked the myth of the noble pirate and smuggler. In 1856, a major New York City newspaper published "The Slave Smugglers," depicting Lafitte as a sadistic buccaneer trading in illicit human cargo.[31]

The tariff and slavery had played havoc with traditional views of smuggling. By 1850, the merchants of New England who had once defied Jefferson's embargo demanded protection for their infant industries. These Yankees now viewed the contrabandist as a threat to the fragile republic. By contrast, southern states once support-ive of trade restrictions now detested federal power. Enraged by the tariff, dependent upon foreign markets, and fearing the emancipa-tion of their slaves, planters celebrated the legend of the patriotic smuggler.

LAZARUS

Charles Lewis Lazarus was born on the Fourth of July, Independence Day, in the year 1833, just months after the Nullification Crisis. His obituary in the *New York Times* stated his birthplace was "Scarborough, Scotland," presumably meaning Scarborough, Yorkshire, the North Sea resort where his grandfather owned a jewelry store. But his descendants claimed his hometown was the Midlands city of Nottingham, where his father worked in the early 1830s. Charley's children—several of them theater folk—may have wanted to associate him with Nottingham's most famous resident, the mythical tax protester Robin Hood.[1]

Charley's parents, Isaac Lewis Lazarus and Deborah Jacobs, were British Jews, the descendants of immigrants from central Europe. Most of the thirty-five thousand Jews in England in 1850 had come in the previous half century, drawn to wealth created by the industrial revolution, empire, and trade. Charley hailed from a family of importers, brokers, jewelers, and maritime suppliers. His mother, Deborah, came from Kingston-upon-Hull, where her father Israel "Gentleman" Jacobs was a gold- and silversmith. Israel's success allowed him to open a second store in Scarborough, as well as to become a local benefactor. Deborah's brother Bethel was still more prosperous, making timepieces still prized today. His sons practiced law, engineering, and architecture, while his daughters married into wealthy families.[2]

THE DETECTED SMUGGLER.
'Farewell, a long farewell, to all my greatness!'
HENRY VIII., ACT III. SCENE FIRST.

THIS 1834 CARTOON SHOWS HOW JACKSONIAN INSPECTORS SEARCHED FOR CONTRABAND ON THE BODIES OF MORTIFIED TRAVELERS. Courtesy The American Antiquarian Society, Worcester, Massachusetts

Lewis Lazarus, Charley's paternal grandfather, was a "respected" naval agent in the south-coast city of Portsmouth, who made his living provisioning ships and lending to seamen. In 1817, with Napoleon in permanent exile, and the profits of the naval trade in decline, Lewis became a pawnbroker. He must have been an upstanding dealer indeed, for his synagogue elected him president. In 1829, he moved to the resort town of Bath and then to Dublin, where he became a goldsmith on Parliament Street. He was again elected head of the local temple, leading one newspaper to call him "the president of the Jews" in Dublin. Two of his sons followed him to Ireland, where they flourished.[3]

Charley's father, Isaac Lewis Lazarus (also called I.L. and J.L.), was less fortunate than his brothers. Though "a cultivated, educated man," his "intense fondness for drink" diminished his prospects. Born in Portsmouth in 1806, he followed his brother Samuel to Bath around 1828, where the two owned a jewelry store. But the partnership soon dissolved. He improved his position by marrying Israel Jacobs's only daughter in 1830, but the family's subsequent movements suggest more troubles. They migrated to Nottingham, and then moved again to Deborah's hometown of Hull. There Isaac ran another jewelry store until 1840, when he suffered a bankruptcy, prompting him to take a job as a traveling salesman.[4]

Young Charles was probably more impressed by his flamboyant uncle Samuel Lewis Lazarus, who dabbled in steamships, horses, and, perhaps not coincidentally, a soap factory. Samuel ran an agency for a line of packet ships running from Southampton to the Channel Islands, Le Havre, and Brittany. He pursued prospects on the Continent, selling horses to British soldiers stationed in Belgium. In 1832, he wagered on a 140-mile harness race from Bath to Reading, betting that his steed, *Greyhound*, could defeat a cob named *Gypsey*. Though an underdog, *Greyhound* won, earning Samuel £100 (about $11,000 today). In 1833, he dissolved the soap firm and left Bath for London, where he owned the Age Stables, "the fastest stage coach in England."[5]

A gambler, Uncle Samuel knew both luxury and penury. He declared insolvency four times, earning a year sentence in debtor's prison on one occasion. When he was free, however, he was a well-known character in Victorian London. His equine interests connected him to a smart set of dissolute young horse-racing aficionados. Offering his clients credit, Samuel also operated as a "bill discounter," a street banker who lent money and purchased bad debts at shillings on the pound. Lazarus induced payment through public harassment and legal wrangling.[6]

Uncle Samuel's pursuits drew him into contact with British aris-

tocrats with names such as Paget and Huntingtower. In 1848, he
became involved with Lieutenant Walter Lockhart Scott, the "trou-
blesome" twenty-four-year-old grandson of novelist Sir Walter Scott.
Learning that Lieutenant Scott was deep in debt, a man named Moreton promised Scott £1,000 in cash in return for two £500 bills of
debt. Scott mailed his checks to Moreton, who sent nothing in return.
Uncle Samuel obtained the bills and then sold them to an investor.
"Mr. Scott," Lazarus allegedly gloated, "is well known to me, and is as
green as grass. I can suck him like an orange." When the speculator
declared bankruptcy, Lazarus came forward as a creditor and asked
the court to force Scott to pay in full. The judge refused, concluding
that Scott was the victim of a conspiracy. But he lambasted the young
wastrel for poor judgment. Unimpressed by this scolding, Scott continued his debauched ways and died just three years later.[7]

ISAAC LAZARUS DEPARTED England for New York in July 1845. He left
his wife and five children, including Charley, with his in-laws in Hull.
Isaac had obtained a job as the authorized agent of J. B. Carey & Co.,
a Manhattan manufacturer of ornamental show cards. These were
advertisements, often 3½ by 2½ inches, printed with color images
on one side and trade information on the other. That year, Edgar
Allan Poe, the editor of the Broadway Journal, touted Carey's "beautiful specimens, displaying much taste." Isaac's job was to thwart
"imposters" claiming to be their salesmen, stealing customers, and
hawking inferior products under their name.[8]

Isaac must have imagined brighter prospects in New York City, for
he brought his three teenaged sons—Charles, John, and Frederic—to
the U.S. in 1847. Manhattan was already the commercial capital of
the United States. Its deep harbor appealed to shippers, while canals
connecting the Hudson River to the Great Lakes to the Mississippi
River made it the hub of a grand circuit, from Europe to Chicago and
then south to New Orleans and the Caribbean. The main business of
the city became commerce itself: importing, wholesaling, retailing,

transportation, and finance. In 1850, only 16.8 percent of New York residents toiled in factories. The docks were the real source of the city's wealth and employment. Between 1820 and 1860, 60 percent of America's imports passed through New York, not to mention 33 percent of the country's exports. New York was also the main entry point for immigrants. Between 1845 and 1850, over half of all newcomers to the country landed in the city. For this reason, no one in New York could afford to ignore the port and its guardian, the custom house.[9]

But the family also fled the restrictions of Victorian England. Until 1832, the City of London permitted only twelve Jews to purchase the right to trade in what was then the world's greatest financial market. Jews could not legally vote until 1835. Britons who refused to take a Christian oath on the New Testament were barred from election to Parliament. Laws forbidding commerce on Sunday hindered Jewish merchants, who rested on Saturday and worked on the Christian Sabbath. Indeed, in 1827, six years before Charles's birth, police arrested a "C. L. Lazarus" for peddling fruit on a Sunday in London. Though British Jews endured little of the mob violence that plagued their kinsmen in continental Europe, they were nonetheless second-class citizens. And every attempt to promote Jewish equality had occasioned protests from those who worried that Britain was losing its Christian character.[10]

Many British writers depicted Jewish merchants as thieves, chiseling merchants and unscrupulous moneylenders. Frederick Marryat, the inventor of the modern sea story, viciously libeled port Jews in his fiction. Edmund Hodgson Yates named a smuggler "Old Lazarus" and wrote about borrowing "silver" from a "shy" named Lazarus on Jermyn St. (possibly Uncle Samuel). Even the liberal Charles Dickens succumbed to stereotype in 1838, introducing the character Fagin, a Jewish fence who leads a gang of child pickpockets. This bias declined over time. Dickens avoided ascribing a religion to the usurer Krook in his 1852 novel *Bleak House*, while Yates later described Jews with a certain condescending fondness. But well into the twentieth century, British authors disparaged their Jewish characters.[11]

Charles's relatives experienced this anti-Semitic derision. In 1842, Charles's grandfather Lewis Lazarus testified in a Dublin court on behalf of a Michael Coote, the owner of a jewelry store accused of selling stolen property. The judge, Baron Richards, asked Lazarus, "What is your Christian name?" Before he could answer, the defense attorney interjected "Oh, my Lord, he has no Christian name, he's a Jew," prompting the audience to laugh. Lazarus sought to recover his dignity by replying "My names are Lewis Lazarus; I am a Jew and a proprietor of a *large* establishment in Parliament Street." In 1847, Uncle Samuel's son, John Zachariah Laurence, had been obliged to attend the fairly new University College London, as Oxford and Cambridge still did not accept Jewish students. He would subsequently become the father of British ophthalmology. [12]

England offered the Lazarus family wealth but not status, arguably the real coin in what George Orwell later called "the most class-ridden country under the sun." As early as 1829, Uncle Samuel began intermittently using the Anglicized surnames "Lawrence" and "Laurence." Seeing himself as an international banker, he bragged of his dealings with the aristocracy and his speculations in notes worth "hundreds of thousands of pounds" in both England and on the Continent. Yet, the British establishment mocked his pretensions. The *Times of London* explicitly referred to him as a "Jew." Satirical journals considered him little more than a con man, viewing his attempts at assimilation as deceptive. *Punch* lamented the fact that "the names of the patriarchs and princes of Israel . . . are capable of an expansion or contraction by which they are effectively disguised. . . . The name of LAWRENCE is one which several Englishmen have rendered honourable; but LAWRENCE is also convertible with LAZARUS unconverted."[13]

In New York City, Charley's father Isaac could see an appealing alternative. There, Jews had an easy defense against those who attacked them as alien, namely the fact that coreligionists from Holland and Brazil had lived in New Amsterdam since the 1650s. In the colonial period, they suffered under Dutch and British restrictions on their enterprise, but these limits gradually disappeared in the eighteenth century. The state did require businesses to close on Sunday, a law placing Jewish merchants at a disadvantage, but the rule was often unenforced until the 1860s, and even then it inspired significant protest from many different groups. The wealthiest Jewish merchants had unprecedented opportunities, including a place in high society.

In the United States, Jews could obtain full citizenship. The Constitution itself barred religious tests for office holding, while the First Amendment prohibited the federal government from establishing a national religion or interfering with religious practice. In 1790, President Washington wrote parishioners of Rhode Island's Touro Synagogue that "happily the Government of the United States . . . gives to bigotry no sanction" and "requires only that they who live under its protection should demean themselves as good citizens." That same year, Pennsylvanians changed their commonwealth constitution to allow Jews to run for office and elected Israel Jacobs, a namesake of Charles's grandfather, to the second U.S. Congress. By the 1830s, nearly every state had eliminated religious qualifications for office and voting.

Indeed, other Lazaruses had succeeded in New York. A religious leader at the Sephardic synagogue Shearith Israel, Eleazer S. Lazarus, edited the nation's first "Spanish-rite" prayer book. Eleazer's son Jacob Hart Lazarus was a painter dubbed "a nineteenth-century Copley." His other son, Moses, owned a sugar refinery and distillery. Moses's daughter Emma later wrote "The New Colossus," a poem inscribed inside the Statue of Liberty, whose words—"Give me your tired, your poor, Your huddled masses yearning to breathe free . . ."— helped redefine America's historical mission around the principle of immigration.

The freedom experienced by American Jews was best demonstrated by newspaper editor and playwright Mordecai Manuel Noah. In 1813, President James Monroe appointed Noah as consul to Tunis, one of the Barbary States that harbored pirates, and assigned him the clandestine mission of obtaining the return of American hostages held in Algiers. Though Noah negotiated the return of the captives, he failed to keep the affair secret, prompting Monroe to recall him in 1815. Looking to disguise the diplomatic failure, Monroe cited Noah's Judaism as a justification. But in a democracy like the United States, such official anti-Semitism was politically dangerous. Under pressure from the Jewish community, Monroe apologized.

As their numbers grew, Jews like Noah could actually demand that Gentiles accept their leadership. Styling himself as the leader of his community, Noah outlined a scheme for colonizing the world's Jews in Grand Island, New York, near Buffalo. At the 1825 dedication ceremony for this proto-Zionist experiment, Noah dressed as an Israelite judge, wearing a costume from the Shakespeare play *Richard III*, complete with gold medallion. The plan never materialized further, but Noah's clout among Jews remained very real. In 1829, newly elected President Andrew Jackson nominated him to be the surveyor of the Port of New York, the second highest position in the custom house. Though his rivals tried to use his Jewishness to prevent his appointment, he nonetheless secured confirmation from the Senate.[14]

IN 1850, SEVENTEEN-YEAR-OLD Charles L. Lazarus declared his independence, setting out on a career as a daguerreotypist. Daguerreotyping was an early form of photography perfected in France, using a copper plate coated with silver and sensitized to light with iodine vapor. Many jewelers had turned to photography in the 1840s, perhaps because of their interest in art, their experience with metal plating, and their interest in selling frames. Lazarus opened two studios in Manhattan a block apart at 271 Broadway and 74 Chambers St., not far from City Hall. This was a popular location for artists; master jeweler Charles Lewis Tiffany occupied the same building, while painter Jacob Hart Lazarus worked across the street.[15]

Charley was not the only New Yorker intrigued by photography; in 1850, the city boasted seventy-seven daguerreotypists. Within

MORDECAI M. NOAH. Courtesy New York Public Library, New York, New York

a short walk, one would find famed photographers like Mathew Brady and Martin M. Lawrence. Perhaps seeking a less competitive environment, Charley moved to the elite resort of Newport, Rhode Island, in July 1850. His ads promised "colored daguerreotypes with all the latest improvements in the first style of art" as well as "fifty different kinds of the most splendid and varied" cases at "moderate" prices. Vacationers may have doubted the teenager's abilities. He lowered his prices, charging one dollar for a portrait in a morocco case, and promising a "magnetic process which shortens the time of sitting." By the end of the month, he was begging customers to view his "Daguerrean Gallery" as well as his selection of "inlaid cases, gold breast pins, lockets, &c." Shortly thereafter, Lazarus abandoned the business.[16]

Charley then turned to his true love, the theater. His mother's family included several performers, and over the course of his life, he befriended leading artists and impresarios. In 1852, he opened a music store at 493 Broadway, selling "American and Foreign music, for the Voice, Piano. Guitar, violin, Cornet, Flute, Sachorn [sic] . . . Instruments, Military Concert or Orchestral Music Books, Paper. &c.," as well as tickets. His partner was Harvey B. Dodworth, a member of a family of musicians who had also emigrated from Yorkshire. In addition to leading the city's best-known brass band, the Dodworths ran a dancing school and a gallery.[17]

The two Englishmen joined the Broadway scene at a dangerous moment. Pundits were calling for Americans to consume local culture rather than the books, plays, music, and performers of Europe. Disputes over the theater grew heated. In May 1849, a Democratic custom-house clerk named Isaiah Rynders urged patriotic citizens to shower British thespian William Charles Macready with insults, rotten fruit, bottles, and stink bombs as he performed Macbeth at the Astor Opera House. The leader of a gang of pugilists, gamblers, and ward heelers, Rynders's attack on Macready turned into a riot, the military response to which left at least twenty-three people dead. The opera house closed, leaving the city's bourgeoisie with nowhere to hear the classical repertoire.[18]

Following the Astor Place Riot, a shop selling European music might have been a target for nativists. But Dodworth had established his all-American identity playing before rallies and parades. And the partners further burnished their patriotism by petitioning for an honorary concert featuring the works of William Henry Fry, an American composer and the music critic for the *New York Tribune*. Fellow petitioners for the Fry concert included several well-known newspaper editors, including Henry Raymond of the *Times*. But for Lazarus, the most important signatory was Manuel M. Noah, the son of late editor Mordecai Manuel Noah. Though a mere shadow of his late father, he vied with his brothers for the media's honorary title of "King of the Jews."[19]

On September 11, 1854, Charley became an American citizen, swearing allegiance to the United States government and renouncing his former sovereign, Queen Victoria. By 1854 all four of his grandparents were dead, weakening his ties to his homeland. He also may have feared that the nativist American (or Know-Nothing) Party might win November's election and lengthen the time required for immigrants to obtain civil rights. In any case, the decision was relatively painless. He did not need to abandon his English heritage insofar as Great Britain did not acknowledge the naturalizations of other countries.[20]

Still only twenty-two years old, Lazarus opened a brokerage on Pine Street in the financial district, less than a block from the custom house. He published the 1855 West Point class song ("The purple shadows of the past, are closing on the grey Cadet . . ."), but otherwise sold his interest in the music store to Dodworth. As a broker, he helped merchants pass their goods through the customs bureaucracy. He had to know the Byzantine tariff schedules. Charley had to be chummy with the clerks who calculated the duties and liberated each shipment. He needed to convince the assessors to favorably categorize each object. Lazarus had to watch for drawbacks, or refunds of duties paid, which a merchant could claim for breakages and other causes.[21]

On November 12, 1856, Charles vaulted himself into America's Jewish elite by marrying Zipporah Noah, the twenty-one-year-old daughter of Mordecai M. Noah. Called "Zip" by her family, she was a "pretty, lively little lady," educated at boarding schools. Though newspapers later claimed that the Noahs had opposed the match, the wedding was a loving, happy, and not inexpensive occasion. The rabbi of Shearith Israel officiated at the family home at 153 East Twelfth Street. The bride, "elegantly arrayed in richly embroidered white silk," walked down the aisle to the sounds of Mendelssohn's "Wedding March" and stopped below a *chuppah* (or canopy) made of "crimson damask." Charley's eighteen-year-old sister Rose left England to attend. At the reception, eight bridesmaids and "a cortege of intimate acquaintances" enjoyed "viands and delicacies of the choicest description." At six o'clock, the couple traveled to Washington, D.C., for their honeymoon. All over America, newspapers reported the wedding.[22]

To all appearances, at the age of twenty-three Lazarus had settled down. The couple moved into the Noah family home, where Zipporah's mother Rebecca lived with her teenaged sons Henry and Lionel. They organized the synagogue's annual fair at Academy Hall at 663 Broadway to benefit the Jewish poor. As an attraction, Charley hired his old partner Harvey Dodworth and his band to play every night of the event. He solidified his brokerage by adding a storage business with a well-connected fellow parishioner named Elias Wolff. Soon, the couple greeted two sons, Walter Noah Lazarus (1858) and Percy Noah Lazarus (1859) before moving into their own home at 269 East Ninth Street, about four blocks away.

Like many other entrepreneurs, he hunted for price spreads, eking out returns by moving goods from one place to another. In January 1857, Charley took out an ad in the *New York Herald*, appealing to "CAPITALISTS AND OTHERS" to purchase ten thousand flint muskets and two thousand rifles, all with bayonets, "at a bargain." He was acting on behalf of his cousin Benedict S. Bernard, who had acquired the guns from the British government and was holding them on a London dock. Later that year, he advertised a "handsome and commodious three-story house" at 121 Mercer Street for lease.[23]

But Lazarus's businesses depended upon the general prosperity. The early to mid–1850s were an exuberant time. The world's desire for California gold, midwestern grain, and southern cotton had created new fortunes. With this success came a surge in foreign speculation in U.S. firms. With tariffs at their lowest since 1816, Americans bought European manufactures, leading to a trade deficit. When the Crimean War ended, however, grain prices declined, and investors

dumped U.S. securities. By 1857, the situation had become perilous. When bankers realized they were insolvent, they suspended
payments in hard currency, leading depositors to pull their money.
Bank runs quickly led to a general depression. By the end of October,
twenty-five thousand New Yorkers had lost their jobs. In November,
the president ordered soldiers led by General Winfield Scott to protect
the custom house against unemployed men gathering in Tompkins
Square Park.[24]

Amid this disorder, Charley's business affairs turned suspicious.
In 1858, he invested in a ninety-ton schooner called the *Express*,
importing Cuban sugar, honey, molasses, and tobacco. No one
accused Lazarus of dishonesty, but the *Express* was a notorious vessel.
The year before, the customs had seized it for the illicit importation of
forty-eight thousand cigars. The charges were dismissed, but in 1859
an *Express* crewman allegedly pistol-whipped a Buffalo deputy sheriff
to avoid capture. The next year, the schooner, painted black, carrying
"mostly colored persons," arrived in New York after spending time in
the Outer Banks of North Carolina. After giving suspicious answers
to questions, the captain sailed the ship out of port during the night
without clearance.[25]

To further his international wheelings and dealings, Charley
traveled to Europe and the Caribbean. In March 1858, he sailed to
Paris and back for purposes unknown. At this time, no special documents were required from the federal government for travel between
nations, but in 1859 Lazarus applied for a United States passport. In
the winter 1859–60, he put the documents into use by steaming to
Havana, returning home through New Orleans.

In 1859, Lazarus obtained an appointment to a two-year term as a
notary public, a position helpful to his broker business, but an omen
of his future troubles. The state commissioned notaries to guard
against fraud by certifying oaths. They were essential to the function-
ing of the port, as customs collection depended upon sworn statements about the value of merchandise. Though less romantic than

the hollowed-out cane, lying about the price of foreign goods was the most common form of smuggling, and notaries had the power to enable such deceit.[26]

Charley scrambled. He took over a pawnshop started by his brother Frederic, who had returned to England to marry the daughter of a wealthy sponge merchant. Charley scaled back the business, going from loans of $50,000 to much smaller advances on "valuable personal property." He promised to keep all transactions "strictly private," and offered to meet "parties at their own residences." The firm still struggled. In August, he loaned a shady aristocrat named Louis De Pennevet $80 at 5 percent monthly interest, with a diamond cross as collateral. When De Pennevet failed to pay, Charley sold the jewelry, leading the former owner to accuse him of usury. Lazarus defended his innocence, but closed the pawn brokerage in 1859.[27]

His storage business was failing as well, with politics the likely culprit. Republicans swept the elections of 1858, putting them in charge of New York's Assembly and congressional delegation. Charley was a Democrat because his late father-in-law had once been a Tammany Grand Sachem, while his brothers-in-law were Democratic editors and appointees of President James Buchanan. Any loss of patronage would have devastated the firm, which depended upon friendly inspectors, assessors, and warehouse clerks. At this same moment, the courts assessed a judgment against Lazarus and Wolff, which forced them to dissolve the partnership.[28]

Then, on August 11, 1860, Charley experienced the shock of losing his mother, Deborah Jacobs Lazarus, at the age of fifty-one. Described as a "wealthy and cultured Yorkshire lady," Deborah had raised five children to secure adulthood. Her oldest son, Frederic, had become a gentleman dentist in London. Charles had married well and was working alongside his brother John at the port. Her daughter Rose had wed George H. Davis, a wealthy dry goods merchant in Petersburg, Virginia, and she promised to care for her sister Emily.[29]

Little more than a decade after his arrival in the United States,

Charley was at a crossroads. Once a happy-go-lucky artist, Lazarus
was now an orphan, a father to two children, and the master of several fragile businesses. He was not yet a smuggler, but he worked
near the port, engaging in murky deals taking him to Europe, Cuba,
and New Orleans. Yet during the same decade, his adopted homeland faced a crisis of its own. Disagreements over the future of slavery tested the compact between the states. And these debates drew
a range of other Americans into the orbit of the custom house, the
agent of American nationalism.

{ 4 }

SLAVES

During the years preceding the Civil War, slavery overshadowed smuggling and everything else. Abolitionists demanded emancipation, while politicians suggested limiting the South's "Peculiar Institution." Congress lurched from compromise to compromise, trying to satisfy slaveholders fearing the liberation of their human property. But planters refused to be appeased. Indeed, their demands only grew more extreme, some radicals calling for the repeal of laws banning the importation of African slaves. Finally, following the election of Abraham Lincoln in 1860, seven Southern states declared their independence, forming the Confederate States of America. By April 1861, four more states had joined the C.S.A., and the nation itself was at war.

Yet smuggling still provided Americans with a metaphor for understanding disunion. The tariff was a pillar of Lincoln's Republican Party platform. And slavery could not be disentangled from trade. Yankee mills competed with British factories to purchase Southern cotton and sell slaveholders clothes, tools, and shackles. For Northerners unoffended by Southern bondage but committed to the sovereignty of the federal government, smuggling existed on a continuum of treachery with slave importation, piracy, and secession. When war finally erupted, these American nationalists joined the fight for the Union and applied the smuggling simile to runaway slaves, who became "contraband," free from the rule of their former masters.

ANTEBELLUM AMERICANS supported moderate tariffs, staunchly collected. After the Nullification Crisis, Congress lowered rates but strengthened enforcement, expanding the definition of smuggling to include the undervaluation of imports using a "false, forged, or fraudulent invoice." The Treasury also hired "secret inspectors" to patrol the Canadian border, the ports of Boston and New York, and later the new state of Texas. Even free-trade Democrats argued these covert agents were necessary to catch "smugglers" who were "both criminals and enemies of the country."[1]

Despite regional opposition to tariffs, Southern Unionists condemned contraband. Ports like Charleston, Savannah, New Orleans, and Mobile began building new custom houses, temples of commerce that embodied the local hope that Southern businessmen might someday import finished goods directly rather than through New York City. Illicit trade symbolized secession. In 1844, one Tennessee Whig accused politicians opposed to western expansion of harkening to the "jingle of British gold," leaving Texas ripe for English invasion, where it might "corrupt our slaves," "destroy our revenue by smuggling," and "assist the crowned heads of Europe to pull down the fairest fabric ever reared to freedom on this earth." In 1851, none other than Preston Brooks—then a member of the South Carolina legislature, but later a congressman notorious for his caning of antislavery senator Charles Sumner—condemned disunionists as "smuggling secessionists."[2]

Southern judges severely punished smugglers. In 1855, San Francisco federal district court judge Matthew Hall McAllister, a "fervent Unionist" from Georgia, heard the case of Julius Levy. A Prussian-born tobacconist, Levy was accused of lying to customs officials, claiming crates filled with cigars contained less expensive cigarettes.

Levy hired antislavery attorney Edward Dickinson Baker as his counsel. When the jury voted to convict, McAllister confiscated Levy's $30,000 shipment and sentenced him to one year in prison and a $5,000 fine. Levy appealed to President Franklin Pierce, who pardoned him shortly after his conviction.

But the slaveholders who embraced secessionism slowly began defending these same offenders. In 1850, New Orleans customs agents seized packages belonging to a man coincidentally named Jules Levois, claiming that the clothier had undervalued his imports. In 1855, the case rose to the United States Supreme Court, where Justice Samuel Nelson, a New Yorker, wrote the decision giving the government broad authority to confiscate the goods of deceptive merchants. Advocating leniency was dissenter Justice John Archibald Campbell, an Alabaman who retired in 1861 to become the Confederate assistant secretary of war.[3]

And the forces of disunion destroyed the tariff's strongest advocate: the Whig Party. Founded by a southerner, Henry Clay, the Whigs favored federal laws designed to promote economic growth, including the protective tariff, a banking system, infrastructure, and the security of the slaveholders' human property. But this nationalist program became unpopular in the late 1840s. The Whigs' support for the Compromise of 1850, containing a Fugitive Slave Act requiring free-staters to return runaways, demoralized the party's Yankee base. Southern Whigs defected over the nomination of an antislavery candidate, General Winfield Scott, in the presidential election of 1852. By the end of that year, Clay was dead, Scott defeated, and the Whigs all but defunct.

ON THE FOURTH OF JULY 1839, Benjamin Franklin Butler entered American public life, giving a patriotic toast at a picnic attended by Massachusetts Democratic luminaries. Bald, homely, with a limp moustache, drooping eyelids, and a severe strabismus that prompted some to nickname him "Cockeye," Butler relied not on his figure, but upon his brilliant advocacy of Lowell's workers. He began helping injured laborers sue their employers. Butler subsequently denounced wage reductions at the factories. Within two years, he had led the campaign for a ten-hour workday, riding the issue to the Massachusetts House and Senate. With an eye on higher offices, he advocated for a secret ballot and a protective tariff with exemptions for necessities. Meanwhile, Butler wove an elaborate patronage web by securing his supporters jobs in the state's custom houses, post offices, and the Springfield Armory. Over the ensuing decades, this network served him well as a Union Army general, U.S. congressman, and presidential candidate.

Butler's environment nurtured this combination of nationalism and sympathy. He was born to a family of New Hampshire Jeffersonians, and raised to revere Andrew Jackson, his father's commanding officer at the 1815 Battle of New Orleans. Shortly after his birth, his father died captaining a privateer in the Caribbean. The family moved to Lowell, where his mother opened a boarding house. Mingling with laborers sensitized him to their problems, and a rejection from West Point deepened his sense of class resentment. After graduating from Waterville (now Colby) College in Maine, he returned home, working as a fisherman, teacher, and law clerk.[4]

Yet this champion of the mill hand defended slavery. He endorsed it not only in the South, but in the territories taken by purchase and conquest from Mexico. This marked Butler as a conservative within his party, which contained a Free-Soil faction opposed to the extension of slavery into new lands. In 1848, Butler endorsed the presidential campaign of Lewis Cass, a New Hampshire native who believed the territories should make their own laws regarding servitude. This position, called "popular sovereignty," appeared democratic, but actually put the balance of power in the U.S. Senate into the hands of the tiny number of settlers who controlled the new legislatures.

Butler had no special affection for the South. In 1837, while attending Waterville College, he undoubtedly heard how Missouri slavers murdered abolitionist Elijah Lovejoy, who had graduated from the school in 1826. Butler would have also recalled the 1838 death of his cousin, Representative Jonathan Cilley of Maine, in a duel with a Kentucky congressman named William Graves. Northerners eulogized Cilley as a martyr to Southern lawlessness and brutality.

But conservative Democrats believed that the perpetuation of slavery was essential to the survival of the federal union. Moreover, slaveholders had control over the federal patronage that Butler needed to ensure an army of campaign workers come Election Day. Finally, many of his Catholic working-class constituents still supported slavery. When abolitionists came to Lowell and other mill towns, mobs gathered to harass them. Such riots reflected not only commonplace racism, but also distrust of Protestant reformers, and fear of disunion. These workers saw themselves as beset not by the "slave power," but by foreign trade and the employers' stinginess.

In 1850, Butler surprised his critics by joining a reform coalition including Free-Soilers and antislavery Whigs, eventually winning himself a seat in the Massachusetts legislature. The move excited *New York Tribune* editor Horace Greeley, an abolitionist and protectionist. Greeley imagined Butler a "champion of the working classes," who could unify the crusade to liberate slaves with the movement to defend laborers. But when the ten-hour-day bill stalled in the assembly, Butler discovered that he had alienated Southern party leaders without attaining his signature goal. He returned to the conservative fold. Though he refused to indulge in racist demagoguery, Butler supported proslavery candidates until secession in 1860.[5]

IF NATIONALISM LED northern Democrats like Butler to endorse bondage, then hatred of slavery prompted Richard Henry Dana Jr. to reject blind patriotism. Dana hailed from the kind of elite Cambridge Brahmin family that Butler resented. Dana's grandfather signed the Articles of Confederation. His father was a poet best known for a tale in verse titled "The Buccaneer" (1827). In 1834, declining vision led the younger Dana to quit Harvard and sign on as a seaman on a ship bound to California. Two years later, he returned to complete college and law school. In 1840, his sea diary, *Two Years before the Mast*, became a bestseller, but Dana supplemented his writing as a maritime attorney, making him a familiar figure at the custom house.[6]

Dana possessed strongly benevolent convictions. Early in his career, he campaigned for an end to the flogging of seamen. By 1848, the nomination of slaveholder Zachary Taylor for president led Dana to become a "Conscience Whig," supporting the Free-Soil candidate Martin Van Buren. And new concessions to the South fed his resolve to resist laws protecting slavery. In 1854, he took the case of Anthony Burns, a black man who had allegedly smuggled himself from slavery in Virginia to freedom in Massachusetts about three months earlier. His purported master argued the Fugitive Slave Act of 1850 required federal officials in Boston to return Burns upon his assertion of his ownership. At a time when New England mills depended on slave-grown cotton, northern mobs pelted abolitionists, and politicians truckled to their southern copartisans, Dana's defense of Burns cost him friends and clients.

But Dana often disdained actual humans. He bristled that democracy prevented him from obtaining the high offices he felt he deserved based on his talents, education, and antecedents. He filled his private journals with disparaging comments about poorer Bostonians, especially Irish Catholics. An equal-opportunity snob, Dana condescended to his fellow Brahmins as well. One friend stated that Dana had an "incurable . . . repellent mannerism, behind which lay a want of tact." Another observed that Dana was "a learned lawyer, an aristocrat by nature" who "scorned the opinions of inferior men."[7]

At the time of Burns's arrest, the president was Franklin Pierce, a New Hampshire Democrat known for his servility toward Southerners. Eager to show his support for the Fugitive Slave Act, he ordered federal officials in Boston to imprison Burns pending his return to Virginia. Abolitionists stormed the jailhouse in an unsuccessful effort to free Burns, killing James Batchelder, one of his warders. Only twenty-four years old, Batchelder was a teamster at the custom house, who had migrated to Boston from New Hampshire like so many others. He was popular, and his memorial service was well attended. Burns's rescuers claimed marshals had accidentally shot the deputy, or perhaps that an errant shard from their blunderbuss had hit him. But Benjamin Butler insisted that the emancipators had intentionally stabbed Batchelder in the heart.[8]

To prevent abolitionists from freeing Burns, the U.S. marshal hired 120 guardsmen. In his opening remarks defending Burns's right to freedom, Dana lambasted these Democrats for enforcing federal law:

> The city has never been so safe as while the marshal has had posse [sic] of specials in this court-house. Why sir, people have not felt it necessary to lock their doors at night, the brothels are tenanted only by women, fighting dogs and racing horses have been unemployed, and Ann Street and its alleys and cellars show signs of a coming millennium.

Even more inflammatory was Dana's claim that the martyred Batchelder was a mercenary, driven by greed rather than patriotism. He said he was "glad" that Batchelder had died because he "did not belong there, but he went in for his pay; and . . . he has got his corn."[9]

Louis Bieral, the lead guardsman, took special offense at Dana's comments. Black-haired and mustachioed, Louis had a stout, muscular body "tattooed from head to foot," with "a large picture" labeled "Our Saviour" on his back. He was born in 1814 in Valparaiso, Chile, but kidnapped to the United States in 1823. He took the English name "Lewis Clark," joined the navy, and sailed on the U.S.S. *Columbia*, fighting Sumatran pirates and circumnavigating the globe. Mustered out, he moved to Boston, where he was charged with but not prosecuted for drowning his mistress in Mill Creek in 1841. Over the ensuing years, Louis established a reputation in the city as a pugilist, pimp, saloonkeeper, and gambler. In 1849, he tried his luck in the California gold rush but fled home after being convicted of shooting a prostitute. In 1850, he reassumed his birthname, Louis Bieral, either to confound San Francisco police or perhaps to avoid confusion with Lewis Clarke, a fugitive slave living in Cambridge. But under any sobriquet, he was a dangerous man.[10]

The court ordered Anthony Burns back to slavery, but the government's victory did not satisfy Louis Bieral. As Dana walked down the street, Bieral offered a crony named William Huxford ten dollars to "give" the attorney "his corn." Hitting Dana with a "slung shot," a weight on a rope tied to the wrist, Huxford wounded his scalp, blackened his eye, and broke his tooth. Huxford escaped, inverting the typical fugitive slave's northward flight from bondage by heading to New Orleans as a crewman on a merchant vessel. Slaveholding Louisianans were surprisingly unsympathetic. Their police found the perpetrator hidden in the ship's flying jib and extradited him to Boston. Louis Bieral was equally cold. He testified against Huxford, who received over a year in jail for the mugging.[11]

After the assault, Bieral returned to his old pastimes: boxing, horse racing, and the bordello. He ran a well-known brothel near Bunker Hill in Charlestown and made a name for himself as a "sporting man." Between 1856 and 1860, he umpired several bare-knuckle donnybrooks, including the heavyweight championship bout between Tom Heenan and John Morrissey. He was equally respected by horsemen, who asked him to judge the $1,000 race between two of the period's finest trotters, *Flora Temple* and *George M. Patchen*. He participated in Democratic politics, joining the Empire Club of Isaiah Rynders, the man responsible for the Astor Place Riot. In 1857, Bieral obtained a job in the New York Custom House.[12]

But the Burns case achieved a concrete political result. The new Republican Party emerged out of the anger over the Fugitive Slave Act and the Kansas-Nebraska Act. It drew together Conscience Whigs, Free-Soil Democrats, nativist Know-Nothings, and mem-

CAPTAIN LOUIS BIERAL. Courtesy Bird Library, Syracuse University, Syracuse, New York

bers of the Liberty Party. The goal of the new organization was to bar slavery from the western territories, preserving those lands for whites. Yet, such a platform could not attract a majority of voters in a national election. The Republicans needed the support of workers in cities like Lowell, whose more immediate concerns were higher wages and shorter hours. To broaden their appeal, the GOP adopted a version of the Whig program, advocating policies promising not only a general prosperity, but enabling manual laborers to advance in status. By the election of 1860, the Republicans favored protective tariffs on imports, federal support for the construction of a transcontinental railroad, and the distribution of national lands to farmers.[13]

WHILE NORTHERN DEMOCRATS called for Americans to obey the laws protecting slavery, Southerners began defending the illegal smuggling of slaves into the United States. In 1858, off the coast of Cuba, the navy captured the *Echo*, a schooner carrying four hundred kidnapped Africans. Towing the ship to Charleston, the very center of secessionist sentiment, the U.S. attorney prepared to try the crew for piracy. Confident of a sympathetic jury, the defense attorneys asked the jury to nullify the statute, calling the prosecution a front for "the Black Republican bloodhound." Though newspapers like the *Charleston Courier* urged the rule of law, the defense tactic worked, as the two juries swiftly acquitted the crew of the *Echo*.

Southern editors even suggested repealing the 1808 ban on the international slave trade. James D. B. DeBow, the man who had helped create the legend of Jean Lafitte, founded an organization to convince Southerners that blacks benefitted from being abducted to the United States since it introduced them to Christianity and western civilization. Likewise, the *Charleston Mercury* called for the resumption of the African slave trade, mocking the "sickly sentimentality" of those who enjoyed the fruits of slavery but bridled at the horrors of the Middle Passage.[14]

In the past, this unlawful traffic had divided Northerners. In 1820, Congress enacted the Piracy Act, which made kidnapping Africans a capital offense. The president dispatched the navy to capture slavers, while revenue cutters patrolled the coasts of the United States to prevent them from landing. Yet northern politicians showed little interest in prosecuting offenders. One slave trader claimed that eighty-five ships sailed from New York City in 1859 carrying back at least 30,000 slaves. Despite this activity, New York courts had convicted only one person for the crime during the prior decade, and that verdict was overturned by the Supreme Court. As a consequence, as many as 250,000 slaves were illicitly spirited into America between 1808 and 1861.[15]

Yet the acquittal of the *Echo*'s crew unified the free states. The Republican *New York Times* criticized the government's "very timid and hesitating" prosecution. Northern Democrats were barely less frustrated. At the 1860 Democratic Convention in Charleston, Benjamin Butler sought a compromise: a Southerner such as Senator Jefferson Davis for president, but a moderate platform. His fellow delegates did the opposite, nominating Illinois senator Stephen Douglas and producing a platform that was a slaveholder's wish list. By the time the deadlocked convention reconvened in Baltimore, Butler had to hire a prizefighter to guard him against his fellow Democrats. A Georgian delegate's "homily" for the international slave trade was the last straw; Butler withdrew from the convention, declaring that he refused to associate with men advocating "piracy." As he exited, a Douglas supporter jeered, "There goes the Boston custom house. . . ."[16]

THE ELECTION OF Republican presidential nominee Abraham Lincoln, a man who hated slavery, marked the beginning of the secession crisis. On December 21, 1860, South Carolina declared its independence, charging the North with breaching the Constitution by refusing to guarantee the property rights of slaveholders. The Palmetto State sent commissioners to Washington to negotiate the status of federal buildings, such as custom houses, post offices, and forts. By the end of January 1861, six other states had left the Union. On April 12, 1861, fighting began in earnest when Confederate cannons bombarded Fort Sumter, the U.S. garrison in Charleston harbor.

Given the secessionist's complaints, Republicans naturally saw the war as an expression of their political values, namely the incompatibility of freedom and slavery. But the war also forced Democrats to reconsider their principles. Benjamin Butler felt betrayed. He had believed Southerners who claimed that the Union depended on northern compliance with the Fugitive Slave Act. Supporting that law in hostile Massachusetts had cost him the governorship in 1859. Now it was clear that secessionists did not care about his sacrifice.

In December 1860, Butler advised President Buchanan to arrest the South Carolina commissioners before the other states could follow. The conversation steeled Buchanan temporarily, but the elderly executive soon returned to a condition of impotent despair. Unsuppressed by prompt action, rebellion flowered, and the war came.

War meant raising an army, and the Republicans needed men like Butler capable of convincing working-class Democrats to fight the rebellious South. Dreaming of military glory since childhood, Butler had risen from private to colonel in the Lowell militia. Now, he asked his state's Republican governor how he might aid the state's war preparations. Appreciating Butler's denunciation of the secessionists and believing he could marshal Democrats behind the Union, the governor named him commander of the Massachusetts volunteers.

As a general, Butler became slavery's staunchest foe. Originally sent to Washington to protect the capital, he was shifted to Fort Monroe in Virginia in May 1861. Only two days after arriving, Butler's captain of the guard arrested three black men who had fled their work on Confederate fortifications. In need of labor, Butler confiscated the human property as "contraband of war," impressing the runaways into federal service and sending a receipt to their master, Captain Mallory. Essentially freeing any slaves who could reach the Union lines, Butler's order constituted the beginning of the end of the "Peculiar Institution" and made him an idol among the Republicans who had loathed him in the 1850s.

"Contraband" became the Union's term for slaves escaping their plantations amid the chaos of war. The word seemed to depict freedpeople as property even as it gave them their liberty, yet Butler's choice reflected his father's exploits as a privateer, his hero Jackson's response to nullification, his expertise as an attorney, and his experiences with the custom house. Butler chose to call fugitives "contraband" not because he believed them commodities in human form, but rather because it legally justified taking slaves away from their masters. With the word "contraband," Butler harkened to the authority navy captains wielded to seize enemy merchantmen as "prizes," as well as the power of Treasury officials to claim illicit cargo. The term defined secessionists as smugglers whose human property could be seized and liberated by the Army.[17]

Tattooed, rowdy Louis Bieral also threw himself into the fight, winning a captain's commission in the First California infantry regiment, led by Oregon Republican senator Edward Dickinson Baker. Before his election to Congress, Baker had been one of the finest attorneys in the west (he represented smuggler Julius Levy in 1855), as well as close friends with Ben Butler's brother Andrew and the new president, Abraham Lincoln. To fill out the regiment, Bieral recruited "every sporting and muscle man known to fame and the Police Courts for the last five years."[18]

Bieral redeemed himself in combat. On October 21, 1861, Colonel Baker ordered his men to cross the Potomac River from Maryland to Virginia, just outside Leesburg, to reinforce a scouting mission by the Sixteenth Massachusetts Infantry. But Confederates trapped Baker's troops against the shore, then shot the commander "four or five" times in the head. The Southerners "rushed in to seize Col. Baker's body," but Louis "and a dozen comrades of the California Regiment sprang forward." He seized the "huge red haired ruffian" who had killed Baker "by the throat and blew out his brains." Bieral then "drove the rebels off, and bore" Baker's corpse "down to the river." Lacking enough boats to retreat, 223 Union soldiers died, many drowning after jumping into the water. The Confederates wounded 226 more and captured 553. To save face following the debacle, the northern press labeled Bieral the "hero" of the Battle of Ball's Bluff.[19]

Disunion had turned the men of the northern custom houses against slavery. Shortly after the Ball's Bluff catastrophe, New York City's district attorney began prosecuting Captain Nathaniel Gordon of Maine for slave smuggling. In 1860, the navy had captured his schooner, the *Erie*, near the mouth of the Congo, carrying nearly nine hundred kidnapped Africans, half of them children. On November 8, 1861, a jury convicted the captain under the 1820 piracy statute. On February 21, 1862, the United States hanged Gordon at the House of Detention known as "The Tombs."[20]

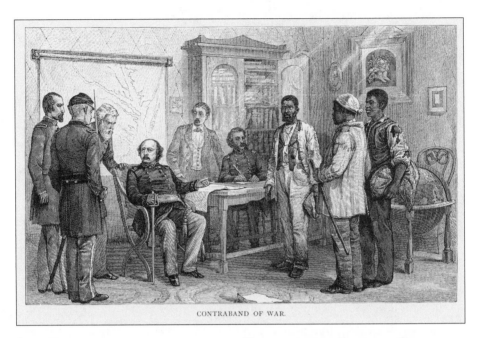

CONTRABAND OF WAR.

STEEPED IN THE LORE OF THE PRIVATEER, UNION GENERAL BENJAMIN BUTLER JUSTIFIED THE CONFISCATION AND LIBERATION OF ESCAPED SLAVES BY DEFINING THEM AS "CONTRABAND." Courtesy New York Public Library, New York, New York

BLOCKADE

On the afternoon of May 1, 1862, General Benjamin F. Butler disembarked the U.S.S. *Mississippi*, marching from the New Orleans levee in search of the United States custom house where Union Marines had raised the Stars and Stripes three days prior. A soldier familiar with New Orleans led the way "along the Levee to Poydras Street . . . to St. Charles Street . . . to Canal Street and the Customhouse," a route that passed close to what had once been the continent's largest market in human chattel. But even a cross-eyed, nearsighted man like Butler could have found the building, then the largest structure in America—32,000 square feet bigger than the Capitol. A locksmith would have been more useful, as the last occupant had secured the door. Butler's men had to force their way into the "huge sarcophagus of granite" to make camp inside.

Butler based the Union occupation of New Orleans in the custom house, but he did not remain overnight, choosing to stay with his wife on the *Mississippi*, and subsequently in the luxurious St. Charles Hotel. The building lacked a roof, permanent windows, and a finished floor, its completion having been delayed by serious structural problems. Wartime neglect had done the building no favors. Since the firing on Fort Sumter, the Confederacy had used it not for tax collection, but as a post office and arms depot.

The general reveled in his control over the Crescent City. As he marched past the grand mansions of St. Charles Street, he likely thought of his late father, who had once served there with Jackson and Lafitte. He also knew the port's potential. As commander of the Army of the Gulf, he now controlled the South's largest city. Before the war, New Orleans was the port through which 2.26 million bales of cotton, 195,000 hogsheads of sugar, and 314,000 barrels of molasses per year passed on their way to foreign markets. The builders of the custom house had dreamt that New Orleans could be a center for imports, where Southern merchants could buy manufactures directly from Europe, cutting out middlemen in New York. Butler's command gave him control over this trade, and it was smuggling on his watch that ended his reign in the Gulf.[1]

THE CIVIL WAR amplified the implications of smuggling. Before secession, in 1860, a Republican House of Representatives passed a new tariff doubling the rate of taxation on imported manufactures. Its sponsor, Justin Smith Morrill, represented the transformation of northeastern opinion. Having been born in Vermont two years after the trial of the *Black Snake* smugglers, he became the nation's foremost protectionist. Southern congressmen had uniformly opposed the Morrill Act, and the Democratic Senate would have reduced his rates, but by the time that body voted on the bill in February 1861, most Southern politicians had resigned their offices, allowing the remainder to enact the House version. With the onset of war, Congress further increased tariffs to fund the construction of the Union Army.

Then, on April 16, 1861, just weeks before Butler liberated the Virginia "contrabands," President Lincoln announced that the Union Navy would blockade Southern ports and confiscate all Confederate trade. On May 2, Treasury Secretary Salmon Chase ordered the customs to assist the military. By the end of the month, Union commanding general Winfield Scott had outlined his "Anaconda" plan, which proposed the navy throttle Southern commerce while the army drove down the Mississippi River valley to hew the Confederacy into pieces.

The blockade targeted the South's dependence on international

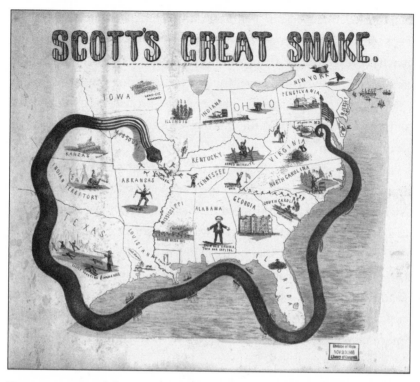

BLOCKADE MAP, 1861. Courtesy Library of Congress, Geography and Map Division

trade. Antebellum Southerners produced less than 10 percent of all American manufactures and less than 5 percent of the nation's iron, clothing, shoes, and firearms. Rather, businessmen invested in cotton production, selling 78 percent of their crop in England. To wage war, the Confederacy needed to trade cotton for British-made guns, ammunition, and uniforms. Secessionists reinforced this relationship in their fiscal policies, lowering taxes on imports to 15 percent and banning tariffs protecting specific industries. Though ideologically satisfying for Southern free-traders, this placed Confederate soldiers at the end of a long supply chain.[2]

War policy thus came to embody the existential rhetoric of antebellum tariff debates. For Southerners, suffocating effects of the Union cordon reinforced their dedication to free trade. And for Northerners, Confederate blockade running ratified the insinuated connection between smuggling and disloyalty. Much as the Emancipation Proclamation of 1863 took the cause of the conflict—slavery—and made its extinction a war objective, the blockade turned the struggle into a test of divergent economic philosophies, a clash between the fast ships of the free-trade South and the blockade squadrons of the protectionist North.

But could such a blockade be enforced? Lincoln had repeatedly argued that states could not void the Union except by mutual consent. And international law permitted the blockade only if the Confederacy was a separate nation. If the war was an insurrection, then Confederates were merely U.S. citizens living in rebellious states, and the Union had no lawful authority to seize their imports. Since Congress would not declare war until July 13, 1861, the president lacked the authority to capture foreign ships, normally considered piracy under international law. Enforcing the blockade thus risked giving the European powers a *casus belli* for intervention.

Lincoln anticipated these objections. In his proclamation of 1861, he defended the blockade as necessary to enforce the uniform assessment of customs duties required by the Constitution. In essence, the North's inability to collect tariffs equally in northern and southern ports justified the closure of Confederate harbors. Lacking confidence in Lincoln's argument, and fearing offending foreign powers, the government sought an opinion from the U.S. Supreme Court.

A test case arose on July 10, 1861, when the U.S.S. *Quaker City* captured the Richmond-based brig *Amy Warwick*, carrying 5,100 bags of Brazilian coffee off the coast of Virginia's Cape Henry. A fast sidewheel steamer, the *Quaker City* had captured two schooners, four barks, and one ship that spring and summer. But the *Amy Warwick* was the real prize, the vessel and cargo together worth over $130,000 (nearly $3 million today), owned by three Virginians and a British firm based in Rio. Thus, when the *Quaker City* towed the brig north to Boston for confiscation and sale, the owners naturally sued for the return of their cargo.

Richard Henry Dana Jr. represented the government. By this time, the antislavery attorney had recovered from William Huxford's attack and returned to practicing law. When the war erupted in 1861, the forty-six-year-old Dana did not follow his similarly middle-aged rivals, Benjamin Butler and Louis Bieral, into the army. He stayed in Cambridge and accepted Lincoln's appointment as U.S. attorney for Massachusetts.

Considering the seizure of the *Amy Warwick* was a largely Democratic Supreme Court, led by Chief Justice Roger Taney, the author of the infamous 1857 *Dred Scott* decision. The owners of the vessel argued that, absent a declaration of war, the executive lacked the authority to seize the assets of loyal U.S. citizens, innocent of any crime, who merely happened to live in a state that had declared its independence. Submitting a brief called a "legal masterpiece," Dana replied that an insurrection of such a scale gave the president war powers, even if the hostilities were technically civil in nature. In a 5-4 decision, the court legalized the expropriation of Southern importers.[3]

Having established the constitutionality of the cordon, the Union scrambled to implement it. At first, the Northern navy had too few vessels to patrol 3,500 miles of Southern shoreline. Of the ninety ships in the federal service, only three armed crafts were available on the Atlantic coast at the start of the war; the rest were in disuse, under construction, or abroad. Moreover, Union steamships possessed drafts too deep to follow smugglers into the shallow coastal waters between Norfolk and Charleston. Rather than trying to stop small craft from landing on beaches, the navy focused on ports where larger vessels could dock, unburden, and load. On land, Union troops were often too busy battling the Confederacy to police the long border between the sections. And the restrictions only increased the profitability of smuggling, tempting otherwise loyal merchants into trading manufactured goods for raw cotton, whose global price had exploded.

Because international law forbade belligerents from enforcing a porous blockade, smuggling increased the risk that one of the European powers might intervene on the Confederacy's behalf. On June 29, 1861, Napoleon III of France told diplomat James Watson Webb his country would obey the blockade if, and only if, it was effective. Blockading was one of Britain's favored tactics, so the English acknowledged the cordon was lawful, but whined about its inadequacies. Thus, if the United States could not stop Confederate smuggling, European nations might cease to recognize the blockade and then use the harassment of their shipping to justify ending their neutrality.

Southerners sought to exploit these holes in the cordon to exchange their agricultural products for gold, materiel, food, medicine, and clothes. During the Civil War, traders exported nearly two million bales of cotton, worth as much as $327 million, over half of which was smuggled past federal forces. Likewise, the South obtained 60 percent of its armaments by skirting the Northern blockade. Most runners steamed to and from neutral ports in the Caribbean, either Bermuda and the Bahamas, so close to the Carolinas, or Cuba, which allowed access to Gulf cities like Mobile and New Orleans. Using these harbors allowed merchants to avoid the Treasury's restrictions on exports to the South. To obtain clearance to sail from Union custom houses, shippers had to swear their goods were not destined for the Confederacy and post bonds as security against violation of their oaths. Merchants could take their goods from New York to Nassau on larger ships and then transfer their cargoes to faster, smaller Southern steamers for transportation to nearby Charleston. As the blockade drove prices higher, smuggling profits exploded, and trade with the British West Indies rose to double its prewar levels.[4]

The Confederate Navy itself purchased a few ships to run the blockade. The most famous smuggling vessel was the C.S.S. *Robert E. Lee*, a former Scottish steamer built to carry mail quickly from Glasgow to Belfast. Between her purchase in 1862 and capture in 1863, she ran twenty-one missions between Bermuda and Wilmington, North Carolina, bringing valuable war materiel into the South and exporting almost seven thousand bales of cotton worth more than $1 million in gold. The ship's commander, Lieutenant John Wilkinson, had fought with Jackson at New Orleans in 1815. Born in Virginia to a wealthy slaveholding family rooted in naval service, Wilkinson denied any selfish motivations. "Being a gentleman of the purest integrity," one author noted, Wilkinson forewent the "large fortune" he might have accumulated and "returned to his family" after the war "dead broke," but with a "clear conscience."[5]

The rebel government, however, delegated the responsibility for provisioning the South to private citizens, many of them ordinary Southerners. Presidential assassin John Wilkes Booth bragged that he took advantage of the liberty given him as an actor to smuggle quinine—then the only effective treatment for malaria. Louisa Buckner, the niece of the postmaster general, was caught carrying one hundred ounces of the drug sewn into her skirt. Likewise, at the start of the war, First Lady Mary Todd Lincoln's half-sister fled to Alabama carrying medicines and a uniform bearing solid gold buttons worth as much as $40,000.

The privatization of smuggling left Southern supply in the hands of merchants motivated by a mix of self-interest and sympathy. One historian has counted seventy-seven London firms engaged in supplying the Confederacy and many more traders invested in contraband cotton. These merchants seldom did their own smuggling, choosing instead to book transit on blockade runners like the famous *Margaret and Jessie*, a side-wheeled steamer that carried goods primarily between Nassau and Wilmington. A Glaswegian ship similar to the C.S.S. *Robert E. Lee*, the *Margaret and Jessie* was purchased for £24,000 by South Carolina financier (and later Confederate treasury

secretary) George Trenholm whose business interests stretched from
Liverpool to New York to the Caribbean. Its captain, Robert Lockwood, left a position piloting a packet ship for the glory of blockade
running. But unlike Wilkinson, Lockwood grew "rich" before the
Union Navy captured his vessel in November 1863.[6]

THE BLOCKADE REQUIRED that the federal government assert an
authority over trade unimagined since the War of 1812. The Congress
appropriated funds for new employees in the Treasury and custom
houses to collect the higher tariffs and prevent the flow of goods
to the Confederacy. The War Department not only gained two million soldiers, sailors, and marines, but also whole divisions, such as
the Union Intelligence Service, the army's spy agency and the sole
national police force in the era before the Secret Service and the Federal Bureau of Investigation. The new mandate of the government
was just as noteworthy as its enlargement. The application of the
blockade enabled U.S. officials to arrest the bodies and confiscate the
property of Confederates crossing the line between North and South.

The superior United States Navy held primary responsibility for
policing commerce. Though initially opposed to the blockade, Navy
secretary Gideon Welles performed admirably, purchasing private
vessels and building new ironclad steamers to police the shore, control the rivers, and capture Confederate ports. During the ten months
preceding Butler's victory at New Orleans, three hundred ships ran
the blockade of the city. But then the Gulf Coast Blockading Squadron
arrived, led by Flag Officer David Farragut and his adopted brother
Commander David Dixon Porter, the son and namesake of the captain
who fought Lafitte in 1808 and the British in the War of 1812. Cotton
exports through the port dropped from 1,800,000 bales of cotton to
fewer than 40,000 between 1861 and 1862. Even as cotton prices rose,
the total value of exports from the city dropped by two-thirds.

Such efforts prevented the Confederacy from resupplying. While
smugglers completed over five thousand runs to Atlantic and Gulf

ports during the war, nearly two-thirds of these occurred during the year 1861, when the cordon was not yet established. After 1862, few ships completed more than two trips before being captured. Over time, merchants focused exclusively on exporting cotton, concluding that the returns of importing no longer justified the risks. Private interests having failed to guarantee the South sufficient food, clothing, and materiel, in 1864, the Confederate Navy took responsibility for running the blockade. This effort proved too late to save the Southern war effort, but it further solidified the Northern sense that smuggling and rebellion were intimately entwined.[7]

The Lincoln administration also hired spies to police the trade in cotton and war supplies. Lincoln's first chief of the Union Intelligence Service was Allan Pinkerton, a Scottish immigrant and abolitionist who ran an eponymous private detective agency in Chicago. Pinkerton nabbed several blockade runners, but focused on gathering military intelligence for Union commander General George McClellan, rather than looking for treason among citizens. In November 1862, after Lincoln replaced McClellan with Ulysses S. Grant, Pinkerton resigned in protest. Though he continued to work for the Union cause, he no longer led the secret service.

Pinkerton's replacement was Lafayette C. Baker. Neither an experienced detective nor an active Republican, Baker was a baffling choice for the job. Born in Stafford, New York, in 1826, Baker worked as a mechanic in Philadelphia and New York City before moving to gold rush San Francisco at the age of twenty-six. In 1855, he joined the reborn Vigilance Committee, but his commitment must have been lackluster, for the official organ of that group, the *Evening Bulletin*, remembered him as "sharp, shrewd, and unscrupulous," capable of "any wickedness in private life or any treason in public employment." By contrast, Democratic editor Manuel M. Noah (Charley Lazarus's brother-in-law) praised Baker's "quickness and intelligence." He served two years with the local police, started a business that failed, and then moved to New York City.[8]

At the start of the war, Lafayette Baker enlisted in Senator Edward D. Baker's First California regiment. But he quickly changed his mind and signed on as a messenger for Benjamin Butler's Thirty-First Massachusetts Volunteers. After serving with Butler, Baker drifted to the famous Willard's Hotel in Washington, D.C., where he regaled various congressmen with his exploits in the romantic west. Striking looking, with pale eyes, a strong nose, a thick head of hair, and a fashionable full red beard, he radiated confidence, which convinced the politicians to arrange a meeting with General Winfield Scott. Scott sent Lafayette on a mission south that was successful enough to persuade Secretary of War Edwin Stanton to hire him as the Union's chief intelligence agent when Pinkerton resigned in 1862.[9]

Baker spent much of his time chasing blockade runners. He disguised himself as a secessionist to gain the trust of Confederate agent Felix Wyatt, British merchant William Gilchrist, and Baltimore businessman James M. Haig. Fooling his suspects, Baker arranged with the trio to hide fifty thousand gun caps, fifteen thousand cannon primers, as well as a "large quantity of surgical instrument," in bales of hay on a ship that would "accidentally" run aground at Aquia Creek, Virginia. Upon Baker's information, detectives arrested Haig, Gilchrist, and Wyatt. The latter two spent months in various prisons, were indicted for treason, and then finally released in April 1862. By contrast, Haig succumbed to mental illness and was freed upon swearing his loyalty in December 1861. His mind never recovered.[10]

For Baker, the blockade seemed less a military tactic than a tool for uncovering "sympathizers with secession." Blockade runners were incarcerated in Fort Lafayette. Called "the American Bastille" by its critics, the prison housed as many as 135 perceived enemies of the war effort at any one time, many of them held without charge. Jailed communally in the casements (from which the guns had been removed) were not only contrabandists but Democratic foes of the administration, including newspapermen critical of the war effort. Union officials saw blockade runners as criminals not merely because they broke the law or impeded the war effort, but because they demonstrated a treasonous association with the enemy. To obtain their release, they had to swear loyalty to the U.S. government.[11]

Baker bragged he could penetrate any disguise to uncover rebel smuggling. He claimed he once found fifty-six Sharps rifles with ammunition buried in a Maryland Catholic graveyard, his men digging as the priest decried the desecration of "the resting place of the dead." Baker seized an entire Baltimore bank whose owners had used army travel permits to carry gold across the lines. Nor did he ignore petty contrabandists. He gleefully recalled how a smuggler with twenty ounces of quinine in his "peculiar" hat fired a derringer pistol at him through "his pantaloons pocket." Likewise, he reminisced about confiscating forty pounds of silk from a woman boarding a steamship whose heavy steps did not match her slender appearance.[12]

Like many policemen in this era, Baker thought in terms of criminal cohorts, deeming particular types of people to be treacherous. Seeing Jews as natural blockade runners, he sometimes donned the costume of an "itinerant Jew" in his undercover work. Baker declared the Jewish fraternal society, B'nai B'rith, a "disloyal organization" and arrested its fiercely Republican president for daring to represent Southern refugees. Likewise, his memoirs depicted the blockade runner James Haig as a cowardly "money-making Jew," despised even by the Confederates he was assisting. Blue-eyed, high-browed, and straight-nosed, the London-born Haig had lived in Baltimore for over a decade, yet Baker portrayed him as speaking in a comic-opera "German" dialect.[13]

Such profiling was common during the war. The most infamous example occurred in 1862, when General Ulysses S. Grant issued General Order No. 11, expelling all Jews from Tennessee, Kentucky, and Mississippi, on the assumption that they were smugglers. Lincoln reversed the command, but Grant's prejudice was pervasive.

One Union soldier stated that the "belief became general" that Jews had "secretly banded together" to thwart the war effort. Newspapers played up the religion of Jewish suspects, reporting that "swarms" had migrated south drawn by the profits of smuggling. Some rationalized their prejudice as a function of Jewish involvement in the cotton trade, but the true source was the North's sense of betrayal, filtered through a Christian "Passion play" narrative. It could not have helped that Judah Benjamin, the Louisiana Senator with a name so close to "Judas," was a key figure in the Confederate cabinet.[14]

The suspect groups tried to counteract generalizations about their patriotism by joining the military. Six thousand Jewish men fought for the North, over twice as many as for the Confederacy, yet this did not stop the anti-Semitic insinuations. One anonymous Jewish letter writer erupted in frustration, comparing the situation to the Spanish Inquisition:

> Has the war now raging been inaugurated or fostered by Jews exclusively? Is the late democratic part composed entirely of Israelites? Are all the blockade-runners and refugees descendants of Abraham? Are there no native Americans engaged in Rebellion? No Christians running the blockade or meek followers of Christ within the folds of Tammany?

Meanwhile, Democrats described Baker as more dictator than detective. In 1862, *New York World* editor Manton Marble bitterly complained about Baker's "despotic and illegal arrests of innocent Union men." Two years later, Marble himself was arrested and held in Fort Lafayette.[15]

BLOCKADE ENFORCEMENT was never perfect. At the outset of the war, Union officials noticed suspicious traffic between New York and the West Indies, and enacted precautions governing Caribbean trade. To gain clearance to leave port, the custom house required merchants to submit bonds guaranteeing that their shipment was not destined for the Confederacy. Under these rules, however, officials cleared 7,932 ships to the islands between 1861 and 1864.

These trips attracted increased scrutiny in the fall of 1863. First, in October, New York collector of customs Hiram Barney received evidence that men in the custom house were selling clearance bonds at large discounts. Barney was a handsome fifty-three-year-old attorney, with a cleft chin, moustache, and mane of graying hair combed back off of his large brow. Joining the antislavery movement as a teen, Barney had married the daughter of abolitionist (and former smuggler) Lewis Tappan. Friends with Treasury Secretary Salmon Chase and a major fundraiser for Lincoln's campaign, he won one of the administration's plum jobs.

Investigation soon revealed that a clerk with antislavery connections had abetted the smuggling. Evidence pointed to Daniel Cady "Neil" Stanton, the son of deputy collector Henry B. Stanton and women's rights pioneer Elizabeth Cady Stanton. Described by one historian as "untrustworthy, mendacious, and sly," Neil had long disappointed his parents, who hoped that a job might improve his behavior. Neil instead cancelled bonds worth tens of thousands of dollars for bribes as small as $25. Barney had no choice but to remove Neil and suspend his father.[16]

Then, in November, Barney received letters from an anonymous Bahamian loyal to the Union. The letters claimed that a partnership called "A. Wolf & Co." was smuggling between New York City, Nassau, and the Confederacy. In England, the firm's principal, Abraham Hoffnung, purchased "1,200 colt revolvers, 2,000 badges, made of velvet, for Confederate officers, with a small golden palmetto, 13,000 pairs of Army shoes and 1,200 blankets." In New York, Lewis Benjamin shipped the cargo under a false name, forged bonds, and distributed bribes of between £500 and $10,000 for each clearance. Hoffnung's brother-in-law Samuel G. Levey transported the goods with another shipper named Joseph Eneas. And in Nassau, brothers-

in-law George and Aaron Wolf transferred the goods to blockade runners headed for the South.[17]

These men were international merchants, not buccaneers. A mustachioed young goldsmith partial to cigars, Hoffnung was already
a seasoned traveler. At the age of three, he had emigrated from his
birthplace in Kalisz, Poland, to Exeter, England, where his father had
been offered a position as rabbi. In 1852, at nineteen years old, Abraham moved to St. Louis, where he sold watches for three years, then
left for Montreal. There he married the daughter of tobacconist John
Levey and built an international export business. By 1860, Hoffnung
was prominent enough to be commissioned by the city to produce a
silver medallion for the visiting Prince of Wales. Yet his background
remained murky to outsiders. A reporter for a credit agency groused
that Hoffnung "belongs to a class regarding whom it is next to impossible to learn anything certain."[18]

The Wolf brothers were hardly less itinerant, leaving their childhood home in Great Yarmouth, England, to spend years in Montreal
and New York before abruptly relocating to Nassau at the start of the
war. In February 1863, Aaron Wolf met former congressman Albert
Gallatin Riddle on a steamer to Nassau. Riddle was on his way to
Cuba to serve as the U.S. consul in Matanzas, where part of his job
would be stopping blockade runners. His diary described Wolf as "a
diminutive dark little man of Jewish aspect," who "had made a fortune on a cargo of shoddy, landed in the dark of a conspiring moon
and sold to the rebels." Riddle "congratulated" Wolf on his venture,
choosing to gather information rather than brandish his authority.[19]

Lewis Benjamin was also an Englishman, but marriage tied him
to the United States and the custom house. His wife was the daughter
of Naphtali Phillips, a Tammany Hall stalwart and an assessor at the
port. This made Benjamin a cousin of Mordecai M. Noah, the former
surveyor of customs, and connected him to Noah's son-in-law, Charley Lazarus. Like other members of his wife's family, Benjamin had
links to Charleston, and he openly invested in Southern securities.[20]

These incriminating letters came at an awkward time for Barney, who was under intense political pressure. Though the collector was friends with the president, he was even closer to Treasury Secretary Chase, who was considering challenging Lincoln for the Republican presidential nomination. As a former Free-Soil Democrat from the swing state of Ohio, Chase had bipartisan appeal in the Border States, as well as support among antislavery Republicans that Barney's praise could only burnish. More significantly, Barney's subordinates in the custom house could help Chase's campaign. When Barney refused to endorse Lincoln in the fall of 1863, Secretary of State William Seward and his political vizier Thurlow Weed called for the collector's removal.

Under pressure, Barney sent a detail of men to arrest George Garcia Wolf, bound from Nassau to New York on the *Corsica*. Subjecting him to a "rigid personal search," they seized his "carpet bag," in which they found "southern bonds, sterling exchange, and gold" worth £9,000 (over $600,000 in current money). When he asked for a receipt, the officers responded with "abusive and violent language." Wolf's belongings contained a note matching the manifest of blockade runner *Margaret and Jessie*, recently captured on the way to Wilmington, North Carolina.[21]

The navy released Wolf for lack of evidence, and under pressure from British diplomats, the U.S. government returned his property. But the investigation continued. Discovering that Lewis Benjamin had signed as surety on nearly all Wolf's bonds, U.S. marshals arrested him on December 31, confining him in Fort Lafayette, where he complained of the rotten food, the "filthy and dirty" and overcrowded privies, lack of bathing facilities, and "deprivation of sunlight and air."[22]

The scandal now drew closer to Barney. Marshals seized Benjamin's papers, accounts, and a locked safe. Cracking the latter, officials found letters from Barney's twenty-six-year-old secretary, Albert M. Palmer, demanding money from Benjamin. Further examination showed that Palmer's friend, clerk William A. Smalley, had signed several of Benjamin's bonds. On January 7, detectives arrested Palmer at the custom house. "The accused," the *New York Times* reported, "trembled violently and became very much agitated at the suddenness with which he had been taken." He was confined to Fort Lafayette for seven months without trial before being released.[23]

The alleged smugglers denied the charges, then fled the country. On January 18, Abraham Hoffnung steamed from Boston to Liverpool on the *Arabia* with his wife, four children, and a maid. The Wolf brothers avoided the United States for the remainder of the war. While free on bail visiting his family after more than two months in Fort Lafayette, Lewis Benjamin bolted to Montreal, where he filed charges of attempted kidnapping against a federal marshal who tried to extradite him. Authorities arrested Samuel Levey on the twenty-sixth of May in Boston. After ten days in prison, he secured his discharge by posting $5,000 bail, then hustled back to Canada. Rather than defending themselves in court, the conspirators instead sought redress through diplomatic pressure. Levey filed a protest with the British Foreign Office, as did George Wolf, who demanded the return of the items taken from Lewis Benjamin's safe.[24]

The scandal provoked an outpouring of casual anti-Semitism. Congressional witnesses blamed Jews in the custom house. Testimony described various figures as "a Jew," an "old Jew," and a "confiding, clever, and soft-mouthed Jew." One key witness stated his desire to lay bare the "great number of Jews doing a large business in running the blockade," telling the congressmen about another "French Jew organization" engaged in smuggling led by a man named "Rothschild." The *New York Times* asserted that Hoffnung and Wolf had conspired with an "English Jew" to abscond with borrowed money to fund their smuggling. The article continued, describing them as "notoriously irresponsible and insolvent." This final charge infuriated Hoffnung, who denounced the "vile slanders" in the article. On January 15, from Montreal, he sent a letter to the *Times* firmly denying any allegation that "a single individual, either in Canada, the United States, or Europe, who has a just claim upon me to the amount of one farthing" [sic].²⁵

But the press's target was the Lincoln administration's radical wing, not Hoffnung. Democrats joyously repaid Republicans for past aspersions. The *New York World* commented:

> While an earnest and patriotic people were duped with the loud-mouthed bigotry and the political intolerance which passed for loyalty and patriotism a few months ago; while honest Democrats, whose hearts are in a war for the Union, were being so violently denounced as traitors for not approving a war of extermination and abolition, these Republican politicians were already laying their plans for sending arms and supplies to the rebels.

The *Brooklyn Eagle* declared "Abolition Malfeasance," noting the antislavery vita of Collector Barney. The *Albany Atlas and Argus* condemned Treasury Secretary Salmon Chase and "the criminals, high and low, of the administration, who are turning this bloody war to profit, and who are trying to prolong it, by all means, in order to profit by it."²⁶

Though the collector had committed no crime, Congress flayed Barney for hiring subordinates who had been caught "treasonably aiding the rebellion." President Lincoln hesitated to punish his friend Barney, but the pressure eventually grew too great. In September, Lincoln replaced the collector with Simeon Draper, Thurlow Weed's "whimsical bagman" and a supporter of the president's reelection. The events had worked so clearly to the benefit of Seward's faction that some insisted they had plotted the scandal from start to finish.²⁷

FROM HIS HEADQUARTERS in the New Orleans custom house, General Benjamin Butler faced a range of problems: hunger, crime, disease, the insubordination of city officials, and the resistance of the populace. Their faith in the Confederacy's eventual victory unshaken, residents defied Butler's authority. A local gambler removed the U.S. flag from the top of the Mint. Women heckled and even spat upon infantrymen, assuming their gender protected them against being jailed. The mobs that surrounded Butler had to be held back by bayonets, a reminder that while New Orleans belonged to the Union, the hearts of its citizens did not. Though Confederate forces could not hold the city, secessionist sympathizers could still resist the occupation.[28]

In Butler, Louisianans endured an occupier seemingly concocted to antagonize them. His emancipation of slaves at Fort Monroe terrified planters, but their distaste was as personal as it was political. Southerners preferred leaders to be patrician, tall, and handsome like Jefferson Davis. If Butler bragged about his Revolutionary forebears as a defense against his childhood poverty, he cultivated the hatred of the elite and despised the very notion of aristocracy. Despite his homely physical appearance, women liked him, in no small part because he treated them as equals. Reared by a widow, he married a beautiful, successful, independent-minded actress two years his senior, Sarah Jones Hildreth, who refused to give up her trade until after their wedding.[29]

Through a combination of force and sarcasm, Butler tried to reestablish respect for federal authority in the Gulf. He ordered the execution of the flag thief, believing that this punishment was necessary to deter "blacklegs and blackguards" from engaging in acts of petty terror. Even more controversial was General Order 28, designating ladies who insulted soldiers "women of the town" (i.e., prostitutes). The order mocked the South's "cult of true womanhood," which depicted white women as delicate vessels of morality needing the protection of chivalrous men. Ladies haranguing men in uniform were not, in Butler's view, too pure to be jailed with drunks and thieves. But he also reasoned that women who prized their virtue above all else would want to avoid being labeled streetwalkers, especially in a city known for vice. More ominously, Butler exploited the fear that being classified as prostitutes made Confederate women vulnerable to sexual assault. Though he promised to punish rapists, the "woman order" enraged an already hostile South.[30]

Butler's wrath fell hardest upon Eugenia Levy Phillips, the wife of former Alabama congressman Philip Phillips. Eugenia was a southern belle, related to Charleston's oldest Jewish families. The Phillips house was divided. The congressman supported the Union, but Eugenia was a fire-eating secessionist, who spied for the Confederacy, leading to the couple's 1861 arrest in Washington, D.C. The family was allowed to move to New Orleans with their slaves, but when Butler took the city, the Phillipses found themselves in Union territory again. With tensions high, Eugenia angered Butler by laughing at the passing funeral cortege of a Union soldier, blaming her snickering on her "good spirits." Shocked by her insolence, Butler announced, "I do not call you a common woman of the town, but an uncommonly vulgar one, and I sentence you to Ship Island for the War." During her four-month stay, she complained bitterly of the prison's food, hygiene, and, naturally, the mixing between blacks and whites.[31]

The carrot, however, worked in tandem with the stick. Having established his authority, the general aimed at improving living conditions in the city. Almost immediately, he relieved the starving population by allowing delivery of supplies. In June, Butler convinced Lincoln to lift the blockade on the city. The New Orleans Custom House resumed its former duties, with the cousin of Treasury Secretary Salmon Chase in charge. Butler retained authority over exports, granting residents permits to sell products like cotton and sugar. He hoped that the restoration of lawful commerce, under federal supervision, could earn the loyalty of the city's rebels, the respect of his superiors in Washington, and the love of the voters.[32]

Butler distributed trading permits to his political allies, leading to allegations that he was using his power to run the blockade. The worst offender was his older brother, Andrew Jackson Butler, a "blustering and overbearing" conniver. Once a "Monte dealer" on San Francisco's Barbary Coast, he now found himself in New Orleans, the

"Great Southern Babylon," with his devoted sibling in command. The collector of the Port of New Orleans complained that Andrew cared for nothing besides "making money" and viewed Benjamin's role as "suspicious." In time, even Butler's defenders grew exasperated. Treasury Secretary Chase wondered why Butler "so embarrassed" his friends "with his commercial connections."[33]

His enemies went on the attack. Fearing that Butler or Chase might challenge Lincoln in 1864, using customs officers as campaign workers, Secretary of State Seward dispatched former attorney general Reverdy Johnson to the Gulf to investigate claims made by foreign consuls that Butler was profiting from smuggling. A conservative Marylander with ties to Butler's rivals, Johnson called the corruption "without parallel in the past history of the country."[34]

Confederates redirected these accusations against the Union itself. C.S.A. president Jefferson Davis sought to arouse international opposition to the occupation by issuing a resolution alleging that Butler and his men were "robbers and criminals deserving death," not "soldiers engaged in honorable warfare." Davis asserted that Butler had confiscated property and driven slaves from the plantations until "their owners" consented "to share their crops." The planters having been "extorted," Butler restored the slaves and then required them "to work under the bayonets of the guard of United States soldiers." Davis's allegation that Butler "compelled" the slaves to labor at gunpoint seemed rather rich, given that fifty-seven enslaved African-Americans toiled on the Confederate president's plantation without pay. But Davis correctly surmised that such stories defaced portraits of Butler as a heroic emancipator.[35]

The charges had their effect. On December 14, Butler learned that Lincoln had replaced him as head of the Department of the Gulf. A shocked Butler observed that his critics had reasons for wanting him discredited. If diplomats complained of thievery, it was only because they sympathized with the Confederacy. When other officers like Commander David Dixon Porter charged the general with "supplying the rebels," he did so to steal credit for the New Orleans victory from Butler. If the professional officer corps deprecated Butler as a corrupt amateur, calling him "gas bag" and the "fatty from Lowell," it was because they identified with Porter, the son of the naval hero of the War of 1812, who had once fought smugglers in the Gulf.[36]

Butler claimed he had neither broken the law nor hurt the war effort. Contrary to rumors, cotton exports from beyond enemy lines actually declined during his administration; his rule increased only the flow of food and necessities. Distributing permits to loyal merchants undercut Confederate smugglers, and loosening the blockade helped regain the allegiance of the hostile residents. Cotton sales reduced the price of clothes and Northern unemployment. Commerce with Southerners lengthened the struggle, but so did all compassionate action on the part of the North. Butler favored his friends, but so did every politician in America. And, finally, the law had always allotted the spoils of war to officers who vigorously performed their duties. If the awful toll of war had eroded such traditions, no one ever informed the general.[37]

When logic failed to sway his critics, Butler resorted to demagoguery, deflecting blame for smuggling onto Jews and Englishmen. On April 2, 1863, he spoke in New York, lambasting British blockade runners and their ally, "the Jew banker in Wall Street." The next year, as a commander in Virginia, Butler publicized the capture of "five Jews" trading unlawfully. When criticized for labeling the captives, Butler apologized. Having met few "men of the Jewish faith" during his youth, his attitudes had been shaped by his experiences enforcing the blockade. Though Butler had commanded Jews in the army, they apparently made no impact.[38]

As the Union loosened the blockade in other regions, enforcement grew further politicized. The textile manufacturers of Lowell needed cotton just as desperately as did the mills of Lancashire. And as the Union Army made headway, officials called for the suspension of the blockade to resupply their troops, reduce the profitability of illicit trade, and obtain the loyalty of local residents. Between the fall of 1862 and the end of the war, Lincoln experimented with a range of policies to alleviate misery among Southern Unionists and direct cotton to Northern factories.

Southerners saw such business as proof that antislavery rhetoric was a front for greed. If secessionists believed the Confederacy was glorious crusade, then they painted the Union as a hustle perpetrated by grifters like Butler, who were willing to assist the enemy if it proved lucrative. Such critics were untroubled by the fact that trade between Confederate cotton farmers and Yankee manufacturers necessarily implicated both sides. And they loudly voiced these complaints after the war's end, when a national consensus emerged condemning slavery as an evil.[39]

Victory in 1865, however, guaranteed that such Southern charges of hypocrisy won few immediate adherents above the Mason-Dixon Line. The blockade's success only strengthened Northern support for continued regulation of international trade. The economically diverse, self-sufficient, industrial, high-tariff Union had subdued the cotton-obsessed, Europe-dependent, agricultural, free-trade Confederacy, which had focused on its area of comparative advantage to its eventual doom. The North's superior railways, roads, and canals had proved as invaluable as the South's underdeveloped transportation system had proved disastrous. The war thus demonstrated the strategic value of improvements long favored by Whigs and Republicans, as well as the benefits of developing national economic networks. Finally, the victors concluded that internationalism had fed secessionist sentiment. From now on, the survival of the nation demanded that Americans be forced to trade with one another, even at great cost to themselves.

EXPATRIATE

The South's departure from the Union doubtless left Charles L. Lazarus feeling abandoned. The newly dominant Republicans distrusted Charley because he was a member of a prominent Democratic family. He had ties to slavery, both professional and personal. He had done business in Cuba and New Orleans. Charley's sisters Emily and Rose lived in Petersburg, Virginia, with the latter's husband, George H. Davis. Though George hired a substitute to serve for him in the Confederate infantry, the family owned slaves. Those adhering to the period's anti-Semitism and Anglophobia doubted Lazarus for his religion and birthplace.[1]

The Noah family sought to establish its loyalty. Zipporah's brother Jacob accepted a captain's commission with the Second Minnesota Volunteers and campaigned in Kentucky. As the naval supply agent in Rio de Janeiro, Robert Noah worked with U.S. consul Robert G. Scott Jr., an elite Virginian transformed by war into "an open mouthed traitor and loud" advocate of secession. The consul sailed home to run for the Confederate Congress, absconding with notes on the movements of American ships and thousands of dollars meant for injured sailors. Before Scott left, he lowered the Stars and Stripes from the consulate and replaced it with a Confederate flag. Enraged, Noah secured the building and restored the U.S. flag to its proper position.[2]

Only twenty-seven years old, Lazarus was young enough for military service, but he instead accepted a diplomatic posting in Brazil.

The new minister plenipotentiary to the Empire of Brazil was James Watson Webb, the editor of the *New York Courier and Enquirer*. Tall, handsome, well dressed, with ample cavalry whiskers, Webb was a vain, pompous, and pugnacious man. In his youth, he had been an army officer denied military glory by peacetime. Becoming a newspaper editor, Webb satisfied his bloodlust by challenging rivals to duels. His attacks on James Fenimore Cooper were so vicious that the author sued Webb for libel. The duel that killed Rep. Jonathan Cilley, Benjamin Butler's cousin, began when the congressman slighted the hypersensitive Webb. A profligate spender with little business sense, Webb ran through several fortunes seeking high offices his personality precluded him from ever being given.

Webb had once been partner with Charley's father-in-law, Mordecai Noah. It was an odd relationship. The year before the merger of their newspapers, Webb had argued that Noah's religion disqualified him for office. And the dissolution of their partnership required litigation. Yet the two editors remained on friendly terms. Noah described Webb as a "very honorable man ... possessing about as good a character generally speaking as his colleagues," faint praise in an era when most editors were partisans, ruffians, and opportunists, but tribute nonetheless.[3]

In 1856, Webb abandoned his prior support for slavery to follow his friend William Seward into the new Republican Party. In 1860, Webb used his newspaper to stump for Lincoln. He further cultivated the president early in the war by offering his residence for the funeral of their mutual friend, Sen. Edward D. Baker, Louis Bieral's martyred commander. In 1861, Webb begged Seward, the new secretary of state, to name him ambassador to England. But Webb overrated himself; many men wanted the appointment to the Court of St. James, the nation's premier diplomatic posting. Webb instead received nomination to Brazil, a country where he was friendless and could communicate only through an interpreter.

Webb's disappointment at the Brazil appointment belied its actual

importance as a diplomatic posting. Before the construction of the
Panama Canal, ports like Rio were essential stops for merchantmen
on the way to the Pacific Ocean. To harass Union trade, the Confederate Navy needed harbors to weigh anchor. And as an agricultural
slave empire that had won its independence from Portugal less than
four decades earlier, Brazil's leaders sympathized with the South.
Rio was home to many Englishmen, who pressured the emperor to
endorse the British position on the blockade. But Brazilians mostly
desired peace, for the war had cut coffee exports in half, causing "a
perfect stagnation in business."[4]

Charley's opportunity came when Webb fired the secretary of the
legation, Rev. James Cooley Fletcher, an expert on Brazil, antislavery
author, missionary, and naturalist. The status-conscious Webb was
concerned about rumors that Fletcher had been cuckolded by a prior
ambassador, Robert Schenck, a statesman who later figured prominently in Charley's life. Lazarus seemed almost ideal as a replacement; he was charming, fluent, and familiar with local expatriates.
There was only one problem in Webb's mind; he was "a Jew, and his
social position is not what it should be." Given the mortifying title of
"temporary secretary," Lazarus worked in the legation until December 1861, when Webb found a blue-blooded replacement. Never content, Webb complained that the new secretary was good for nothing
but copying.[5]

Lazarus displayed no resentment upon leaving the embassy in
Petropolis, a city north of Rio, where the emperor lived during the
summer. While his brother-in-law Robert Noah sailed home to the
United States, Lazarus opened an importing business in Rio with
a man named Marcos Weyl. To advance the firm, Charley flattered
Minister Webb and his wife. In May 1862, he wrote, "I take this
opportunity of thanking you for the many kindnesses and the hos-
pitality received at your hands and from Mrs. Webb," and begged for
the "opportunity of reciprocating." He obeyed the "little commands"
of Mrs. Webb, purchasing rheumatism ointment, pins, and a bonnet

from France. In return for this obeisance, Webb named Lazarus his attaché and granted him a diplomatic passport, which smoothed his travels between Rio, Paris, London, and New York.[6]

Beginning in mid-1862, scandal enveloped the Noah-Lazarus family. On July 13, the military governor of Kentucky ordered the arrest of Major Jacob Noah and confined him in an Indiana penitentiary for five months without a hearing. One of the few slave states to remain in the Union, Kentucky was not only strategically invaluable, but also a center for rebel guerrilla fighting. Noah managed to contact the editor of the local newspaper, who convinced officials to release him. But in return, Noah had to post bonds worth $10,000 and promise to exile himself to New York. Only after a senator threatened to investigate did the government void Noah's bonds and grant his unconditional release. Jacob never learned why he was incarcerated, though he supposed it was for befriending a recently paroled Confederate surgeon.[7]

Meanwhile, Charley ran afoul of Brazilian officials. Permitted to import goods for their own use without paying local taxes, diplomats imported more than they needed and sold the rest at a profit. On November 3, a Brazilian customs inspector wrote Webb that Weyl & Lazarus had tried to import forty cases of candles from Havre free of duty by claiming the goods belonged to the minister. "I entertain the suspicion," the inspector wrote, "your respectable name had been involved in this matter without the knowledge of that gentlemen, or your consent."[8]

The inspector probably gave Webb too much credit. Despite marrying two heiresses, he lived so opulently and invested so speculatively that he was constantly short of funds. One enemy described Webb as a "bully, a brawler, a blackguard, and a bankrupt" whose "venality and corrupt conduct as a politician are so flagrant that no one wishes to see him entrusted with the affairs of others." Webb tried to profit from his ambassadorship by pressuring Brazil to grant his son Robert a concession on steamship travel to New York. He wrangled with the U.S. government over reimbursement for his move to Brazil. And after he departed from Petropolis, his critics accused him of pocketing £9,152 given to him for the settlement of a diplomatic claim, then lying about the money's dispensation. In short, many considered him a high-toned hustler.[9]

Webb nevertheless thundered at Weyl & Lazarus's alleged crimes. He assured the inspector "that this transaction is a base and impudent fraud." Webb insisted that he had imported nothing but furniture, candles, wine, paté, and ham. "I indulge the hope, Sir," he wrote, "that as a simple act of justice to me, as well as from a sense of duty to the Customs of Brazil, you will not fail to pursue and punish this disgraceful fraud to the full extent of the law."[10]

To investigate the matter, Webb hired George North Davis—not to be confused with Charley's brother in-law, Virginia retailer George H. Davis—as attaché. A Maine-born rubber merchant who had married into a Boston missionary family, Davis had the background Webb preferred in an aide. Davis went to the custom house to discuss the matter, and on November 13, 1862, he informed Webb that Weyl & Lazarus had done a "very pretty business through you. Your consumption of merchandise has quite astonished the Brazilian office." He then informed Webb that Charley had dissolved the partnership with Weyl, but was still importing goods, a move Davis described as "probably some Jew scheme for swindling."[11]

Lazarus shifted the blame onto his Brazilian dispatcher. On November 15, Davis complained to Webb that the minister of justice had decided to prosecute Charley's employee rather than the principals. "He must go to prison," he wrote, "and W&L go 'scott free'" [sic]. But Davis's righteous anger was short lived. Just two days later he told Webb, "I think you have to congratulate yourself that you are rid of Jewish attachments." Webb continued to correspond with Lazarus, but only to express his displeasure. "I appointed you acting secretary of the legation," he wrote, "& you presumed on the fact to introduce into my House a <u>German Jew Pedlar</u> without my sanction." Davis became Webb's new attaché, a position he used to acquire great wealth.[12]

Chastened, Lazarus left Rio for Paris in 1863. In cooperation with a Brazilian merchant named Alphonse Gatto, Charley exported French goods to South America. When this partnership soured, Lazarus relocated to London with Zipporah and his three sons, Walter, Percy, and newborn Lionel. Believing that his former partner owed him money, Charley began borrowing in London in the name of A. Gatto & Co. In reply, Gatto posted an advertisement in the *Times of London* disavowing Lazarus. Under the name, "Gatto & Co.," Charley began a consignment business, offering cash advances to merchants for goods to be sold in "India, China, Brazils [*sic*], and the Mediterranean." He also traded in commercial paper, freely lending and borrowing money around London.[13]

In London, the Lazarus-Noah family dabbled in a range of pursuits, including blockade running. Though Robert Noah was still less than thirty years old and a veteran of the U.S. Navy and the British Army, he chose to become a director of a Leicester Square music hall rather than fight for the Union. He also entered into partnership exporting wine, beer, and spirits to Brazil. After little more than a year, the business found itself £56,508 (about $6.5 million today) in deficit. Robert had squandered money on racehorses, while his partners had lost £9,135 in the stock market. But their biggest failure was their foreign consignment business, which mislaid £16,728 trading in a range of unfamiliar objects "including swords, guns and gunpowder, hardware, sugars, cement, calf skin, &tc." At least £2,022 of this sum disappeared in "adventures to the Confederate States."[14]

Robert rebounded by starting a similar concern with his nineteen-year-old brother Lionel Noah. Calling themselves "Jackson's Nephews," a play on their mother's maiden name, they exported "wine, pickles, muskets, porter, cement and paving stones" on commission. Jackson's Nephews collapsed in October 1864, having already purchased preserved foodstuffs worth £390 (today, about £26,600, or $53,900) from a provision company. Learning of the Noahs' insolvency, the firm asked the wharfinger to seize the pickles. Lazarus responded by suing the warehouseman, asserting that he had already purchased the goods. When the case went to court, the brothers-in-law had exchanged so many bills that they could not properly explain their finances to the judge. Befuddled, the court sided with the provision company.[15]

Amid the hurly-burly of nineteenth-century commerce, such ploys were suspicious but hardly criminal. It is worth recalling, however, that Lazarus and his brothers-in-law were wheeling and dealing in London while one of Webb's sons was at Gettysburg. They were selling arms to the South while so many other Northerners were dying on the nation's battlefields.

Crawling from the wreckage, Charley took out an advertisement in the *New York Herald* on December 15, 1864, announcing his renunciation of the surname "Lazarus" in favor of "Lawrence." On his formal application, Charley noted that his relations had already changed their appellations and that his notorious Uncle Samuel had offered him a legacy should he do the same. Yet he probably had other motivations. "Lawrence" was less recognizably Jewish, and a new name could help him escape not only the allegations lodged against him in Rio, Paris, and London, but also various creditors in the United States.

Though the war had been tumultuous, Charley seemed as buoyant as ever upon his return to New York. He had managed to avoid both military service and a South American penitentiary. By July, he was back in his element, subscribing to a benefit for the victims of a fire at showman Phineas T. Barnum's famous museum. The gala was a success; "most of the dramatic artists in the city volunteered their services," and the celebration helped convince the showman to rebuild. And on August 30, 1865, by special statute, he officially became a new person: Charles Lewis Lawrence. Now, all he needed was a job.[16]

THE PARSEE

In the fall of 1869, a series of letters ridiculing the tariff appeared in New York's leading Democratic newspaper, the *New York World*, signed "Adersey Curiosibhoy, Parsee merchant of Apollo Street, Bombay." The letters were addressed to Horace Greeley, the protectionist editor of the *New York Tribune*. Styling himself a Zoroastrian trader of western India, Curiosibhoy described his travels around the nation's manufacturing centers. In florid language, he recounted his efforts to buy wondrous American manufactures, discovering to his dismay that taxes on imports made their prices far higher than their British competitors. Through such anecdotes, Curiosibhoy tried to convince "sahib" Greeley that high tariffs deprived Americans opportunities to sell their wares to consumers in India and around the globe.[1]

The letters were an immediate hit. The *New Orleans Times* called them "adroit" and "inimitable" while the *Boston Evening Times* declared them "decidedly humorous" and observed that "there is considerable curiosity to ascertain the name of the author." The *World* published as many as eleven notes from the "Parsee Merchant" each week and reprinted the first forty in a special volume. In time, Curiosibhoy grew more expansive. Writing to a range of "sahibs," he wittily discussed money, politics, art, and theater. But he always returned to the tariff, and Greeley remained his most noteworthy correspondent.[2]

Now recalled for popularizing the phrase "Go West, young man," Horace Greeley was perhaps the most influential journalist of the nineteenth century. A migrant to New York City from rural New England, he worked at several newspapers before founding the *Tribune* in 1841. Enlisting a slate of brilliant writers to add to his distinctive voice, Greeley built the most successful daily in the country. He did not sacrifice radicalism to achieve popularity. Indeed, it was his highly personal, frequently disruptive moral passion that appealed to his audience. Greeley opposed not only slavery, but racism and sexism. Braving the mockery of his competitors, he endorsed experiments in communal living, vegetarianism, and temperance. A committed friend of labor, he advocated a shorter working day and high tariff walls protecting domestic industry.

Greeley eventually learned that the "Parsee" was a middle-aged customs clerk named Joseph Solomon Moore. Though Moore was no Zoroastrian, he and Greeley were opposites in appearance and attitude, as well as politics. The editor was slender, bespectacled, and often wearing a white overcoat with a matching top hat covering his bald crown. Greeley kept his face clean-shaven, but allowed the remaining hair on his head and neck to grow so long that it flowed out of and around his collar like a fur scarf. By contrast, Moore sported muttonchop whiskers on his round head, which made him look "strikingly like the old Emperor William I of Germany." Greeley styled himself a simple Chappaqua farmer; Moore was a globe-trotting immigrant, fluent in five languages. While the *Tribune* editor was a vegetarian, Moore enjoyed a banquet. Greeley was a neglectful husband, who often slept at a boardinghouse rather than at home, whereas Joseph's happy marriage produced seven children, all of whom lived to adulthood.[3]

"The Parsee" and Greeley were leading figures in the bitter intellectual struggle over the tariff that raged after the Civil War. Americans violently debated whether the United States imported too much or too little, whether the tax on foreign goods was too low or too high.

JOSEPH S. "PARSEE MERCHANT"   HORACE GREELEY. Courtesy New York Public
MOORE. Courtesy HathiTrust   Library, New York, New York

Such topics today seem less gripping than race riots, labor strikes, and
women's rights conventions, but voters of the time were enthralled,
making the custom house the center of American politics. Editor E. L.
Godkin complained in 1898: "During the last thirty years . . . it would
have been almost useless to consult the voters on any subject except
the tariff. . . . All other matters would have been passed over." Nor
could the tariff be disentangled from matters of race, class, and gender, for contrary to modern expectation, protectionists were the firm-
est advocates of African-Americans, workers, and women, whereas
free-traders were libertarians allied with former Confederates.[4]

For both sides, smuggling exemplified the errors of their opponents. For reductionists, smuggling proved that taxes were too high.
Prohibitive duties tempted honest merchants to bypass the custom
house and deal in contraband, whereas lower rates meant more legit-

imate trade and higher revenues. For protectionists, such defenses of smuggling merely proved the disloyalty of the reductionists, whose policies threatened to impoverish workers, upset the harmony of the home, and reverse Union victory in the Civil War.

THE "PARSEE MERCHANT" was born Joseph Solomon Pincus in the small city of Lobsens, Prussia (now Łobżenica, Poland), in 1822, the son of Solomon and Fanny Pincus. There, he likely received schooling in German and Hebrew. At the age of seventeen, he migrated to Birmingham, England, where his uncle Benjamin Pincus Moore was a merchant. Joseph learned English and read widely in the language, particularly Shakespeare, whom he often quoted.

In 1849, taking the surname Moore, Joseph left Birmingham for the United States, just two years after Charley Lazarus. He first traveled in the South, perhaps interested in the cotton trade, but soon made his way west to the California gold rush. Luck, however, was not with him. After only one year, fire damaged his general store to the tune of $6,000. Though proud of being one of the "Argonauts" who first settled San Francisco, he later recalled the city as home to fifty thousand "schemers and workers," similar numbers of rats, and "millions of fleas." Scarcity had inflated prices to absurd heights, and the markers of civilization like houses, hotels, and coaches were absent almost altogether. Still worse, the city's rulers were "thieves . . . robbers, cutthroats, and cowards," who "tyrannized" residents. After less than two years in San Francisco, skeptical about the government's ability to solve problems, Joseph steamed back to England.[5]

When Joseph returned to Birmingham, he found his uncle Benjamin living "in some style." His business, Moore, Phillips & Co., traded guns and other manufactures for "exotic luxuries" from Hong Kong, Tientsin, Shanghai, and Manila. Seizing the main chance, Joseph sailed off to establish branch offices of the firm in Cape Town, South Africa, and Melbourne, Australia, where gold had been discovered in 1851. Selling items ranging from musical instruments to prefabricated housing, Moore spent three years in Oceania before returning to Birmingham again, this time to marry his cousin Amelia. Departing his uncle's business, however, he established his own firm, J. S. Moore & Co., with offices in London and Bombay.

Like many British merchants during the Civil War, Moore invested in Southern blockade runners. In March 1865, however, with the Confederacy toppling and cotton prices dropping, his firm collapsed. Moore blamed his employees, but the creditors suspected that the clerks had absconded to avoid responsibility. As the bankruptcy court dissected the remains of his business, Moore fled to New York City, perhaps hoping to recoup almost $6,000 from the federal government for cotton seized by the Union Army from a Louisiana warehouse in 1863. But he likely stayed in America to distance himself from bill collectors. In June 1867, much to the frustration of his English creditors, Moore completed his bankruptcy under New York State law, defaulting on debts of £34,241 ($2.28 million today).[6]

Lobbyist Samuel Ward introduced Moore to Treasury Secretary Hugh McCulloch, who offered him a customs clerkship paying $1,800 per year. Moore knew Ward from his time in San Francisco. A banker's son holding a doctorate from the University of Göttingen, Ward was an unlikely friend to a self-taught Polish Jew. But the two men shared a deep love of food, European culture, and conversation. The job at the port saved the Parsee, who thanked the "King of the Lobby" by naming his seventh child Samuel Ward Moore.[7]

From his desk at the custom house, the Parsee Merchant begged Greeley to change his views while writing more equivocal government reports under his true name. In 1872, having risen to the position of chief of the Bureau of Statistics, Moore produced a brief for Congress considering which tariffs produced the highest return. He admitted that tariffs were "considered the easiest mode of collecting revenue" because they allowed the government to collect through "twenty or thirty thousand merchants," a tax on "forty millions of consumers." But he could not resist giving legislators a history lesson, charging that the tariff's origins were "neither very pure nor honorable," having been initiated by feudal lords, Barbary pirates, and Prussian aristocrats. Moore granted that "many now firmly seated and flourishing industries in different lands" owed their existence to "indirect subsidy," but he begged for a reasoned debate "in the great controversy on the tariff," without accusations of "selfish motives."[8]

Greeley slowly acknowledged Moore's letters, but remained unmoved. Indeed, the argument grew personal in 1871, when the usually genial Curiosibhoy remarked in frustration that Greeley was "the poorest merchant in the world" and "knew nothing." The *Tribune* editor responded in kind, referencing Moore's checkered past by observing that "a bankrupt merchant is presumptively an unsafe teacher of Political Economy" while touting his own faithful repayment of notes worth millions of dollars. Greeley continued writing paeans to protection, even as his friends in reform circles began warming to free trade.[9]

THE BACKDROP FOR the tariff debate was the drama of Reconstruction. In the aftermath of the Civil War, Americans faced the problem of reintegrating the defeated Confederate states into the Union without allowing secessionists to regain control over the government and restore the antebellum status quo. A Tennessee native who despised the slaves more than he hated slavery, President Andrew Johnson implemented a plan for reunification so lax that it allowed Southerners to restrict the civil rights of African-Americans and send former Confederates to Washington. Americans responded at the ballot box, electing a radical Congress that swept away Johnson's scheme, installed military governments in the South, enacted legislation to guarantee equality, and created institutions to assist freedpeople.

When Johnson vetoed the new laws, the radicals struck back. Elected to the House of Representatives, Benjamin Butler became a leading advocate of a robust reconstruction plan. The Republicans had embraced Butler since his liberation of "contraband" slaves and his severe but effective administration of New Orleans. Butler's longtime advocacy of working people also linked him to radicals such as representatives Thaddeus Stevens and William D. Kelley, who saw in the Civil War an opportunity to promote both economic and racial equality. Together, these congressmen pushed for a protective tariff, a shorter workday, the expansion of the money supply, and the extension of the suffrage to African-Americans.

Radical Republicans found Butler's talent for vengeance useful. In 1868, in just his first term in Congress, he managed the unsuccessful impeachment of President Johnson, who had impeded their agenda. In November, Richard Henry Dana Jr. decided to challenge Butler's congressional seat. The two men had long been on the opposite sides of Massachusetts politics, dating back to when Dana was counsel to fugitive slave Anthony Burns, and Butler was a slavery-defending Democrat. Though they made peace during the war, the class-conscious Butler loathed Dana, while the snobby Dana saw Butler as an arriviste, a demagogue, and very nearly a socialist. The general easily retained his office, but he never forgave his opponent.[10]

The 1868 election of a more sympathetic president, Ulysses S. Grant, cleared the way for Congress to act, yet serious fiscal problems impeded strong action. The federal government had borrowed almost $2.8 billion to pay the costs of defeating the Confederacy, equal to one half of America's gross national product. Of this debt, $450 million was in the form of paper money, called "greenbacks," and the rest was borrowed through bonds of varying lengths and interest rates. The Internal Revenue Act of 1864 was still in force, allowing government to tax "the gains, profits, and income of every person residing in the United States" at rates up to 10 percent, as well as the sale of whiskey, tobacco, matches, and other goods. But three-quarters of federal revenue came from the tariffs on foreign imports enacted by Congress in 1861 amid the secession crisis. With some small tinkering, these duties remained in place during Reconstruction. By the time Grant took office in 1869, the Treasury had managed to pay down the principal debt to just over $2.5 billion, but the nation still needed significant revenue to pay the remaining bondholders.

Meanwhile, the Civil War had transformed the U.S. economy itself. Prior to secession, the North's manufactures were not yet truly competitive with those of western Europe. Profits from selling slave-grown cotton to mills in Lowell, Lancashire, and Lyon had made the South the nation's wealthiest region. War inverted this. The costs of the war had sapped the former Confederacy's wealth, while emancipation had eradicated billions invested in slaves. The South's roads and railways, never especially well developed, were ruined by invading Northern armies. While guns and disease had diminished the white labor force, thousands of freedpeople fled the plantations for cities, and those who remained refused to accept the brutal work conditions of the past.

By contrast, the demands of war production had accelerated improvements in metallurgy, transportation, and engineering in the North. The ironmasters of Pennsylvania began producing quality steel, adopting the British Bessemer process. By 1870, states supporting the Union during the war accounted for over two-thirds of the nation's railroad mileage. Telegraphy spread through the inventions of tinkerers such as Ezra Cornell, the organizer of Western Union. In 1866, the son of a Massachusetts minister, Cyrus Field, organized the first transatlantic telegraph cable.[11]

But the growing distance between workers and their employers loomed ominously. In 1860, the Republican Party had promised laborers opportunities to become independent entrepreneurs, but the rise of mass production only seemed to increase the number of workers for wages. The costly new machines made it harder for tradesmen to compete, while the speed of work introduced new dangers to the shop floor. In 1866, William Sylvis, a Pennsylvania Civil War veteran and president of the Iron Molders International Union, began organizing the National Labor Union, a federation that rapidly enlisted seven hundred thousand members. The NLU soon disappeared, but the existence of an organization dedicated to promoting workers' interests suggested the class resentments that had been brewing since the emergence of the factory in the 1820s.

Congress tried to improve work conditions through the tariff. Legislators did so partly because they thought that the Constitution denied the federal government any other way to regulate manufacturing aside from taxation. But it also reflected the laborers' own belief in protection. The National Labor Union proposed a tariff on all imports, except for necessities, to "develop the resources of the country, increase the number of factories, give employment to more laborers, maintain good compensation, cause the immigration of skilled labor" and "enable us to successfully compete with the manufacturers of Europe in the markets of the world." In 1872, the National Labor Reform Party recommended an eight-hour day, paper currency, public ownership of the railroads, and a protective tariff.[12]

To its proponents, the tariff was more than a tax; it was a complex form of economic regulation produced by sincere, if sometimes corrupted, legislative deliberation. Congress tried to determine not only which sectors needed protection, but the exact levels of insulation each type of product required. The level of taxation often depended upon the grade of merchandise. For instance, the rate of tax on wool flannel rose as the value of the cloth increased. Representatives used the tariff to guard the people against luxuries that they believed undermined social equality, such as diamonds, and products that promoted immorality, such as opium, pornography, condoms, lottery tickets, liquor, and tobacco. Congress debated the mode of assessment. The government taxed some imports a proportion of their value (*ad valorem*), others according to their weight or size (*specific* tariffs), and some goods faced both types of calculation. As a consequence, tariff schedules ran hundreds of pages and only the most seasoned clerks, importers, and brokers knew the particulars of the law.

Ordinary Americans perceived the tariff issue in terms of narratives, not statistics. Indeed, then as now, people found the facts and figures of the tariff sleep inducing. The *Brooklyn Eagle* praised the Parsee Merchant, noting that "Mr. Curiosibhoy knows that a daily deliverance on Free Trade, Protection and other politico-economics must be a dreadful bore to the public. He therefore varies his essays with sprightly dramatic critiques." To engage a public more interested in art than science, protectionists and free-traders focused on values, interests, and priorities. The questions were: who should pay taxes, does patriotism oblige citizens to trade with one another, and how big should the government be?[13]

The protectionist narrative posited that tariffs safeguarded the "harmonious" republic, endangered by industrialization, consumerism, and global trade. Writers such as Henry C. Carey worried that market forces were eroding equality among men, concentrating financial power in cities like London, and destroying community control over the economy. Trade across long distances created resentment between workers and employers, farmers and urbanites, and men and women. The anonymity of an extended supply chain promoted immorality, Carey argued, as producers had little incentive to deal honestly with customers that they did not know. Protected from competition, capital could afford to be generous with labor, allowing workers to improve their condition.

Protectionists like Carey further believed that the tariff harmonized the domestic sphere. In their vision, women were soft, nurturing, and pure, responsible for maintaining the piety of their homes and the education of their innocent children. By contrast, men were hard and corruptible, destined to go out into the world to win sustenance for their families, but in need of female civilization at home. Mechanization might have liberated more affluent women from traditional tasks such as weaving, giving them greater time to attend to their families, but the rise of mill towns drew poorer men, women, and even children away from the farms, forcing husbands to compete with their own wives and progeny. Carey believed such rivalries were dangerous, and he proposed a high tariff to enable men to be the family's sole provider.[14]

If protectionists saw the custom house as the guardian of the American family, then they equated free trade with free love and other radical ideas. Labor reformer Clinton Roosevelt observed in 1870 that "to buy cheap and sell dear that things may regulate themselves . . . the free trader, free lover, and freebooter and slave dealer utter the same cry, 'Let us alone'." Roosevelt associated attacks on regulation with secessionists, who had preferred "cheap merchandise of Old England and cheap negroes in Africa" to "dear goods in New England" and free black labor. Critics of marriage used the tariff as a metaphor for marriage, leading Horace Greeley to complain, "The free trade sophistry respecting marriage is already on every libertine's tongue; it has overrun the whole country in the yellow-covered literature which is as abundant as the frogs of Egypt and a great deal more pernicious." The *New York Telegram* mocked a convention attended by women's rights advocates such as Elizabeth Cady Stanton and Victoria Woodhull as favoring "free love, free trade, free suffrage, free labor and free soil." Such attacks now seem reactionary, even hysterical, but the convention indeed endorsed an end to tariffs on necessities.[15]

Imagining citizenship as a marriage between the American and the United States government, where the former vowed eternal fidelity to the latter in return for the law's protections, commentators conceived of smuggling as akin to sexual infidelity. The young writer William Dean Howells penned his first novel, *Their Wedding Journey*, in 1872, telling the story of Isabel and Basil March, bourgeois newlyweds, returning from their honeymoon in Quebec. Isabel purchases umbrellas, laces, and silk, then refuses to pay duty. When Basil refuses to lie to the customs inspector, Isabel agrees, but demands that her husband sneak the goods into the United States some other way. A former consul in Venice appointed by Abraham Lincoln, Howells portrayed his heroine's smuggling as a threat to male honor and the Victorian family.[16]

The protectionist world view flattered American workers, depicting them as the agents of the nation's modernization. For instance, in 1859 Careyite writer William David Lewis declared that the tariff was necessary not only to increase wages and raise the mechanic's "intelligence," but also to spur the "higher development of mankind." Embracing the Protestant work ethic, they defended a policy promoting producers over consumers. Greeley argued in his descriptively titled 1869 volume *Essays Designed to Elucidate the Science of Political Economy, while Serving to Explain and Defend the Policy of Protection to Home Industry, as a System of National Coöperation for the Elevation of Labor*:

> They [workers] do not, as a class, believe it the chief end of man to render Shirtings or Sugar inordinately cheap; they believe it more important that the maker shall be well fed, well clad, well lodged, well developed, and well taught. Every spontaneous, instinctive movement of this class looks to fair payment for honest, useful effort first; cheapness of product—if such cheapness be compatible with the primary requisite—afterward.

At a time when many workingmen felt direct assistance threatened their masculinity, tariff subsidies to labor were almost invisible. Protection did not seem like charity; it gave workers an opportunity to earn a living. The Lowell mill hand could argue that import duties were a penalty paid by "unfair" foreign rivals employing ostensibly "degraded" workers. Conversely, laborers could fight for laws limiting the workday to eight hours knowing they were protected from competition with residents of undemocratic countries who could not demand such reforms.[17]

For some protectionists, the tariff guarded the Founders' dream of

national economic independence. Greeley truly believed that manufacturing was essential to America's survival:

> The agricultural nation falls into debt, becomes impoverished,
> and ultimately subject. The palaces of "merchant princes" may
> emblazon its harbors and overshadow its navigable waters; there
> may be a mighty Alexandria, but a miserable Egypt behind; a
> flourishing Odessa or Dantzig, but a rude, thinly peopled south-
> ern Russia or Poland; the exchanges may flourish and roll in
> luxury, but the producers famish and die.[18]

Greeley thus saw protection as an antidote to not only the poverty
of rural life, but the inequality and fiscal insecurity of agricultural
economies, which made them prone to foreign domination. To open
America's borders to British manufacturing, Greeley believed, was to
risk making the United States an English colony, bound to produce
commodities for an industrial parent.

The hyperpatriotism of the Reconstruction era intensified such
sentiments. Tariffs retained their association with the Union war
effort, when a high-tariff north blockaded a free-trade south. Duties
paid pensions for the Union Army veterans and supported the military occupation of the former Confederacy. Moreover, the tariff
enforced nationalism, penalizing cotton farmers who sold their fiber
abroad rather than sending it to the mills of Massachusetts. Believing, in the words of Henry Carey, that "British free-trade gave us
sectionalism," protectionists argued that trade restrictions prevented
future rebellion.[19]

And if tariff supporters deprecated foreigners, it was not for
their color. The two most ardent protectionists in Congress, Thaddeus Stevens and William D. "Pig Iron" Kelley, were also the strongest racial egalitarians in the House. For Henry Carey, the problem
with foreign workers was their poverty and distance, not their race.
Carey specifically argued that African-Americans needed protection,

and sympathized with Chinese victims of the British free trade in opium. Horace Greeley denigrated Asian immigrants but demanded their admission to the United States. "If millions of 'coolies' are to be thrust upon us merely because their labor is cheap," the editor noted, then the nation needed to provide them with education, citizenship, and a living wage. Oppressed nonwhites, according to Greeley, were the workers who needed the tariff most.[20]

All nationalist melodramas have villains; during the Reconstruction period, America's nemesis was England. Protectionists argued that British merchants funded the American Free Trade League (A.F.T.L.), bribing Congress with their "gold." Greeley's *Tribune* predicted that tariff reduction would leave "manufactories . . . crippled and broken," putting the nation "at the mercy of English capitalists," whose workers toiled for "pauper wages." The A.F.T.L. mocked Greeley's conspiracy theories, commenting that "the peculiar dent noticed last Monday in Mr. Greeley's hat was received in a struggle with the miscreants, who invaded the sanctity of his private residence, and sought to carry him off to Nova Scotia by main force." But Greeley's Anglophobia did not seem ludicrous to a nation that recalled the American Revolution, the War of 1812, the Irish potato famine, and British assistance to the Confederacy.[21]

Anti-Semitic elements sometimes leeched into protectionist conspiracy theories. Two authors complained of the nation's billion-dollar debt to "the Jews." Likewise, Henry Carey identified Jewish financier Nathan Rothschild as representative of "the speculators of every kind, in England, who live at the cost of the laborers of the world." The "Hebrew loanmonger," Carey argued, was the "high priest of the temple of Janus" who raised funds for a "despotic state." Free-traders certainly believed that protectionism had a bigoted component. Late in his career, Parsee Moore complained that "Jew baiting" and "feudal taxation" worked "hand in hand."[22]

But at its root, protectionism depended less on bigotry than on the mystical notion of American exceptionalism. By isolating the domes-

tic market from the wicked world, the tariff seemingly maintained
Congress's sovereignty over business, allowing it to democratically
address industrialization. Even better, having protected workers from
competition with the world's paupers, many Americans could imagine they needed little additional government at all.

AN ELITE GROUP of writers and politicians offered the main critique
of the protectionist vision. These men called themselves "independents" or "liberals," in honor of the British Liberal Party, whose ranks
included men like John Stuart Mill, Richard Cobden, and William
Ewart Gladstone. These men were not liberals in the modern sense,
favoring social spending. Gladstone, for instance, rose to the leadership of the Liberal Party by developing a reputation for cutting government costs through administrative reform, dedicating his career
to eradicating the institutions that he believed created human misery, ranging from slavery to war to discrimination. No existing policy
aroused liberal ire so much as tariffs. Their first great success was the
1846 repeal of the Corn Laws, taxes on foreign grain that protected
aristocratic landlords at the expense of the poor. Over the course of
his career, Gladstone continuously pressed Britain towards the goal
of total free trade.

American liberals belonged to both major parties, their number
including Republicans such as Richard Henry Dana Jr. and Democrats like his fellow attorney David Dudley Field. In some respects,
they were cosmopolitan. They were conspicuously Anglophilic and
their leading lights included immigrants such as German-born senator Carl Schurz and Irish Protestant editor E. L. Godkin. But most
liberals were from old New England families, smugly confident of
their superiority to arrivistes. And while independents generally rallied behind Lincoln, they were dissatisfied with the political choices
following his assassination. They viewed the contemporary Republican Party as tainted by zealotry and corrupted by greed. And the

Democratic Party seemed no more appealing, torn as it was between the ex-Confederates in the South, machines like Tammany Hall in the cities, and increasingly radical western farmers.

Liberal reformers wanted to replace the Reconstruction-era state, composed of tariffs, custom houses, patronage appointees, and military governors, with a small, efficient government administered by honest, apolitical, educated men of business. They generally agreed upon four concrete goals. First, they wanted to make government workers into professional civil servants, who earned their jobs through merit rather than favoritism. Second, liberals sought to prevent politicians from expanding the money supply to assist debtors. Third, independents wanted to end the political experiment in the South by removing federal troops from states that passed the constitutional amendments banning slavery, establishing formal equality for African-Americans, and granting all men the right to vote. And, finally, they aimed at reducing the protective tariff, which they contended enriched manufacturers at the expense of farmers, merchants, and consumers. In sum, the reformers of the late 1860s and early 1870s wanted government to be effective, but they saw the state itself in largely negative terms, as a barely necessary evil.[23]

Among American liberals, faith in tariff reduction was relatively recent, and wrought by a mixture of philosophical debate, social research, and self-interest. The best example is special commissioner of revenue David A. Wells. The grandson of a paper manufacturer, Wells initially supported tariffs. But he had a change of heart after visiting England in 1867, where he frequented the Cobden Club, a meeting place for free-trade reformers named in honor of British activist Richard Cobden. While in Washington, he befriended Ohio congressman James Garfield, a fellow graduate of Williams College and that rare beast: a Republican free-trader. At the same time, Wells embarked upon field research that convinced him that protection added more to living costs than it did to wages.

And finally, Wells's friends in the textile industry informed him that protection increased their costs, making them noncompetitive in world markets.[24]

Quite convinced of his own indispensability, Wells believed that new president Ulysses S. Grant would appoint him secretary of the treasury. But this was impossible, for Wells had called for tariff reductions specifically at odds with the GOP platform in 1868. Still worse, Wells supported Richard Henry Dana's electoral challenge to Rep. Benjamin Butler in Massachusetts. Butler made it his mission to punish Wells, seeing him as a hypocrite who called for an end to tariffs only after inheriting a fortune earned in a protected industry. Butler convinced Grant to choose a practical politician, former Massachusetts governor George S. Boutwell, to run the Treasury. Not content with denying Wells the plum job, Butler allegedly convinced Grant to silence him altogether by suspending his position as special commissioner of revenue in 1870.[25]

Feeling stung, the independents routinely questioned the intelligence, honesty, and sobriety of President Grant, perhaps the war's greatest hero. They highlighted Butler's failures in battle and alleged corruption, describing him as a "socialistic demagogue," a "carrion-bird," an "unprincipled rascal," and a "blackguard by nature" with "a following among the ignorant and corrupt and young." They attacked Boutwell as an unlettered shopkeeper. Hatred of Grant and his allies drove much of the liberal rebellion and blinded the independents to issues on which the administration proved much more perspicacious, such as the condition of African-Americans.[26]

At this moment, Joseph S. Moore joined the liberal circle. Though cosmopolitan in principle, the reform community was an ambiguous place for Jews like Moore. The liberals were a clubby bunch, bound by blood, history, and education. Several independents, notably Henry Adams and E. L. Godkin, viewed Jews as vulgarians responsible for the nation's materialism. But the movement's leader was August Belmont, financial titan, the owner of the free-trade *New York World*, and a convert from Judaism to Episcopalianism. And the Parsee's wit, charm, and skill overcame any potential coolness. Moore had traveled in England, California, the Isthmus of Panama, Australia, India, South Africa, the Philippines, and China. He could tell tales of meeting Hindus, Muslims, Parsees, Chinese, and Zulus. He had not attended college, but his wide reading and regular attendance at the theater and opera made him a boon companion conversant in many subjects besides political economy.

The "Parsee Letters" made Moore a leading independent. His adoption of an Asiatic persona allowed him to mask his true identity from protectionists. Indeed, Charley Lawrence's father-in-law, Mordecai Noah, once wrote a popular column called "Oriental Correspondence" under the pseudonym "Muly Malak," a Turkish tourist reporting on his travels through America. Such masquerades built upon the popular notion of Jews as pseudo-Asian interlocutors who could explain the "inscrutable East" to a western Christian audience. Moore chose to present himself as a Zoroastrian not only because he had once traded in South Asia, but also as a winking reference to the common belief that "the Parsees" were "among the heathen what the Jews" were "to the christian [sic] nations of the earth." Expelled from Persia for refusing to abandon their ancient religion, Parsees facilitated exchange between Europeans, Muslims, and Hindus.[27]

The persona allowed Moore to joke without incurring rancor. Most reformers damned their rivals as hell-bound imbeciles. By contrast, Moore flattered opponents as "sahib" and "my august master," insisting they were too intelligent not to see the truth. People enjoyed Moore's stories of a befuddled foreign merchant trying to understand why the American goods he desires are so expensive. Moore's "charming" letters overcame this sensibility by making the driest figures "alive and nervous." An obituary recalled that "while prosy essayists knew how to 'bore their readers to death,' he knew how to encourage and interest them."[28]

Moore argued that America's destiny lay in selling its products abroad. He often began his letters by praising the United States, the country's natural features, as well as the workers' ingenuity and cleverness. The U.S. had "pure" copper, "the finest cotton," as well as "the most skillful machinery and best manipulators." He expressed special admiration for American umbrellas. "There is a perfect magic about the Yankee touch in manufacturing goods, it combines the grace of France with the durability of England; above all the American manufacturer makes it practical." But he inevitably reported his surprise that American goods were too expensive to be profitably traded, breaking down the rough costs of production and then comparing it to the British price. Because of tariffs added at every level, umbrellas, sugar mills, corrugated metal houses, and calicos were pricier in the United States than in England, effectively confining American manufacturers to the home market. And the decline in imports and exports had the added disadvantage of eradicating the nation's once strong position as a shipper.[29]

To undercut the protectionists' hypernationalism, the Parsee appealed to formative American values like antimonopoly. His main villains were the corporations that had grown from infants into giants under the careful nurturing of protection. These firms built a "lobby engine . . . moved by a mystic key, made of pure gold" to secure their "well-bought and vested interests" against the threat of foreign competition. He offered as an example bleached cotton long cloth, a product upon which the duty was 35 percent. The mills of Lowell could raise their prices 30 percent above the rates in England and still hold the entire U.S. market. Still worse, because it was never profitable to import British cloth, the government received no proceeds from the tariff at all; the entire benefit went to the manufacturer. The Parsee called this a "tyranny worthy of native Indian princes."[30]

Moore also appealed to workers' interests as consumers. He granted that laborers earned higher wages in the United States, but offered figures to show that taxes inflated the cost of necessities, making their advantage illusory. Taking aim at the contention that tariffs promoted "harmony" between labor and capital, the Parsee cited the authority of John Roach, an iron founder destined to become the foremost ship builder in the nation. Roach insisted that there were "no strikes, no distress, either for work or sufficiency of wages" under the tariff rates of the 1850s. But under the higher rates of the 1860s, "They are always in distress.... Men cannot live ... because all those necessities of live [sic] which they buy with their wages have advanced in price 20 per cent, more than the advance in wages they earn." Moore did not ignore the workers' stake in continuing employment. Again, he cited Roach, who argued that the tariffs on the production materials raised his bottom line so high that he could not compete with Scotland, Belgium, and France. The result, he claimed, was to chase 75 percent of the iron manufacturing jobs out of the City of New York.[31]

Instead of advocating free trade, which would have left the nation with no way to repay its bondholders, the Parsee contended that lower rates would increase revenue by reducing smuggling. Borrowing an argument from David Hume and Adam Smith, he contended that excessive duties effectively barred taxable foreign products from the market altogether. High rates on silk and opium encouraged unlawful traffic in these items, leading to lost revenues and defeating the protective qualities of the tariff itself.[32]

Moore could not resist, however, teasing Greeley about the tariff's effect on less weighty matters such as women's couture. The Parsee wondered why wealthy American women wore frocks that appeared "second-hand." He learned that the 60 percent tariff on heavy silk had prompted French manufacturers to add "dressing or glue or gum," which made low-quality fabric as stiff as luxurious taffeta. But because the resulting cloth was more vulnerable to stress, heat, sun, and moisture, the dresses quickly became "shabby." Moore's interest in fashion differentiated him from Greeley, who saw gowns as un-American fripperies and whose belief in women's rights never conquered his faith that women belonged in the home. The Parsee also heightened the gap between protectionists who argued that male breadwinners needed high wages to support female domesticity and free-traders who imagined a more liberated, if still decorative, role for women as consumers.[33]

Posing as a Parsee allowed Moore to compare protectionism to dogma. He described protectionists as "blind followers" and those who rejected the tariff as "heretics." Moore likened protection to the "superstition" of his own countrymen, who allegedly spend one hundred years building a "bloodstone temple" to house a brass statue. "We worship the idol of protection," Moore quoted a "cloth manufacturing sahib," which "proves to be the most impotent brazen image one can possibly think of." Coyly presenting himself as the representative of supposed Asian backwardness and mysticism, Moore challenged Greeley and his peers to justify the tariff in modern, scientific terms rather than patriotic slogans.[34]

DESPITE MOORE'S BEST EFFORTS, tariffs remained popular nearly everywhere but the former Confederacy, a fact that only reinforced the contrast between protectionism and disloyalty. In 1870, Henry Adams observed, "The suspicion of free trade sounded to the ears as terrible a charge as that of having worn a rebel uniform or having been out with the Ku Klux Klan." The tariff was a sacrament in Pennsylvania, where protected industries such as steel were the main source of employment. And while New Englanders showed enthusiasm for civil service reform, they demonstrated little desire to open their markets to foreign competition.[35]

Yet the fight had just begun. In 1870, reformers founded the new Liberal Republican Party to promote expert administration, lower tariffs, and hard money. Their goal was to replace the Grand Old Party, a sectional organization confined to the north and west, with a new national coalition dedicated to business principles. They looked south and imagined that a more conservative version of Republicanism, promising to end the Reconstruction experiment, could win white voters hostile to the party of Grant. But the key to their plans was New York, where elite Democrats were overthrowing Tammany Hall, and merchants raged against the power of the custom house.[36]

LEVIATHAN

Approaching the New York Custom House, merchants trembled before a former salesman named Benaiah Gustin Jayne. Looking like an Old Testament patriarch, with a foot-long beard, wild eyes, and a crutch he waved like a club, Jayne was a "special treasury agent." Hired in 1869, he quickly uncovered a scheme by sugar refiners to bribe customs weighers to underreport their imports, leading reformers to call Jayne "one of the most trustworthy and skillful detectives in the service." He then scourged the nation's foremost importing houses, convincing clerks to implicate their bosses, promising them they would share in any revenues recovered. Confiscating private documents and using them to expose deceptive customs declarations, Jayne made over eighty seizures and earned the government over $3 million between 1869 and 1873.[1]

Jayne's status had risen dramatically during Reconstruction. Born to a family of farmers outside Philadelphia in 1831, he received minimal education in youth, and he dabbled in various businesses like daguerreotyping during the 1850s. Though Jayne later claimed to have spent the Civil War as a secret messenger for the Lincoln administration, he was actually a common clerk in the War Department in Washington. Turned out of office by President Andrew Johnson, he moved to Ithaca, New York, where he sold sewing machines and ran a clock company. But in April 1869, somehow sensing Jayne's talents

TREASURY AGENT BENAIAH G. JAYNE SCOURGED CORPORATE SMUGGLERS
UNTIL 1873, WHEN MERCHANTS BEGAN CHALLENGING THE CONSTITU-
TIONALITY OF HIS SEIZURES. Courtesy of the author

as a bloodhound, Gen. Benjamin Butler secured him an appointment
as an investigator at the Port of New York.[2]

In the winter of 1872, Jayne made his biggest bust, charging the
renowned global firm Phelps, Dodge & Co., with defrauding the revenue. Scouring their accounting ledgers, Jayne learned that the merchants had undervalued their imports by $7,000 to avoid less than
$2,000 in taxes. This was a trifling sum for the company, possibly an
accident, but the law empowered Jayne to seize their entire shipment,
worth $1,750,000 ($31 million today). Keen to avoid a huge loss and
further scrutiny, Phelps, Dodge & Co. negotiated a settlement, paying
the government over a quarter of a million dollars in fines and duties.[3]

William Earl Dodge, the owner of Phelps, Dodge & Co., was the very model of the merchant philanthropist, descended from leading clergyman and reformers. A fervent evangelical, William had generously supported missionaries, sabbatarianism, and temperance, as well as moral-uplift organizations such as the Young Men's Christian Association. He had much to share; in 1863, his personal income was a staggering $344,171 ($6 million today). In 1866, Dodge secured his reputation as a reformer by running for Congress as a Republican, and then dipping into his own fortune to overcome election fraud and take his seat.

Dodge's public piety failed to impress Radical Republicans like Jayne. Though Dodge criticized slavery, his firm traded southern cotton for British metal. When war came, Dodge attended the Peace Convention of 1861, which proposed appeasing secessionists by allowing slavery's continued expansion. Taking "a business view of this subject," Dodge believed that "true Yankees" should negotiate a profitable armistice. Once the war began, Phelps, Dodge funded Union regiments, but allegedly shirked the taxes necessary to fund the war. In 1865, Rep. Thaddeus Stevens of Pennsylvania accused Phelps, Dodge of cheating the customs by molding highly taxed lead into busts of patriotic figures, which were not subject to duty, recasting the metal into more useful shapes after the statues left the custom house.[4]

With Radicals triumphant at the polls, plebian officials like Jayne no longer feared aristocrats like Dodge. The antagonistic machinery of the modern nation-state was replacing the clubby antebellum custom house. Needing funds to repay $2.7 billion in war debt, Congress granted the Treasury new authority to pursue contrabandists of all types, including corporations. Yet this new state was hardly neutral. Staffed heavily with Republican partisans and Union army veterans, the custom house extended the nationalism of the war into the ensuing peace. Reflecting the biases of its officers, the custom house profiled specific populations: Democrats, independents, Jews, Asians, and women. In other words, through its pursuit of smugglers, the government defined the loyal American of the Reconstruction era.[5]

DURING RECONSTRUCTION, the custom house served as the locus of federal power in the Northeast, along the Great Lakes, and on the Pacific coast of California. If the U.S. Army still occupied the former Confederate states and clashed with tribes in the plains and Southwest, the authority to tax made the Treasury the most potent agency in the country's cities and along its borders. Every ship arriving in an American port endured customs inspection of its invoices, manifests, and cargo. No person entered the country without declaring the value of his or her chattels, stating the origins of their manufacture, and paying any duties owed to the government. By the early 1880s, officials were not only examining hundreds of thousands of immigrants, travelers, and sailors each year, but also supervising the importation of over thirteen million tons of merchandise worth $723 million, the warehousing and appraisement of over $515 million in goods, and the collection of over $214 million in taxes.[6]

The growth of the Treasury's power had begun during the Civil War itself. At this time, there was no federal constabulary like the modern-day FBI; a small number of postal inspectors, U.S. marshals, and the District of Columbia metropolitan police force combined to enforce national law. General Lafayette Baker, spy chief of the Union Army, also had the authority to investigate crimes such as counterfeiting, embezzlement, and smuggling. Perhaps hoping to confine the attention-seeking Baker to military matters, the Treasury Department created a new unit to prevent Confederates from forging the new "greenback" paper currency in 1864. On July 5, 1865, almost three months after Appomattox, Secretary of the Treasury Hugh McCulloch appointed Colonel William P. Wood, the warden of the Capitol jail, the first director of the Secret Service. With the end of the war, this arm of the Treasury became the federal government's primary police force.[7]

Fearing that smuggling might undermine support for protective tariffs, Congress built a newly muscular custom house. The anti-smuggling act of 1866 sanctioned the Treasury secretary to appoint agents as "the exigencies of the revenue service may require." It gave "any officer of the customs" or any "authorized agent of the Treasury" the power to search any vessel, "person, trunk, or envelope" and "to use all necessary force to compel compliance." The statute stipulated only that the agent's suspicion be reasonable. The law sanctioned officials to examine structures on land if "deemed necessary." It enabled federal magistrates to order firms to produce account books, letters, and receipts that might reveal undervaluation. The law permitted the seizure of not only the smuggled, undeclared, or undervalued cargo, but the shipments of which they were part, as well as the boats, carriages, and trains that carried them. The statute forced defendants to prove that they did not know they carried contraband. And, finally, it instituted punishments of as much as two years in prison and a $5,000 fine, to go along with the forfeiture of the goods themselves.[8]

The bill frightened many congressmen. Arguing that the bill's presumption of guilt violated the Fifth Amendment's privilege against self-incrimination, one Buffalo, New York, Democrat compared it with the medieval rack. Concerns were not confined to the opposition. Libertarians and border Republicans also worried about the legislation. But with the South still largely absent from Congress, the legislation's Radical advocates easily obtained majorities for the bill. At a time when the survival of the nation itself depended upon the legitimacy of oaths, an importer who lied on a customs declaration was in some ways worse than a smuggler; he was a potential traitor.[9]

IMPORTERS ENCOUNTERED the expanded Treasury as soon as they purchased goods abroad. Because many tariffs were assessed as a percentage of value, or *ad valorem*, the law required the merchant to present an invoice demonstrating the purchase price to the U.S. consul and swear to its validity. Formally part of the State Department's

United States Custom-House, Wall Street, New York.

In the domed interior of the New York Custom House, merchants negotiated the importation of the world's goods into the United States. Courtesy Bird Library, Syracuse University, Syracuse, New York

Befitting their status as outposts of the U. S. government and financial centers, custom houses were often imposing classical structures. Courtesy Bird Library, Syracuse University, Syracuse, New York

diplomatic corps, responsible for protecting the interests of the U.S. government abroad, consuls were also an essential component of the Treasury's antismuggling machinery. Making three copies of the declaration, the consul kept one in his files, sent a second to the importer, and a third to the destination port.

More and more travelers directly experienced the custom house. Between 1861 and 1882, the number of steamship lines running from New York rose from two to twelve, with several others landing in Boston, Baltimore, Philadelphia, and New Orleans. In 1850, steamers crossed from New York to Ireland in sixteen days; by 1869, the trip took less than eight days. The cost of ocean travel decreased, enabling tourists to travel to Europe itself and select from the full range of continental products. To the elite American, novelist Henry James observed in 1879, "The world . . . was a great bazaar, where one might stroll about and purchase handsome things."[10]

The law permitted individuals to wait and declare their purchases upon arrival in the United States, resting the system of tax collection upon the traveler's sense of honor. Tourists testified to the origin and value of their belongings in a written statement, which the individual swore to be accurate. The absence of any check at the site of purchase created several problems for customs officials. Purchasing bargains unmindful of future duties, travelers often arrived home with insufficient cash to pay the customs. And the laxity of the rules concerning individuals prompted some professional smugglers and merchants to pose as mere tourists.

As a vessel neared the shores of the United States, lookouts at the edge of the harbor alerted customs officials of its arrival by telegraph, and they sent a revenue cutter, usually a single-masted, lightly armed craft, to meet the incoming vessel at sea. By 1886, the Revenue Marine Bureau, the antecedent of the Coast Guard, had forty ships, fourteen of them "sloops, steam-launches, or harbor boats," one "sailing bark," and twenty-five "steamers ranging from 130 to 500 tons burden." Though potent enough to be sent into combat, these ships were more useful for patrolling the shore, rescuing foundering vessels, collecting duties, and forcibly interdicting smugglers.[11]

Leaving the cutter, inspectors boarded and took possession of the cargo. The inspector examined the baggage to see if passengers had "forgotten" to declare any goods. He rummaged thoroughly through personal items not only because foreign goods were not labeled as such, but because valuable items like jewelry could be hidden in bags and upon the body. Inspector Charles Edwards even declared the necessity of examining picnic baskets of food carried by Canadians walking to the American side of Niagara Falls, stating that "no customs officer with ordinary human eyes by only looking on the outside of an opake [sic] bundle, basket or traveling-bag, could see the contents." It was his "duty to prevent any smuggler from taking such an opportunity to bring a huge basket full of kid gloves into the United States, instead of sandwiches."[12]

For Americans of the nineteenth century, bodily inspection was an unfamiliar experience. Governments accorded a good deal of deference to the white middle classes; inspection, like suspicion, was reserved for criminals, people of color, and perhaps the poor. Police themselves were scarce. Upon departing the United States in 1863, one Prussian sojourner commented that he "never met a single uniformed policeman or soldier" in over a decade spent in the U.S. "except in New York on my trip home during the Civil War." If Manhattan was an exception, it was because the city was one of the first in the United States to replace constables with uniformed police, and many cities would not follow until the late nineteenth century. As a consequence, few Americans of the 1860s had experienced government scrutiny, much less physical examination.[13]

Thus American men and women were shocked to discover that inspectors considered them potential smugglers. Upon "the slightest suspicion ... of prevarication," customs officer Thomas Bangs Thorpe observed, "a strict search ensues." The inspectors took the suspect into a room, asked him to disrobe, and searched his body, checking his ears and nostrils for small items such as gemstones. Thorpe described a "very pretty ... polite and affable woman" with "a full bust, broad hips, and plethoric person generally" who aroused the doubt of the customs inspector. A female officer took her aside for "a private interview," after which "the apparently well fed and portly dame of a few moments before, stripped of innumerable dry-goods, stepped into public gaze reduced to a wonderfully thin and rather skeletonized individual."[14]

Nor were the inspectors satisfied with surface examinations. Secret Service chief Hiram C. Whitley told the story of a diamond merchant he called "Haman Bosch." A frequent traveler to and from Europe, Bosch attracted the attention of customs officials, who demanded he undress so they could search his garments. They found nothing. But before Bosch could be released, he began complaining of stomach problems. The captain of the ship called for the ship's surgeon and asked him to administer a "cathartic." The "pallid" Bosch refused to take the laxative. "Then we will force it down your throat," the captain insisted, "to the last drop." A defeated Bosch drank the dose, and within an hour the custom house had seized $4,000 in diamonds.[15]

The law scarcely limited inspectors. Refusing to submit to examination was itself a crime punishable by a $1,000 fine. Agents could seize valuable goods upon suspicion alone, temporarily putting the burden of proof on the alleged offender. Though the Fourth Amendment of the Constitution theoretically guaranteed individuals the right to freedom from unreasonable searches, judges scarcely enforced this right in practice. The appellate court heard no cases where a defendant challenged the legality of a body search. And the courts invariably upheld the government's authority to seize contraband and demand potentially revealing personal records.[16]

Such exams inspired indignation, not least because travelers believed their outrage might dissuade officials from examining them. To dissuade officials from questioning his honor, one man suspected of smuggling diamonds affected to be a German count. But the indignation was often real. Having never before endured any sort of inspection, American travelers found government distrust insulting and examination degrading. For instance, one businessman crossing the border at Niagara Falls protested being treated like a common "thief" whose word was without value. "When I tell you I have nothing dutiable," he insisted, "that's enough." Inspector Charles Edwards found a bit of taxable tobacco hidden in the bag, which he amiably passed without fines, but this did not appease the traveler, who demanded the officer repack his bag as he found it. Similarly, travelers asserted their right to privacy, one woman complaining, "It's no country at all, at all, if we haven't the liberty of our own pockets."[17]

Such sensitivity could lead to violence. The unusual shape of one eccentric woman prompted customs inspectress Marie Louise Ellis to request an examination. When Ellis felt her "suspicious ridge," the suspect attempted to throw her out the window into the river below. The traveler nearly succeeded before the inspectress's shouts prompted her colleagues to restrain the suspect. In the woman's dress, they found meerschaum pipes, morocco bags, fishing flies, and a stuffed pheasant. In another case, Ellis asked a lady milliner to submit to examination. When the hatmaker refused inspection, protesting "loudly at both the indignity and the suspicion it conveyed," Ellis gave her three minutes to decide, after which she promised to call in a male inspector to "perform the operation, forcibly if necessary." Only when a man actually entered the room did the milliner acquiesce, revealing rolls of silk, lace, and various trimmings.[18]

To determine whom to search, inspectors looked at external traits, such as irritability, anxiety, and awkward movement. Custom-house employee T. B. Thorpe noted that "many a smuggler has escaped detection after the severest personal examination, but at last excited suspicion, and subsequent exposure, by a want of power over his or her nervous system." He told the story of a man who had been examined twice. Left to himself in a room, he began sweating profusely, eventually sinking back "in a chair utterly prostrated." A final inspection revealed two small ladies' watches, rolled in pitch and concealed in his armpits.[19]

Having followed his hunches, searched the baggage, and seized any contraband, the inspector collected the duty from travelers. Insofar as no supervisor checked the inspector's judgment, individuals often tried to bribe the official to accept their valuation of their imports. The distribution of what were called "moieties," however, encouraged the inspector's rigor. Moieties were portions of all forfeitures guaranteed informers, arresting officers, and supervising collectors, established shortly after the founding by the Revenue Act of 1799. An incentive to do one's duty, moieties were similar to the prize shares distributed to naval officers who captured an enemy ship, as well as the "contraband of war" permitted to soldiers in the army.

The inspector then turned to the ship's cargo. The officer ensured the freight matched the manifest and the invoices, and then assigned the goods to a warehouse pending evaluation. Meanwhile, the merchant hired a broker, who knew the tariff rates on each product, the cost of merchandise, and the responsibilities of each port official. The broker filed an entry form declaring the invoiced value of the goods and paid estimated duties. Next, the goods were appraised. Some products, like art, were taxed upon their market value as determined by an expert appraiser. Other imports were subject to specific tariffs, assessed according to the weight and quality of the goods. For instance, sugar was first weighed, then a sample was assessed by an appraiser (eventually, a chemist), who determined the grade and the rate of duty. Likewise, a textile appraiser measured the yards of fabric, then used a microscope to determine the thread counts and the consequent tax rate. This appraiser then revised the entry to reflect his view of the tariffs due.[20]

Some goods were simply barred from landing. The Tariff Act of 1842 introduced America's first restrictions on the importation of sexually explicit items, including ordinary objects with salacious decoration and stereoscopic prints of naked women. The Comstock Law of 1873 required that customs agents seize "any obscene book, pamphlet, paper, writing, advertisement, circular, print, picture, drawing or other representative figure or image, on or off paper or other material, or any cast instrument or other article of an immoral nature or any drug or medicine," then deliver the contraband to federal marshals for destruction. Over the next five years, agents impounded

$200,000 (about $4.5 million today) in so-called obscene material, much of it "articles well known to the drug trade," i.e. contraceptives, but also prints, books, and goods with erotic ornamentation.[21]

If a significant discrepancy existed between the assessor's valuation and the merchant's sworn testimony at the time of export, customs officials could seize the entire shipment for fraud. To prove that firms had intentionally fabricated invoices, agents like Jayne began grooming informers at the great importing houses, men who knew how their employers skirted the law and wanted shares of the revenue recovered. The agents asked the U.S. courts to command companies to produce private documents proving intent to defraud, looking for inconsistencies between balance sheets and customs declarations. Many famous merchants were snared between 1872 and 1874, including the glass importers Platt & Boyd, linen manufacturer Barbour Brothers, the dry goods firm Jordan, Marsh & Co., and, of course, Phelps, Dodge & Co.

If the importer's declarations were sound, however, the process then returned to the broker, who attempted to lower the assessment and tariff rates paid by his client. The science of classifying imports was highly interpretative. Just as lead busts of Washington could be heavily taxed metal or tax-free statuary, cargo could be defined in different ways. A mouth harp could be a toy or a musical instrument. Moreover, the law did not require importers to pay tax on goods broken in transit, so many merchants claimed what were called "drawbacks," or refunds on previously paid taxes on shattered glass, for example. Finally, the naval office of the port performed all this assessment and calculation a second time, to provide a check on the initial process. Finally, the importer paid the duty and received his merchandise for sale.[22]

IN 1873, THE UNITED STATES had 136 custom houses, spanning the nation from Machias, Maine, to San Diego, California, from Sitka in the Territory of Alaska to Savannah, Georgia. Some of these custom houses regulated the modest foreign trade at river ports like Natchez, Mississippi, or Burlington, Iowa, employing only a surveyor and perhaps a deputy or a janitor. But others guarded major border crossings like Brownsville, Texas, and Port Huron, Michigan. Nearly one-quarter watched the comparatively ancient ports of New England, the tiny inlets and craggy shores used by smugglers since the time of King George III. And the largest cities capable of harboring seagoing vessels—Boston, Philadelphia, Baltimore, New Orleans, and San Francisco—contained custom houses employing from two to four hundred civil servants each.

America's most important customs district was New York City, where two-thirds of all imports were landed and five-sixths of the nation's tariffs collected. With over 1,500 workers, the custom house was one of the metropolis's largest employers, and the rotation of personnel each election meant an even larger number of New Yorkers had worked there at some time. Over seven thousand sailors and over thirty thousand merchants in Manhattan and Brooklyn felt the port's gravitational pull. The city's thirty-five thousand garment workers depended upon the custom house not only for protection against foreign clothes, but also for access to highly taxed imported fabrics like wool and silk.[23]

Offering the most desirable unelected positions in the entire federal service, the port employed politicians, merchants, and newsmen. At the top was the collector of customs, responsible for receiving all tariff payments. Next was the surveyor of customs, who oversaw the inspection and assessment of all imports. And third was the naval officer, whose office independently duplicated the efforts of the surveyor, to ensure correct administration. Collectors controlled hundreds of patronage positions, allowing them to marshal an army of campaign workers, who were obliged to kick back a portion of their salary to their political organization. They distributed plum business opportunities, such as warehousing. Within limits, they could rule favorably upon the tariff disputes of their friends. And perhaps most significantly, the heads of the custom house received a share of all moieties. In 1873, New York collector of customs Chester Arthur earned $56,000, over one million dollars in contemporary terms, more than the newly increased salary of President Grant.

The Treasury expanded its reach through the Secret Service and its special agents. President Grant's choice for Secret Service director was Hiram Whitley, a former cattle drover, saloonkeeper, and slave catcher who rose to the rank of colonel in the Union Army working as a military policeman in occupied New Orleans. Another protégé of Gen. Benjamin Butler, Whitley lived a storied life as a lawman, memorialized in two memoirs and numerous newspaper features. Best known for his pursuit of counterfeiters and Klansmen, Whitley also saw smugglers as a threat to the restored Union. Between 1869 and 1871 alone, Whitley's staff of twenty agents confiscated fifty-one illicit shipments of lace, diamonds, wine, liquor, and cigars. The Treasury also employed fifty special agents like Benaiah Jayne to investigate smuggling rings, look for fraud within custom houses, and detect smuggling away from the ports.[24]

These men obtained their jobs through a combination of political patronage and talent. For instance, Charles N. Brackett earned his position as a special treasury agent by working as a police officer, a fire fighter, and a leader of the Seventh Ward Grant Club. But legends of partisanship were somewhat overstated. In 1877, 150 employees at the Port of New York had held positions since the presidency of Andrew Johnson, and thirteen of these since the administration of President Buchanan. The port's oldest officials possessed encyclopedic knowledge of customs affairs. John L. Van Buskirk, the assistant to the surveyor, had served since the presidency of Andrew Jackson, retaining past of the age of eighty a "perfect" memory and mastery of the "details of the duties of unlading ships."[25]

The custom house also employed quite a few of the nineteenth century's finest American authors. At one moment in 1869, one could have held a salon at the port, with attendees including novelist Herman Melville, editor Charles Frederick Briggs, poets Robert Barry Coffin, George W. Bungay, and Richard Henry Stoddard, musician Harrison Millard, essayists Joseph S. "Parsee" Moore and Richard Grant White, humorists Thomas Bangs Thorpe and Francis Durivage, and playwright Charles Powell Clinch. Some, like Melville, viewed their work at the port as a chore to support their less lucrative artistic ambitions. Even before he ever landed a position at the custom house, Melville called such occupations "inglorious . . . worse than driving geese." But the position offered time to write. Busy only when a ship came into port, Inspector Melville could work on his poetic tome, *Clarel*, a meditation upon the clash between science and faith.[26]

Other writers took public service more seriously. As chief of the revenue marine division for seventeen years, Richard Grant White had responsibility for the Treasury's seagoing cutter force, the defense of the coast, and the rescue of accident victims. Best known as an authority on Shakespeare, he humbly called himself a member of the "class of superior, substantial, high-minded men, from whom their less notable fellow-citizens would select those to whose care they would commit the public interests." Other writers were less pompous but just as dedicated. Charles Powell Clinch served four decades in the port. One colleague claimed he would have been one of the "most eminent and successful of our leading business men" had he directed his talents "to his personal interests." The brother-in-law of department store tycoon Alexander T. Stewart, Clinch could certainly have obtained a job paying more than his salary of $5,000 per year. But he chose to remain at the port, "his clear head, vast experience, and entire recollection of all laws of precedence" saving "the government millions of dollars."[27]

Through these appointments, government subsidized American art. But jobs were not allotted according to merit alone. In the 1840s,

Edgar Allan Poe allegedly sank into alcoholism after being unable to land a position at the Port of Philadelphia. Nathaniel Hawthorne lost his surveyorship in the Salem custom house when Whig William Henry Harrison won the presidential election of 1848. Authors needed either to find political patrons, or to cultivate the ruling party by writing speeches or campaign biographies. Having no interest in campaign work, Herman Melville was fortunate that he had politicians in his family. By contrast, the painter, novelist, and short-story writer Thomas Bangs Thorpe justified his appointment by delivering speeches at Republican rallies and working in the Reconstruction government of Louisiana.[28]

When educated writers lacked the skills appropriate to the job, customs officials turned to downtown merchants who knew the prices of imports. In 1871, the Port of New York's chief assessor hired his nephew, stationer Daniel Webster Lee, as examiner of oil paintings. Despite this nepotism, Lee proved worthy of his position, having "few equals" as "a judge of pictures," and knowing the "value in dollars and cents of the works of every artist of note." The port expanded its technological sophistication in 1878 when it engaged Professor Edward Sherer to evaluate the chemical composition of imports like sugar. But most positions required no special knowledge, just literacy and intelligence. For instance, the port employed several medical men as clerks, including Dr. Emmanuel J. Attinelli, a well-known authority on rare coins.[29]

Union Army veterans claimed custom-house appointments as a reward for their sacrifice. Some were officers who had gained administrative experience in the service. Others received berths as representatives of powerful voting blocs. Half of the men in the North had served in the Union Army, and 1.9 million survived the conflict. These soldiers, sailors, and marines lobbied the collector through their former commanding officers, as well as through organized groups like the Grand Army of the Republic (GAR), a fraternal society for northern veterans.[30]

Because the dominant Republican Party was an overwhelmingly Protestant organization, the custom house employed Anglo-American men in the positions with the greatest pay and responsibility, leaving immigrants from Ireland and central Europe to work as inspectors, openers, and packers. Though Jews like Mordecai Noah and Emanuel Hart had served as surveyors of the port during Democratic administrations, their coreligionists had little power during the Grant presidency. Of the 183 New York Custom House officials earning salaries of more than $2,000 in the year 1872, no more than three had identifiably Jewish names.

Educated and politically active African-American Republicans found jobs in southern custom houses. One Texas editor noted in 1869 that the Galveston collector had "selected colored men for most of the places in the customhouse" because "there would probably have been some difficulty in finding within his party white persons enough to fill the places." Though the newsman exaggerated, the Port of Galveston did hire several local men of color like Norris Wright Cuney, as well as Yankee transplants like brothers George T. and Horatio F. Ruby of Maine.[31]

Yet ironically, if not surprisingly, northern custom houses refused to employ African-Americans in executive positions. In 1869, there was talk in the black press of George T. Downing becoming collector for Newport, Rhode Island. Anointed "the foremost colored man in this country," Downing's credentials were impeccable. His father, Thomas Downing, was a wealthy New York oysterman, barkeeper, and caterer, as well as an active member of the antislavery movement, known for defending his equal rights. George attended Hamilton College and learned the restaurant trade before moving to Newport, where he opened the luxurious Sea-Girt House. Like his father, George was active in politics, connections that helped him when he took charge of the congressional cafeteria. And he possessed many friends inside the New York Custom House, where his brother Peter ran a lunchroom. Yet his nomination for collector never came.[32]

African-Americans struggled to obtain positions in New York. In 1861, abolitionist customs collector Hiram Barney hired Robert Vosburgh to be the first black clerk in the history of the federal service. Vosburgh was a pharmacist raised by an African-American father and a white mother in Erie, Pennsylvania, and light-skinned enough to be recorded as white in two censuses. But Democratic newspapers raged that "to turn out of employment a citizen because his skin is white, to put in his place a black negro, would be a movement so odious that the entire race of white men would rise in vindictive rebellion against it." The editorial concluded that "to be ruled by negroes" was a "humiliation and disgrace" and "criminal to the last degree." By 1873, Vosburgh had worked his way up to a job as a statistician in the auditor's division, making him the second-highest-paid African-American in the New York Custom House.[33]

The highest-paid black clerk at the Port of New York was Alexander Powell. Appointed a messenger in 1870, "Aleck" was only twenty-three years old, and described by whites as "a remarkably intelligent looking man." He was born in the Hudson River boomtown of Troy, to southern-born free black parents. His father, William F. Powell, was a steward on the People's Steamship line, and his mother, Julia Crawford Powell, a "marvel of industry," ran an agency supplying servants to the affluent congregants of Henry Ward Beecher's Plymouth Church.[34]

Like Vosburgh, Powell was mistaken for white. But he identified himself as a man of color. In the 1860s, the family sent him to the all-black Ashmun Institute (later known as Lincoln University) in Pennsylvania. Powell served in the navy, then worked for the Freedman's Bureau before his mother presumably asked Beecher to secure him a job at the port. During the 1872 election, Aleck worked to turn the African-American vote away from Democratic candidate Horace

Greeley, whose abolitionist credentials made him appealing to some blacks. After Grant's victory, Powell passed the civil service exam and was rewarded with a clerkship paying $1,200 per year.[35]

Powell developed a close friendship with Collector Chester Arthur and eventually followed him to the White House. When critics charged that Powell was nothing more than a valet for the fashion-conscious president, he publicly rebelled:

> I am not, have not been, nor do I expect ever to be in the remotest degree "a valet," "body servant" or any kind of private servant to any man, even though that man should chance to be the President of the United States. . . . I was appointed to act and be his private messenger.

Yet even at his most defiant, Powell actually minimized his stature. He was in fact, Arthur's confidant. As evidence of their relationship, the president gave him a framed photograph, signed "To Alexander Powell, from his friend Chester A. Arthur," as well as an engraved gold watch. Powell also received something more valuable, a voice in Arthur's patronage decisions.[36]

For most African-Americans, messenger was the highest position to which they might aspire. In 1869, the New York customs collector hired Brooklyn resident Peter Vogelsang. Though a mere porter before the Civil War, Vogelsang was a member of the city's free black elite. His father, a merchant from St. Croix, was a voice for racial equality, while his mother was esteemed in the African-American church. He was connected by blood or marriage to three distinguished free black families: the DeGrasses, the Downings, and the Fortens. At the age of forty-six, Vogelsang had enlisted as a sergeant in the storied Fifty-fourth Massachusetts Volunteer Regiment. Surviving severe chest wounds, he was commissioned first lieutenant. After Appomattox, he helped freedpeople in North Carolina, then returned to the city, where he led innumerable other clubs and societies.[37]

A PROMINENT AFRICAN-AMERICAN, LIEUTENANT PETER VOGELSANG
RECOVERED FROM WAR WOUNDS TO BECOME THE LONGTIME MESSENGER
FOR THE COLLECTOR OF THE PORT OF NEW YORK. Courtesy Massachusetts His-
torical Society, Boston, Massachusetts

But instead of obtaining a job as a customs clerk paying $1,400,
Vogelsang received a position as a messenger at a salary of $1,000
per year. Despite his age, he managed to have a long and distinguished career at the port, carrying messages and manning the door
for seven collectors. Newspapers claimed that there was "no man who
knows so many distinguished public men," including "every politician, merchant, or other habitual caller" at the custom house for over
two decades. He brought more than a war record to his task, being as
"polite as a French diplomatist," the "personification of good humor,"
and a man who "could say 'No' to a persistent office seeker . . . with
as much grace as another man would have said 'Yes.'" Though he

was removed in 1886, in his seventies, his relative Robert continued as one of only five African-Americans whom Democrats allowed to remain at the port.[38]

The Port of Boston was more open, but even at the center of the antislavery movement, positions went only to extraordinary black men. For instance, in 1869, the custom house offered a clerkship to Charles L. Mitchell, a disabled veteran of a celebrated black regiment, the Fifty-fifth Massachusetts Volunteers. He was one of the hundred or so African-Americans commissioned as officers during the war, as well as one of two blacks to serve in the Bay State legislature. In 1871, Charles Lenox Remond, the famous antislavery lecturer, worked briefly as a stamp clerk in the Boston custom house. And later in the decade, Isaac S. Mullen, a navy veteran who had worked for several years in the Norfolk custom house, earned a white-collar job at the port.[39]

But in the North, most African-Americans had to settle for menial positions. The New York Custom House employed several black porters, Cornelius Williams being the best known. "Uncle Corneel," as he was condescendingly known, began working at the port in 1861, likely obtaining the job through the patronage of a powerful New Jersey Republican. Even at the age of eighty, his head bald, but his black moustaches and sidewhiskers giving him a youthful appearance, Williams still shoveled the snowy sidewalks outside the custom house.[40]

IMMEDIATELY AFTER THE WAR, the New York Custom House was nearly devoid of women. One of the exceptions was janitress Louise Chester. In addition to sweeping floors and washing towels, Louise ran a "knickknack stand" in the vestibule of the naval office selling fruit and other items. Called the "Juno of the Custom House Rialto," she was a beloved fixture at the port for over three decades, remembered as "very pretty" and "buxom" when young, but eccentric in her dotage. Her Brooklyn house was filled with flowers and "a small menagerie" including "three parrots; a couple of tropical birds, several sweet-singing canaries and four or five cats" and "the finest collection of King Charles Spaniels in the country." Though observers claimed "her education was so deficient that she could not make change or tell time by the clock," she nonetheless managed to accumulate an estate of over $50,000 and bragged "that she never worked for an Irishman."[41]

Ports with passenger traffic needed female inspectors to stop women from concealing their imports. For years, the Port of New York called upon Mary E. Wadham, a young widow who operated a Broadway hair salon, to examine any female suspects, but in 1866, Congress empowered the collector to hire inspectresses at a healthy wage of $3 per day. Several of the new employees were writers, not unlike the male authors who depended upon the custom house for a stable income. When Lillian Foster was widowed in the 1850s, she decided to preserve the "respectable position" of her family "by the efforts of her pen," writing a well-reviewed travel diary. In 1866, Foster curried favor with the White House by writing a biography of President Andrew Johnson. But by the time positions had opened for women at the custom house in 1867, Johnson was focused on preventing his own impeachment. Thus, it fell to Johnson's enemy, *New York Tribune* editor Horace Greeley, to intervene to secure Foster a berth at the port.[42]

Other inspectresses were elite women motivated by the desire for citizenship. Margaret C. C. Steele, the sister of Senator Roscoe Conkling of New York, grew up in a family dedicated to public service. The daughter of a congressman and federal judge, she worked for her widowed father, attended political events, and met statesmen such as William Seward. But as a woman, she was not permitted to participate directly in politics and was even mocked at times for asserting herself in the public sphere. Thwarted, she became a writer, penning several books and many articles under her own name, as well as the pseudonym Henry Lunettes. A "refined and cultured woman," she studied history, foreign languages, and pseudosciences like phrenology. In middle age she married Dr. Albert J. Steele, a self-styled "professor" and the founder of Brooklyn's Electro-Medical College, who lectured frequently on the "curative powers of electricity." In 1869, after the couple had separated, Margaret asked her brother for a position in the custom house.[43]

Tragic histories were often the female inspectors' main qualifications. Mary Wadham, Lillian Foster, Genevieve "Gennie" Ferris, Mary Dominguez, Marie Louise Ellis, and Sarah Genet were all widows. Politicians viewed these jobs as a form of alms reserved for veterans and widows, whose poverty resulted from factors outside their control. Yet, even a relict had to have connections. For instance, Sarah Genet's brother-in-law Henry was a Tammany state senator descended from the founders of New York's Democratic Party.[44]

THE TREASURY NEVER adopted an official policy of discrimination, but officials were permitted to act upon their own biases. In his memoir, Inspector Charles Edwards of Niagara—a religious Protestant businessman and author—expressed distaste for the Irish, as well as a marked antipathy to alcohol and tobacco users. And yet his *Reminiscences* continually restated the impossibility of detecting crime from poverty alone. Edwards described how elites attempted to defeat the wheels of justice, while innocent paupers meekly succumbed to inspection.

Discrimination against Jewish travelers continued after the Civil War. Secret Service chief Hiram Whitley's memoirs featured several anti-Semitic caricatures, including the story of "Haman Broun," a "keen, wiry, subtle, black-eyed" and "money-loving Jew" who smuggled diamonds in his boot heels. Likewise, Colonel Lewis B. Grigsby, New York deputy collector, informed an 1869 Congressional commit-

FEMALE SMUGGLERS AND FEMALE CUSTOM-HOUSE DETECTIVES.—THE OFFICIAL IN CHARGE FINDS A PIECE OF VALUABLE SILK VELVET SKILFULLY ARRANGED EN JUPON BENEATH A WOMAN'S DRESS.—SEE PAGE 571.

GILDED AGE PUBLISHERS LOVED PRINTING IMAGES OF CUSTOMS INSPEC-
TRESSES SEARCHING THE BODIES OF DISHABILLE WHITE WOMEN. Courtesy
The American Antiquarian Society, Worcester, Massachusetts

tee that "nine-tenths of the smugglers" over the Isthmus of Panama
were Jews. And Dr. John T. McLean, the special treasury agent for
San Francisco, stated that "German and French Jews" were responsible for "a large portion of our undervaluations." "Without intending
to disparage that race," McLean observed, "I think the Israelites a little more prone to that sort of business than persons who are not of
that religious persuasion."[45]

As during the Civil War, Jewish merchants complained bitterly
about bias in the custom house. San Francisco Jews published a
pamphlet accusing McLean of a "gross slander." If Jews had smuggled, then why had he declined to cite specific firms rather than

stigmatizing "a whole community of Israelites." Reminding him
that they were American citizens, the authors asked, "If our religion promotes immoral conduct or acts of turpitude, how is it that
our criminal courts are so seldom troubled with charges against
Israelites?" The pressure succeeded. In 1871, the Grant administration replaced McLean with Jewish politician Louis Cohn, a
man praised as "a popular citizen and consistent Republican" who
would "serve the government without prejudice or fear," not with
"petty oppression, espionage and vexatious intermeddling as in the
manner of some."[46]

Chinese travelers aroused the fiercest scrutiny. According to a sympathetic missionary writing in 1877, "relays of customhouse officials"
greeted Chinese immigrants to San Francisco with body searches,
looking for "a little opium or silk goods or curiosities":

> The officer stops him, makes him hold up his hands, then
> manipulates him from head to foot, fumbling over all the nooks
> and corners of the ample folds of the sleeves and legs of his
> clothing. The Chinaman seems to consider the process as a part
> of our peculiar civilization, and quietly submits to the perfor-
> mance. Sometimes a flash of the eye and a burning face tells
> that the process is distasteful even to the Chinaman, but no
> resistance is ever offered.

The minister observed that the inspectors were "singularly care-
less in handling the personal effects of these poor fellows." Though
sometimes willing to let contraband pass for a price, inspectors often
"wantonly destroy[ed] or . . . unlawfully appropriate[d] to their own
benefit many little articles of personal baggage not subject to duty."[47]

Treasury officials—including inspectresses committed to fur-
thering women' rights—claimed women were prone to smuggling
because their consumer desires trumped their patriotism. Moreover,
they worried that merchants exploited gender assumptions by hiring

"regular female smugglers" to carry their goods across the border. To stop this, in 1872, a Michigan custom house initiated a dragnet on the Detroit River. Beginning at two o'clock in the afternoon,

> [o]fficers walked fifteen or twenty women up stairs into the customs rooms and bundled them over to a woman to be searched. Every boat load which landed for about three hours was treated in the same manner—that is, all the female portion. Some were indignant and appealed to their husbands, who vainly appealed to the customs officer. Others wanted to faint away, but after looking at the planks and dust concluded not to. Others wept, laughed or turned pale, but none of them were permitted to escape. . . . Another one indignantly denied "the right of search," but after remaining a prisoner for an hour or two told the searcher to "take it and go to grass," throwing a package of ribbons and laces on the floor.

Searching 150 women in all, inspectors had "a good deal of fun," caught at least thirteen smugglers, and seized pins, ten yards of English flannel, a pound of tea, calico, and velvet.[48]

MANY WRITERS PAINTED this world as a cesspool of corruption, filled with dishonest, incompetent, or merely superfluous people, who spent their days on politics rather than the business of the government. Nathaniel Hawthorne famously prefaced his 1850 classic, *The Scarlet Letter*, with a screed against his former colleagues in the Salem custom house. In part, such criticisms were merely sour grapes, the cries of scandal heard after every adverse election. Yet, such sentiments grew more common with the rise of the Liberal Republican movement in 1870. Government, they argued, should employ the "best men," determined by experience, expertise, and competitive examination. Economist David A. Wells argued that the poor qualifications, haphazard organization, and partisan orientation of employees at the New York Custom House cost as much as $25 million per year. Reformers believed that professionalization would improve the efficiency of the custom house while denying political machines their patronage fuel.[49]

These detractors simultaneously, and somewhat paradoxically, described the custom house as tyrannical. The port was filled with "spies and informers" who operated a "terrible" and "appalling" "system of terrorism" that afflicted merchants. To these observers, the reality of taxes and the possibility of seizures, indictments, convictions, and prison seemed wholly oppressive and un-American. If a custom house could hardly be both inefficient and too rigorous, it was no matter. Reformers fired a blunderbuss at the port, hoping to undermine the president, his appointees, and the protectionist policies they favored. Though sincere in their support for an honest, nonpartisan, and economical port, reformers never endorsed a more aggressive collection of duties.[50]

Yet, the port had its defenders. Thomas Bangs Thorpe complained, "It is the fashion of the day to speak derisively of Customhouse officials. They are supposed to be idlers, and, if opportunity offers, dishonest," but "the integrity of customs officials compares most favorably when brought in contrast with the almost daily published record of defalcations of . . . officers of banks and other monetary institutions." Thorpe noted that the custom house collected duties "at a cost of from one to one and a half per cent.—greatly less than in the internal revenue department, and just half of what it costs to collect the imposts in England," a nation civil service reformers deemed a model for the United States. Indeed, according to Thorpe, the costs of the customs service in New York were so small that the fees paid the port's entire expenses.[51]

At the time, a striking number of Americans agreed with Thorpe. Elections regularly returned protectionist Republicans to power. Though certainly willing to expose corruption at the port, newspapers proudly reported the "celebrities" and literary figures working in the custom house and printed laudatory obituaries for its leading administrators. When inspectors caught a smuggler, the press conveyed the government's view of the arrest and seizure. Cartoons and illustrations depicted custom-house officers as authorities trying to prevent professional criminals and wealthy smugglers from evading the law. In other words, the public was concerned about dishonesty, but largely sympathetic to the tariff system itself. This support would be tested in the years to come.

DECEIVERS

Rose Eytinge was a smuggler, though not by trade. A leading actress, described by one critic as "talented, handsome, and of an exceedingly formidable character," Eytinge was most famous for playing the bibulous prostitute Nancy Sykes in the 1868 stage version of Charles Dickens's *Oliver Twist*. In August, the thirty-seven-year-old star left for a vacation in England. In London, the manager of her hotel escorted her to the horse races and introduced her to Albert Edward, the Prince of Wales. With "every glass on the racecourse" watching her, Eytinge so charmed the prince that he gave her tickets to the queen's box at the opera. After a delightful week, she returned home, carrying "beautiful silks and satins and laces and furbelows" that she "dishonestly intended to smuggle." But as the steamer approached New York, Eytinge lost her nerve. "Frightened" of the "much-dreaded customhouse officer," Eytinge convinced the ship's disapproving but ultimately obliging captain to help her skirt the inspector.[1]

Eytinge lived an ambiguous life. As a celebrity, Rose needed to present herself as a great lady, but she could only afford the trappings by smuggling. Eytinge identified herself as a Christian, even Anglo-Saxon, yet her dark hair and Levantine profile suggested her Jewish origins. She bragged of meeting dignitaries like President Lincoln, but spent her nights in Pfaff's Beer Cellar with New York's bohemians. Her loves were also split between Olympus and the demimonde. First

ROSE EYTINGE. Courtesy New York Public Library, New York, New York

Rose married a newspaper editor, but the relationship suffered in 1869 when gossips whispered that his boss, *New York Times* owner Henry Raymond, had died in her loving arms. After obtaining a divorce, she married George Butler, the son of Benjamin Butler's notorious brother Andrew. Rose followed George to Egypt, where the State Department posted him as a consul. But when President Grant removed him for corruption, drunkenness, and mayhem, the couple returned to the United States, where Rose resumed her career on the stage.[2]

Eytinge's dual existence mirrored the contradictory nature of smuggling itself. It was a profitable business for career criminals, but far more so for politically powerful merchants and corporations dealing in imported goods. It was an offense associated with foreigners, Jews, Asians, and women, but it was also a "respectable crime" committed

by upper-class whites and Protestant businessmen. Americans condemned smugglers, yet they avidly consumed contraband. In the act of
collecting close to a billion dollars (today, around $18 billion) in import
duties between 1869 and 1874, officials seized over 3,600 shipments for
smuggling-related offenses, obtained sixty-eight criminal indictments,
and collected fines worth over $4 million (about $82 million today).[3]

These were merely the smugglers caught. During the fiscal year
1872–73, the commissioner of customs estimated that 36,830 travelers smuggled nearly $130 million ($2.4 billion today) in merchandise. In 1877, Parsee Moore claimed that $11.7 million in silk, or 25
percent of the total imported, entered illegally. That same year, an
expert claimed that sugar frauds amounted to $6 million per year.
If other experts offered smaller figures, smuggling was nonetheless
commonplace. Illegally imported goods from Europe, the Caribbean,
and Asia filled store shelves, graced the dinner tables of fashionable
houses, and swathed the bodies of chic women.[4]

In the aftermath of the Civil War, Americans consumed smuggled goods even as they demanded protection against contraband. At
the Port of New York between 1866 and 1873, seven of the ten largest
smuggling seizures involved tobacco, alcohol, sugar, coffee, and tea:
pleasurable products that had been taxed for centuries. Opium was
legal in the United States, but fearful politicians enacted a tariff that
doubled its price, leading to extensive smuggling. Illegal trade boomed
in luxury goods like silk, lace, and diamonds, which were taxed not
only to protect domestic industries, but also to discourage consumption of products deemed threatening to social equality. And when they
could get away with it, offenders sought to avoid the tariffs on protected
manufactured goods, ranging from lumber to iron to machinery.

SINCE THE 1820s, American readers had devoured adventure stories
featuring contrabandists operating at sea or on the perimeter. Illustrated periodicals like *Harper's* published etchings depicting sailboats streaking across the sea, gun fights between smugglers and

revenuers, and convoys of men crossing the Rio Grande, knapsacks filled with swag upon their backs. Treasury officials blamed criminal bands for the smuggling problem. Investigating a ship's master for the mundane crime of importing fifty gallons of French brandy, Secret Service chief Hiram Whitley melodramatically declared his determination to "break up the gang of smugglers that has been so long defrauding the revenue of the State with impunity" and "put an end to the contraband trade in New York."[5]

Such accounts had some factual basis. The nation's long borders offered smugglers many gaps through which to carry goods into the United States. In 1858, the Mexican state of Tamaulipas, just across the Rio Grande from Texas, had declared a *zona libre*, allowing the free importation of goods into the province. The effect of the policy was to make foreign manufactures cheaper in the town of Matamoros than in nearby Brownsville. Gangs naturally began sailing products into the Mexican port, then carrying them across the river to the U.S. in knapsacks and on burros. Few complained before the Civil War, when American tariffs were low. And between 1861 and 1865, Texans actually appreciated Mexico's policy, which helped Confederates undermine the Union blockade. But by the late 1860s, with American tariffs at their highest levels in history, the smuggling problem became acute, as the Mexican government was not yet strong enough to collect its own tariffs, much less to put down armed gangs.[6]

Contraband traveled by water, carried by blackened ships into secret inlets under cover of night. Arriving in Puget Sound in 1864, Larry Kelly rose to "the front rank of contraband runners" by dint of his "thorough seamanship," his "disregard to danger," and shrewd "ability to keep his own counsel." Beginning by importing silk, Kelly eventually branched out into new fields. By the 1880s, he was carrying Chinese laborers and opium from British Columbia to Washington State.[7]

But most professionals smuggled their goods alongside legitimate merchandise upon ordinary ships. John "Boots" Cantlon was arrested repeatedly during the 1870s and 1880s. Boots was a boat-

man, a "burly laboring man," paid to row people from the shore to
their ships and known for once trying to drown a dodgy passenger.
His first brush with the law was in 1867, when harbor police accused
him of paying sailors aboard the S.S. *Andrews* to throw imported
cigars in rubber bags into New York harbor where he could gather
them. Officials finally convicted Boots in 1885, only to see his conviction miraculously reversed the next year. After that, Cantlon took his
ill-gotten gain and became a "wealthy saloon keeper."[8]

For others, smuggling was the gateway to a career in crime. The
leader "of a notorious gang of juvenile smugglers," John Talbot,
pretended to be a "young cripple," taking advantage of observers'
assumptions about his innocence. In 1871, a night inspector caught
Talbot, John Collins, and another boy in the act of removing seventeen boxes of cigars from the *Morro Castle*, a passenger steamer that
ran between Cuba and New York. The officer had caught the boys
several times before, but "always let them go on getting possession
of the cigars." But when the gang pitched the boxes overboard and
threw stones at the crates and the inspector, he decided to prosecute
them. After spending thirteen months in the penitentiary, Talbot,
a.k.a. Jacob Travers, a.k.a. The Hatter, became a well-known burglar
and thief throughout the Northeast.[9]

Talbot's colleague John Collins stayed in the contraband business,
eventually joining Boots Cantlon's gang. In 1880, officials spied Collins in a boat in the North River alongside the Havana line steamer
Alexandria receiving packages containing 1,800 cigars. The agents
demanded he surrender, so Collins came over and gave them the
goods, but when they attempted to arrest him, he began rowing
away. Unconcerned for his rights or safety, they fired their pistols at
him. Hit by a bullet, Collins screamed, "Oh! What a shot!" and then
escaped into the darkness under a pier. They later found the smuggler in a "Water Street den," his clothing torn and right arm injured.
In 1884, he would be arrested again, this time for driving a wagon

filled with cigars illegally imported by Boots, prompting him to testify against his boss.[10]

Professional smugglers exploited societal taboos to avoid inspection. In 1872, officials were surprised to hear a "ringing sound" coming from a coffin being carried to a hearse surrounded by mourners.
Inside the box, they discovered French clocks. Likewise, another customs inspector asked the ship's carpenter to remove the lid of a black
walnut casket containing a "slightly decomposed" man. Satisfied, the
inspector asked that the crate be taken away. When the next steamer
contained a similar long box, he again ordered the casket opened,
finding the "blue cold face and head and neck" of a dead man. This
time, however, he removed the entire lid of the coffin, revealing that
the corpse's "trunk and bowels" had been replaced by tin boxes containing $8,000 in "choice Mechlin and other valuable laces."[11]

Smugglers also played on reluctance to probe beneath the surface.
Because gemstones were small, valuable, and highly taxed, contrabandists often hid them in packages taped to their skin, in false
teeth, and in their stomachs. In 1874, an article described a "New
York Jew" named Max Fischer found to be carrying $1,000 in stones
in the lining of his boots. A subsequent time Fischer returned from
Europe, the inspectors closely examined the "nervous and agitated"
traveler. Searching his pocketbook, they found a receipt for eighteen
diamonds. Then they examined his vest, discovering eighteen stones
hidden behind a "strip of chamois skin." The inspectors triumphantly
confiscated the gems and freed Fischer. Only later did they discover
that they had seized mere glass. The smuggler had encased the real
stones in a plaster on the small of his back, to be removed with warm
water upon his arrival home.[12]

Smugglers sometimes used force to defeat the customs. For
instance, in 1879, Inspector Peter Carley received information that a
man named Claudius Benice, a Frenchmen by birth and a barber by
trade, had managed to sneak 175 glazier's diamonds past the inspec-

tors at the Port of New York. Carley found Benice at the corner of Leroy and Washington streets in the company of two other men, but when he tried to arrest him, the Frenchman bit his finger and "drew a pistol," forcing the officer to let him escape. Carley found Benice at a Christopher Street saloon and arrested him. When the parcel was opened, the officers discovered not only the diamonds, but a "lot of India rubber goods the sale of which is prohibited under the Comstock laws," presumably either sex toys or condoms.[13]

The violence sometimes went beyond mere finger chewing. Gangs retaliated against customs officials who tried to arrest them and confiscate their swag. In 1866, inspectors in Buffalo seized four kegs of smuggled liquor and then exchanged a "dozen pistol shots" with the owners, who escaped. In the summer of 1869, the authorities investigated the murder of a Hoboken Ferry night watchman named William Lawrence, whose body had been found standing erect in the shallow water between the scow and the piles supporting the dock," his "feet and legs being far imbedded in mud." Concluding the perpetrator had struck Lawrence with a blunt instrument, the police pursued seven suspects, including a young carpenter named William "Buggy" Nattas, a prostitute named Victorine Hugg, a seaman named Michael Quinn, and "a Spaniard" named Manuel Lasso de la Vega. Witnesses testified that Lasso de la Vega had threatened Lawrence's life when he proposed to arrest the "Spaniard" for smuggling cigars. But the official suspicions could not be proven, and no one was ever convicted of the crime.[14]

This violence grew worse the farther one got from the major custom houses. Around 1870, Secret Service chief Whitley sent three men to break up a smuggling ring based on the Canadian border, near Derby Line, Vermont. The detectives seized several items—a carriage, horses, brandy, and silk—and "put the iron ruffles upon" several smugglers, before the locals became "exasperated." "Squads" of Canadians stormed over the border, and declared they would "clean out the dam Yankee informers." The detectives "soon found they had no friends there save their ever trusty six shooters." A local sheriff then arrested the three agents upon a "trivial trumped up charge." Though the officers secured their release, they failed to do more than inconvenience the smugglers, whose local popularity made them immune to prosecution.[15]

MOST CONTRABANDISTS, HOWEVER, were not career criminals. In 1870, Augustus Radcliffe, a twenty-two-year-old Englishman, decided to sneak $30,000 in gems into the United States. Radcliffe was from an affluent family of industrial diamond manufacturers, but his debts made him desperate. At Euston Square railway station, Radcliffe met an American engineer named Henry Justice, who was in England selling Colorado mining rights. Together the two men bought passage on the steamship *Java*, bound from Queenstown to New York. To fool the customs, Radcliffe signed the manifest as "Stephen Chamberlain," taped the diamonds to his calves, and asked Justice to carry a package in his overcoat pocket. At the landing, they met an associate, Friend Esmond, a former captain in the Union Army, who agreed to sell the gems in Chicago. But Secret Service chief Whitley somehow learned of the plot. He suborned Esmond, posed as a diamond merchant named "Mr Lipman," and obtained the evidence he needed to arrest the desperate English gentleman.[16]

Measured by arrests, the most persistent offenders were seafarers, who supplemented their meager incomes by carrying liquor, cigars, and textiles ashore to sell to local merchants. In 1870, Treasury agents in Philadelphia arrested John Kammett, the steward of the ship *Stadacona*, for smuggling $3,000 worth of silks and Irish poplins from Londonderry boarded up above the vessel's bread locker. That same year, officials in New York held Charles Knight, the British first mate of the ship *Hudson*, in jail until he could pay a $500 fine for smuggling lace. The next year, officials caught Thomas Littleton, the bedroom steward of the steamship *City of Washington*, with contraband

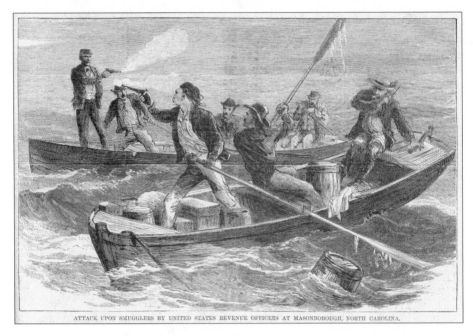

ATTACK UPON SMUGGLERS BY UNITED STATES REVENUE OFFICERS AT MASONBOROUGH, NORTH CAROLINA.

THE TREASURY ARMED OFFICIALS TO ARREST SMUGGLERS WHO RESISTED INSPEC-
TION. Courtesy Bird Library, Syracuse University, Syracuse, New York

lace wrapped around his body. Littleton claimed he had been paid
$10 by a passenger to bring the lace ashore, but officials believed he
intended to sell it for cash.[17]

Rough men engaged in a physically demanding trade, seamen
could be dangerous when confronted. In 1874, two customs inspectors seized a load of cigars from a Manhattan saloon that had been
erroneously passed free of duty by another agent. Very quickly, a
crowd of Spanish and American sailors and longshoremen surrounded the officers and "threatened their lives if they did not
surrender the cigars." "In self-defense," the inspectors drew their
revolvers and "kept the weapons in their hands all the way to the Custom House." The "smuggler's gang" chased them as far as the seizure room before being "forcibly ejected" by officials.[18]

But many smugglers were simply travelers like Rose Eytinge who
wanted to avoid paying duties on their purchases. Inspector Charles

Edwards described how Kansas senator James Lane once tried to pass his station without declaring "Indian curiosities" purchased in Canada. Caught in the act, Lane laughingly retorted, "Is it possible? I wonder if I ever aided in making *that* law." Both rich and poor, according to Edwards, sought to buy clothes across the river, where the absence of tariffs made them cheaper. Individuals often snuck bottles of alcohol into the United States in violation of statutes barring the importation of liquor in quantities less than thirty gallons. People carried cigars and packages of tobacco in their baggage, sometimes inadvertently, sometimes to avoid the small cost of declaring them.[19]

Immigrants smuggled to recoup the cost of the passage to the United States. Some tried to exploit tariff exceptions allowing individuals freely to import "tools of the trade" and household goods in use for more than one year. On May 18, 1870, for instance, customs officials caught a German immigrant carrying "three large cases containing scrub brooms made of birch twigs," presumably for sale ashore. That same day, officials caught an Englishwoman named Laura Thompson carrying a case filled with "fine goods, which she intended to use in her trade as a milliner and dressmaker."[20]

Affluent tourists loved to shop for what seemed to be underpriced foreign luxuries. One paper alleged that "the universal habit of polite smuggling" was so common among the wealthy that many travelers had no sense it was immoral. The *New York Telegram* likewise complained that "wholesale smuggling by wealthy New York citizens" was costing the government "millions of dollars." When the commissioner of customs estimated that over thirty thousand railroad and steamship passengers smuggled nearly $129 million in their baggage, he was complaining not about working people, but about the upper and middle classes who could afford to travel.[21]

Upper-class women had the responsibility for furnishing the freshly built mansions, bejeweling the white necks, and adorning the corseted bodies of the nation. For these ladies, cities like Paris seemed a paradise, offering miles of shops selling the luxury goods at low prices. But the bargains hid looming costs at the port. In May 1870, a Philadelphia woman arrived in New York on the steamer *Pennsylvania* from Europe, carrying clothes worth $125 to be worn on her wedding day. Hoping to pass the trousseau quickly through the custom house, she petitioned the ship's former captain, who promised to pass the goods free of duty and send them to her.[22]

Diplomats possessed special opportunities to smuggle. Since embassies were technically foreign soil, their imports were not subject to U.S. duties. Moreover, agents of foreign governments were immune from prosecution. In June 1874, in the midst of delicate negotiations between the United States and Spain, customs officials seized crates of smuggled cigars consigned to the Spanish minister, José Polo de Bernabé. Polo may have been framed by his enemies, but other diplomats definitely abused the perks of office. For instance, in April 1870, a Guatemalan consul was arrested for using diplomatic mail pouches to smuggle $63,000 in lace. Nor was smuggling reserved to foreign statesmen. According to one former consul, American attachés living abroad commonly used "official mail bags" for "sending silks, laces, etc." to "friends" in the United States.[23]

But the essence of smuggling was deception. Most amateur smugglers simply lied about the extent, value, or nature of their imports and hoped the customs officer did not notice. In 1869, General Ramón Páez, a naturalist, author, and the exiled son of Venezuela's late president, returned from Europe to the United States. Considering his manner suspicious, customs officials examined his baggage, finding "seven or eight" undeclared "packages containing ladies jewelry and an indecent picture in a case." The general deflected the inspectors by accusing them of stealing his studs, but he later discovered them in a jacket pocket. Desperate to avoid arrest and the seizure of his goods, Páez used his connections to bring pressure on the deputy collector, who "destroyed" the obscene image but passed the jewelry in return for the required taxes.[24]

Others sought to stretch holes in the law. In 1875, wealthy New York ladies including a "well known actress," probably Rose Eytinge, commissioned Frenchwoman Leonie Juvin to import silk dresses worth between $7,000 and $20,000 on the steamer *Ville de Paris*. Her ruse was to join an opera troupe and then tell customs inspectors that the garments were her "wardrobe" because, under the tariff law, foreign performers owed no duty on costumes brought into the country for their work. The trick succeeded several times before Treasury officials discovered that she was a milliner, not a performer, and the gowns were specifically ordered by society matrons.[25]

Many amateur smugglers tried to bribe inspectors to look the other way. In 1873, rumors flew around New York that the brother of the king of Sweden had offered customs officials a bribe to prevent them from arresting him for smuggling kid gloves. A British milliner accused of smuggling in 1870 unsuccessfully offered a customs officer £5 in gold to move on. Yet other inspectors actually demanded emoluments. One well-traveled gentleman complained that each person "thus dunned for a bribe becomes an advertiser to travellers that smuggling is made easy and safe for all who will pay a small fee."[26]

IMPORTERS LEARNED HOW to skirt the tariff, and they applied this knowledge toward illicit ends. On May 16, 1870, United States federal marshals raided the fashionable Manhattan home of José de Bessa Guimarães, seeking $30,000 in diamonds smuggled from Rio de Janeiro. Guimarães had come from Portugal to the United States as a young man and made a fortune importing cork and other goods. As an agent for a sewing machine company, Guimarães routinely sent and received shipments from Brazil, which allowed him to bring the stones to New York. The officers found nothing until an inspector "intercepted" Guimarães's American-born daughter Celia fleeing the house. Searching the five-year-old girl, agents discovered a box containing "several thousand dollars" in gems. Federal marshals did not hold the child, but they did arrest the foreign merchant, holding him on $50,000 bail (equal to over $850,000 today). Guimarães avoided prison by settling with Treasury officials, paying the government two installments totaling nearly $20,000.[27]

More frequently, businesses smuggled the merchandise they sold or used. In May 1870, for instance, the government arrested brothers David and John Tilton for smuggling $3,000 in nutmeg from Canada. They were butchers who used the seasoning to preserve meat, to make sausages, and perhaps to sell in their shop. In June of that year, a magistrate heard the case against wholesale druggist William Hall for purchasing bottles of illegally imported bay oil. In 1871, Secret Service chief Whitley seized $15,000 in diamonds allegedly smuggled on the *Merrimac* from Rio de Janiero by Benjamin F. Moore, a Nassau Street jeweler. In all these cases, smuggling served as a natural extension of trade, a means by which businessmen edged their competitors.[28]

In the early 1870s, Treasury agents caught eminent firms undervaluing their imports. Importing houses such as M. & E. Solomon, Alva Oatman, Felix Miranda, Henry Knight, Joseph M. Mayorza, J. J. Almirall, and José A. Vega, bribed chief weigher General George F. Sherman to accept the declared weight of their shipments without actually putting them on the scales. In June 1867, Oatman imported 289 bales of tobacco on the steamer *Columbian*, claiming for them a weight of 25,802 pounds net. Sherman taxed Oatman on 25,809 pounds of tobacco, an impossibly small difference given the time the goods had spent in the hold of a Havana steamer. In fact, the shipment weighed 29,082 pounds. By getting his false declaration certified, Oatman had cheated the U.S. government out of over $1,100 ($17,000 today). Agents uncovered similar practices in the assessment of coffee, tea, sugar, spices, oils, and other products.[29]

Importers of finished goods similarly enticed assessors to accept fraudulent declarations, taking advantage of the Treasury's inability to examine all imports. Appraisers usually checked the merchant's declaration against only one of every ten crates. They were supposed to choose at random, but importers induced officials to scrutinize only a specific container. For instance, the Guiterman brothers were Jewish immigrants who had made their fortune as dry goods dealers, Union Army contractors, and importers of European luxury goods. Aided by another downtown firm, they introduced shipments of silk, kid gloves, and meerschaum pipes as "clocks and glass shades, &c." subject to lower value and duty. They bribed an appraiser to examine a correctly declared marked box filled with pearl buttons, then pass the rest. By this process, they saved an estimated $20,000 in duty for each shipment.[30]

Wealth did not protect businessmen against charges of smuggling. In 1873, Special Agent Benaiah Jayne claimed that the plate-glass firm of Platt & Boyd had defrauded the government to the tune of over $1 million. The company's founder was Isaac L. Platt, a well-known New York financier. In the late 1860s, Platt retired, leaving his importing house to his son John, an indolent yachtsman, who let the firm's junior partner, Edwin A. Boyd, run the firm. Emigrating from Northern Ireland, Boyd had risen from a $3 per week clerkship to amass a fortune, with which he later built a $75,000 house just "a stone's throw" from the Fifth Avenue residence of William H. Vanderbilt, the richest man in the world.[31]

Jayne accused Platt & Boyd of paying foreign manufacturers to falsify measurements and remove charges from invoices. He alleged they declared their imports to be samples, free of duty. They purportedly lied about the grade of their plate glass and exaggerated the amount of glass broken in transit. According to the special agent, Platt & Boyd even smuggled "silks, laces, bonnets, dresses, gloves, boots, stockings, watches, diamonds, champagne, port, sherry, grouse, mutton, shirt bosoms, studs, china, Cashmere shawls, opera glasses, ale, porter, kiramell, mineral water, engraved table tops, bronzes, and Parisian trifles" in their crates. Finally, they supposedly distributed bribes to ninety-seven customs officers, including the deputy surveyor.[32]

Major corporations also schemed to defraud the government. Consider sugar. In 1870, the nation's 38,555,983 inhabitants consumed 530,692 tons of sugar, or 27.5 pounds per person annually. This sugar was subjected to two distinct import taxes, which combined cost the consumer 50 to 90 cents (in constant dollars) per pound. The first tax was to guard the beet, sorghum, and cane farmers of states like Michigan and Louisiana against Cuban planters using slave labor. Feeling pinched by the cost of raw materials, American sugar refiners lobbied hard for a second tariff on refined sugar, with higher rates depending on the grade of the product. These taxes created extraordinary incentives for refiners to smuggle, making it virtually inevitable that every American ate contraband sugar at some time.[33]

Officials repeatedly charged sugar corporations with smuggling. In July 1869, newspapers reported the seizure of over 1.3 million pounds of unrefined sugar worth $4 million in present-day dollars by New Orleans port officials. In December, a San Francisco district court condemned $3.2 million (in 2012 dollars) in sugar smuggled from Hawaii. That same month, special treasury agents in New York uncovered another scheme by sugar refiners. These cases lingered for years, competing with other major scandals for headlines into the mid-1870s. Then, just as the smoke cleared, a new sugar ring was exposed in 1877, leading to five contentious years during which fraud accusations were bandied about in the newspapers, in public hearings, and in published books and pamphlets.[34]

Sugar firms skirted inspection through a mix of corruption and masquerade. Refiners paid custom-house weighers to underestimate the weight of their shipments, cheating the government out of $5 million each year. In one 1869 case, prosecutors accused New Orleans port officials of intentionally miscalculating one shipment of sweetener by a staggering eighty-eight thousand pounds. Likewise, customs assessors determined the quality of the sugar, and thus the rate of duty, using what was called the Dutch standard, a measure emphasizing the color of the crystals. They then bribed assessors to lower their subjective evaluation of imported sugar, and even tried to darken their imports with dyes and additives. In 1876, a San Francisco Treasury agent discovered that importers had made refined sweetener appear raw by mixing burned crystals into each shipment. Such frauds amounted to an "annual loss" of "over $2,000,000" (about $43 million today).[35]

Importers even killed to protect their smuggling profits. In July 1869, customs officials at the Port of New Orleans hired police captain Robert L. Bradley to investigate "colossal frauds" in the valuation of sugar by men loyal to former President Johnson. One day, Bradley discovered that his superiors had passed refined sugars worth $119,000 as raw material, allowing the importer August Couterie & Co. to evade over $30,000 in taxes. Bradley seized the lot, refusing Couterie's offers of champagne and a $50,000 bribe. The next year, three men stabbed Bradley on the street, leading to his death. Though no one was convicted, Bradley's brother Joseph insisted that "the sugar merchants . . . killed him to get him out of their way. . . . He was a politician and a republican, and they did not want such men in the customhouse."[36]

RADICAL REPUBLICANS SAW corporate fraud as a serious problem. On the floor of Congress, Benjamin Butler argued that undervaluation represented a "much more extended and injurious crime" than smuggling. He observed:

> The smuggler must hide in nooks and inlets, and bring in his goods by stealth under the cover of darkness. Of necessity they are few and of little cowst. The fraudulent importer by a false valuation brings in his goods by the cargo, in three thousand ton steamers plying weekly between New York and Liverpool, and passes them through by a bribed officer at under valuation on a perjured invoice of a confederate partner house in Europe, cheats the people of the United States out of millions, thereby becomes a "merchant prince."

One newspaper cartoon depicted "'Old Cockeye' on the Warpath." Well-muscled rather than rotund, naked but for a feathered head-dress, tooth necklace, loincloth, and moccasins, Butler waved a knife at "mercantile corruption." With the aid of his "Shoo Fly," an insect with the head of Benaiah Jayne, Butler provoked "terror and dismay among 'Christian' merchants and statesmen," scattered the textile trades, and frightened the district attorney. In Butler's mind, the importers defied the federal government and shirked their responsibility for America's war debt. Moreover, by importing goods from undemocratic Great Britain and enslaved Cuba, merchants revealed their contempt for workers, white and black, forced to compete with workers lacking basic rights.[37]

Many Americans agreed with Butler. Smugglers symbolized the anxieties of the Reconstruction era, aroused by immigration, racial conflict, sexual license, and rebellion. An article with the headline "Millionaire Importer Imprisoned" described the arrest of John A. Machado, an Azorean merchant caught with "thousands of cigars, cases of liquors of all kinds, furniture, sewing machines, ornaments, &c." The reporter reminded readers that Machado had been tried in the 1850s for outfitting illicit slave ships. He claimed that the defendant had recently abandoned his wife and was living with her sister. Machado was "visited by suspicious persons of both sexes," including "notorious women." Finally, the smuggler was caught in front of Booth's Theatre, the playhouse recently built by Shakespearean actor Edwin Booth, the brother of Lincoln's assassin.[38]

Reports of smuggling played on popular fears that the era's economic growth had forged a class-ridden nation, where elite citizens shed all-American homespun for silk gowns smuggled from Europe. Hiram Whitley falsely asserted that diamond smuggler Augustus Radcliffe claimed to be an "English Lord or something of that sort." The New York Daily Graphic editorialized that a "London court tailor" was smuggling "richly made suits, rolls of silk, ladies shoes, &c." in the captain's cabin of the City of Chester to please the "aristocratic"

"OLD COCKEYE" ON THE WAR PATH

U.S. CONGRESSMAN BENJAMIN BUTLER LED THE "WAR" AGAINST CORPO-
RATE SMUGGLING. Courtesy The American Antiquarian Society, Worcester, Massachusetts

patrons of Fifth Avenue demanding "its things cheap." And others
attacked the "polite smuggling of wealthy people" who felt "inexpress-
ibly indignant" about allegations of wrongdoing, but cost the government "as much as by all other kinds of smuggling put together." Even
tariff critics complained of "wholesale smuggling by wealthy New
York citizens," arguing that such behavior cost the government "millions of dollars" and thus justified lower duties.[39]

Some observers blamed foreigners for the problem. The press cus-
tomarily noted the national origin of defendants: a "Frenchwoman"
here, an "Englishman" there, and "Cubans" everywhere. Newspapers published lurid reports outlining extensive smuggling rings,
run by seemingly respectable Canadian merchants, only to drop the
matter and never report on it again. The blame fell somewhat harder

upon foreign-born residents of the United States. The *Daily Graphic* complained of tobacco merchants such as Emanuel Solomon, Felix Miranda, Joseph M. Mayorza, J. J. Almirall, and José A. Vega, whom it claimed were largely "unnaturalized" and uninterested in the display of "American commercial respectability."[40]

Others focused on Jewish merchants. Relying on stereotypes that became prevalent during the Civil War, newspapers identified smugglers as "Jews," "Hebrews," or "Israelites." A *National Police Gazette* cartoon depicted an inspector stopping two men with beak-like noses, full lips, and enormous downturned mouths, one wearing a loud suit, proclaiming, "Dose is only a present to my bruder, s'help me." For those incapable of deciphering the image, the paper explained it was a picture of "the Hebrew gentlemen who, in their simple honesty, are so unlearned in the ways of the world as to suppose that they can burden themselves with superfluous trinkets as presents to their numerous relatives on this side and be passed on that somewhat diaphanous plea."[41]

Smuggling stories exploited Victorian men's fears that their society was becoming feminine. Again and again, newspapers published articles about female smugglers, ranging from the factual, to the anecdotal, to the fictional. And such articles exploited stereotypes about women's nature. Drawn to the crime by their consumer desires, women used their talents for deception. "Every lady" was "at heart a smuggler, and professional contrabandists displayed an "ingenuity. . . born of that crafty serpent which beguiled their mother Eve." An editorialist observed, "The subtle brain of the feminine has devised many neat schemes too deep to be fathomed by the short line of man's philosophy." And another paper claimed that "men may smuggle clothing now and then, but it is the female sex which carries the burden of guilt," alleging that "at least every tenth woman" who crossed the Detroit River carried contraband.[42]

Such stories traded not only in the oddity of a respectable white woman being arrested, but also the public's prurient fascination with the examination of female bodies. These articles frequently included etchings of female smugglers before, during, and after inspection— lurid pictures of prim matrons undressing voluptuous maidens hiding illicit goodies under their skirts. In an era when federal law strictly controlled the distribution of publications deemed obscene, such pictures offered newspapers a patriotic justification for depicting scantily clad women.[43]

Such articles suggested that emancipated women threatened to replace the masculine, egalitarian America with an effete, European free-trade aristocracy. One bragged that inspectors had seized "costly silks, laces, &c.," which the wife of the French ambassador "intended to air among the simple Republicans who congregate at matinees and soirees in the Nation's Capital." Customs official T. B. Thorpe observed that inspectors "never saw a woman, whatever may have been her social condition, who did not, under any and all circumstances, complain of tariff laws as . . . legalized robbery." "When the sex achieve suffrage," Thorpe added, "free-traders will ever be in ascendancy in the halls of Congress." This exaggeration had some factual basis. In her newspaper *The Revolution*, feminist pioneer Elizabeth Cady Stanton published a letter from the Parsee Merchant complaining of the silk duty, stating, "[W]e . . . hope it will rouse the women of the country to some interest in the question of Free Trade."[44]

If newspapers published smuggling arrests on the front pages, they printed the results in the back pages. The thousands of Americans accused of fraud, undervaluation, and smuggling usually simply forfeited the contraband and paid any duties and fines. In the case of large importers, the customs usually offered them the option of paying substantial settlements in return for a suspension of any criminal sanctions. Augustus Radcliffe was indicted, but simply paid $4,500 to the customs to have it quashed. Tobacco merchants gave the government hundreds of thousands of dollars in return for not prosecuting them in criminal court. Coffee importers John Dymond and Ezra Wheeler respectively paid $40,000 and $120,817.70 (combined, over $3 million today) in duties and fines.[45]

The government tried just a few offenders and convicted even fewer. Boston alcohol wholesaler Dexter T. Mills, one of the few importers who allowed his case to go to a jury, received a fine of $21,000. Of those sent to prison, nearly all were sailors like Michael Gallagher, the fireman on the *Crescent City*, who received a six-month sentence for smuggling cigars, or professional smugglers like Charles Marxen, who suffered an identical fate for smuggling watches into the United States in a false-bottomed trunk. Only one female smuggler spent time in prison: "actress" Leonie Juvin, who resided in Ludlow Street Jail for three months. Most smugglers suffered only the financial punishment imposed by the condemnation of their goods.[46]

Observers found this divergence unsettling. Some protested the disparity in punishments. Upon sentencing two travelers to thirty days in jail for smuggling cigars, Judge Charles L. Benedict "took occasion to denounce the practice of allowing wealthy importers to compromise the crime of smuggling, while poor ones" were "brought to trial." Others saw this disparity as a sign of corruption. In 1872, the reform-minded *New York Sun* complained that "trials have been extremely rare." Instead, the government obtained indictments "indirectly to frighten" businessmen "into making settlements in civil cases . . . on account of the moieties." Assistant District Attorney Ambrose Purdy similarly lamented "disreputable cases . . . put through by irresponsible persons for motives of their own," to wit, the expectation of shares.[47]

Critics suggested that Treasury officials were motivated by greed rather than patriotism. They pointed to Jayne's personal earnings of $316,700 in moieties between 1870 and 1873. Spectacular battles over moieties fed this perception. In April 1871, a letter written by "Fiat Justitia" chastised the *Herald* for attributing the silk arrests to customs officials, who were more interested in "delicious morsels" than "the suppression of the illegal traffic." "The proper authorities" the author insisted, knew that Secret Service chief Whitley was "entitled to the credit." Soon thereafter, Whitley sued another informer for a share of Augustus Radcliffe's $4,500 settlement. When the other claimant refused to budge, the detective allegedly pushed for his indictment as well.[48]

The nation's merchants denied that they were smugglers at all. Businessmen insisted that Butler and his allies had magnified "the charge of Custom House irregularities . . . into an absolute charge of little less than wholesale smuggling." They argued that undervaluations were not frauds on the government, but rather errors discovered by agents poring over records with no attention to similar mistakes made in favor of the United States. Nor were the settlements admissions of guilt. With their shipments in warehouses, indictments hanging over their heads, and their credit dependent upon their reputation for honesty, merchants had no choice but to negotiate with the Treasury. They were not perpetrators, but rather victims of blackmail.[49]

Merchants deflected investigations by appealing to traditional notions of status and authority. They highlighted their reputations, earned through decades in business, politics, and philanthropy. Before the war, their pursuers had been nonentities with checkered resumes, such as Benaiah Jayne, a mere clerk, and Hiram Whitley, a slave catcher. The editor of the *New York Post* complained that one Treasury agent had been a "slave trader and a professional smuggler" as well as a "felon in several points of view" who "had passed immediately from an arrest for smuggling into the service of the United States as a special custom house detective."[50]

The importers' feelings of victimization turned them into potent critics of the United States government, which they painted as tyrannical, corrupt, and even terroristic. During the war, this dissent might have marked them as Copperheads. But as the years passed, calls for lower tariffs, honest administration, and stronger individual rights became more acceptable. Though their demands for the reorganization of the custom house allied them with former Confederates seeking to overthrow the interracial Republican governments of the South, this fact legitimized the latter rather than stigmatizing the former. For this reason, smuggling remained on the front pages, linked as it was to the largest questions of the day.

GILDING

The son of a jeweler, Charles L. Lawrence knew the difference between solid gold and plate. And as a literate man, Charley may well have read *The Gilded Age: A Tale of Today*, Mark Twain's 1873 novel, written with a fellow newspaperman, which satirized the events of the previous decade. Drawing upon the political scandals, financial schemes, sexual affairs, and murders of the years since the Civil War, Twain described a period that glittered like a golden age, but was in fact composed of base metal. To the authors, current events showed that wealth had corroded the grand republican ideals fought for at Gettysburg.

Fear of corruption drew attention to the custom house. But Americans could not agree on what was more scandalous, smuggling or the government's response to it. For Republicans, the tariff was an extension of the Civil War, so a strong custom house protected the nation from lying importers, unfair European manufacturers, and rebellious Southern free-traders. By contrast, Democrats and liberals argued that the Radicals' war on smuggling had made America's ports into sites of extortion and boss politics. They even found themselves defending accused smugglers against the extraordinary powers of Treasury agents. In doing so, they enunciated some of the earliest arguments for the constitutional right to privacy.

———

IN THE YEARS after Appomattox, Charley dreamed of becoming a world-renowned impresario. On October 2, 1867, he hosted a supper catered by the famed Delmonico's for the cast of his new ballet, "The Devil's Auction, or the Golden Branch." New Yorkers desiring haute cuisine depended upon Swiss restaurateur Lorenzo Delmonico for dishes such as *Bass à l'Italienne*. At the end of the meal, Lawrence— the "head and brains" of the production—thanked the performers, and "all retired at an early hour to dream of *houris*, floating female forms, and all the attractions of Terpsichore." The following night, "The Devil's Auction" opened at Banvard's Opera House, featuring a trapeze, dancers, jugglers, and "gorgeous" costumes. Written and directed by veterans of the Spanish stage, the extravaganza offered the sort of story the Founders of the United States deemed frivolous, aristocratic, and un-American: the tale of a count, a maiden, her beloved shepherd, a fairy, magic, and a donkey turned human. But crowds poured in to see the foreign ballerinas, whom publicists naughtily suggested would wear no "further clothing" than an ass.[1]

Lawrence was business manager at the new opera house built by showman John Banvard. This theater was adjacent to a museum, which displayed a "three mile-long" (in fact, between 1,200 feet and one-half mile) panoramic painting of the Mississippi River valley constructed by the proprietor years before. A competitor of Phineas T. Barnum, Banvard was best known for displaying the original Cardiff Giant, a ten-foot-tall gypsum stone statue purported to be either a petrified prehistoric man, or one of the "Nephilim," titanic demigods mentioned in the Book of Genesis. To supplement these static attractions, Banvard had staged plays, but the construction of the new theater marked a substantial foray into the city's still nascent dramatic scene.[2]

Banvard hoped that Lawrence's spectacular would attract patrons to his Thirtieth Street complex, which was a mile northwest of the theater district. He even agreed to expand the stage to fit the imported French scenery, at a cost of $75,000. Some critics predicted financial ruin, but the initial reviews for "The Devil's Auction" were positive. The *Times* deprecated the dialogue and acting, but praised the "beauty" of the performers and the dancing "as equal to any of the artists we have had the pleasure of seeing in New York," predicting a "pecuniary success." The *Tribune* also mocked the show's theatrical elements, but lavishly praised the ballerinas and congratulated the producer, Lawrence. German-born star Augusta Sohlke performed a Hungarian polka with such "abandon and witchery" that she became "the most popular dancer in New York." After three weeks, the producers doubled down by importing Italian sensation Giuseppina Morlacchi, insuring her legs for a reported $100,000. But by November, box office receipts began to decline. The director stopped paying his players, leading his stars to quit. He moved the production downtown to the Academy of Music, cut the number of weekly shows, and then finally closed the production. "So much for *The Devil's Auction*," wrote the *New York Clipper*, "going, going, gone."[3]

While Charley managed Banvard's and produced "The Devil's Auction," he moonlighted as a publisher, merchant, and inventor. He patented a process for manufacturing rubber "floor cloths." When his mother-in-law died in June 1866, he inherited a share of several valuable properties, including the family home near St. Mark's Place and a newspaper, the *Sunday Times and Noah's Weekly Messenger*. Charley brokered tickets out of a "neatly constructed . . . booth" in Chickering & Co.'s piano sales room at 652 Broadway. But he still leapt at new opportunities. In February 1868, for instance, he learned that a man sought a loan offering suspicious bonds as collateral. Feigning interest, Lawrence examined the stolen securities and turned the dealer in for the reward. Lawrence also won a position as an advertising agent for the Paris *Exposition Universelle* of 1867. From his kiosk, he also became "an intimate friend" of foreign-born music promoters and sold tickets for Charles Dickens's celebrated 1867–68 tour of New York City.[4]

In the summer of 1868, Zipporah's fourth pregnancy combined with old debts to strain Charley's finances. He decided to seek a position at the Port of New York. His experience as a broker, his familiarity with foreign trade, and his knowledge of Spanish, Portuguese, French, and Hebrew actually made him well qualified. But to obtain a coveted appointment, he likely needed help from his influential in-laws. Zipporah's father had once been surveyor of the port, and her uncle had long served as a customs appraiser. Her brother Jacob was working for a Radical Republican senator from Tennessee. Another sibling, Manuel, edited the San Francisco *Alta California*. It was probably this last connection that convinced a California senator to secure Charley an inspectorship, earning $4 per day plus moieties.[5]

Lawrence's boss at the port was surveyor Abram Wakeman, an "affable, insinuating, and pleasant, though not profound" attorney. Wakeman was a Republican allied with conservatives such as President Andrew Johnson, Secretary of State William Seward, and political boss Thurlow Weed. This made him an enemy of the emerging Radical Republican caucus in Congress. The Seward-Weed bloc had pushed for Benjamin Butler's 1862 removal from command in New Orleans, as well as collector Hiram Barney's 1864 dismissal following the Hoffnung-Wolf blockade-running scandal. Upon his election to Congress, Butler retaliated by leading the Radicals' unsuccessful impeachment of President Johnson. Perhaps for this reason, Surveyor Wakeman was willing to cross party lines to befriend Charley, a Tammany Democrat.

Charley might have met Joseph S. "Parsee Merchant" Moore, who sat in a carrel in the custom house tabulating statistics. Both men were British Jews, as well as theater buffs. Both were associated with the newspapers. There were differences too. Moore was affiliated with the elite reform Democrats who congregated at Apollo Hall, a theater on East Twenty-eighth Street, while Lawrence identified with the Tammany Hall regulars. The two men attended rival synagogues, Moore frequenting the Ashkenazi B'nai Jeshurun, and Lawrence preferring the Sephardic Shearith Israel. But it is tantalizing to imagine conversations between the free-trade theoretician and the practical smuggler.[6]

At the port, Lawrence might have seen Louis Bieral, the tattooed pugilist dubbed the hero of the 1861 Battle of Ball's Bluff. After being court-martialed for behavior unbecoming an officer, Louis obtained a medical discharge from the Union Army and returned to New York City. There he worked as a bailiff for Judge George Barnard, a reward for helping Tammany Hall frighten Republican voters away from the polls. Though Louis was an officer of the court, he also appeared as a defendant before the bar, charged with deadly assaults on a thief and a Democratic committeeman. But rather than being punished, Bieral received a party to celebrate his Civil War heroics, and a raise in pay compliments of Boss Tweed.[7]

Bieral's 1867 appointment as a storekeeper in the custom house had dismayed civil service reformers. The Brahmins still remembered him as the leader of the "marshal's guard" that sent alleged fugitive slave Anthony Burns back to Virginia in 1854. They also recalled Bieral's role in the assault on Burns's attorney, Richard Henry Dana Jr., as well as his involvement in violent crimes dating back to 1841. Critics protested to Congress that an "indicted murderer" should not be working in the government service. Surveyor Wakeman defended Bieral, speciously insisting that the inspector had neither "committed," nor ever been "indicted for any such offence." The surveyor called him as "a man of unquestioned honesty . . . faithful and reliable," who had been "seriously wounded" in "numerous battles." A skeptical Congress passed a resolution calling for the immediate removal of the collector, a request ignored by President Johnson.[8]

Meanwhile, Charley joined Surveyor Wakeman's so-called Flying Brigade, noted for their aggressive pursuit of contraband and moieties. Lawrence earned far less than his superior, who took in over $100,000, but he caught several offenders, most of them small-timers carrying contraband pocket knives, macaroni, nutmeg, watches, or a few hundred dollars' worth of brandy. He participated in a few major busts, helping seize thousands of dollars in swag from the famed yacht *Fleetwing*, one of the fastest sailboats in America.[9]

Lawrence's time with the Flying Brigade ended with the 1868 presidential election, in which the Republican candidate, Ulysses S. Grant, defeated New York governor Horatio Seymour. The new administration removed Abram Wakeman as surveyor, fired Louis Bieral, and dismissed Lawrence, charging him with stealing kid gloves from a storage room by hiding them in his boots. Facing bankruptcy, Charley won reinstatement by petitioning his friends. But as penance, he was exiled to the barge house, "the most dilapidated and repulsive . . . of any public edifice in any Christian country under the sun," which rocked each time a wave crashed on the shore.[10]

Tiring of his assignment discharging vessels, Charley began idling around the surveyor's headquarters, where he received an education in the smuggler's craft. He heard the case of the Guiterman brothers, importers who conspired to declare cases of silks as buttons and other lightly taxed objects, bribing a customs appraiser to feign scrutiny of the imports. The firm's principals evaded prison only by negotiating a compromise obliging them to pay fines totaling over $33,000 (over $500,000 today). He likewise witnessed the arrest of Isidore Wolff and Myrtle May for smuggling $500,000 in silk with the help of a "Deputy Collector, who was so affected by drink that he hardly knew what he was about, and always did as requested."[11]

In 1870, an inspector accused Charley of smuggling cases of brandy, but his superiors declined to do anything. Then on April 13, Special Treasury Agent Newton Martin Curtis obtained a warrant for Lawrence's arrest, charging that he had smuggled four trunks containing velvet and silk ribbons from Canada into the United States with the help of the Grand Trunk Railway baggage master. An imposing figure, well over six feet, with an enormous beard and "built proportionately," Curtis had served with distinction at the battles of Bull Run, Antietam, and Fort Fisher, where he traded his left eye for the Congressional Medal of Honor. Caught in "flagrant delicto," Lawrence surrendered himself for examination by the federal magistrate.[12]

The arrest made national headlines. The *New York Herald* accused

Charley of being "head centre" of a "custom house ring." Lawrence and his fellow inspectors aimed only to seize contraband and collect moieties, the *Herald* argued, not to convict smugglers. And many officers, the article claimed, smuggled themselves. Reflecting the rising anti-Semitism of the period, the *Herald* blamed Lawrence's Judaism. "Almost from the day of his appointment," the reporter asserted, "a brisk trade sprang up among a certain class of Jews who make a profession of defrauding the government of the revenues due on importations of silks, laces, velvet, ribbons and other costly fabrics." The newspaper insisted that Charley had changed his surname from Lazarus to Lawrence to obtain a job at the port, "doubts arising as to the eligibility of Israelites holding government office."[13]

Before the Civil War, such an article might have obliged Charley to challenge the author to a duel, but Lawrence chose a gentler approach. He wrote a letter that prevailed upon the editor's "sense of justice" to prevent his newspaper from being used "as the medium of private malice." Charley protested accurately that he had changed his name "over three years before" he "was appointed an Inspector of Customs." He then turned the *Herald*'s anti-Semitism to his advantage. "The slur" showed the writer's "personal animus." The "record" of his "co-religionists" either "in the Custom House or general commerce, will compare favorably with that of any other sect." He then correctly predicted his exoneration. In May, Charley's colleagues impeached the government's witnesses, prompting the U.S. commissioner to dismiss the case.[14]

Time in the custom house strengthened Charley's finances, if not his reputation. By 1870, he lived on an affluent block of West Twenty-third Street, near the theater district, in a home complete with servants. Charley had befriended the city's most powerful politician, William M. Tweed. In January 1871, Lawrence and safe manufacturer John M. Davidson gave Tweed $10,000 in "elegant paintings." Davidson allegedly ran "a private bar" in the back of his warehouse serving "the best vintages of wines" to Tammany favorites. In return, New

York had awarded Davidson contracts worth over $400,000 for safes
to furnish the county courthouse. The Republican paper joked that
one painting should "represent a crowd of millionaires gathered, hat
in hand, in front of the City Hall . . . gently commanding them to
'Stand and Deliver'." Lawrence was now socializing in the highest
strata of the Tweed Ring.[15]

Lawrence returned to the broker business, splitting his time
between New York and a second home in London. He continued reg-
istering patents: first, a padlock devised by an Ithaca clockmaker connected to Benaiah Jayne, and second, a special ink for use on bank
checks. In New York, he campaigned unsuccessfully for a position as
election inspector. He had to satisfy himself with an appointment as
a commissioner of deeds and a position as a notary public, which put
him in contact with merchants applying for passports. All told, his
future seemed very bright, the sole dark spot being the death of his
younger sister Rose in Virginia.[16]

As time winnowed his blood relations, he developed a wide-ranging
network of in-laws, allies, partners, and friends. One of New York's
best-known bon vivants, Charley "spent money lavishly," and was "a
popular man about town" who lived "in fine style . . . sporting his
horses and carriages." He was invited to join the Americus Club.
Originating as Tweed's fire brigade, Americus Engine #6, the club
had moved to Greenwich, Connecticut, on Long Island Sound. For an
initiation fee of $1,000 and monthly dues of $250, members received
access to three steam yachts and a $300,000 clubhouse containing
a bar, barbershop, billiard room, and a "grand dining hall one hundred feet long." Reports claimed that Lawrence himself imported the
club's English carpets, "thick as a beefsteak," as well as the enameled
gold tiger-head badges worn by members.[17]

WHILE LAWRENCE ROSE in Tammany circles, the nation girded itself
for the 1872 presidential election. Grant's opponents were optimistic,
as the president had shown some vulnerability in the midterm elec-

tions of 1870. Not only had the Democrats narrowed the GOP advantage in the House from 86 to 30, showing special strength in New York, but also the new Liberal Republican Party had won the governorship of Missouri. Adding to the Democrats' hopes was the recent readmission of three Confederate states—Mississippi, Texas, and Virginia. Lacking opinion polls, the participants could not predict the result, and this uncertainty fired the intensity of the race.[18]

The great issue of the day was Reconstruction, specifically the equality of African-Americans and the erection of responsive governments in the former Confederacy. But Grant's opponents downplayed these matters, vaguely proposing to restore friendship between the sections, and emphasizing instead the alleged corruption of the administration. Many reformers sincerely believed that the scandals of the time imperiled republican government. For others, the focus on corruption was a "dog whistle," inaudible to most, but loud and clear to southern whites, as well as northern Democrats who had become leery of "black" Reconstruction. By attacking Grant's honesty, they metaphorically diminished the African-American voters who put him into office.

Democrats and liberals in both major parties argued that the custom house was the core of the administration's corrupt misrule. Their newspapers raged at "rings," "gangs," "mobs," and "cliques" based at the nation's ports. Opponents charged that Republicans stashed their regulars at the custom houses, and then unleashed these partisans upon every meeting of not only their own faction, but also the opposition. Seeing their jobs as dependent only on their political pull, some employees did little work. To create more slots for their friends, officials expanded government payrolls. To fund GOP campaigns, they demanded that port workers pay kickbacks to the party. And by this logic, such a system of hiring led to a demoralized customs service, prone to seeking moieties, demanding bribes, and allowing smuggling.

Critiques of the custom houses often turned into attacks on

African-American participation in government itself. In article after article, black voters were described as nothing more than dupes controlled by customs "rings" who promised them employment. In Philadelphia, August Belmont's *New York World* alleged, the "rascally Republican ticket" had promised African-Americans "fat places in the Customhouse." In Louisiana, the *World* claimed, the "Customhouse party" achieved its goals through the efforts of "ignorant Negroes." The *New York Herald* alleged fraud when Savannah customs officials issued certificates testifying that black voters had paid their poll taxes when the local tax collector refused to accept their payments. Allegedly too ignorant to know their own names, the African-American voters dispersed, lacking "any interest in the election at all, except a few surly-looking disappointed darkies, who hung about some of the corners."[19]

For some liberals, the problem was neither corruption nor race, but rather power. Some attacked the Revenue Act of 1866, which had given Treasury agents the power to confiscate importers' private records. In 1870, Richard Henry Dana Jr. took the case of Davis Stockwell, a Maine lumber merchant. During the Civil War, Stockwell had bought 4.7 million shingles from a relative, who claimed they had been manufactured in the United States. In 1868, customs officials concluded the shingles had come from New Brunswick, seized Stockwell's records, and demanded half a decade's worth of tariff duties. Once an antislavery defender of the Union blockade, Dana now opposed the seizure of Stockwell's records. Charging the law had violated the Fourth Amendment protection against unreasonable searches, Dana asked the Supreme Court to invalidate the seizure of Stockwell's goods. The majority ruled against Stockwell, upholding the Revenue Act, but dissents by younger justices suggested the potential for future litigation.[20]

Critics also pressed Congress to abolish the payment of moieties to government officials, which made the exposure of smuggling as profitable as the crime itself. Many people were appalled by the earnings of Treasury agents like Jayne and disgusted by greed of men like Hiram Whitley. If moieties induced rigor, critics argued, they also encouraged overzealousness. By turning agents into entrepreneurs, Treasury attracted grasping men who were more concerned with taking moieties than prosecuting offenders. Overall, the civil service reformers attacked moieties for the same reasons they attacked the patronage system—a belief that professionalism rather than profit or politics ought to guide government officials.

The White House sought to appease critics with statements of concern. In December 1870, President Grant called for civil service reform, surprising members of Congress who were currently debating radical bills requiring applicants for federal jobs to pass examinations and banning congressmen from lobbying the president on appointments. Lacking the support to pass anything so extensive, on March 3, 1871, Congress enacted a vague statute empowering the president to appoint commissioners to assess new appointments. Grant then named a reformer to head a committee to design a "comprehensive set of civil service rules."[21]

Grant also condemned moieties, charging the system with working "perniciously" to the benefit of "dishonest" men. His Treasury secretary, George S. Boutwell, likewise censured the practice. Boutwell was the perfect man to appeal to Republicans enticed by the Liberal movement. One of the most able, honest, and progressive members of the administration, Boutwell was a self-educated Massachusetts shopkeeper whose humble origins connected him to the average voter. He was aware that the colossal incomes of custom-house workers like Jayne threatened to alienate the farmers who paid the tariffs on imported goods. By calling for an end to such fees, Boutwell distanced the administration from the greed of its appointees, seizing one of the reformers' issues for the Grant administration.[22]

At the same time, reform Democrats sought to deflect charges of hypocrisy by abandoning their own "uneasy alliance" with Tweed and Tammany. Their opportunity came in 1870, when the *New York*

Times uncovered evidence that contractors building the new county courthouse had paid kickbacks to Democratic officials. A granite neo-classical structure complete with Corinthian columns and rotunda, the beautiful building cost $13 million, a large percentage of which was estimated to have been skimmed by Tammany contractors. Fearing that the scandal would damage the party's reputation, Swallowtail Democrats sought the impeachment of Judge George Barnard and the prosecution of Tweed for conspiracy, perjury, and grand larceny.[23]

Grant eagerly adopted any Tammanyites alienated by the Swallow-tails. The president knew that the Democrats' hopes in 1872 depended upon taking New York. And port workers, the city's most effective campaigners, were the key to winning the state. In 1870, Grant appointed Thomas Murphy, a friend of Tweed's, as collector. The next year, he replaced Murphy with Chester Arthur, a former abolitionist with the wardrobe of a fashion model and the mind of a machine boss. Arthur stacked the new civil service committee with "henchmen," ensuring the appointment of partisans. For instance, the collector managed to secure an inspectorship for Louis Bieral. Since being fired in 1869, Louis had worked as bodyguard, assaulted reformer Dorman Eaton, witnessed the assassination of infamous financier Jim Fisk, and fought in the battle for control over the Erie Railroad.[24]

In May 1872, the Liberal Republicans chose to run Horace Greeley against President Grant. It was a bizarre selection. A utopian eccentric, Greeley possessed scant experience as a campaigner, having not run for major public office since before the demise of the Whig Party. In a period when veterans of the Civil War dominated politics, Greeley had not served in the military. Greeley's avid protectionism clashed with the party's commitment to tariff reduction. The situation grew even more perverse when the Democrats, a party that Greeley excoriated for three decades, nominated the antislavery Yankee as well.

Greeley focused his campaign on the alleged corruption of the Grant administration and the need to reform the custom house. Once the enemy of the slaveholder, the *Tribune* editor now called for the nation to bind its wounds and remove U.S. troops from the South. By contrast, President Grant sought to neutralize Greeley's long-time support for tariffs and other labor reforms by emphasizing the working-class credentials of the Republican ticket. Grant reminded voters that he had once been a tanner, while his running mate, eight-hour-day advocate Henry Wilson, was once a cobbler. But more than anything, Republicans simply emphasized that a vote for Greeley gave white southern Democrats control of the federal government, effectively reversing the Union victory in the Civil War. Northern voters needed few reminders, for news of Klansmen and other terrorists murdering blacks had been on the front pages of Republican newspapers since the war's end.

Men like Louis Bieral did their work. For instance, on August 17, 1872, the Cooper Institute hosted a debate between two well-known African-American leaders, Rev. Henry Highland Garnett and Hon. William U. Saunders. The question was whom black voters should support in the coming election. Garnett spoke for Grant, citing his embrace of black suffrage as president. Saunders reminded the audience that Greeley had opposed slavery and supported civil rights decades before Fort Sumter. The friendly conversation ended when someone—possibly Chester Arthur's confidant, Aleck Powell—suddenly admitted the "Custom House gang" and members of the Eighth Ward Grant Club. Producing a "continuous howl" of "Banshee cries" intended to drown out Saunders, the Republicans showered "epithets and the foulest abuse" upon the speaker, crying "shoot him" and "hang the __." Saunders completed his speech, but only after the police arrested several Grant men.[25]

Such tactics helped Grant win New York and the White House. He took 56 percent of the popular vote, thirty-one of the nation's thirty-seven states and 286 out of 352 electoral votes. Greeley's muted calls for an end to the military occupation of the South earned him the support of states such as Maryland, Kentucky, Missouri, and Tennessee, but lost him the support of newly enfranchised black voters, now a potent bloc in the old Confederate states such as Mississippi, Louisiana, and South Carolina. Greeley's association with tariff reductionists undermined his credibility as a protectionist, alienating the workingmen of the industrial Northeast. And worst of all, the campaign so drained the editor that he died before the states finished tallying the ballots.

DEFEAT AT THE NATIONAL LEVEL did not staunch the reform impulse in New York City. Independents, Liberals, and Swallowtail Democrats bristled at the continued freedom of Tweed and his circle nearly two years after the "ring" was uncovered. The state had managed to secure the impeachment of Louis Bieral's old employer, Judge George C. Barnard, but several other indictments ended in mistrials. In the first trial of the "Boss," the jury was unable to reach a verdict. Fearing a loss of momentum, reformers determined to try Tweed as many times as needed to secure a conviction. Thus, the gray clouds of criminal prosecution shadowed machine Democrats like Charles L. Lawrence in New York City during the years 1872 and 1873.[26]

Unfazed, Charley continued his hustling. With his brother Frederic, he obtained the British patent for an "apparatus to be used in boilers for washing or cleansing clothes." He became an attorney. At this time, aspiring lawyers did not have to attend law school. They could "read for the bar," obtaining a license through the sponsorship of a senior attorney who vouched for their knowledge. Charley's patron was Philip Phillips, the former Alabama congressman whose wife Eugenia had been imprisoned by Benjamin Butler during the war. In the summer, he hobnobbed at Long Branch, the popular New Jersey resort frequented by the president and others, displaying his team of horses and watching the races from the Monmouth Clubhouse.

Charley remained a showman. He reportedly took the stage in Boston as the Indian leader Captain Jack in a "war drama" called "The Modocs, or the Red Friends of the Lava Beds." His family had loaned over $17,000 to Dr. Louis J. Jordan, the British proprietor of a worldwide chain of anatomical museums, including Kahn's Grand Museum in downtown Manhattan. At a time when much of young men's sexual education occurred in the barnyard, the museum featured a titillating and illuminating exhibit showing a cross section of a woman's body, including her private parts. The museum also sold patent medicines, most notably a treatment for venereal diseases called "Treisemar" patented by Jordan's father.[27]

Lawrence was named secretary of the Americus Club, a social triumph deflated by the prevailing gloom surrounding Boss Tweed's organization. Excepting funerals, members had barely met as a group since the start of the trials, and the investigations dampened their enthusiasm for the sort of entertainments that had once been "the wonder of the world for lavish expenditure, prodigal waste and Oriental magnificence." He tried to buoy members' spirits with a dinner dance in Greenwich on August 9, 1873, but observers deemed Lawrence's party melancholy for the absence of any women save the wives of the members.[28]

Lawrence soon found himself in the papers again. The *New York Herald* dredged up the four-year-old accusations of General Ramón Páez, who alleged that Charley had stolen diamond studs worth $500 from his baggage. Identifying Charley as a "Hebrew Jew of various linguistic accomplishments," once known as Lazarus, the author claimed that Lawrence had led "a smuggler's gang on the Canadian frontier." As he had in 1870, Lawrence asked the *Herald* to publish his rebuttal. Noting his acquittal on smuggling charges three years before, he recalled that Páez had acted suspiciously, leading the inspectors to examine him. Páez had indeed accused officials of robbing him, but he later admitted to finding his property. Charley's version appeared plausible, and the case came to nothing.[29]

During Tweed's second criminal trial, Charley became the Boss's closest confidant. Rumors circulated that Tweed had given Charley $100,000 to bribe the jury. If so, the prosecution must have pro-

vided some counterinducement, for on November 19, 1873, the jury
returned with a verdict of guilty. A bespectacled Charley looked at the
judge hoping to see some glimmer of sympathy, but the face of the
jurist was "the face of a rock set against the storm." Tweed's entou-
rage was similarly dour. Seemingly unable to resist a religious slur,
the *Herald* observed the Boss's brother bore the "marked Jewish features that are noticeable in all the male members" of the undeniably
Protestant Tweed family. The ordeal was not over. While the Boss
relocated to Blackwell's Island prison, New York's corporate counsel
prepared lawsuits for the return of hundreds of thousands of dollars
allegedly stolen from the city.[30]

MEANWHILE, POST-ELECTION public opinion turned against Grant's
custom house. In early January 1873, the news broke that Special
Treasury Agent Benaiah Jayne had forced a $271,000 settlement with
metal importers Phelps, Dodge & Co. Reformers initially declined
to defend their ally, merchant prince William Earl Dodge, lament-
ing that his "almost irresistible influence" would allow him to evade
punishment. But they did begin to question Jayne's motives, accusing
him of selling "out to the guilty parties." Jayne favored a settlement
because he would "get a nice whack out of the $280,000 . . . due the
Government."[31]

    Then the plate glass importers Platt & Boyd rebelled by refusing
to relinquish private records to Jayne, arguing that his request constituted an unreasonable search barred by the Fourth Amendment.
At this time, the argument had little purchase among lawyers. Congress had ignored the voices of civil libertarians when debating the
Revenue Act of 1866. Four years later, the Supreme Court had explicitly refused to limit the power of officers to demand records. Jayne
ranted, "I'll lock the whole gang in Ludlow street jail to-night, and
take the books and papers if it takes the whole army and navy of the
United States to do it." The Treasury agent further retaliated by leak-

ing a ledger to the press showing Platt & Boyd's bribes to over fifty customs officials. Nonetheless, the cases of 1873 led lawyers to reevaluate whether the newly powerful Treasury exceeded the limits set by the Founders.[32]

On September 18, 1873, a financial disaster aroused new anger towards the Grant administration. News that Republican financier Jay Cooke was bankrupt sent security prices tumbling, forcing the New York Stock Exchange to close for ten days. Meanwhile, the Treasury's decision to end the production of silver coins shrank the money supply, causing prices to plummet. The United States lapsed into a business depression. In the coming year, thousands of firms were reduced to insolvency and millions of workers were left without employment.

The panic provided the reformers with the initiative they needed. In February 1874, Congress initiated hearings into the distribution of moieties. The press naturally latched onto Jayne's shocking earnings. Between 1870 and 1873, in the process of making over eighty seizures and recovering over $3 million dollars for the government, the special treasury agent had earned $316,700 in moieties. Merchants complained of unfair, arbitrary, and coercive treatment at the port. One eminent attorney decried the "means of extortion which have been placed in the hands of corrupt Custom House officials and more corrupt informers." William Earl Dodge himself testified that the government had intimidated his firm. "There was terror on that first day when we went into that dark hole in the Custom House," Dodge observed, and "there was terror throughout."[33]

Merchants enlisted the public in their campaign against the custom house. The New York Chamber of Commerce, of which Dodge was president, paid economist David A. Wells to publish several books defending the firm. The Chamber also hired attorney Shelburne Eaton to prove the unconstitutionality of the 1867 Revenue Law. Eaton's pamphlet evoked the spirit of the American Revolution, noting that the nation had fought British tyranny only to enact intrusive customs laws of its own. But Eaton concluded with a utilitarian argument, arguing that "[a] sense of freedom is essential to the largest prosperity." By calling "honest merchants" smugglers, the government had destroyed the "possibilities of exchange" and reversed the "march of trade."[34]

Jayne responded by explaining that he only seized private records when the collector, the U.S. attorney, and a federal magistrate agreed he had cause. He declared merchants' complaints about employee spying to be "mock morality" that privileged the obligations servants owed to their masters over the responsibilities of "good citizenship." Moieties were needed "to make" customs officials "more vigilant in the detection of fraud." And, finally, Jayne insisted that "all the moneys that ever came from the mines of California," were insufficient compensation for the withering criticism he endured.[35]

Jayne's patron Rep. Benjamin Butler agreed that moieties encouraged performance in office. Butler's war experience convinced him that a strong Treasury was necessary to defeat treason. Though the pursuit of moieties appeared ignoble, the inspectors could scarcely manufacture infractions where none existed. He savaged the "fraudulent importer," the "merchant prince" who cheated "the people of the United States out of millions," then covered "his sins perhaps by building churches." Butler insisted that Dodge was less a martyr than a greedy man who had opposed the Civil War and cheated the customs for decades.[36]

The reformers lost in court, but won minor victories elsewhere. A federal judge affirmed the constitutionality of the Revenue Act, which had allowed Jayne to seize Platt & Boyd's papers. But Jayne himself resigned his position with the government. And Congress passed legislation making it harder for the Treasury to seize private records. Customs officials now needed court orders rather than mere warrants. The new statute also limited moieties to undeclared goods brought directly ashore without passing through customs, denying shares to agents who discovered errors in merchant's declarations. In doing so, the law discouraged officials from investigating established importers. And it differentiated merchants from smugglers by looking at methods rather than the intent or result. It was the inadequacies of this definition of smuggling that Charley Lawrence determined to exploit.[37]

SILK

Amid the personal advertisements (addressed to "St. Valentine" and "Black Eyes") on the front page of the February 29, 1873, edition of the *New York Herald* sat an unusual notice. Appealing to a "Chevalier De Follone of 238 West 21st Street," the small box asked for a current address and "advices" to be sent to "Charles L. Laurence [*sic*]" at Box 4452 at the post office. This random appeal, a single blurb purchased in the hopes that a European aristocrat would read the *Herald* that day, was one of several ads printed in the newspaper referencing the same address or postal box during the surrounding months. One offered to sell a "REMARKABLY HANDSOME, intelligent, well trained white Spitz Dog," another solicited mortgages for inclusion in a trust fund, and a third offered "pleasant and cheerful rooms to let with Board, for gentleman and wife, or single gentlemen speaking "English, French, and Spanish.""[1]

On the surface, the advertisements offered a cozy picture of Charley's life as a cosmopolitan Manhattanite. Here was a man living off secure investments in real estate, troubled only by his difficulty caring for his family's snowy purebred and his desire to connect with an old friend. No man named "Chevalier De Follone" lived in New York in 1873, but a Count Camillo Nomis Di Pollone did. Lawrence may well have known Di Pollone, a Torinese nobleman familiar to society-page readers for his association with transportation tycoons, bankers, music aficionados, art collectors, and the Tweed Ring.

Or perhaps Charley's misspellings of the count's name—and of his own—were intentional. Maybe the "Chevalier De Follone" was not a reference to Count Di Pollone, but rather code for Lawrence's accomplice Colonel Robert Des Anges, whose artist brother styled himself a French chevalier. Perhaps the Spitz dog was not a pet at all, but a signal. It is possible that the "cheerful rooms" referred to something besides apartments. The ads' apparent domesticity may have masked their true purpose, which was to relay information to Charley's far-flung co-conspirators, operating in Lyon, Liverpool, and at the Port of New York. For by 1873, Lawrence was no longer merely a downtown merchant, impresario, high-living clubman, or Tweed's close confidant. He was the leader of the America's most extensive smuggling ring.[2]

Silk was Charley's contraband of choice. First produced in China around 4,000 BCE, the fabric was uniquely light, strong, and soft. As demand grew, so did cultivation of *Bombyx mori* larvae, whose cocoons provided the raw fiber, and white mulberry trees, which fed the worms. Silk became China's most valuable export, familiar to the Greeks, the Hebrews, and the Romans, the last of whom coveted the material but also worried about its effects on the larger public. The poet Juvenal, the philosopher Seneca the Younger, and the historian Tacitus all disdained silk as too feminine for men, a sentiment that extended to the Roman Senate, which actually forbade men from wearing it in 16 CE. Seneca further reviled his fellow Romans for sending their wealth eastward to an "unknown people" in return for a revealing material he believed best befitted adulteresses.[3]

The development of the famous Silk Road allowing trade between China and the Roman Empire suggests that this ambivalence did little to staunch the craving for the fine cloth. But suspicion of silk existed in tension with desire for the product, kindling the search for a local source. Hindered by ignorance of the fabric's manufacture, and thus unable to break the Chinese monopoly, the sixth-century CE Roman emperor Justinian taxed silk importation, while funding espionage to learn the mystery of its production. He reportedly hired two Nestorian monks to smuggle silkworm eggs back to Constantinople "concealed in the hollow of their palmer staves." Over the next millennium, silk manufacture spread westward into Asia Minor, Europe, and even the Americas. King James I of England, "almost insane" in his desire to build a silk industry, not only obliged Englishmen futilely to raise silkworms, but also required Virginia colonists to plant ten mulberry trees for every hundred acres cultivated.[4]

Despite sericulture's early arrival, the American silk industry remained weak in the 1870s, prompting manufacturers to demand government protection against the established factories of France. The political result was a 60 percent tariff, which made finished products like ribbons and dresses much more expensive in the United States than in Europe. Drawing upon classical republican and Protestant values, supporters of high taxes on silk argued that the expensive, sensuous fabric was a divisive symbol of conspicuous wealth and a threat to the nation's masculine strength. Advocates also defended the tax as a check on women, who, having been displaced from traditional tasks by the mills of Lowell, had begun working for wages, starting businesses, asserting themselves in public, and spending money on luxuries.[5]

DURING ECONOMIC DOWNTURNS, many people live unscathed by the destitution around them, and some individuals can even thrive. By 1874, scandal and panic had shattered New York's political and financial systems, ruining several of Charley Lawrence's associates. It was at this moment that Charley decided to establish a new firm at 62 Wall Street. He lavishly decorated his offices with luxurious European carpets, "gorgeous furniture and books," and contemporary features such as a "speaking tube" connecting his "private sanctum" with that of his counselor, well-known Democratic attorney Thomas Bracken. Charley likewise shared the space with his brothers-in-law, attorneys

Robert and Lionel, perhaps drawn closer by the recent death of their sibling, newspaper editor Manuel M. Noah.

Lawrence's official business was the United States Pipe Company, a $500,000 concern that owned the patent on a new type of drain pipe made from sand, clay, and limestone rather than iron or ceramic. When public construction stalled in the city after the Tammany revelations, Charley dispatched his brother-in-law Robert to sell one-quarter of the firm to Alexander R. Shepherd, the so-called Boss Tweed of Washington, D.C. The District of Columbia's second governor, Shepherd was a Radical Republican who supported racial integration and women's suffrage, but as a member of the territorial board of public works he was better known for leading the drive to improve the capital's infrastructure. Naming Shepherd's assistant Richard Harrington as the attorney of the newly formed Washington Silica Pipe Company, Charley soldiered on in the hopes of winning federal contracts.[6]

Charley placed Judge Jacob J. Noah, another brother-in-law and a behind-the-scenes figure in the District, on the board of the new firm. Imprisoned without charge during the Civil War, Jacob made a new career for himself during Reconstruction, becoming an ally of Tennessee governor William Brownlow. An anti-Semitic, evangelical Radical Republican, Brownlow was an unlikely patron for Noah. But the "Parson" took Jacob with him to Washington when he accepted a Senate seat in 1869. By 1874, Jacob had become the personal secretary for the Republican chairman of the Senate Committee on the District of Columbia, the body responsible for financing the Shepherd administration's construction projects.[7]

Lawrence remained in New York, speculating on equities and real estate without regard for the nation's fragile economy. In May, he lost over $800 in a stock trade. In October, Zipporah bought a property on Twenty-seventh Street and Sixth Avenue. Just a few weeks later, Charley himself purchased a three-story building at 243 West Twenty-

second Street, east of Eighth Avenue. Taken together, the buildings cost the couple over $43,000, money without any clear origin.
Though now a licensed attorney, Charley appeared in no high-profile
cases in 1874. Nor were his financial dealings profitable enough to
earn notice anywhere aside from the classifieds.[8]

Gambling played no less a role in Charley's social life. At his "elegant" West Twenty-third Street home, the Lawrences hosted "brilliant
gatherings, and numerous heavy games of cards." The pastime was
poker, a game that had evolved in Persia and Europe before being
imported into the United States by way of New Orleans. Poker had
become highly fashionable in the United States and England in the
1870s. Gen. Robert C. Schenck, the ambassador to the Court of St.
James, introduced the British royals to the game, writing a set of
rules for their use. Charley may have learned the game in his visits to
the Crescent City, or perhaps from a pupil of Schenck, who had once
served as minister to Brazil, where Lawrence was the legation's secretary. Whatever the source of his knowledge, Lawrence became known
for playing poker at the Blossom Club, another Tammanyite haunt
where he was a "favorite."[9]

Charley also attended card games at the home of George Garcia
Wolf, the Nassau-based blockade runner whose high-profile 1864
arrest had cost Hiram Barney his collectorship, Henry Stanton his
reputation, and Salmon Chase his chance at the presidency. Unlike
his brother and in-laws, who had fled the United States, George was
held in the military prison at Fort Lafayette. He lost his shipment
of goods intended for the Confederacy. But Lord Lyons, the British
ambassador to the U.S., obtained Wolf's freedom and the release of
his personal property: "gold coin, bills of exchange, and other securities" worth £9,000 (over $1 million today).[10]

The ensuing years treated George well. In 1865, he popped up in
the Mexican border town of Bagdad, a center of Confederate cotton
trafficking. After Appomattox, he owned businesses in New Orleans
and New York City. Wolf climbed the city's social ladder, winning

an invitation to Charley's Americus Club's pleasure cruises. Soon, George had settled into a "fine private stone residence" about a mile up Eighth Avenue from Lawrence. "Prodigal with money" obtained in a mysterious fashion only "suspected and whispered," Wolf provided his guests "with the best the market could afford." He held parties nearly every night, filling the streets with the sounds of "revelry" and "the noise of coming and departing carriages."[11]

Also attending the parties were Lewis and Henry J. Levey. Born in England, the Leveys had grown up in Montreal. Though their father John was a tobacconist, the brothers had branched out into "all sorts of commercial pursuits," including importing, storage, and the marketing of a "patent hand fire extinguisher." They were related to the Wolfs through Abraham Hoffnung, who had wed their sister Esther during his stay in Canada, and whose sister Bertha Hoffnung had married George Wolf in Montreal in 1859. The three families were close. When the Leveys' mother passed away, her two youngest children, Caroline and Alfred, went to live not with their siblings, who were bachelors at the time, but with George and Bertha Wolf.[12]

Abraham Hoffnung did not attend the poker games, and not only because he lived across the Atlantic in Liverpool. Unlike Charley Lawrence, Hoffnung invested in no frivolous enterprises; no dramas, ballets, or operas. He took colossal risks, but only when the returns promised to be equally enormous, as they had been when he ran supplies to the Confederacy. And even then, he refused to risk his own imprisonment, leaving the dirty work to his in-laws. After the war, he had left the colonies for England itself, using his ties to British capitalists to establish a Liverpool importing business, trading in guns, clothes, and cigars (tobacco was his one evident vice). Even his charities were run as businesses. When the Liverpool Jewish community needed funds, Hoffnung proposed they run a bazaar, soliciting gifts from around the world and selling them to raise revenue. Though many found this idea embarrassing, under his administration it was a great success.

George Wolf's younger brother Aaron tied himself tightly to Hoffnung's coattails. Together, the two ran an importing firm, with Aaron
handling business in America and Abraham managing affairs across
the Atlantic. Though the partnership dissolved around 1870, the split
must have been amicable, for when Aaron moved back to England,
he settled into a home near Liverpool, in the suburb of West Derby.
And while little is known of his business affairs at that time, he had
money, perhaps from an inheritance; in 1871 his house held not only
his wife and four children, but also his wife's mother, her sister, and
four servants.

How Lawrence met the Leveys and the Wolfs is unclear, but culture, experience, and sensibility bound these merchants. All were
from Jewish families that had migrated from the Continent to
English port cities such as Hull, Great Yarmouth, and Liverpool in
the eighteenth and early nineteenth century, then scattered again to
the United States and the ends of the British Empire. In the 1850s,
Abraham Hoffnung's brother Sigmund left Montreal for Sydney, Australia, where he thrived. Others were less successful. Joseph Wolf, the
elder sibling of Aaron and George, sailed as a teenager from England
to America, joined the U.S. Army in Baltimore, was discharged in
New Mexico, married in Montreal, sold crockery in New Orleans,
ran an auction house in Manitoba, and moved to Washington State.
Though they established roots in each place they settled, becoming
citizens and participating in indigenous institutions, the Wolfs never
stopped steaming across the globe in search of new opportunities.

The husbands and wives mingled freely, in defiance of the period's gender conventions. George's Wolf's "handsome affable" wife
Bertha hosted his poker parties. An "elegantly" dressed woman in
her early thirties, described as possessing "fascinating" manners, the
"fairest of fair skins," blonde hair, and beautiful hands, she herself
played a "good game" of cards. George was accustomed to feminine
attainment: his mother Matilda Wolf had run a jewelry store, and his
widowed sister, Harriet Wolf Samuel, founded "H. Samuel," which

later became one of the world's largest jewelry corporations. With her indomitable will and political contacts, Charley's wife Zipporah fit right into the group.[13]

Financial pressures likely pushed them to dabble in crime. In the spring of 1872, George Wolf abruptly moved to New Orleans and sold his entire Manhattan household, including "elegant . . . carved walnut and rosewood" furniture, "Brussels carpets," clocks, candelabras, "Florentine bronzes," Dresden china, fine oil paintings, a "Marvin parlor safe," and two Steinway pianos. Shortly thereafter, his brother Aaron was forced to meet with his creditors to renegotiate his debts. Then the Panic of 1873 began. Amid the wreckage, the courts rendered a $100,000 judgment against George Wolf's firm, forcing him to flee the United States entirely. No legacies would save them; Lawrence, the Noahs, the Wolfs, and the Leveys were all orphans by 1872.[14]

As the depression worsened, the fear of poverty may have strengthened the allure of contraband. Charley's new plan exploited a flaw in the collection of customs he had observed during his time as an inspector. In 1869, the Guiterman brothers were charged with avoiding the tariffs on silk and kid gloves by hiding them in shipments of clocks, which were subject to lower duties. The Guitermans had exploited the inability of officials to assess the massive quantity of goods now steaming into New York. They corrupted an appraiser, who agreed to examine only the goods conforming to their official declaration. Lawrence would have recalled that while the brothers were forced to pay a settlement to the government, they did not receive any criminal punishment, inasmuch as they were seen as merchants, not smugglers.[15]

The conspirators reproduced this deception on a larger scale. Abraham Hoffnung provided the silks from St. Etienne, France, packed them into crates, and shipped them to Liverpool. In that port city, one of the firm's agents, William Benjamin, swore before the U.S. consul that the boxes contained jute, burlap, buttons, and other cheap materials subject to low tariffs.

It was Charley's job to slip the silks unexamined through the Port of New York. Growing up in England, he had seen his paternal uncle Samuel bend the law to his purposes, using British courts to expropriate various aristocrats. Charley himself had dabbled in smuggling since the 1860s, when he had used his diplomatic post to undermine Brazilian customs. A showman, he possessed few inhibitions about falsifying his identity and his imports. Charley's many friends, his parties, his political connections, and his charm all made him a talented corruptor, capable of suborning men with unblemished records. Yet even after his arrests, his reputation for frivolity prevented officials from viewing him as a criminal mastermind.[16]

To do his bidding at the port, Lawrence chose officials with spotless reputations. His first kept man was Henry Melville Williams, the deputy collector of the Warehouse Division. Like Lawrence, Williams was cosmopolitan in outlook and lavish in lifestyle. The two men likely first met during the Paris Exposition Universelle of 1867, where Williams was the state's official representative and Charley an advertising agent. They probably reconnected at the Port of New York in 1869, as well as in the convivial spaces of the Americus Club and Delmonico's. Yet politically Williams was seen as a Liberal Republican reformer. Speculating as to why the collector removed him from office in 1871, newspapers concluded that he was "too independent." Unaware of Williams's ties to Lawrence, prosecutors put him on Boss Tweed's first jury, only to be horrified when he voted for acquittal, obliging them to try the Boss a second time.[17]

After Williams left the port, Lawrence turned to Rev. Noah Murray Gaylord, the deputy collector in charge of appraisal. Like Williams, Gaylord appeared to be incorruptible. A Universalist minister from Ohio, he had called for the abolition of slavery in the early 1850s. He was a man of many talents, who ran newspapers, wrote pamphlets, practiced law, and legislated. During the Civil War, Gaylord served as a chaplain in the Thirteenth Massachusetts Infantry and headed the Campbell Hospital in Washington, D.C., where he was described as "indefatigable" in his care for the wounded and "untiring . . . in every good work." If he possessed any moral failings, no one mentioned them in his lifetime. Perhaps Charley persuaded Gaylord to pass contraband by promising to aid his daughter Julia, a young opera singer. Or maybe, having spent his life as a minister, Gaylord simply needed the money. At any rate, his usefulness to the smugglers came to an end in 1872, when he retired from his position and died of tuberculosis at the age of fifty.[18]

Gaylord's replacement, both as deputy collector and as the smugglers' chief servant, was Colonel Robert Des Anges. Des Anges probably first met Lawrence in 1869 at the port's putrescent barge house, where the Civil War veteran worked as a bookkeeper, and the showman had been exiled for stealing kid gloves. The two men had much in common. Both were transplanted Englishmen. Like Lawrence, Des Anges had changed his name, having been christened Robert William Burdett Desanges. Both had a strong interest in the arts. Des Anges's brothers were a composer and a famous painter. His uncle had been sheriff of London; Lawrence's father-in-law held the same office in New York. Coming from a family of Huguenot silk dyers, Des Anges not only knew the material, but may have had ancestors who smuggled. And finally, they had common associates. George Lewis, a solicitor for the Desanges family, had several connections with Charley's family.[19]

In the United States, Des Anges's sterling reputation deflected suspicion. To Anglo-Saxon reformers who saw British administration as a model, the upper-class Englishman seemed the ideal government official. His antecedents were impressive; his uncle was a knight, his grandfather an Anglican chaplain of the Duke of York's own regiment, and his brother, a self-styled "Chevalier." In 1863, Robert came to the U.S., won a captain's commission in the Eighty-first U.S. Colored Infantry, and rose to the rank of brevet colonel in another black battalion, the Sixth Louisiana. Friends recalled him as "a soldier of fortune," but also a "gentleman . . . by instinct, education and association," pos-

sessing "one of the most amiable dispositions, together with a cheerful, contented mind that, like his stories and songs, was a 'continual
feast.'" As a political figure, Des Anges was equally well regarded. Liberal Republican reformers cheered his nomination as deputy election
marshal for New York, charged with checking "any fraudulent tactics
of Grant's minions at the polls." An educated man, he was the first port
worker to pass the new civil service examinations.[20]

But in reality, Des Anges was even more a refugee from Victorian
England than Charley. When he served in the British Army, it was
as a paymaster, a noncommissioned position. His family was listed
in *Debrett's Peerage*, but their fortunes were in decline. In 1856, poor
investments in sugar beets, chimney brushes, and South American
mines forced his uncle, Sir Francis, into debtors' prison. One judge
described the knight as "one of those luckless mortals" whose "san-
guine expectations of being made rich in a hurry, often made them
rapidly poor." In 1857, Robert defied his parents and married Louisa Elizabeth Barnard, the daughter of a silversmith. But in January
1862, Robert filed for divorce and sued Lieutenant Charles John Griffiths for £1,000 in damages, charging that he had slept with Louisa. The divorce was never finalized, suggesting that Robert really
wanted Griffiths, who stood to lose his commission if his actions
were exposed, to pay restitution. Shortly thereafter, his regiment "dis-
pensed with" Robert's "services" as paymaster, charging him with
embezzling £1,400 (today, over $210,000). Though Robert's father
prevented any criminal charges by paying the deficit, the young soldier left shamefaced for America.

Charley's contacts in London may have told him Des Anges's
secrets, but Robert probably aided Lawrence for the money. Since the
war, Des Anges had lived alone in hotels, accumulating no assets,
but in 1870 he brought his wife to the United States, buying her a
$10,000 home in rural Plainfield, New Jersey. Perhaps inspired by
these new responsibilities, Des Anges agreed to accept $100 ($1,800
today) for each shipment he shepherded through the port.[21]

What remained was to dispose of millions of dollars in silks. If any one man took possession of the textiles, officials would quickly realize that the consignees on the paperwork were imaginary, and they might begin to suspect that the boxes contained more than burlap, buttons, and corsets. To prevent this, Aaron Wolf sold some goods directly to importers such as Haas & Sons, but also auctioned the silks to vendors through sixteen accounts in the names of fictitious persons with the auction house of Field, Morris, and Fenner. In 1872, George Wolf decided to leave New York City to run a commission business in New Orleans, where he may have received shipments or helped dispose of the contraband. Henry Levey hired a private carting firm to pick up the crates and bring them to his place of business, from which he sold them in secret. And Charley sold some silks "on his own account" to firms such as Alfonso & Co., which dealt in artificial flowers, and Simmons & Fisher, a neckwear retailer.[22]

Charley developed a working relationship with a young liquor dealer named Lafayette Graff. Short, dark, with an "aquiline" nose and prominent chin, Graff was the conspiracy's only native-born American. Born in Wheeling when it was a center for Virginia Unionists, Lafayette's immigrant father presumably named him in honor of the Revolutionary War hero. Lafayette and his brother Abraham migrated to New York, where the latter married into the extended Noah family. In 1871, Charley notarized Lafayette's passport application, and within a few years, Graff was a significant part of the ring. Sending his assistant Gustavus W. Ball to the port to collect the imports, he sold the silk to houses like H. B. Claflin & Co., the largest dry goods wholesaler in the United States, as well as to Justinian Hartley, the former president of the New York Silk Mills.[23]

MULBERRY TREES AND SILKWORMS never became common in the United States. The problem was less the difficulty of cultivation than the expense of unwinding cocoons and reeling fibers. American laborers were never able to equal the skill and cost of Chinese workers, nor were domestic manufacturers able to match the quality of raw silk from France. But by the end of 1872, an industry dedicated to spinning and weaving imported raw silk had become reasonably well established. The largest factories were in Paterson, New Jersey, but 147 plants dotted the industrial areas of the Northeast and stretched as far west as Kansas and California. These facilities produced over $25 million worth of silk, employed over eleven thousand workers, and paid these operatives nearly $5 million dollars in wages each year. Moreover, the domestic industry was growing. Two years hence, in the midst of a business depression, the nation possessed 180 firms employing 14,479 workers, 9,245 of them women. Crowning their success, the manufacturers founded the Silk Association of America, its main goal the perpetuation of the tariff.

Yet, despite Congressional protection, Americans still imported almost half of all their silk, especially expensive dress material, as most factories in the United States specialized in cheaper products such as thread, trim, and tassels. Dress silks came primarily from France, in particular from Lyon, the nation's industrial capital, and St. Etienne, a manufacturing city approximately forty miles to the southwest. Thus, while members of the Silk Association might see the development of their industry as bolstering the case for high tariffs on imports, there was little evidence that the tax on higher-quality textiles encouraged local production of silk suitable for clothing and handkerchiefs. The tariff helped pay America's national debt. It discouraged the purchase of expensive gowns. But it protected few workers and employers.[24]

Silk manufacturers and importers sold their goods primarily to firms such as H. B. Claflin & Co., owned by Horace Brigham Claflin. Bald, with a large round skull, discerning eyes, prominent nose, and frowning mouth, Claflin's miserly appearance masked his "mellow," "accessible," "large and judicious," as well as "quiet and altogether unassuming" character. A Yankee from Massachusetts, he apprenticed in his father's country store, eventually settling in Brooklyn, where he developed a reputation as a generous employer. Claflin was a benefactor of the city's most exalted religious institution, Plymouth Church, led by the famous Rev. Henry Ward Beecher. By 1872, over seven hundred people worked in Claflin's "dry goods palace" at the corner of Church and Warren streets, with six acres of space packed into a seven-story Nova Scotia–sandstone structure containing "the products of a thousand factories, and the work of hundreds of thousands of people in every quarter of the globe."[25]

But the dry goods magnate's standing had suffered since the election of 1872. Claflin's problems began when Theodore Tilton, Horace Greeley's campaign manager, privately alleged that the Rev. Beecher had seduced his wife. Another of Beecher's parishioners, silk importer Henry C. Bowen, the son-in-law of former smuggler Lewis Tappan and brother-in-law of former collector Hiram Barney, alleged that the minister had bedded his wife as well. Seeking to bury the matter, Claflin arbitrated a secrecy agreement between Beecher and the alleged cuckolds. But Tilton had already revealed his shame to Victoria Woodhull, a carnival medium turned feminist journalist. Just weeks before the presidential election, Woodhull published articles accusing Beecher of practicing his own version of "free love." Seeking to suppress the scandal, Claflin met with Woodhull to ascertain whether she could prove Beecher's infidelities. Against Claflin's wishes, the press reported the conference, tying him ever more closely to the tawdry matter.[26]

The Panic of 1873 further tarnished Claflin's reputation. Middlemen caught between manufacturers and retailers, wholesalers were both lenders and borrowers. Claflin not only owed mill owners for textiles they had delivered, but also had issued or endorsed $25 million in commercial paper. He had insufficient cash to repay the owners of this debt, for he had himself given millions in credit to couturiers, tailors, and other retailers. When Americans stopped buying suits and dresses, these firms went bankrupt, leaving Claflin holding their worthless debts. And neither Claflin nor the manufacturers could turn to Wall Street for loans to bridge the gap, as the panic had decimated financial markets. Meeting with his creditors, he received two months of relief, which proved sufficient to return to profitability. Claflin's recovery showed his personal dependability, but it destroyed any sense that his benevolence immunized him against insolvency.[27]

Some claimed that H. B. Claflin & Co. was the first to suspect that someone was flooding auctions around the nation with smuggled silk. Others suggested the reverse; Claflin's low prices aroused its competitors and suppliers, the silk importers, who demanded the government take action. The Silk Association also expressed concern to customs officials, but with less urgency. Despite the tariff, few U.S. mills produced the expensive dress silk that Lawrence's ring imported, so his crimes were not an existential threat to them.

In any case, in the fall of 1874, "several of the leading dry goods merchants" in New York hired a private detective agency, Mooney & Boland, to investigate declining silk and lace prices. Two years earlier, detective James Mooney and sheriff John Boland had established a firm to uncover fraud for a business clientele. The partners chased Alfred Eugene Lagrave, a Frenchman accused of fleeing to Europe without repaying $600,000 in credit tendered by H. B. Claflin & Co. and others. Detective Mooney, a twenty-six-year-old "stout . . . Irishman with clear eyes and fresh, round features," hopscotched from Montreal to Liverpool to New York to Belfast, Brussels, Paris, and the Pyrenees resort town of Bagnères-de-Luchon to capture Lagrave in October 1872. Over the next two years, businessmen used Mooney & Boland to retrieve fugitive debtors, cheats, and swindlers, as well as politically sensitive fugitives like filibusters to revolutionary Cuba.[28]

IN OCTOBER 1874, Mooney & Boland began following the clues to their source. Stationing a man outside the Broadway warehouse of a firm selling discounted silk, the detectives observed the delivery of three cases of goods marked B.C. 926, 927, and 929. Tracing these numbers in the custom-house records, they learned that the company had declared the goods as "cotton corsets." They contacted the collector of the port, Chester Arthur, who informed them that the importers had paid no duties for two years. Arthur also told Mooney that the goods had been consigned to "D. Bamberger & Co.," a company with "no existence." When Mooney asked Arthur who had made the entries on, and signed bonds on behalf of, the mythological "Bamberger," his answer was downtown customs broker Charles L. Lawrence.[29]

Collector Chester Arthur was one of the leading Grant supporters in the State of New York. Though Arthur succeeded to the presidency of the United States in 1881, no one imagined such a position for him in 1874. A forty-five-year-old abolitionist attorney, classically educated at Union College in Schenectady, Arthur might have been mistaken for a reformer. Contemporaries described him as tall, strong, and well dressed, with a pleasant if rather porcine face, and impressive mutton-chop whiskers. Yet Arthur's true asset was his mastery of Republican patronage. He knew every soldier in the vast army of officeholders, the men who had recommended them for their positions, and their constituencies. He spent little time at the port, showing up for work "at 12 or 1 o'clock in the day" and passing "one or two hours there" before "leaving it to be run by" a subordinate. For his labors, he received over $65,000 between 1871 and 1873. When Congress limited moieties in 1873, Arthur's salary plummeted to $12,000. This was still more than double the pay of a U.S. congressman.[30]

New scandals increased the pressure on both Collector Arthur and Charles L. Lawrence. In 1874, reporters exposed the so-called Whiskey Ring, revealing that a federal agent had received unseemly fees for investigating delinquent distilleries, forcing the president to dismiss his secretary of the treasury. Just as damaging was the bizarre "Safe Burglary Conspiracy," in which a bumbling crew of Grant supporters staged a phony robbery in a desperate attempt to silence a Democratic critic. The farce ended in the resignation of Secret Service chief Hiram Whitley and the removal of District of Columbia

public works commissioner Alexander Shepherd. Shining light upon
the Treasury, the exposures strengthened advocates of a professional
civil service. Yet Shepherd's disgrace also crushed Charley's dreams
of becoming a sewer millionaire. With his connection to District
government now unemployed, the Washington Silica Pipe Company
went the way of the United States Pipe Company.[31]

Arthur likely wanted to bury Mooney's report, which revealed
a major breach in security and endangered his job. But the detectives had been hired by dry goods merchants with close ties to the
president. In 1872, Horace Claflin had resisted the appeal of Liberal
Republicanism and supported Grant. After the Civil War, department
store king A. T. Stewart had helped buy the triumphant general a new
home. In 1868, Stewart had been a generous contributor to Grant's
campaign, leading the new president to try and appoint him to the
cabinet. The collector could not ignore the complaints of the president's close supporters.[32]

Arthur called in the subordinate who passed Lawrence's shipments: Deputy Collector Robert Des Anges. Despite the circumstan-
tial evidence, Arthur refused to chastise the former Union Army
colonel. He found Des Anges "thoroughly trustworthy and one of
the last to be suspected of being engaged in any attempt to defraud
the Government." Des Anges had promoted policies seen as reforms,
including a rule prohibiting merchants from seeing their competitor's entries. Though the decree made it harder for importers to detect
foul play by their rivals, the *New York Times* celebrated it as a boon to
privacy. Arthur was so sure of Des Anges's innocence that he enlisted
him in the investigation, asking him to have customs lawyers Dudley
F. Phelps and Isaac D. Balch scrutinize the bonds for Lawrence's next
shipment. Arthur then instructed these attorneys to give Mooney &
Boland "all the assistance in their power to further . . . plans for the
detection of the smugglers." Phelps had known Des Anges as a fellow officer in an African-American regiment in the Gulf, but he was

an upright official, trusted by Democrats and Republicans alike; his older brother Benjamin had helped prosecute Tweed.[33]

Mooney and Boland assigned a man to shadow Lawrence around town. With Arthur's authority, they searched ship manifests from Europe and watched the docks for the Hamburg-American steamship line, looking for any large cargoes of textiles. Then the detectives received word that an agent of Lawrence's, presumably Aaron Wolf, had made heavy silk purchases in Europe. Communicating with Phelps and Balch, but not Des Anges, the investigators waited for papers to be filed. The detectives soon learned that Lawrence and another broker had eight cases of "cotton hosiery" on the S.S. *Pommerania*, which had steamed into New York harbor on January 7, 1875, carrying goods and immigrants from Hamburg, Cherbourg, and Plymouth.[34]

On January 10, John Boland headed to Lawrence's Twenty-third Street home. Ignoring the record-low temperatures that made it "one of the very worst" days "of the whole winter," he followed Charley, hoping to catch him signing for his boxes at the custom house. When Lawrence realized he was being followed, he cut through hotels and changed cabs several times. Boland kept Lawrence in sight until they arrived at the port, where the smuggler got lost in the crowd. "Too well known" to enter the Rotunda unnoticed, Boland sent a subordinate into the building. The man witnessed Lawrence signing the bonds for the release of seven crates of what purported to be cheap socks consigned to the fictional house of "Freeman and Powell," leaving one for inspection. The officer granting the discharge was Deputy Collector Robert Des Anges.[35]

Des Anges realized he was under investigation when customs lawyer Isaac D. Balch asked him about releasing the boxes on the *Pommerania*. To allay Balch's suspicions, Des Anges reversed his order, allowing Mooney & Boland to move the cases to the government warehouse in Hoboken. The colonel scrawled a note to Lawrence, begging him, "No further communication verbally or in writing. You are followed and so am I. Let everything go to the devil. Export all you can. Just let me alone to try and save myself for the future." Alarmed, Charley tried to distract detectives by having his associates send a new shipment containing "cotton corsets," exactly as listed on the declarations. But this blind fooled no one. Between January 16 and 18, Phelps and Arthur ordered the inspection of the *Pommerania* boxes, which were found to contain "the finest silks . . . fine suspenders and kid gloves" worth $50,000. The only case to contain "cotton hosiery" was the one Des Anges had initially chosen for examination.[36]

In the meantime, anxious customs officials sought to prove their honesty by catching smugglers. In late December 1874, officials tried their colleague David P. Harris for accepting $500 to pass twenty thousand smuggled Cuban cigars belonging to Spanish importer Francisco Avellanet. A farmer from Poughkeepsie, Harris was a man of no special importance, just a crooked official. His prosecutor was Ambrose Purdy, the assistant U.S. attorney who had five years before criticized Treasury settlements with smugglers. Now a seasoned veteran, Purdy settled with Avellanet in return for his testimony against the inspector. On January 23, 1875, Judge Charles Benedict gave Harris a two-year sentence in the Brooklyn Penitentiary, and shortly thereafter, the government sold the cigars at auction for over $5,000.[37]

Meanwhile, Collector Chester Arthur headed for the nation's capital, ostensibly to discuss the reorganization of the port, but just as likely to inform his superiors about the developing smuggling scandal. Eager to show its seriousness about reform, the administration had promised to fire inefficient employees and recommit itself to enforcing the law. Rumors echoed through the city's newsrooms that customs officials were about to announce an immense conspiracy to defraud the revenue. No names were offered, but some hints suggested the direction of the investigation. Articles mentioned that officials had seized eight cases from the *Pommerania*, finding silks

where cottons had been declared. They bragged of evidence "to convict a dozen firms in New York of fraud and deceit," in all "the most
gigantic series of swindles against the revenue, carried on by men of
capital and influence, ever broken up by the Customs Department."[38]

On January 26, Treasury agents arrested Gustavus Ball for
"defrauding the Government by concealing imported goods liable to
a high rate of duty," committing him to Ludlow Street Jail in default
of $10,000 bail. Ball was "a respectable-looking, well-dressed man
of about thirty years of age" who worked for liquor dealer Lafayette
Graff, one of the men Lawrence had chosen to sell the silk. Detectives
suspected him when they noticed that crates seized from the *Pommerania* had the same marks as boxes purchased earlier by H. B. Claflin & Co. Mooney and Boland went to Claflin's silk buyer, William
H. Talcott, who stated that he had obtained the fabric from Ball. Ball
had cemented his guilt by signing a false name to release the cases
held in Hoboken.[39]

It was clear that the young clerk was part of a larger intrigue. Ball's
counsel, Stephen G. Clarke, was too expensive a lawyer for a wage
laborer, no matter how "respectable-looking," to afford. Clarke was
not only the predecessor to Dudley Phelps as the port's leading attorney, he had made a name for himself since 1873 helping corporations,
such as Platt & Boyd glass, protect their records from Special Treasury
Agent Benaiah Jayne. His law partners, such as Edwards Pierrepont,
the former U.S. attorney for the Southern District of New York, were
similarly distinguished and thus unlikely to appear for a mere clerk.

On February 4, 1875, the grand jury indicted Robert Des Anges for
"complicity" in Ball's frauds on the revenue. The indictment charged
him with deliberately sending only special marked cases to the
appraiser for valuation, releasing the crates containing valuable silks,
laces, gloves, and other goods to Ball. Surrendering himself to the
U.S. attorney, Des Anges nonetheless declared his innocence, as did
his friends, who insisted that it was "physically impossible" for the

well-regarded deputy collector to examine "2,000 invoices per day," 15 percent of them for A. T. Stewart & Co. alone. The court held Des Anges upon $5,000 bail.[40]

With Des Anges under arrest, Charley Lawrence, Lafayette Graff, and the Levey brothers "disappeared from the city" just ahead of newspaper reporters and the grand jury. A few days later, the *New York Sun* became the first source to mention Lawrence's and Graff's involvement, describing them as "the principals in the frauds." The *Sun* connected Charley with Tweed, describing him as "the ex-Secretary of the Americus Club." Other papers followed. On February 6, the *Daily Graphic* added that he was the "son-in-law of Mordecai," no surname offered, and blamed "certain merchants" fearful of his testimony for delaying his arrest. By the time the grand jury finally indicted Charley and his co-conspirators, they were all safe in Montreal and England.[41]

FLIGHT

N ever in American history had it been easier for a man to escape. Rails now crisscrossed the continent, allowing travelers to arrive in Canada, Mexico, or Cuba in just a day or two. Steamships plied the rivers, lakes, and oceans. And while no canal yet allowed passage across Central America, the Panama Railroad offered ground passage from the Caribbean to the Pacific. Custom houses guarded nations against foreign products, but most governments sought to attract rather than repel immigrants. Borders were not walls barring entry, but rather the limits of sovereignty, the line beyond which a state could commit no legitimate acts of violence save for self-defense or war. And to catch a fugitive required international cooperation at a time when countries were scrambling to win new territory, retain old empires, and consolidate their hold over their citizens.

Lawrence and his friends absconded to Montreal, which was the closest foreign city to New York, less than a day away by rail. It was also familiar. Henry Levey had grown up in Montreal, and his brother Samuel still lived there. Lafayette Graff's wife Isoline had been raised in Quebec. Five years before, Lawrence had been caught smuggling silk ribbons from Canada. Moreover, Montreal was known for intrigue. In its bars, Union spies had once eavesdropped upon Confederate agents. With over a hundred thousand people, Canada's largest city was a comfortable place for Charley to wait for Gotham's newspapermen to tire of him. He stayed at the "first-class" Ottawa

Hotel on St. James Street, not far from the Old Custom House. There he was joined by his pal John P. Morris, a Brooklyn lawyer and the publisher of *Noah's Weekly Messenger*, the newspaper partly owned by Charley's wife Zipporah.[1]

By fleeing the United States, Lawrence escaped American jurisdiction to the dominion of international law. In the U.S., Charley was a wanted man, but in Canada, he was simply another merchant. At this time, few nations limited immigration, and most welcomed travelers with money. Though Canada had achieved home rule in 1867, the mother country still managed its foreign affairs. The British, untroubled by Lawrence's oaths of American citizenship, still viewed him as a natural-born subject, possessing all the rights of Englishmen. The United States could ask Canadian officials to arrest and extradite Lawrence, but treaties with England defined the terms of their obligation to do so. England might have seen any attempt by U.S. officials to arrest Lawrence in Montreal as grounds for war. With the most powerful empire in the world on his side, Charley possessed substantial security against seizure.

International law made little allowance for the rendition of fugitive smugglers. In this case, the guiding document was the Webster-Ashburton Treaty of 1842, best known for settling the border with Canada and committing the two nations to suppressing the African slave trade. But the agreement also established seven crimes that justified extradition: "murder, or assault with intent to commit murder, or piracy, or arson, or robbery, or forgery, or the utterance of forged paper." Under pressure from British abolitionists, Secretary of State Daniel Webster and British diplomat Lord Ashburton deliberately excluded petty crimes, such as theft, which slaveholders might use to extradite slaves fleeing to Canada. But the list also codified the standing principle that countries should not extradite individuals charged with political crimes, such as "[t]reason, misprision of treason, libels, desertion from military service, and other offences of similar character." It was this broadly accepted notion that enabled mid-century revolutionaries like Hungarian Lajos Kossuth to travel to England or the United States without fear of rendition.[2]

This principle proved both popular and frustrating. Americans opposed to returning Irish revolutionaries to England for trial favored excluding "all political offences, or criminal charges arising from wars or intestine commotions." But this treaty also made it difficult for the United States to demand the extradition of secessionist leaders who fled in 1865. Confederate president Jefferson Davis tried to bolt to Europe, but was caught in Florida (Northerners claimed he was disguised as a woman in his wife's coat and shawl) and spent two years in prison awaiting trial for treason. Secretary of State Judah Benjamin and Secretary of War John C. Breckenridge were luckier; they escaped separately to England. Benjamin stayed in London, where he became a well-known solicitor. Breckenridge traveled in Europe before settling in Niagara, Ontario, just across the river from Buffalo, pending the 1868 amnesty that allowed him to return to his Kentucky home.[3]

Moreover, even in the cases of apolitical criminals, the Canadian government took the pact seriously. Though Canadian authorities remanded forger Augustus T. Berch (alias Charles Baker alias Thomas Wilson) and arsonist Israel Rosenbaum, they refused to give up shoplifters Catherine Martin and Mary "Black Lena" Morris because larceny was not an extraditable offense. In 1872, when banker Henry R. Conklin fled to Montreal leaving defaults valued at $170,000, his employers convinced the grand jury to charge him with forgery so he could be extradited. But Conklin hired "the ablest lawyers in Canada," who persuaded the Montreal court that it could not send him south to face prosecution. The judge ruled that "the indictment as drawn" came "under the statute of exceptions to the extradition treaty."[4]

Frustration with the extradition process sometimes prompted American officials to violate international law, forcing the diplomats to negotiate a solution. In October 1867, a Michigan sheriff crossed the Canadian border to capture Allan McDonald, a British smuggler. London strongly disapproved, forcing Secretary of State Seward to order that U.S. officials set McDonald "at liberty in Canada." More commonly, American prosecutors claimed fugitives had committed offenses listed in the treaty, but after extradition, they tried those defendants for other crimes. England attempted to abolish this practice with the Extradition Act of 1870 that established the principle of "specialty," that is, a nation's obligation to try a defendant only on the charges listed in the petition for extradition. But the United States ignored this law, and fugitives found themselves accused of one crime abroad only to be prosecuted for different offenses in America. When detective James Mooney retrieved defalcating clothier Alfred Eugene Lagrave in 1874, he did so on a charge of burglary, an extraditable offense. But once in the U.S., Lagrave faced not the promised criminal prosecution, but rather the civil suits of his creditors.[5]

Around February 10, 1875, Lawrence received a telegram informing him that a federal grand jury had charged him with forgery, shattering his assumption that as a smuggler he could not be extradited. Just as unsettling, he learned that John Boland was in Montreal to arrest him. Charley decided it was time to go to England. Though his birthplace offered him no more diplomatic protection than Canada, he had more resources in Great Britain, including his brother Frederic and his co-conspirators Abraham Hoffnung and Aaron Wolf. From England, he could flee to Spain or another country lacking an extradition treaty with the United States. Charley knew well the recent story of Tammanyite William Sharkey, a convicted murderer who avoided execution by escaping from jail and disappearing into the Spanish empire.[6]

For Lawrence, the question was how to get from Montreal to England without meeting an American Treasury agent. Steamers traveling to Europe docked at Halifax, Nova Scotia, over six hundred miles to the east as the crow flies. But the border between Canada and the United States was not straight, so anyone traveling directly from Montreal to Halifax had to cross the State of Maine and endure its custom officers. The Grand Trunk Railway had begun building an all-Canadian rail line to Nova Scotia that curved around the tip of the United States through Quebec and New Brunswick, but this route was not yet complete in 1875.[7]

On February 12, Charley abruptly departed his hotel, leaving his friend John Morris to pay the bill, and headed up the St. Lawrence River. With Boland in pursuit, he embarked upon a "memorable sleigh ride" to cross the frozen landscape of New Brunswick. Wearing a "grey overcoat, trimmed with Astrakhan," he schussed the entire two hundred miles to St. John and then made his way to Nova Scotia. In Halifax, he found a letter warning him not to go to England. "The doctors in consultation advised the air of Bermuda or the South of France for Mr. Gush," it recommended; "he would possibly find the English climate too severe." Ignoring this counsel, on February 25, Charley boarded the steamer *Caspian*, bound for Ireland. He signed the manifest "George G. Gordon," a winking reference to romantic poets, corsairs, and confidence men.[8]

Lawrence's co-conspirators remained in Montreal, despite the best efforts of U.S. attorney George Bliss to summon them back to New York City. To dislodge Lafayette Graff, Bliss sued him for $36,000 in duties owed to the government, obtaining permission to attach a "tin box" the smuggler had deposited in a bank. Perhaps tipped off, Graff sent his wife Isoline to claim the property first, but when she arrived, the marshal had already officially sealed the lock of the safe. Bliss then obtained warrants for the arrest of Mrs. Graff and the seizure of their "costly and well-furnished brownstone" residence at 207 East Sixty-first Street. Isoline convinced the deputies that the property was hers and thus not liable to attachment. The disappointed agents left, but when it became clear that she was preparing to leave for Montreal the next day, they demanded she post bonds worth $2,000 against her failure to return to New York.[9]

Bliss similarly tried to rouse Henry Levey by seizing cases of silverware and imported silk neckties from his business. But Levey remained concealed in Montreal, adopting the alias "Goodwin," and hiding among friends and relatives. Boland finally discovered Levey "in disguise" at "a Jewish Ball," but Bliss ordered the detective not to arrest him for fear of violating international law. Levey took his own sleigh ride to Mont St.-Hilaire and boarded a train under the name "Carter." Boland headed for Richmond, the railway junction one hundred miles from Montreal, where he borrowed "a conductor's cap" and searched each train that passed, finding Levey "enveloped in furs," "snugly" hidden in a Pullman car. Pretending not to notice, Boland remained on the train and followed Levey to Quebec City, where he had police arrest the fugitive. But when Boland failed to appear in court, Levey convinced the Quebec magistrate (perhaps with a bribe) to release him on March 9. He steamed to Europe.[10]

While Charley sailed on the *Caspian*, his brother-in-law Robert Noah calculated the costs of fraternity. Noah worked in New York City's corporation-counsel office, a bureau suing the Tweed Ring for the millions of dollars stolen during the prior decade. The mayor had recently named William C. Whitney as Noah's boss. Whitney was an aristocrat, who had graduated from Harvard and Yale, inherited immense manufacturing and shipping interests, and then moved to New York, where he became a leader of the Swallowtail Democrats. Eager to save his party from its association with Tweed before the 1876 elections, Whitney may have pressed Noah to inform on his sister's husband. Noah himself was likely anxious, having just endured his wife's suit for divorce on grounds of desertion, adultery, and cruelty. But whatever his reasons, he informed Bliss of Charley's location.[11]

Upon learning that Charley was on the *Caspian* posing as George G. Gordon, Bliss contacted Secretary of State Hamilton Fish, who consulted with President Grant and then cabled the U.S. minister to Great Britain, Robert Schenck, to request Lawrence's arrest and extradition. Displaying no sympathy for his fellow poker player, Schenck complied, as did the British, who were told Lawrence was a forger. When Charley arrived in Queenstown (now Cobh), Ireland, police arrested him and brought him to London. On March 10, he came before magistrate Sir Thomas Henry, who ordered him imprisoned in the Clerkenwell House of Detention, where he was put in solitary confinement, permitted minimal exercise, and allowed slight access to his family. While the *Caspian* was still at sea, Bliss sent detective Mooney to England to escort Charley home.[12]

If Lawrence's accommodations in the Clerkenwell were dismal, he had reasons for hope. Abraham Hoffnung predicted that Americans would tire of the matter while waiting for the English to process Charley's extradition. George Wolf secured for Charley the services of George Lewis as his solicitor. Lewis later became the premier fixer in England, earning a title by representing everyone from Oscar Wilde to the Prince of Wales. But at the time, Lewis was a hungry young "police court hack," not the baronet known for his fur coat and monocle. Lewis likely felt a bit of empathy for Lawrence; the two men were of the same religion and almost the same age. He had attended school with Charley's brother Frederic. And both men were connoisseurs who enjoyed the fine arts and the society that attended them.[13]

Lewis's first task was to dispose of incriminating documents, including a cipher revealing the "secrets" of "the contraband business in the United States." The book contained "about 1,500 separate key words." For instance, Lawrence's code name was "Mr. Gush," an appellation possibly taken from the British painter William Gush, a neighbor of Robert Des Anges's brother. But the encryption was often doubled. So the key defined the word "vertical" as the phrase "let fabulous make leave." Looking deeper, the word "fabulous" referred to co-conspirator William Benjamin, and the word "leave" was translated as "consular invoice," so that the single word "vertical" actually meant "let William Benjamin make the Consular invoice." Aaron Wolf offered Lewis £500 to recover the book from Scotland Yard. Lewis puckishly responded that he could obtain it for nothing, as he was "on very friendly terms" with the government's attorney. Lewis did as promised, and Wolf burned the code book in a fireplace at his home.[14]

Lawrence's attorneys also contested his extradition. To bolster his case, Lewis solicited opinions from two eminent authorities. One was former Confederate secretary of state Judah Benjamin. If hiring a leading secessionist seemed likely to reinforce the sense that Charley was a traitor, then this may have been Lewis's intent, since Benjamin's freedom stood as a tribute to the principle that the Webster-Ashburton Treaty did not permit the extradition of political criminals. As expected, Benjamin argued that Britain could not render Lawrence to the United States for trial on charges of smuggling. To reinforce this argument, Lawrence also hired Edward G. Clarke, author of a treatise on extradition, who wrote "I concur in this opinion" on Benjamin's brief.[15]

On March 23, Charley was brought to Bow Street Magistrates' Court to have his fate considered by Sir Thomas Henry. By coincidence, Sir Thomas had written the Extradition Act of 1870, which prohibited English officials from releasing a prisoner to a nation intending to prosecute him for crimes not listed in the treaty. But the prosecutor insisted that Lawrence had been charged with forgery, not smuggling. The matter was deferred until April 15, when a handwriting expert confirmed that Charley had signed incriminating documents and a Scotland Yard detective produced the scrawled note from Des Anges. Having heard enough, Sir Thomas ordered that Lawrence be returned to the United States. Charley asked to be sent home immediately, but the judge told him that "the law required" his incarceration in England for an additional fourteen days.[16]

Charley's associates did not abandon him. His family had already hired prominent attorney Edwards Pierrepont to plead his case in New York. Aaron Wolf agreed to hold onto Charley's jewelry to prevent its confiscation by customs officials. Fearing rumors of a rescue mission, Sergeant Shaw of Scotland Yard helped James Mooney escort Charley to Queenstown. But instead of executing a daring escape, Hoffnung merely offered Mooney $5,000 in gold to release

Lawrence. When the investigator refused, Wolf upped the offer to $10,000 (one report claimed the number was $30,000). The private eye again balked. Finally, Charley's supporters hired a lawyer to plan his defense on the cruise home, but Mooney threatened to put Lawrence "in irons on the trip if any of his friends were among the passengers." On May 1, 1875, the detective accompanied Charley onto the Cunard steamer *Scythia*, bound for New York City.[17]

As the *Scythia* approached New York harbor during the second week in May, importers fretfully telegraphed the docks to learn whether, when, and where Charley had landed. Federal officials were eager as well. U.S. Attorney Bliss had ordered the revenue cutter *P. J. Washington* bearing deputy U.S. marshals to wait in quarantine three days early to ensure that Lawrence could not escape. Then finally, before daybreak on the morning of May 13, 1875, the *Scythia* landed. The deputies relieved Mooney of his prisoner and seized Charley's baggage, merely an "old leather valise" and worn lap blanket. They then brought him to the federal courthouse on Chambers Street, where his "two young sons . . . embraced him." Lawrence was then taken into the presence of Judge Samuel Blatchford, who ordered him taken to Ludlow Street Jail, where Des Anges was also being held. The marshals courteously asked the accused smuggler whether he preferred to drive or walk the mile to his place of confinement. Perhaps eager to stroll along the city streets again after three months away, Charley chose to travel by foot.[18]

Newspapers around the world reported Lawrence's capture and extradition. They dubbed Charley the "Prince of Smugglers" and his gang "Credit Mobilier," alluding not only to the infamous 1872 scandal, but also the peregrinations of the alleged perpetrators. The *Sun* reckoned that Charley "organized a system of fraud on the revenue almost unparalleled in ingenuity and execution in the whole record of great frauds." Most reporters claimed the smugglers had illicitly imported $3 million in merchandise, cheating the United States out of an astronomical $1.5 million in duties. Reporters believed that the conspiracy was "very far reaching" and predicted that Lawrence would assist the government in the prosecution of prominent businessmen and politicians.[19]

Anxious merchants exhaled when the earliest reports implicated Tweed. Nearly every newspaper emphasized Charley's position as secretary of the Americus Club and his friendship with "the Boss." Some claimed that Lawrence had not paid duties on the imported furnishings for the luxurious Greenwich clubhouse or the famous jeweled tiger-head pins worn by Tweed and other Americus members. Such an association distanced the newly elected Democratic governor Samuel L. Tilden from "the Ring." The connection helped the Grant administration present Collector Chester Arthur as the nemesis of customs corruption. And for Liberal Republicans, spotlighting Lawrence obscured the embarrassing arrest of Des Anges, the first port worker promoted under the new examination regime and the beau ideal of the civil service crusade.

Articles about Lawrence evoked the stereotype of the Jewish smuggler. Most papers, including the esteemed *New York Tribune*, mentioned his decision to change his name from Lazarus to Lawrence. The *New York Sun* noted his "Jewish parentage," while the straitlaced *New York Times* described Charley's "Hebrew cast of countenance." Having derided Jews in prior years, James Gordon Bennett Jr.'s *Herald* took the high ground in 1875. But Bennett's more salacious evening paper, the *Telegram*, described Lawrence's original name, his Yorkshire forebears, and his alcoholic father. In the *New York Independent*, silk importer Henry C. Bowen called Charley an "Israelite" possessing a "good deal of guile." Outside New York City, the accusations were more bizarre. The *Bucks County Gazette*, published near Philadelphia, called Lawrence a descendant of "a crumb eater," a scavenger who picked at scraps rather than working honestly to purchase his own meal. Upon changing his surname, Charley's nose took "a Yankee shape" and his feet "arched at the instep," losing two imagined markers of Jewish appearance.[20]

Reporters embellished Charley's wealth. The *London Week's News* and *Madras Mail* both claimed that police had found that Lawrence was traveling with three hundred gold sovereigns (between $30,000 and $100,000 today) concealed upon his person. The *St. Albans Daily Messenger* claimed he carried only 280 gold coins, but also "diamond studs" given by Tweed. The *Anglo-American Times* mentioned a three-carat diamond pin, also alleged to be a gift from the Boss. The *Sun* reported that he possessed $250,000 in property and carried "$10,000 in diamonds on his person." The *Sabbath Recorder* claimed he held assets worth "half a million." The articles often mentioned that this property could not be seized, as it had been transferred to his wife. Since much of Lawrence's wealth came from Zipporah's inheritance, such assignments may have never occurred, but these claims further underscored the shiftiness of the smuggler.[21]

Observers tried to turn the scandal to their advantage. Dry goods importers joined civil service reformers in blaming the "evils of the smuggling system" upon corrupt officeholders appointed by politicians. Skeptics of reform responded that Robert Des Anges was the first official promoted under the touted examination regime. Opponents of moieties noted that customs officials had needed no cash incentive to ferret out Lawrence. Supporters of the old system replied that they might have caught him sooner had moieties not been banned. One Republican former deputy U.S. attorney complained that "so-called reformers claiming great importance and responsibility," merchants making "hue and cry," and "an interested press" had convinced Congress to remove "every safeguard against illegal importations." And a *Daily Graphic* editorial protested that without the motivation of moieties, customs officials became so lax that honest merchants had to hire private detectives like Mooney and Boland to catch smugglers.[22]

SMUGGLING SEEMED TO BE everywhere. In March, President Grant ousted Attorney General George H. Williams, whose wife had accepted a $30,000 bribe from Platt & Boyd to press her husband not to prosecute the glass importers for customs fraud. It even crept into the ubiquitous reportage of the Henry Ward Beecher trial when it was revealed that a prime witness, Frank Moulton, had hired former Special Treasury Agent Benaiah Jayne. Moulton had made Jayne's acquaintance while negotiating a settlement for his own importing firm's alleged undervaluations. On April 28, after consultation with his cabinet, Grant nominated a new attorney general to replace Williams. Only afterward did the president learn that his choice, New York attorney Edwards Pierrepont, had himself been previously retained by the Lawrence family. Almost as mortifying, Pierrepont's law partners, Stanley, Brown & Clarke, had represented Platt & Boyd, the firm that corrupted Williams. Then, on May 15, days after Charley's extradition to the United States, Grant pardoned cigar-smuggling customs inspector David P. Harris, who was only four months into his two-year sentence. Pierrepont criticized the president's act of clemency, but the series of decisions suggested that administration did not care about revenue frauds.[23]

On May 18, Charley petitioned the president, complaining that U.S. Attorney George Bliss intended to ignore the terms of extradition and try him for smuggling or, worse, sue him for the millions of dollars in duties he had evaded. Four days later, Grant asked his cabinet for their thoughts. New Treasury Secretary Benjamin H. Bristow, who was cleaning up his department, favored prosecuting Charley for all his crimes. The president and the secretary of state, Hamilton Fish, saw the matter as legal, to be determined by the judiciary, not the executive. Attorney General Pierrepont viewed a smuggling prosecution as unlawful, but because his prior commitment to Lawrence barred him from considering the case, the matter was referred to Solicitor General Samuel F. Phillips for his opinion. While they waited for Phillips to render his judgment, Bliss was ordered to "stay all proceedings," continuing only to prosecute Lawrence for forgery.[24]

Grant likely wished the matter would disappear. The scandals were destroying his political coalition. By 1875, most of the wartime radicals had died. For every egalitarian like Rep. William "Pig Iron" Kelley and Sen. George Boutwell, there were now an equal number of lawmakers hostile to equal rights for African-Americans. With nearly all former Confederates restored to citizenship by the election of November 1874, the Democrats had won both houses of the United States Congress for the first time since secession, and even Ben Butler had lost his seat. Moreover, the Democrats now held majorities in state legislatures in Arkansas, Alabama, and Texas. Thus, the rendition of Charley Lawrence not only foretold new investigations of the executive by Congress, but also the unthinkable possibility of a Democratic president and an end to Reconstruction.

Meanwhile, the U.S. attorney focused on the other conspirators. On May 23, John Boland and a deputy marshal arrested Justinian Hartley, the commission merchant alleged to have paid Lafayette Graff to smuggle silks for him. Boland alleged that Hartley had been living "in a very liberal way for some time" under "an assumed name." To capture the incognito merchant, the detective had engaged in subterfuge. Reading in the news "that a man by the name of Hartley had been thrown from his carriage in Central Park," Boland went to the listed address and posed as a "reporter desirous of obtaining information relative to the accident." Hartley admitted his identity, only to become "very anxious that his full name should not be published." But it was too late.[25]

After intense legal wrangling, arrangements were made to open Lafayette Graff's tin container, which was assumed to be a "Pandora's box-full of mischief" containing "papers of dangerous import." Less than a week later, Col. Bliss, Graff's brother, and his attorney, Gen. Roger A. Pryor, examined the box's content, finding documents and $2,000 in valuables. The papers must have been damning, for the next day, after over four months in Montreal, Graff returned to New York City to testify against his associates in return for immunity.[26]

Most shocking, on June 9 the grand jury indicted dry goods tycoon

Horace Claflin, his silk buyer William Talcott, and five others for purchasing contraband silks. The panel also charged Lawrence and Des
Anges, as well as the auction house of Field, Morris & Fenner and
importer Justinian Hartley. When marshals had arrested Talcott on
the fifth, Bliss had stated he had "no evidence to implicate Claflin." But
days later he reversed himself, explaining that the firm knew it was
buying contraband, possession of which was grounds for conviction.
H. B. Claflin & Co. insisted they had run their "business honorably
and honestly," asking their "fellow-citizens to withhold all judgment."
This was likely true; the firm would hardly have hired detectives to
uncover a conspiracy of which they were the beneficiaries. But it was
a blow to the standing of the famous wholesale house. Even those
who viewed the charges as a "false imputation on the great merchant
prince" nonetheless demanded a "thorough examination."[27]

On the fourteenth of June, 1875, the court finally arraigned the
conspirators. As it was the "first time that Lawrence had appeared
in the court-room," the *Times* reported, "he attracted a good deal
of attention." In addition to his "Hebrew cast of countenance," the
reporter described him as "of medium height, rather thick-set," not
to mention "quite bald, having only a narrow fringe of gray hair running around his head," and "a heavy mustache." But the newspaper
was most intrigued by Charley's attire, observing that "he was well
dressed," the "noticeable features of his costume" being "kid gloves
and a white necktie." All of the participants pled not guilty except
Lawrence, whose attorney, Stephen Clarke, obtained a delay pending
the return of his lead counsel, Edwin W. Stoughton. Two days later,
Bliss acknowledged the complexity of international law and agreed
to put off any consideration of Lawrence until the next court term in
September.[28]

So Charley waited in Ludlow Street Jail, his main solace being
the arrival of his friend William Tweed on June 22. The Boss was
being held because he was unable to post $4 million bail in the
city's $6 million civil suit for moneys allegedly stolen by the ring.

The arrangements in Ludlow Street were surprisingly comfortable. Its seventy-eight cells were nearly the private domain of the sheriff, who received seventy-five cents each day from the county for each prisoner but paid for their accommodations out of his own pocket. One reporter described the rooms as "large well lighted clean and neat" not to mention "thoroughly ventilated." Outside the cells, the corridors were "cheerful," reminiscent "of the lobby of a large hotel." Inhabitants were at liberty to move within the prison during the day-time. Moreover, those with money could buy superior accommodations. Lawrence allegedly paid $50 per week, while the Boss paid $75. For this price, Tweed received special food, the attentions of a black waiter, Louis "Luke" Grant, as well as a pleasant room that had once served as the warden's parlor. Tweed's chamber adjoined Charley's, allowing the two friends to socialize at will.[29]

THE DEFENDANTS' DAZZLING legal talent indicated the enormousness of the stakes. After losing Edwards Pierrepont to the attorney-generalship, Lawrence engaged Edwin Stoughton, Gen. Benjamin F. Tracy, and the firm of Stanley, Brown & Clarke. Stoughton was a leader of the city bar, representing clients like Jim Fisk and Mayor Oakey Hall. Tracy had received the Medal of Honor during the Civil War and later served as secretary of the navy. Stanley, Brown, and Clarke were experts on smuggling and customs cases. Nor did the other defendants skimp on representation. Lafayette Graff's attorney, Roger A. Pryor, was a former congressman and Confederate general. Justinian Hartley hired Sidney Webster, the son-in-law of Secretary of State Fish. Claflin's lawyer, William Evarts, was a former U.S. attorney general. His associate, Elihu Root, was an ascending star, and both men later held the position of secretary of state. Evarts, Tracy, Root, and Pryor were all involved in the public litigation surrounding the Beecher scandal.

These lawyers styled themselves as Olympian figures standing above the petty corruption of the city and nation. They worked not only for individuals and corporations, but also for foreign governments such as Spain. Seeing themselves as the equals of the great orators of antiquity, Pierrepont, Evarts, and Stoughton all commissioned busts of themselves by Augustus Saint-Gaudens, a brilliant young sculptor trained in Rome. These men helped construct the ideal of nonpartisan professionalism, which obliged lawyers to represent clients independent of their political beliefs. Pierrepont, Stanley, and Brown had recently been partners with C. C. Langdell, dean of Harvard Law School and the father of modern American legal education. Evarts and Stoughton helped found the New York City Bar Association in 1870, which led the fight against Tammany judges such as George C. Barnard. And yet they were also dealmakers who managed to work with these jurists, a fact not missed by their critics.[30]

Stoughton's first responsibility was to sway Solicitor General Phillips, who had been chosen to determine whether Lawrence could be tried for smuggling. On May 24, Stoughton filed his brief, arguing that Parliament's Act of 1870 had ratified an understanding between the two nations that they would try prisoners only for crimes listed in the request for extradition. Stoughton claimed that Great Britain had rendered Lawrence to the United States only because District Attorney Bliss had concealed his true intent. The accusation rankled Bliss, who insisted that Stoughton knew the charge to be "not true." He also condemned the counselor's broader goal. Limiting the charges to mere forgery would permit Lawrence to obtain a low bail, allowing him to flee the country again, escaping punishment "without abandoning more than a tithe of his gains." Or if he remained for trial, he could use "the same skill and wickedness" he used in "defrauding" the government "of millions of money" to win his case.[31]

On May 28, Bliss filed his formal response, arguing that the British government had no standing to sue to limit the charges Lawrence faced. The Act of 1870 constrained British officials alone. Bliss cited extensive case law showing that the U.S. courts had never accepted the doctrine of specialty, which required them to try Lawrence only for the offenses listed in the request for extradition. Indeed, the courts had recently upheld lawsuits against Lagrave, another defendant retrieved by Mooney & Boland. On July 16, Solicitor General Phillips submitted his report, arguing that the United States had the right to prosecute Lawrence for any offenses it wished. In requesting Lawrence's extradition, the U.S. had made "no promise" that modified the Webster-Ashburton Treaty, and thus was free to pursue any course it chose. Indeed, President Grant could not "interfere in the civil suit pending" against Lawrence to obtain $1,386,400 back duties and penalties owed to the government.[32]

The report divided the executive branch. Secretary of the Treasury Bristow endorsed the opinion, as did Secretary of State Fish, who wanted to avoid involvement. But Grant was reluctant to authorize Lawrence's prosecution for smuggling. The president seemed to want an external agent, such as England, to prevent a trial. Grant might have feared that Lawrence would implicate close friends like clothier Alexander T. Stewart. Perhaps he simply dreaded another scandal on his watch. In any case, Attorney General Pierrepont recommended Bliss try Charley for forgery. If Lawrence was convicted, then there was no need for a smuggling prosecution. If he was acquitted, then the justice department could seek England's permission to try Lawrence for other crimes. Pierrepont's compromise appeared rather sordid; after all, it negated the millions of dollars his former client owed the government. But Grant liked this advice, and he told Bliss to pursue the forgery indictment alone for the time being.[33]

Charley had won a reprieve, yet he remained in jail under multiple indictments, with a million-dollar lawsuit pending as well. His London solicitors, Lewis & Lewis, wrote to Britain's home secretary informing his office that the United States intended to try Charley for smuggling, a "gross violation" and an "outrage" against an "Englishman" who, "although resident in America for some years, has never forfeited his allegiance as a subject of the British government." Robert Noah appealed to present and former members of Parliament to use their influence with the foreign minister. This correspondence initially had the desired effect. Learning that Secretary of State Fish intended to intervene, Charley's lawyer Stephen Clarke exclaimed, "The skies brighten." Noah followed this up with a lengthy meeting with Sir Edward Thornton, the "universally respected" British minister to the United States, who appeared receptive to Lawrence's plea.[34]

Such optimism was premature. Later in the month, Robert met with Secretary of State Fish at Glenclyffe, his stately home on the Hudson River, where he appealed to the secretary's memory of his father. Whatever Fish thought of the elder Noah, the secretary was not to be moved by mere amity. Fish was an imposing figure, descended from New Amsterdam's first governor, Peter Stuyvesant. An aristocrat, a snob, and even a bigot, he saw himself as a gentleman above petty matters of money and favor. This made him unlikely to side with Charley. Fish told Noah that he could do nothing until England decided to "press its claim and negotiate." The problem was that Thornton "refused to interfere" or even "take official cognizance of the matter unless specially instructed by" the British foreign minister, Edward Henry Stanley, the Earl of Derby.[35]

But Derby declined to intervene. He may have wanted to maintain the newfound stability of U.S.-British relations wrought by the recent settlement of the *Alabama* claims. During the Civil War, British shipyards had built the C.S.S. *Alabama*, a fast Confederate commerce raider that cost Northern merchants millions in damages. Outfitting the *Alabama* was a clear violation of neutrality, so after Appomattox, these shippers petitioned the U.S. government to sue Great Britain. Politicians hostile to England, such as Rep. Benjamin Butler, felt the United States should seize Canada in reprisal. Instead, Fish arbitrated a final settlement of $15.5 million, settling the matter without bloodshed.

Benjamin Disraeli, Britain's newly elected prime minister, also likely preferred to keep his government out of the matter. While Disraeli's parents had baptized him as an Anglican at the age of twelve, his Jewish origins prompted vicious attacks from both enemies and friends throughout his long career. As a supporter of protective tariffs, he could not openly sympathize with a smuggler, even one who had offended another nation. Moreover, at the moment Disraeli was secretly negotiating to purchase the Suez Canal from Egypt's ruler, Khedive Isma'il Pasha, for £4 million borrowed from the Rothschilds, the famous Jewish bankers. All the elements of the agreement, including not only the ethnicity of the parties but also the financial engineering and the "Oriental" location of the investment, inspired anti-Semitic jibes from opponents. Charley could not have picked a more politically inopportune moment to ask the prime minister for aid.[36]

As Lawrence's case gathered attention, he won a new ally in economist David A. Wells, who saw the prosecution as an opportunity to advocate free trade. Writing in the *New York World*, the Democratic paper owned by banker August Belmont, Wells argued that tariffs on silk were so high that even good men were tempted to smuggle. The way to stop smuggling and increase revenues was to lower tariffs, Wells contended. In honor of the nation's upcoming centennial, he compared Charley to John Hancock, harassed by the British for smuggling in 1775. Wells jabbed Bliss, his old associate, coauthor, and first cousin by marriage. The district attorney, he argued, might just as well have jailed "one half the signers of the Declaration of Independence." Even more brazenly, Wells implicitly compared Charley—a Tammanyite associated with blockade runners—to opponents of the 1850 Fugitive Slave Law once defended by Richard Henry Dana Jr. Wells hazarded that freedom-loving Americans would never convict Lawrence of any crime.[37]

This unsolicited support did little to relieve a tense situation. Zipporah sought help from Aaron Wolf, but he was busy trying to keep his businesses afloat. "The fact is," Lawrence's wife complained, "he is so absorbed in his troubles that he is not responsible [*sic*] half the time." In early September, Thornton informed Robert that he refused to take any action until he heard back from his government, prompting attorney Stephen Clarke to recommend that he lobby the minister again. Clarke also promised he would "endeavor to see" his former law partner, Attorney General Pierrepont, when he was in New York on September 24. Zipporah hounded her brother Jacob to use his pull on behalf of her husband, leading him to protest, "I have done the best I could." Living in London, Charley's brother Frederic wrote directly to the foreign secretary to beg for his intervention, but received minimal response. In late October, Edwin Stoughton wrote to his co-counsel Clarke that "Lawrence is to be tried on the charge on which he was extradited, after which the final disposition of the matter will be made and I have no serious doubt as to what that will be." But Stoughton knew that hazards remained, telling the younger attorney, "Now we must strain every professional nerve to succeed."[38]

ON OCTOBER 26, the United States began its prosecution of Col. Robert Des Anges, the former deputy collector of the port. The government presented evidence showing that Lawrence, Graff, and others had smuggled silks and laces through the custom house. But the guilt of the deputy collector hinged on his complicity—in particular, whether he had received payment for inspecting only those crates actually filled with the items on the declarations. Thus, the key piece of evidence was Des Anges's note to Lawrence warning him that their ring had been uncovered. The message suggested not only his awareness of the crime, but his knowledge that Lawrence was not "F. L. Blanding," the false name he signed on the customs bonds. To prove the note was genuine, prosecutors asked Scotland Yard to send Sergeant Shaw to testify at the trial that he had found it on the smuggler's person when arresting him in Queenstown.

On November 9, after a deliberation of only five minutes, the jury returned with a guilty verdict, which Des Anges accepted "without seeming surprise." His lawyer's motion for an arrest of judgment gave him an extra two weeks of freedom. But if he believed his reputation as a soldier and civil servant would earn him lenient treatment, he was mistaken, as the newspapers eagerly revealed his exaggeration of his time in the British Army, his embezzlement of funds, and his flight from England. He arrived at the next hearing "fashionably dressed" in a gray overcoat and "new silk hat" but evidently "very depressed in spirits." On November 27, Judge Benedict denied his motion, giving the former deputy collector the maximum sentence of two years "confinement at hard labor" and a fine of $10,000, a punishment he deemed "hardly adequate to the offence." After one more night and day in Ludlow Street Jail, Des Anges took the 6:40 p.m. train from New York to Albany accompanied by two deputy sheriffs. "He was neatly attired" the papers reported, but being "handcuffed" left him feeling "his humiliation keenly," and he spent the train trip "prostrated" with sorrow. He was given a position as an assistant in the prison infirmary at Albany Penitentiary, and the *New York Times* believed he would "have a comparatively easy" stay. But it was a crushing blow for a man accustomed to comfort, respect, and responsibility.[39]

Just as Des Anges entered prison, William Tweed startled the nation by escaping from Ludlow Street Jail. On Saturday, December 4, Tweed finished lunch, then walked out of the building, entered a coach, and drove to the countryside, accompanied by his son, the warden, and a keeper. This was not odd; it was the fifth time Tweed had been permitted exercise since his arrival. Returning to the city at 6:30 p.m., the group parked and walked to Tweed's brownstone at 647 Madison Avenue, where they sat and chatted with family members. At one point, Tweed stood and said he wanted to see his "very sick" wife. But after five minutes, the warden grew restless and asked Tweed's son to retrieve the "old man." The son went upstairs, but soon returned, calmly stating, "Father's gone." He stayed "gone" for ten months before he was captured fleeing from Cuba to Spain using a false passport made out in the name of "John Secor."[40]

Observers claimed the Boss had learned the laws of extradition from Lawrence, who was Tweed's "constant" companion in Ludlow Street, "intimate friend," and an experienced (if unsuccessful) fugitive. Now, the U.S. attorney had another reason to proceed with Lawrence's prosecution. A trial could allow Bliss, a leader of New York's Republican Party, to blame corruption in Grant's custom house on the Democrats and Tammany Hall. And Charley's trial could provide Republicans with the closure denied them by Tweed's disappearance.[41]

Hoping the diplomatic situation might change, Lawrence fought for delays. He petitioned to quash the indictments and then refused to submit a plea. He begged for postponements. The tactic worked. A scandal broke involving Robert Schenck, Grant's minister to Great Britain, who had backed America's right to prosecute Charley for smuggling. Years earlier, Schenck had encouraged Britons to buy stock in the Emma Silver Mining Company of Utah, a firm in which he was a director. Under pressure from Secretary of State Fish, Schenck severed his relationship with the firm, but delayed publicizing his departure until after he had sold his shares, allowing him to avoid the ensuing decline in prices. When the other stockholders learned the mine was depleted, Congress investigated and the London press flayed Schenck, leading him to resign on February 17, 1876.[42]

Two weeks later, President Grant chose Richard Henry Dana Jr. as the new minister to Great Britain. Many still revered Dana for his representation of Anthony Burns and his defense of the Union blockade, but he had powerful enemies. Former congressman Benjamin Butler had resented Dana as a Brahmin snob long before Dana unsuccessfully contested Butler's congressional seat in 1868. Moreover, the men disagreed about American foreign policy, for Dana was an Anglophile, whereas Butler detested the British Empire. And, finally, Butler sought revenge against Liberal Republicans who had aided his defeat in the election of November 1874. Determined not to allow his enemies any small victories, Butler rallied opposition to Dana's appointment, leading the Senate to reject him on April 4, 1876.[43]

Incredibly, Grant then considered naming Edwin Stoughton,

Charley's attorney, as Schenck's replacement. When the proposal reached the public, immediate opposition arose from several quarters. A woman named Cecilia Kerr met with Attorney General Pierrepont and threatened to expose Stoughton for conspiring in 1869 to have her committed to the Utica Lunatic Asylum. Though Kerr's claims sounded bizarre, they actually received respectful treatment from the New York press. Secretary of State Fish added that Stoughton was tainted by his association with the silk smugglers. Unwilling to invite more criticism, the president turned to Pierrepont himself, who passed Senate muster and accepted the posting in May. In the U.S. ministry in London, Charley now had a former member of his legal team who favored his interpretation of the law. It was a victory, for though Pierrepont could no longer block Charley's criminal prosecution, his new position allowed him to lobby Great Britain to stem the Treasury's million-dollar lawsuits.[44]

After the New Year, the Disraeli government began pressing the United States to quash Lawrence's smuggling indictments. The British home secretary, Richard Assheton Cross, seemed keen to enforce his nation's 1870 Extradition Act, making this point in his correspondence to the Foreign Office. "The right of asylum," his office wrote, "is one above all others of which public opinion would with justice be highly sensitive." Cross threatened to cease sending prisoners to the United States unless that nation accepted the principle of specialty. Cross was close to foreign minister Lord Derby so his letters had an effect. Derby instructed Sir Edward Thornton to impress upon Secretary of State Fish the importance of the issue. When the federal grand jury returned to duty in January, they issued a new indictment for Lawrence mentioning only his forging of the name "F. L. Blanding & Co." on oaths and entries.[45]

On the other side was the wide array of detectives, customs clerks, and politicians angling for rewards for capturing Lawrence. Though Congress had banned moieties in undervaluation cases, eliminating the incentive for agents to investigate importers, the law still promised shares to anyone who uncovered outright smuggling. In October 1875, newspapers named Deputy Collector Phelps as a possible beneficiary, but predicted the fight would be a "lengthy affair." The next month, an article stated that eight "revenue officers and detectives" had claimed the $20,000 moiety, including a customs examiner named Corbett, whose role in cracking the case was negligible. In late January, detectives James Mooney and John Boland petitioned Secretary of the Treasury Bristow for their share, arguing that they were responsible for uncovering the scheme. Unwilling to cede such a prize, port officials argued that Mooney and Boland "simply worked as detectives under the instructions of the Customs officers." To sort out these claims, Bristow ordered an investigation.[46]

Joining this chaotic scene were former general and congressman Benjamin F. Butler and his minion Benaiah Jayne. Butler wanted the Justice Department to trade Lawrence's freedom for evidence implicating wealthy merchants. Jayne told Treasury Secretary Bristow that there were guiltier parties than Des Anges "still in office," protected by the lassitude of Collector Arthur, who left the operation of the port to his crooked assistants. They contended that Bliss pursued Charley not out of any desire for justice, but because he dreaded what the smuggler's testimony might reveal: not only the dishonesty of importers, but also corruption within his own office. Moreover, they felt that Arthur and his backer New York senator Roscoe Conkling were "against doing any thing to make even a ripple on the water" that might hinder Conkling's presidential aspirations.

The courts also pushed Charley to make a deal. First, on March 28, 1876, Judge Benedict ruled that the government could try him for smuggling as well as forgery, upholding the position of Bliss, Fish, and Bristow. It was a blow that eliminated any chance that he would avoid prison and bankruptcy without some new agreement or policy. Then, only four days later, Judge Blatchford upheld Judge Benedict's ruling quashing the indictment of wholesaler Horace Claflin. The opinion held that purchasing contraband was not a violation of the antismuggling law. This meant that several of the most prominent beneficiaries of Charley's crime could not be prosecuted without some testimony implicating them in the actual movement of goods across the border.

On April 8, Butler's wife Sarah Hildreth died. A former actress two years her husband's senior, Sarah had been Butler's love, confidante, and goad. Butler overcame his grief to forge a compromise agreement. At the end of April, Butler arranged to have Attorney General Pierrepont appoint attorney Sidney Webster as a special counsel for prosecuting Lawrence. He had already helped indict silk importer Justinian Hartley, who had testified for the state in the Des Anges trial. Afraid of Butler and desperate for the Treasury to repay him for prior work, Webster took the position. In return, Butler pressed the government to pay its debts, an act that likely pleased incorruptible Secretary of State Fish, Webster's father-in-law, who was embarrassed by his daughter's husband's whining about money.[47]

Through May, the negotiations intensified. On the seventh, a frantic Zipporah wrote Butler begging for help, complaining that Bliss "has again stated he shall try Lawrence next week and no one can prevent him." The U.S. attorney was "villainous," possessing "neither truth nor honor." In desperation, she offered her correspondence with British and American officials to the State Department, believing the letters had value for intelligence purposes. By the middle of the month, the factions had agreed upon a settlement allowing Charley to avoid prosecution and restitution in return for information about corruption and smuggling. On May 25, 1876, with "considerable mystery" in the air, Butler informed the court that Lawrence changed his plea on charges of forgery from "not guilty" to "guilty." With his friend John P. Morris and his wife Zipporah as his sureties, he posted $15,000 bond to await sentencing. Charley was a free man.[48]

ON JULY 4, 1876, the United States commemorated one hundred years of independence from England. The observance in Providence showed "unusual zest," with a "trades procession . . . four or five miles in length . . . a regatta on the Pawtucket River," as well as other exercises and orations. In Charleston, South Carolina, businesses were closed, but "the military part of the celebration was confined to the colored people, who had a parade and a reading of the Declaration of Independence" in front of a crowd of eight thousand. In Philadelphia, a magnificent International Exposition had been built in Fairmount Park. Its stellar features were a dynamo invented by American Frederick Corliss, a telephone devised by Canadian Alexander Graham Bell, and the right arm and torch of the Statue of Liberty, designed by Frenchman Frédéric Auguste Bartholdi. Attending the exposition were advocates of women's suffrage, who "endeavored . . . to show that women were as well calculated to hold positions of trust and intelligence as men."[49]

On the same day, Charley celebrated his forty-third birthday. Since his plea, observers wondered whether Lawrence would ever pay any penalty. When a reporter asked U.S. Attorney Bliss what he expected, the prosecutor replied that he "thought no sentence would be passed" but that he was not "through with him yet." By day, Bliss kept Charley in "elegantly furnished apartments," where he worked with Jayne "concocting a scheme by which a large number of merchants are to be proceeded against." Rumors flew that Butler and Jayne were to receive any moieties for frauds Charley uncovered. Still more sensational, some falsely claimed that Treasury Secretary Bristow's recent resignation had been a protest against the agreement with Lawrence.[50]

Charley's testimony led to few arrests over the coming years. Horace Brigham Claflin was a ripe target for prosecution, as his firm had unquestionably purchased smuggled silk. But Claflin's attorneys, William Evarts and Elihu Root, convinced the appellate courts to uphold the dismissal of the criminal charges and the Supreme Court to suppress the government's civil suit. Charley implicated a few officials and importers, but nearly all of them avoided punishment. One unlucky firm paid a $15,000 tax judgment, but in the end, the only member of the conspiracy sentenced to the penitentiary was Robert Des Anges.[51]

The real consequences materialized as the nation dove into another all-consuming presidential election season in 1876. Weighed down by an endless series of exposures, President Grant declined to run for a third term, something not yet barred by the Constitution. The Republicans looked past dynamic candidates such as Sen. Roscoe Conkling to pick nondescript Ohio governor Rutherford B. Hayes. An antislavery lawyer, Hayes had been a general during the Civil War before winning election to Congress and then the statehouse. Like many former soldiers, Hayes wore a long beard. With his abolitionist wife, he had five children. The Democrats meanwhile picked their third consecutive New Yorker, recently elected Governor Samuel Tilden. Rather than serving in the Union Army, Tilden had worked as a railroad attorney, eventually riding the upheaval against Tweed to the governor's mansion. Childless and never married, Tilden was the first clean-shaven major party presidential candidate since Sen. Stephen Douglas.

Although Charley was a Democrat, the Tilden campaign tried to tie the silk smuggling ring to the Republican candidate. In June, the New York Sun ran a spoof in which a "Mr. Maguffin" claimed he had asked several men "down at the Custom House" what they thought of the Hayes ticket. An "enterprising young man" from "the Appraiser's Office" who "put the figures in Charley Lawrence's invoices," called it "a roarer." Another called it a "blazer" that would excite the voters like "a house afire." When Maguffin asked him whether "the Governor will pitch in for reform?" the clerk answered, "I don't know what he'll pitch in for but will you just cast your eye on his war record? . . . He'll draw like a blast furnace!" Each of the men then claimed that he had personally served under Hayes, finding him to be a fearless hero who had survived shot and shell at Shiloh, Antietam, Gettysburg, the Wilderness, and Cold Harbor.[52]

Others settled for using the scandal to condemn the Republican

Party of New York. On August 5, 1876, David A. Wells published a screed denouncing his former friend and relative, attorney George Bliss. Bliss, he alleged, had ignored both the law and his superiors to pursue Charley on charges of smuggling. Wells implied that "Jayne, Bliss & Co." had pressured Lawrence to "arrange the necessary machinery" to extract moieties from merchants. The *Nation* amplified Wells's remarks twelve days later, contending that Bliss used the justice system to extract money from importers "for purely technical violations of the most technical and unintelligible system of revenue law in the world." In response, Bliss accused Wells of "an extraordinary combination of errors, falsehoods, and groundless charges and insinuations against one whom, from an intimate acquaintance of forty years, he knows to be influenced by motives as good as his own." Bliss then correctly noted that Butler and Jayne had considered him an obstacle, not an ally. And he defended the Lawrence settlement as necessary to punish importers who "defrauded the Government of hundreds of thousands of dollars of duties."[53]

As the *Sun* predicted, Hayes changed the subject by reminding voters about the Civil War. "Waving the bloody shirt" was still effective at a moment when southern whites were genuinely undermining gains achieved during Reconstruction. Old secessionists were regaining power. Confederate vice-president Alexander Stephens now sat in Congress. In 1873, in Colfax, Louisiana, Democrats had murdered over 150 black Republicans over possession of a county courthouse. Hayes promised to prevent the rebels from seizing control of the federal government. Moreover, the campaign wove the war into a narrative about manhood, family, morality, class, and geography. The Ohioan presented himself as a benign patriarch from the West, dedicated to reforms such as temperance. Unlike his rival, he supported "duties upon importations" as a means of promoting "American labor," in particular the ability of workingmen to support a household on their wages alone. By contrast, Republicans suggested, Tilden was an effete eastern urbanite, a sterile slacker who depended upon the votes of secessionists, Copperheads, and free-traders.

Lacking any combat experience, Tilden sought to harness those who had sacrificed themselves for the Union. As governor he appointed reformer Josephine Shaw Lowell to be the first female commissioner of the New York Board of Charities. She was the sister and widow of combat martyrs Robert Gould Shaw and Charles Russell Lowell; few women more deeply appealed to the sympathies of northeastern liberals and black voters. Tilden thus showed he would enable women themselves to address social problems. But Tilden also promised to move beyond the war. The once-seceded states had been readmitted, and the Constitution had been amended to give African-Americans legal equality and voting rights. Blacks, he contended, could defend themselves, a notion that appealed to voters more concerned with economy than justice.[54]

When November 1876 arrived and the ballots were counted, over half of American voters had selected Tilden as president. But frauds in Florida, Louisiana, Oregon, and South Carolina made twenty electoral votes suspect. In late January, Congress created a commission to determine the next president. Making the argument for Hayes were Charley Lawrence's former counsel Edwin Stoughton, as well as Horace Claflin's lawyer, William Evarts. For his team, Samuel Tilden selected lawyers including Robert Noah's supervisor, William C. Whitney. Commissioners deciding the matter included Rep. James Garfield, a close friend of David A. Wells, and Justice Stephen Field, brother of Tweed's attorney, David Dudley Field.

In the end, party loyalty determined the outcome, as Supreme Court Justice Joseph P. Bradley and seven other Republicans awarded the ten electors to Hayes. Enraged that the commission had denied their candidate the office the majority wanted him to hold, Democrats alleged bribery. Tilden himself said he went to bed believing that he had the support of Bradley only to learn that the Republicans had obtained his vote later in the night. Rumors flew that the Grand Old Party had rewarded the justice with a $200,000 emolument plus a clerkship for his son at the Port of New York. This minor appointment soothed Bradley, who had begun his own career in the Newark custom house and had long complained of his inability to obtain patronage for his relations. And it helped convince his wife, who was worried about her son's future.

Hayes was president. But rather than guarding the Civil War's legacy, protecting interracial Reconstruction governments from being usurped by former Confederates, he spent four years fighting to reorganize the New York Custom House. Hayes even pardoned Robert Des Anges in the hope that he might reveal other smugglers. On August 4, 1877, with four months remaining in his sentence, Des Anges was released from Albany Penitentiary with his debts to the government discharged. The patrician Englishman helped the U.S. attorney with some customs prosecutions, then ran a vinegar business in the city before escaping to Kansas to work as a railway clerk.[55]

PRIDE

On November 1, 1886, seventy-two-year-old Louis Bieral pushed his way into the office of Hans Beattie, the surveyor of the Port of New York, to demand he be rehired as an inspector of customs. When Beattie refused, Bieral responded, "I'll teach you to take my bread and butter" and twice fired his French .42 caliber pistol at his former boss. The first slug passed through the administrator's hand into his groin, and the second struck his heavy desk, neither producing a mortal wound. "Spanish Lew" then put the gun to his own head and pulled the trigger, but the bullet missed his skull, damaging nothing more than his hat and a window. Bieral then fled the custom house to the street, where he saw Joseph Solomon Moore, the Parsee Merchant. Bieral yelled, "You are the — who put up that job on me and got me discharged." But before he could attack the terrified free-trader, a "large and excited crowd" surrounded Bieral, allowing an auditing clerk to hold the gunman until a patrolman arrived. The officer then marched the onetime boxer, gambler, pimp, equestrian, bailiff, deputy marshal, sailor, soldier, and murderer to Old Slip police station, followed by over a thousand curiosity-seekers.[1]

Bieral had been stewing for several months. In early August, he had been working as a baggage inspector at Castle Garden, the city's entry point for immigrants, when the French ship *Champagne* arrived. Louis scrutinized a young Swiss dressmaker named Marie Mertens. Finding no silks or laces, Bieral accused Mertens of smug-

LOUIS BIERAL SHOOTING SURVEYOR OF CUSTOMS HANS BEATTIE. Courtesy
Tom Tryniski, Fulton, New York

gling her sewing machine into the United States and demanded
she pay him four dollars to secure its entry. Mertens insisted the
machine was exempt from duty, as a "tool of the trade," but Bieral
did not understand French, so he forced her to surrender two dollars, which he kept. When news of the extortion reached Surveyor
Beattie, he seized the chance to remove the man who had annoyed
the pundits since the 1850s. On September 8, the federal Civil Service commission fired him. Uncertain as to how he might support
his family, Louis asked his political patrons to plead his case, but they

were rebuffed. Ashamed, sleepless for weeks, "out of his head," Bieral finally sought the satisfactions of violence.[2]

The victim, Hans Stevenson Beattie, was a reformer. Born in Belfast, Northern Ireland, he came to America in 1865, at the age of eighteen, arriving too late and too young to be drafted into the Civil War. Beattie instead went to law school at New York University, eventually becoming the private secretary of William Whitney, the leader of the Democrats opposed to Tammany Hall. Beattie accompanied the reformer into the New York corporation council's office in 1875, where he likely met Charley Lawrence's brother-in-law, Robert Noah. Beattie had been appointed port surveyor in 1885 by newly elected president Grover Cleveland. Like the president, he supported tariff reduction, a professional civil service, and even women's rights. Liberals viewed Beattie as one of the "Best Men," deserving of government appointment. But in fact he had few real achievements. He held office solely through the sponsorship of Whitney. His political fame rested on having, in the words of one wag, "the biggest moustache, the prettiest dimple, and the slowest drawl of any man in public life."[3]

The contrast with Bieral was striking. Though now seventy-two years old, Louis did "not look over" forty; his hair appeared "thick" and his moustache "heavy," but only because he dyed them "raven black." Despite his age, he had kept his physique "square shouldered and muscular." Demonstrating his pride of office, he wore "a customs officer's suit of blue" with "the brass buttons of Uncle Sam's service," not to mention a hat trimmed with medals from his Grand Army of the Republic lodge and Civil War division. Though he was a gangster, gambler, and bully, he had been serving in the U.S. government for nearly fifty years. With the navy, in the 1830s, he had fought Sumatran pirates. As a federal deputy, in 1854, he had helped render fugitive slave Anthony Burns back to Virginia. And as a captain in the Union Army, he had rescued the corpse of Colonel Baker at Ball's Bluff. While reformers like Hans Beattie touted their honesty, intelligence, and education, Louis Bieral predicated his authority upon his death-defying national service.[4]

Bieral's attack on Beattie occurred against the backdrop of a continuing fight over America's purpose in the world. The day before the Beattie shooting, Americans went to the polls to offer their midterm judgment of President Cleveland, the first Democrat elected to the White House since 1856. Louis fired his Gallic pistol one week after the dedication of the Statue of Liberty in New York harbor, the monument to American freedom given to the United States by France ten years before. Indeed, the meaning of that symbol had already taken on a more cosmopolitan cast. Three years earlier, Horace Claflin's lawyer William Evarts had held an event to raise money for the construction of the statue's pedestal. One of the speakers was poet Emma Lazarus (likely Charley Lawrence's cousin) who wrote the words now associated with the copper-clad icon:

> *"Keep, ancient lands, your storied pomp!" cries she*
> *With silent lips. "Give me your tired, your poor,*
> *Your huddled masses yearning to breathe free,*
> *The wretched refuse of your teeming shore.*
> *Send these, the homeless, tempest-tost to me,*
> *I lift my lamp beside the golden door!"*

Lazarus defined liberty not as an idea that America exported to a monarchical Europe, but as a condition that the United States offered to immigrants. Though the poem, titled "The New Colossus," made no statement regarding tariffs, it identified pluralism as the core of American greatness. The golden door needed to be open.

During the prior decade, the fight for the custom house had escaped the confines of congressional speeches. In the aftermath of the Beattie shooting, the headline in the *National Police Gazette* was "GUITEAUED," a reference to Charles Guiteau, the assassin who had murdered President Garfield five years before, in 1881. The parallels were obvious. Bieral wanted to be reinstated at the port, while Guiteau had hoped to be named the U.S. consul in Paris. Observers painted Bieral and Guiteau as the natural products of a corrupt patronage system, which promised jobs to madmen and murderers. But it was the ferocious debate over tariffs that made the staffing of the port and consulates seem like an existential concern. To the reformers, the custom house was the instrument of tyrannical government. To the assassins, the nation was forgetting the economic principles that had saved the Union.[5]

These values had been tested by the desolation of the "Long Depression." When Rutherford B. Hayes entered the White House in March 1877, the United States was still mired in the downturn that began with the panic four years earlier. Estimates of unemployment that year ranged from five hundred thousand to three million (between 11 and 67 percent of all nonagricultural labor). New York City officials claimed that one in four laborers was out of work. The number of vagrants given relief in Massachusetts tripled. Noting the joblessness around him, economist David A. Wells unsurprisingly suggested lowering tariffs and expanding foreign trade, but generously granted that American workers might need to accept lower living standards, including the disappearance of upward mobility. Moreover, though the depression finally subsided in 1879, three years later, growth rates dropped again and continued to stagnate until 1886.[6]

On the nation's railroads, the government had violently thwarted protesting workers. Beginning in February 1877, several firms determined to break the Brotherhood of Locomotive Engineers, the strongest labor union in the nation. In July, workers walked off the job, freezing the nation's transportation network. Governors roused state guard units to forcibly subdue the strikes; then President Hayes ordered federal troops to Martinsville, Baltimore, Pittsburgh, Scranton, Philadelphia, East St. Louis, and Chicago to suppress the "Great Upheaval." Reformers like Samuel Tilden endorsed the clampdown in principle. The mill hand's friend, Benjamin Butler, said little about the strike, but showed his sympathies by inviting railroad magnate Jay Gould on a cruise to escape the stressful situation. Former president Grant announced that the strike "should have been put down with a strong hand and so summarily as to prevent a like occurrence for a generation." In 1877, the idea of a labor movement obtaining higher wages through strikes and boycotts was unthinkable to the political classes.[7]

Frustrated workers contemplated the total redefinition of the relationship between capital, labor, and the state. Not a few embraced the various radicalisms: anarchism, socialism, communism, mutualism, etc. Others chose the new Greenback Party, which proposed goosing growth rates through expanding the money supply and replacing tariffs with a graduated income tax. In 1879, newspaper editor Henry George published his bestselling novel *Progress and Poverty*, arguing that the government should replace all tariffs and excises with a single tax on land. And thousands of workers joined new unions such as the Knights of Labor, founded in 1869 to promote a "cooperative commonwealth" through the enactment of reform legislation protecting workers' rights, limiting the workday, and abolishing monopolies.

Yet neither the horrors of 1877 nor the ensuing ideological experimentation shook the conviction that American citizens needed shelter against imports. Manufacturing areas such as Pennsylvania—then the second most populous state in the Union—remained strongholds of protectionism. When Congress considered tariff reduction, unions like the Amalgamated Association of Iron, Steel, and Tin Workers rallied to defeat it. On February 10, 1878, fifteen thousand people attended a rally in Pittsburgh to hear the president of the Amalgamated proclaim, "Labor may need protection from other dangers, but that menaced by foreign competition is now the most imminent." In 1879, the Knights of Labor elected a new Grand Master Workman, Terence Powderly, who strongly supported tariffs.[8]

With voters demanding protection, the Treasury continued its war on smuggling. In July 1877, Special Treasury Agent Charles Brackett began an investigation into the National Steamship Line, claiming that crew members had smuggled $1 million in silks. Not content with the cargo, the officers seized the S.S. *Denmark* itself, a steamer valued at $300,000. The seizure infuriated the passengers, but delighted the U.S. attorney, who announced that "the Government, as well as the merchants of this city, owe a lasting debt of gratitude to Capt. Brackett and his assistants for their zeal, fidelity and ceaseless vigilance, which have resulted in the exposure of this great fraud." As the months went on, the United States filed a claim against a second ship, the S.S. *England*, worth $200,000. Juries convicted the purser and dock superintendent, sentencing them to two years in prison and a $1,000 fine. After over a year, the U.S. attorney recommended the government release the ships in return for a payment of $10,000, arguing that condemnation was unfair to the unwitting stockholders and bad for commerce at the port.[9]

Investigators also uncovered revenue fraud among the city's sugar refiners, a powerful industry tied to Democratic reformers. In March 1877, refiners insisted that surveyor Gen. George H. Sharpe dismiss customs inspector William H. Grace for drunkenness and blackmail. An immigrant from Ireland, Grace was a popular Brooklyn Republican who had worked at the port for six years. He alleged that the sugar firms feared him because he knew about their bribery and smuggling. Grace's resentment festered. On July 19, 1877, he told a friend that he planned to "catch the cowardly poltroon ... by the throat" and "break every bone in his body" unless Sharpe repudiated the charges. The next day, Grace, a "large powerful man," attacked Sharpe, grabbing his neck, tearing his collar, and using his "fist like a sledge hammer" to bruise "his face and head." Sharpe claimed he was ambushed; Grace insisted that he had tried to shake Sharpe's hand, only to be spat at and called "a damned scoundrel."[10]

An overflow audience composed of "the political and personal friends of the principals" attended Grace's trial. His attorney emphasized the sugar conspiracy, but the judge deemed such evidence irrelevant. The prosecution asked the defendant to apologize, but Grace refused, stating that "he had done nothing that should cause him to blush; had he done less he would have been less than a man." On September 24, the jury found Grace guilty. The judge sentenced him to four months in Blackwell's Island penitentiary. While his lawyer tried to free him, he waited in New York's Tombs, growing steadily more paranoid. He contended his trial was "one of the most outrageous on record" and an outgrowth of "as complete a despotism . . . as ever existed in this or any other country." Sugar refiners had conspired with Surveyor Sharpe, Collector Chester Arthur, and others to destroy him. In his mania, Grace blamed a "German Jew jury" for his conviction, insinuating that such men sympathized with smugglers.[11]

But the convict's fortunes soon changed. After two months, the governor pardoned Grace. The Treasury assigned an agent to investigate whether refiners were coloring their sugar to make it appear cruder and thus subject to lower rates of duty. Grace obtained a meeting with President Hayes and Treasury Secretary John Sherman, both of whom assured him that his reports had been found correct. An unusual combination of protectionist and reformer, Sherman initiated a new set of policies calibrated to stem sugar smuggling and undervaluation.[12]

The allegations of sugar smuggling riled the public as well. In 1878, free-trade advocates initiated a congressional investigation of the sugar frauds. The hearings were so crowded that the New York Times reporter complained about the "great annoyance" caused by the "mob of loafers who seize upon the vacant chairs and force themselves between the witnesses and those having business in the room, rendering the testimony inaudible." In the next year, Grace, economist David A. Wells, and an author calling himself "A Workingman" all published books addressing the problem. In January 1879, citizens called a mass meeting at Chickering Hall, where some accused the "sugar ring" of cheating the government out of $10 million per year (about $225 million today) through discoloration, adulteration, and false weights. The largest firms tried to fill the theater, hiring "rough-looking men," to whom the police denied admission. The refiners denied the charges. As the two sides jockeyed for control, the meeting grew heated, but the police prevented fisticuffs, and they adjourned without enacting any resolutions.[13]

SUCH EXPOSURES ENCOURAGED the Hayes administration to assert control over the Port of New York. In April 1877, Treasury Secretary Sherman initiated the so-called Jay Commission hearings on conditions in the custom house. Explicitly referencing the Lawrence silk scandal and the sugar frauds, the committee argued for a 20 percent reduction in staff, the depoliticization of appointments, reorganization of the weighing division, and the transformation of the port's system of appraisal. Prior hearings had revealed inefficiency, partisanship, and corruption at the Port, and previous collectors, including Chester Arthur, had made similar recommendations. But unlike past presidents, Hayes appeared genuinely committed to acting. In September, he wrote to Sherman announcing that the "collection of revenues" should be "free from partisan control and organized on a strictly business basis." Egged on by Secretary of State William Evarts, Hayes decided to remove both Arthur and naval officer Alonzo Cornell to make room for men who might professionalize the port. With his term about to expire, Surveyor Sharpe declined renomination, allowing his position to be restaffed as well.[14]

The main obstacle to Hayes's plan was New York senator Roscoe Conkling. Now all but forgotten, Conkling was in his time loved and hated by millions of Americans. He was tall and physically imposing, with a handsome face, well-groomed red beard, and hair he carefully wound into a "Hyperion curl" upon his Jovian brow. At a time when speeches could shape politics, he was known as a powerful orator. As the head of the Republican Party of New York, a crucial swing state, Conkling had significant sway over who could become president. Moreover, following Grant's departure from the White House, the senator became the leader of what remained of the post-war Radical majority. Calling themselves the "Stalwarts," these Republicans became the foremost advocates not only of protective tariffs for northern industries, but also of the legal rights of Southern blacks. As a consequence, Conkling was revered by African-Americans in his lifetime, Frederick Douglass classing him with Grant, Sumner, Butler, Wade, and Stevens.

In order to secure the fruits of Northern victory, however, Conkling engaged in the ruthless promotion of his core constituencies: Union Army veterans and black politicians, as well as clients such as Arthur and Cornell. He needed to control the custom house to repay his supporters with jobs. Indeed Conkling's own sister, author Margaret C. C. Steele, had worked as an inspectress at the port since 1869. Liberals caricatured Conkling as a corrupt machine boss because they had soured on Reconstruction, making them blind to Conkling's main virtue: his racial egalitarianism. His egotism deepened their contempt. Conkling brooked no slights from men he considered his inferiors, a group to which the new president belonged.[15]

For many years, historians painted the fight between Hayes and Conkling as the first major skirmish in the war between civil service reformers and corrupt machine politicians. Such authors presented Hayes as an idealist trying to transform the government from a sectional, partisan instrument, benefiting politicians, Union Army veterans, and free blacks, to an institution dedicated to the impartial administration of laws benefiting the whole nation. Other scholars have deflated the reformers' rhetoric, suggesting that liberals simply used concepts such as nationalism, nonpartisanship, and efficiency to place their own friends in positions of power. By this logic, Hayes and Conkling struggled because they were the leaders of rival factions who had both vied for the presidency. Such scholars argue that Evarts spitefully retaliated against the Stalwarts for impeding his own efforts at securing the Republican nomination for governor in 1876.

Such interpretations ignore the fact that the port was an active instrument of protectionism, an agency dedicated to the regulation of international trade. The custom house was not simply a place of employment, and its purpose was not merely to collect revenues. Its mission was ideological. Southern whites and northern reformers formed a temporary coalition dedicated not only to a professional civil service, but also to lowering duties and ending Reconstruction. And the intermittent rigor of the custom house during the Grant administration had infuriated wealthy merchants of both parties. Secretary of State Evarts himself had represented wholesale dry goods merchant Hiram Claflin against charges of smuggling in 1875. By challenging Conkling's control over the port, the president sought to tame what he believed to be a renegade government agency harassing respectable businessmen.

Hayes's choice for the new collector of the port—Theodore Roosevelt Sr., the father of the future president—illustrated his desire for a less aggressive custom house. The scion of one of the city's oldest Knickerbocker families, Roosevelt was not a successful businessman. Indeed, his firm had failed in 1873, forcing his family to live off vast tracts of inherited real estate. He had no government experience, not even in the military. A supporter of the North, only twenty-nine years old in 1861, he nonetheless paid a substitute to serve for him in the Union Army out of respect for his Georgia-born, slaveholding wife. Nor was Roosevelt especially sympathetic to the port's mission. Before the depression, he had owned a window glass–importing firm, plying the same goods as accused smugglers Platt & Boyd. He was also close friends with William E. Dodge, another businessman pursued by Treasury agents. But Roosevelt was a respected philanthropist opposed to Conkling, and this was sufficient. Hayes nominated him to take the port away from Stalwarts and give it to the importers themselves.

To rally opposition in the Senate, Conkling savaged Hayes's supporters, accusing them of being effete amateurs. They were "the

man-milliners, the dilletanti [sic], and the carpet-knights of politics"
and "worthies" who

> [m]asquerade as reformers. Their vocation and ministry is to
> lament the sins of other people. Their stock in trade is rancid,
> canting self-righteousness. They are wolves in sheep's cloth-
> ing. Their real object is office and plunder. When Dr. Johnson
> defined patriotism as the last refuge of the scoundrel, he was
> unconscious of the then undeveloped capabilities and uses of
> the word "Reform."

In a close vote, Conkling convinced his peers to reject Roosevelt.
Then on February 9, 1878, the importer died of a tumor at the young
age of forty-six.[16]

Hayes successfully installed a new surveyor, General Edwin A.
Merritt, but the custom house violently resisted reorganization. Noting that smugglers developed suspicious relationships with particular officers, Secretary Sherman ordered that "[n]o entry clerk" be
"allowed to pass habitually the entries presented by one broker or
firm." But importers often preferred specific clerks because their
knowledge made them more efficient. On February 16, 1878, the
day the rule went into effect, "700 angry, excited men" crowded the
rotunda, "each one striving to get his entry passed so that he might go
about his business." The merchants tried "cajoling, bribery, denun-
ciations, and oaths" but all were "in vain." Soon the clerks "replied
to abuse with abuse," and the importers began "fighting among
themselves," as the "packed mass of sweltering humanity swayed
and struggled savagely for precedence." Some "scrawled" "uncom-
plimentary allusions" about Sherman on the posted announcement.
Collector Chester Arthur—who was still in office, pending the confirmation of a replacement—called for men to suppress the "continual
riot." "Indignant" businessmen argued that "only a few importers"
engaged in bribery, so the new rule did "no good whatever" while

inflicting "great annoyance and expense upon a class of merchants whom the Government should rather strive to accommodate as far as reasonable."[17]

The feud between Hayes and Conkling lingered through 1878, as the senator stymied the president's attempt at replacing the other top officials at the port. Finally, Hayes decided that the wisest move was to elevate Surveyor Merritt to collector. Conkling responded by pointing out the reformers' hypocrisy, releasing their letters to Arthur soliciting custom-house jobs for their friends. One explosive dispatch came from Supreme Court Justice Joseph Bradley, the 1877 electoral commissioner who had handed the presidency to Hayes, requesting a customs clerkship for his son. Nevertheless, on February 3, 1879, President Hayes pinned his opponent. Ignoring the damning correspondence, the Senate confirmed Merritt and two other nominees. The next day, the front page of the *New York Times* declared "The Long Contest Ended." Reformers celebrated. Liberal editor E. L. Godkin called it "an effective blow struck at what is worst in the present system."[18]

LITTLE MORE THAN a year later, in the summer of 1880, the nation once again prepared for a presidential election. The race was wide open, as President Hayes had vowed to serve only one term. After thirty-five deadlocked votes at the Republican National Convention, the delegates chose James Garfield of Ohio. Garfield had a somewhat unusual pedigree for a politician. Losing his father at a young age, he grew up in relative poverty in rural Ohio. Performing odd jobs, he managed to fund his education at Western Reserve Eclectic Institute (subsequently Hiram College) and then Williams College in Massachusetts. After receiving his degree, he became a Classics instructor at Hiram and began engaging in antislavery politics. Sick of teaching and needing to support his family, he became an attorney and won a seat in the Ohio State Senate. By the Civil War, he was prominent enough in Republican circles to be commissioned a colonel in the

Union Army, rising up in time to become a general. After Appomattox, he was elected repeatedly to Congress. There he developed a reputation as a staunch Republican, but one who was honest, intelligent, and liberal in his sympathies.

If Garfield made an attractive candidate in the general election, however, he lacked the support of the party faithful, who had wanted a Stalwart such as Conkling or a rejuvenated Grant. Searching for a vice-presidential nominee who could appease the base, Garfield selected Chester Arthur, the former collector of the Port of New York. The choice was bizarre. Hayes had removed Arthur, seeing him as an obstacle to reform at best, and crooked at worst. Arthur had no constituency among the voters; indeed, he had never held an elected position of any kind. Still more confounding, Arthur's patron, Senator Conkling, wanted him to reject the nod, believing his faction's support worth a position carrying more patronage. But Arthur accepted the offer, risking his backer's wrath in return for a chance at greater glory.

Adding Arthur to the ticket did not dispel doubts about Garfield's protectionist convictions. Close friends with David A. Wells, Garfield belonged to England's Cobden Club, an institution at the center of protectionist conspiracy theories. Garfield insisted that the club had made him an "honorary member" as "a compliment" after he gave a speech favoring "sound currency." To allay fears, the nominee called upon important Stalwarts such as Pennsylvania congressman William Kelley to testify as to his soundness on the tariff question. Yet the rumors did not die. The *Washington Post* called him a "trickster," citing specific speeches to show his disdain for tariffs. The United Labor League inveighed against the Republican candidate, saying he had "sold himself to England," making himself an agent for the "free traders of London," who were sending "one millions of pounds" to Indiana to elect him.[19]

By obscuring his free-trade leanings, Garfield managed to defeat Democratic candidate General Winfield Scott Hancock in November.

Pennsylvania, the nation's second most populous state, was a manufacturing center and thus deeply protectionist. It was to win the Commonwealth that Democrats chose Hancock in 1880, a candidate who not only hailed from outside Philadelphia, but also was a commander of Union forces at Gettysburg. But Hancock undermined these efforts when he told a reporter that the tariff was a "local question . . . that the general government seldom cares to interfere with." Hancock's gaffe scared enough voters to allow Garfield to win the Keystone State by just over thirty-seven thousand votes, only 4 percent of the ballots cast.[20]

Once in office, however, Garfield followed his predecessor in denying the Stalwarts control of the Port of New York. For collector, Garfield chose William H. Robertson, a career politician whose only qualification was his hostility to Conkling. Enraged by Garfield's ingratitude, the senator fought the appointment. But when Conkling realized he did not have the votes to stop Robertson, he decided to protest by resigning his Senate seat on May 14, 1881, pressuring the other member of the state's senatorial delegation, Thomas Platt, to do the same. The two politicians assumed that they would be reselected by the New York Assembly—at the time, senators were chosen by the state legislatures, not by popular vote—so they were startled when that body chose less controversial replacements. Conkling never again held high office.[21]

Stalwarts raged, and none more than Charles Julius Guiteau. Forty years old, Guiteau was raised in a midwestern middle-class family headed by his grandfather, a veteran of the War of 1812 and former customs collector at Sandy Creek, New York. As an adult, Guiteau wandered from one bungled scheme to the next. He decided to join the Oneida Colony, a utopian commune near Utica, New York, whose founder, John Humphrey Noyes, favored the principle of "complex marriage," under which residents chose bedmates according to their changing affinities. The colony manufactured traps, silverware, and silk thread, their products once receiving a prize from none other than Horace Greeley. But Guiteau was a poor worker and unpopular with the commune's women, who nicknamed him "Charles Git-out." After five years, Noyes asked him to depart. Moving to Chicago, Guiteau tried to start religious newspapers, filed libel suits, gave theological speeches, and published a companion to the Bible. When these ventures failed, he survived on money earned collecting bills, borrowed from relatives, or stolen from his clients.[22]

Guiteau dabbled in politics. In 1872, he stumped for Greeley, but by 1880 he fell behind the Stalwarts. Guiteau may have liked Conkling from his years in Oneida, not far from the senator's hometown. Perhaps he identified with Chester Arthur, a customs collector like his grandfather. Or maybe he preferred the Stalwarts because they opposed President Hayes, who was the first cousin of his nemesis, John Humphrey Noyes. In the fall of 1880, Guiteau delivered a stemwinder on Garfield's behalf, contending that the Democratic candidate would deliver the nation to the "rebels," empty the treasury, induce a panic, and provoke civil war. After the election, Guiteau wrote to the victorious president-elect, attributing his victory to the tariff and the Stalwart faction. As repayment for his imagined services during the campaign, he demanded a posting as U.S. consul general to Paris, a position responsible for certifying the value of French imports to the United States. But Secretary of State James G. Blaine refused to see him.[23]

By June 8, 1881, Charles had decided his course. He convinced a relative to lend him $15, then purchased a snub-nosed .45 caliber British "Bulldog" revolver. On July 2, 1881, Garfield was walking with Blaine outside the Baltimore and Potomac Railway station in Washington, D.C., planning to travel to Williamstown, Massachusetts, to attend his alma mater's graduation ceremonies. Having trailed the president for several weeks, Guiteau saw his chance. He fired twice into the president's back and ran for the exit, but a police officer grabbed him in the station's reception room. Guiteau put up no fight. "All right," he replied, "I did it and will go to jail for it. I am a

Stalwart, and Arthur will be president." Guiteau was correct, but not immediately. Though the president's injuries were not initially fatal, his physicians' probing of the wounds led to an infection that killed him on September 19.[24]

In his broken mind, Guiteau sought more than personal revenge. He saw Garfield's betrayal of the Stalwarts as treason. In his mental illness, he believed God wanted to save the United States by bringing Chester Arthur, the foe of smugglers, to the presidency. The background noise for the murder was the long-running scuffle over the custom house. A jury convicted Charles Guiteau on January 25, 1882, and the judge sentenced him to death. Before he was hanged on the last day of June, he read a poem he had written, imagined in the style of a "child babbling to his mamma and his papa" declaring, "I saved my party and my land, Glory hallelujah!"

CONTRARY TO COMMON PERCEPTION, Garfield's death at the hands of an office seeker did not immediately spur a wave of good-government reforms. In fact, President Arthur did not sign the Pendleton Civil Service Act, which began the professionalization of government workers, until January 16, 1883, during the lame-duck session following the bruising 1882 midterm elections. One newspaper mocked "the frantic efforts of the Republican managers to save something from the November wreck." Suddenly, "all up and down the land a chorus of voices is heard in favor of reform." The "mania" for lower tariffs and a nonpartisan civil service consumed both "Garfield Republicans" and "Guiteau Republicans," the "ultra-protectionist" and "his free trade friend," the "rabid spoilsman" and the "top-tier reformer." By passing the act in January, Republicans sought to preempt the new Democratic House from doing the same and getting the credit.[25]

The mourning nation wanted to reduce tariffs, but lacked the political will to do so. Shortly after taking office, President Arthur recommended the creation of a commission to study the matter and make recommendations to Congress. Congress quickly agreed.

Though Arthur appointed protectionists to the commission, the members took their job seriously, traveling around the nation and hearing over six hundred witnesses. Their final report defied expectations and recommended lower tariffs, delighting both liberals and protectionists, who sensed that high rates had become a political liability. But when the president pushed for Congress to enact the recommendations, the legislators balked. Finally, in January 1883, after the Democrats dominated the midterm elections, the lame-duck Republican Congress passed a new tariff act that barely lowered duties at all.[26]

Yet Garfield's death felt like a watershed. The Pendleton Act only made 10 percent of custom-house jobs subject to civil service examinations, but it began the achingly slow transformation of the port into a nonpartisan institution. The new revenue bill was dispiriting, but the tariff commission suggested that protectionism was waning. Combined with the Democrats' overwhelming victory in the 1882 elections, the nation seemed to be rebelling against the nationalism of the post–Civil War era.[27]

THE MODERN RIGHT to privacy emerged from this fight over smuggling and the power of the custom house. And remarkably, the key decision involved Edwin A. Boyd, the junior partner in the glass-importing firm of Platt & Boyd, which had played such a prominent role in the events of the early 1870s. In 1882, the reorganized firm of E. A. Boyd & Sons had won the contract to provide plate glass for the Philadelphia custom house. Under the agreement, the secretary of the treasury allowed Boyd to import, free of duty, 9,222 square feet of glass worth $4,181. To save time, the Treasury allowed Boyd to take glass from his warehouse, then to import later an equal amount of replacement material duty free. But when Boyd asked for permission to land two additional shipments in the summer of 1884, Treasury officials became suspicious, revoked Boyd's permit, and confiscated the second delivery. Upon investigation, they concluded Boyd had imported $48,000 worth of glass free of duty, over ten times the amount stipulated in the contract.[28]

The evidence crossed the desk of Elihu Root, U.S. attorney for the Southern District. Root had dealt with smuggling before, as one of several defense attorneys for H. B. Claflin & Co. in the 1875 silk-smuggling scandal. To strengthen his case, Root obtained a court order demanding that Boyd produce a receipt proving their guilt. In November 1884, the jury returned after only five minutes' deliberation. The windows were contraband, subject to condemnation and sale. The panel also recommended the indictment of Boyd and his twenty-six-year-old son George. The criminal trial began May 1, 1885, and lasted two months. As in the civil suit, the criminal case ended in a rapid verdict for the prosecution. The public sympathy Boyd had enjoyed in 1873 was now gone.[29]

On June 30, 1885, Edwin and George Boyd faced sentencing. Stepping up to Judge Benedict "slowly, with a depressed look on his face," "the old man" asked the court to spare his son from a prison spell. Concluding that George was only a "nominal partner," the court granted the request and sentenced him to a $1,000 fine. But the judge sentenced the elder Boyd to two years in Kings County Penitentiary in the Crow Hill section of Brooklyn (what is now called Crown Heights). For several days, sixty-four-year-old Boyd experienced "nervous prostration and kidney troubles" and was unable to eat. His family physicians were called to Ludlow Street to examine him. They testified that "fright" over "the idea of incarceration in the penitentiary" had "broken him down completely," making it dangerous to transport him across the river. In light of his condition, officials postponed Boyd's transfer, but on July 6 he was taken to Brooklyn. Perhaps to ease his anxiety, his guardians allowed him to get very drunk. He gave his seal ring, scarf pin, and watch and chain to his son, then "staggered" into the prison.[30]

From his prison cell, Boyd appealed the condemnation of his glass, worth $25,000, contending that the section of the Revenue Act of

1874 providing for demand of the receipt proving his guilt violated
the Fourth Amendment prohibition of unreasonable seizures. His
lawyers argued that the customs could seize any contraband, but they
did not have authority to command access to private papers looking
for evidence of guilt. Having litigated this issue in 1874, Boyd knew
the precedents were against him. But the seizures and criminal trials had nearly ruined his business, and he likely hoped to recoup
some sort of legacy for his children. To represent him on appeal, he
hired the successor to the firm that had defended Charley Lawrence a
decade before.

Since the *Stockwell* ruling in 1871, the Supreme Court had changed
markedly. The dissenters, Joseph Bradley, Stephen Field, and Samuel Miller, remained on the court, but newer justices sympathized
with Hayes's effort to reform the custom house. Justice Stanley Matthews was an "intimate" acquaintance of President Hayes who helped
secure Merritt his appointment as collector of the Port of New York.
Chief Justice Morrison Waite was Hayes's "lifelong friend." Justice
Horace Gray was a Boston Brahmin married to the daughter of Justice Matthews. Of the nine justices on the court in 1885, only one,
Samuel Blatchford, an Arthur appointee, could be seen as a Stalwart.[31]

The judges of this era saw legislatures as reckless. Though historians often describe them as hostile to government, they actually
lacked any uniform or absolute view of the state. Rather, judges of
the 1880s detested two types of laws. The first was "class legislation," that is, acts giving benefits exclusively to specific groups. And
the second were laws interfering with the right to property, liberty
of contract, and freedom of association. This made them suspicious of policies designed to assist workers, constrain businesses,
and guarantee equality. For instance, in the *Jacobs* case of 1885, the
New York Supreme Court voided a law barring cigar manufacturing in tenement houses, arguing that the state had no authority to
interfere with an apartment dweller's enjoyment of his rooms. In
the *Civil Rights Cases* (1883), the U.S. Supreme Court struck down

the Civil Rights Act of 1875, which outlawed racial discrimination on railways, buses, hotels, theaters, and restaurants. Writing the majority decision, Justice Bradley concluded that the Reconstruction amendments did not authorize the federal government to prohibit private acts of racism.[32]

In February 1886, the Supreme Court decided in Boyd's favor, overturning the precedents it had set in *Stockwell* and *Platt & Boyd*, and unanimously holding the revenue statutes unconstitutional. Justice Bradley's majority opinion defined a sphere of privacy for defendants, validating Boyd's Fourth Amendment arguments. Moreover, Bradley also enunciated an argument Boyd's attorneys never presented, namely that the seizure of Boyd's glass, though civil in form, was "quasi-criminal" in fact. That is, the government confiscated the contraband from the accused smuggler as punishment for his crime. Thus, Boyd possessed the Fifth Amendment privileges against self-incrimination that permitted him to refuse to produce a receipt showing his own guilt. Though Justice Miller and Chief Justice Waite rejected Bradley's expansive reading of the Fourth Amendment in a concurrence, they agreed that the law had unlawfully forced Boyd to incriminate himself. Even Justice Blatchford—a Stalwart Republican and the author of the *Platt & Boyd* decision—supported Bradley's majority opinion.[33]

In stirring language, Bradley rebuked the government. Like reformer David A. Wells, he harkened back to smuggler John Hancock and the American Revolution. Bradley compared the revenue laws to the writs of assistance, vague warrants that British revenue officers had used to search the property of suspected smugglers. He insisted that Root's demand for Boyd's receipt cut to "the very essence of constitutional liberty and security," applying "to all invasions on the part of the government . . . of the sanctity of a man's home and the privacies of life." Bradley insisted he was not concerned with the mere "breaking of his doors, and the rummaging of his drawers," but rather "the invasion of his indefeasible right of personal security, personal liberty and private property, where that right has never been forfeited by his conviction of some public offence."[34]

The decision also embodied the court's understanding of reform. For lawyers of their time and place, the custom house was the center of political corruption and government tyranny. But Justice Bradley's rhetoric also reflected his own personal grievances. He was still outraged that Senator Conkling had revealed his private letters asking Collector Arthur to appoint his son to the custom house. Publishing the correspondence had fed rumors of his corruption and partiality, destroying what he fancied was his sterling reputation (in fact undone by the casual racism and misogyny of his other opinions). Bradley identified with Edwin Boyd, who seemed the continuous victim of Arthur and his subordinates, Jayne and Root. And the justice wanted to rebuke the Stalwarts who embarrassed him in 1879.

In doing so, the court essentially loosened restrictions on mercantile firms and corporations. The court did nothing to stop the casual inspection of bodies, steamer trunks, and personal possessions. Bradley's opinion clearly distinguished between the unconstitutional seizure of private papers for the purposes of investigation and the lawful confiscation of "stolen or forfeited goods, or goods liable to duties and concealed to avoid the payment thereof." He placed no limits on the overt profiling of Jews, Asians, and other suspect populations. Indeed, by making it more difficult for Treasury officials to catch the undervaluations of importers, the *Boyd* decision actually shifted the focus of custom-house investigations away from corporations and towards the less financially significant frauds of immigrants, tourists, and professional smugglers.[35]

Nor did the Supreme Court immediately use the *Boyd* precedent to expand protection against unreasonable searches. On May 4, 1886, anarchists rallied in Chicago's Haymarket Square on behalf of striking reaper workers and to demand the eight-hour day. Police arrived, but before they could suppress the demonstration, someone detonated an explosive. The blast and ensuing gunfire left seven officers dead and sixty injured. Seeking to connect August Spies, a radical newspaper editor, to the bombing, police broke into his office and seized a letter from the author of a pamphlet on bomb making. Sentenced to death, Spies hired Benjamin Butler, still recalled as the worker's friend, to appeal his case to the Supreme Court. Butler, of course, had long advocated the government's authority to seize private property, but he nonetheless cited the *Boyd* decision, arguing that the letter was tainted evidence. But the Supreme Court refused to consider the anarchists' case. Spies and three others died on the gallows on November 11, 1887.[36]

Only over time did Bradley's opinion become the basis for the modern right to privacy. In a 1928 dissent, Justice Louis Brandeis argued that *Boyd*'s ringing endorsement of freedom would be remembered "as long as civil liberty lives in the United States." It was the key precedent for the exclusionary rule, enunciated in famous decisions such as *Mapp v. Ohio* (1961), and thus central to debates over the authority of police, receiving plaudits from Senate Watergate Committee counsel Samuel Dash and criticism from Supreme Court justice Samuel Alito Jr. It was likewise cited in cases defining a right to sexual privacy, such as *Griswold v. Connecticut* (1965).[37]

Edwin Boyd himself benefited little from the ruling. He won a new civil trial but remained in Kings County Penitentiary, where an illness made his left lung "useless." On April 10, 1886, President Grover Cleveland pardoned him. By then, Boyd was so weak the prison infirmary dared not release him. The next day, Boyd defied doctors and left. Breathing free air did not save him. Boyd died two years later, and by 1890 his business was no more.[38]

THE 1884 ELECTION of Grover Cleveland, the first Democratic president in twenty-eight years, showed that protectionism no longer commanded an automatic majority. Civil War nationalism was waning.

Between 1884 and 1886, death claimed Judah Benjamin, Ulysses S. Grant, George McClellan, Winfield Scott Hancock, and Chester Arthur. Republican candidate James Blaine stumped on the tariff, but many Americans asked why the nation's industries still needed shelter. Why, with neither soldiers at war nor ships at sea, did the government require so much revenue? The Greenback Party nominated Benjamin Butler, but his platform appealed to laborers with soft money, factory inspection, and the abolition of child labor, not with the tariff. In the end, patriotic rhetoric sank Blaine. When one of his supporters claimed that the Democrats were the party of "Rum, Romanism, and Rebellion," Cleveland turned the religious attack against the Republicans to win a narrow victory.

Under the auspices of the new Civil Service Act, Cleveland continued the process of restaffing the custom house. Hit especially hard were African-American Treasury workers. Unable to find black Democrats to appoint to the Philadelphia custom house, Cleveland turned to Greenback supporters like Alexander G. Davis. In the end, he usually replaced African-Americans with whites. He fired navy veteran Isaac Mullen from the Boston custom house. Later that year, his secretary of the treasury ordered the eviction of Peter Downing, who owned a small eatery on the first floor of the New York Custom House. In June 1886, the Democratic management of the port terminated custom-house messenger Peter Vogelsang. By 1888, only five black men held jobs at the Port of New York, all of them messengers and porters.[39]

Cleveland used charges of smuggling to remove old Republicans from the employment rolls. In 1885, the Treasury dismissed two long-serving agents from the Port of New York for accepting bribes from Irish linen importers, but refused to reinstate them after their acquittals. Yet such charges were merely instrumental. In 1887, the *Bangor Daily Whig & Courier* grumbled that President Cleveland had appointed Samuel D. Leavitt, a man once convicted of smuggling morphine, to the position of collector of customs for the district of

Passamaquoddy, Maine. Bordering on New Brunswick, the "Quoddy" had been a center for contraband trade since the Revolution. To the protectionists, it seemed as if the world was upside down.[40]

LOUIS BIERAL'S TRIAL began in January 1887. His attorney was former Tammany judge George M. Curtis, who contended that Bieral had been insane at the time of the crime. Defense witnesses described his confusion before the shooting, his threats to kill himself and his family, and the head injury he sustained during the Civil War. The defense's expert had "no doubt" that Bieral "at the time of the shooting was insane." The prosecution called its own alienist, Allan McLane Hamilton, the grandson of Founder Alexander Hamilton. Spending an hour with Louis, the doctor concluded that Bieral was able "to distinguish between right and wrong" and thus "quite competent."

Curtis sowed sympathy for Bieral by invoking his war heroism. Then, "in stentorian tones," he contended that Bieral had been wrongly dismissed. When Curtis asked Surveyor Beattie whether he opposed "having such old men in the service," the surveyor answered that "the public service should not be obstructed by the presence of dead wood." Curtis called Gen. Daniel Sickles, former congressman, minister to Spain, and a Union commander who had lost his leg at the Battle of Gettysburg. Louis was "as brave a man as ever drew a sword," Sickles testified; "[h]e wasn't a man to do a cowardly act in his right mind." Asked if Bieral was a "political heeler," the general answered, "By no means. He belonged to a class of men that doesn't exist now, such as Bill Poole, Tom Hyer, and Dutch Charlie [Duane]," champion boxers who guarded the polls. Seeing Bieral before the shooting, Sickles found him incoherent. The aging pugilist told the general, with a "desolate, spare look" on his face, "I have no friends. They're tired of me—all of us soldier boys."[41]

Returning on the morning of January 28, the jury found Bieral guilty. But "in consideration of his former services to his country, his extreme age, and previous apparent good record," they "unanimously and strongly" recommended that he receive "the mercy of the court." Before a courtroom full of supporters, Judge Benedict sentenced Louis to five years in Auburn Penitentiary, half as long as it might have been. Auburn released him a year and a half early for good behavior, and later that year, Republican president Benjamin Harrison pardoned him. But his age and past injuries left him "hardly fitted to keep up the struggle for a livelihood." In 1893, he retired to the Hampton Home for Disabled Veterans in Virginia, where he was buried almost seven years later. As they had during his incarceration, newspapers collected charity to support his widow, specifically citing his heroism at Ball's Bluff.[42]

LUXURY

William C. Whitney wanted a new home. In 1889, he was returning to New York City after four years in Washington, D.C.,
working as Grover Cleveland's secretary of the navy. Whitney
was a native of Massachusetts, where his father had once been a collector of customs associated with Benjamin Butler. But Manhattan
was where he had made his political fortune, serving as the city's corporation counsel. And it was the logical place from which to administer his far-flung investments in streetcars, steamships, coal, iron, and
finance. Historian Henry Adams jealously wrote that "after having
gratified every ambition and swung the country almost at his will,"
Whitney "had thrown away the usual objects of political ambition
like the ashes of smoked cigarettes; had turned to other amusements,
satiated every taste, gorged every appetite, won every object that New
York afforded, and not yet satisfied, had carried his field of activity
abroad." Still not appeased, Whitney then brought the fruits of his
global dominance back to the city again.[1]

Whitney hired architect Stanford White to remodel his Fifth Avenue mansion. Thirty-six years old, White was already one of the
nation's most successful architects. With his partners, "Stanny"
defined the neoclassical style, combining modern materials such as
red brick with columns borrowed from ancient Greece and Rome. A
brilliant decorator, White spent time every year in Europe, buying up
antiquities for his wealthy clients. In short, he unchained himself

from the ambiguous patriotism of his father, literary critic Richard Grant White. Though the senior White was called a "thoroughbred man of the world," he spent most of his life working in the New York Custom House, guarding the nation against foreign merchandise. A peerless expert on the plays of William Shakespeare, Richard Grant White only visited England once, at the age of fifty-five.[2]

On April 4, 1889, Special Treasury Agent George Simmonds raided Allard & Son, a French firm with a store on Fifth Avenue specializing in European furnishings. Simmonds alleged that Allard's American representative, Paul Roulez, had hidden paintings, curtains, and tapestries inside furniture, including a $20,000 Rembrandt that, because of its age, could have entered free of duty. The newspaper stories screamed "Smuggling for High Life." Despite his relationship with the Paris firm, Stanford White was not mentioned, but Secretary Whitney was, alongside several Vanderbilts. Reporters concluded that Whitney and the other customers neither knew of, nor benefited from the smuggling, but given their wealth they might never have noticed. If a disgruntled former employee had not reported Roulez to officials, the scam would have continued indefinitely.[3]

If arrests are any measure, art smuggling was something new. Up to 1883, the tariff on paintings was only 10 percent, and the law exempted works intended for museums or produced by Americans living abroad. For this reason, customs officers attended more to obscene images, which were outlawed altogether by the Comstock Act of 1873. They were also concerned with cast statues, such as the lead allegedly converted into busts by Phelps, Dodge & Co. in 1865 to avoid the duties on manufactured metal. More importantly, the great era of American mansion building had not yet begun in the early 1870s, and thus there was less need for imported art and furnishings.

The rise of new fortunes meant greater demand for European paintings and decorative objects, which led to smuggling. In 1876, a Mr. R. Guerrero exhibited Spanish paintings in Peru, then brought them into the United States for sale. Customs officials appraised them at $1,700, only to learn that a merchant named Francis Tomes of Maiden Lane had purchased the lot for $6,000 and was auctioning them off for even more. An embarrassed Treasury sought to confiscate the paintings, but Tomes resisted, arguing that he was not responsible for the agents' blunder. Similar incidents occurred in 1882, when officials seized collections of ancient terra-cottas from French archaeologist Henri de Morgan and Italian paintings from collector Ludovic de Spiridon. In both cases, agents investigated the objects after they had passed through the custom house, alleging that the owners had lied about their value or purpose. Either importers had exploited disagreements about the art's worth, or perhaps subjectivity had stymied assessment itself.

The so-called Mongrel Tariff of 1883 sought to prevent the wealthy from importing foreign art, imposing a 40 percent tax on imported paintings and sculpture produced since 1700. Philadelphia Republican Thomas Corwin Donaldson lobbied for the provision, arguing that American artists needed protection because European painters received direct subsidies from their governments. Though the nation's artists protested, Donaldson had support from his close colleague, William "Pig Iron" Kelley, one of the last remaining Radical Republicans in Congress, a leading protectionist, and the chairman of the House Ways and Means Committee. Legal importations of paintings and statuary promptly fell to one-quarter their prior level, while Treasury agents routinely seized contraband art.[4]

Despite Donaldson's claims, protectionism was becoming less about guarding American workers against competition—though this strain of thought never disappeared—and more about preventing the development of what some saw as a hedonistic, aristocratic country. The maturation of the nation's industry had produced a fabulously rich upper class, free to live in a lavish style. At the same time, periodic downturns worsened the poverty of laborers, while more efficient farming led to falling prices and profits. The currents of modernity were undermining religious morality and gender hierarchy. And all this was simultaneous with the hardening of racial segregation, the disfranchisement of black voters, and the exclusion of Chinese workers. Customs officials remained vigilant against liquor, silks, tobacco, and sugar, but became more concerned about the smuggling of luxuries, opium, and human beings.

THE COSMOPOLITANISM OF the new society was self-evident. Freedom, land, and work drew millions of immigrants to Castle Garden and then its replacement, Ellis Island. And the same steamers returned to Europe and Asia carrying middle-class tourists. By the mid-1870s, liners equipped with compound engines, iron hulls, and screw propulsion had almost entirely replaced sailboats. Fourteen steamship lines served New York. Novels about international travel became more common, initially focusing on wealthy expatriates like Henry James's Isabel Archer, but later on rustic characters such as Tom Sawyer, whom Mark Twain depicted flying a hot-air balloon from Missouri to Africa in 1894. Funded by philanthropists like William Dodge, of Phelps, Dodge & Co., Protestant missionaries expanded their presence in the Levant and China then returned home to write about their experiences.[5]

In 1886, historian Henry Adams traveled to Japan seeking to recover from the suicide of his wife Clover. To plan his wife's tomb, Adams hired Augustus Saint-Gaudens and Stanford White, designers working in the French Beaux-Arts style. But White delayed completing the memorial, busy as he was working for New York's wealthiest men, chief among them William Whitney. Stanny had no sooner finished decorating Whitney's house than the tycoon moved to a new home at 871 Fifth Avenue, purchased from a deceased sugar refiner. Whitney again hired White, who turned the house into a showplace for décor drawn from every corner of the globe. One biographer described White as a "human bridge across the Atlantic, bringing splendor and purchasable portions of nobility to a group of America's best makers of fortune." The final product contained iron gates

Even before the Chinese Exclusion Act of 1882, the customs subjected Asian travelers to humiliating body searches. Courtesy Bird
Library, Syracuse University, Syracuse, New York

from the Palazzo Doria in Rome, a "Henry II–style fireplace from a
French chateau," and glass from a Renaissance chapel. White hired
Allard & Sons again to build and install the ceilings. And through the
efforts of art importer Joseph Duveen, White obtained for Whitney's
dining room Parisian "treasures" once belonging to the Vicomtesse
de Sauze.[6]

Like Allard & Sons, Duveen Brothers was a foreign firm, specializing in helping America's rich decorate their homes with the world's
art. Born to a Dutch Jewish family of merchants, Joseph Joel Duveen
moved to Hull, England, in 1867 at the age of twenty-four to appren-
tice in the grocery business. He stayed in England, married a young
woman named Rosetta Barnett, and went into business with her
brother Barney, an antique dealer (remarkably, Rosetta and Barney
were related to Charles L. Lawrence, whose grandmother was also a

Barnett from Hull). As the business grew, Joseph's sons expanded first to London and then to New York, opening a showroom special- izing in "antiquities" and "bric-a-brac" at 882½ Broadway. By the 1890s, their store had moved to Fifth Avenue and dealt in the most extravagant goods from Europe and Asia, ranging from tapestries to paintings to ceramics.[7]

The globalization of consumption was not confined to the afflu- ent; the styles enunciated on a grand scale by Stanford White also appeared in drawing rooms around the nation. Middle-class home- owners embraced what historian Kristin Hoganson calls "cosmopol- itan domesticity," namely the creation of an attractive living space by borrowing elements from around the globe. This initially meant purchasing European antiquities or reproductions of these items, but in the 1890s Americans expanded their repertoire to include borrowings from China, Japan, Latin America, and the Middle East. Decorators freely mixed these elements; one "small city apartment" contained "Turkish brass, Japanese tables, a Chinese cabinet, carved gourds from Central America, a Mexican fan, a Breton vase, a Bohe- mian chalice, and posters from Paris and London."[8]

International trade affected what ordinary Americans ate. Between 1865 and 1900, per capita consumption of imported food doubled. Sugar, once a luxury good stored in chests to prevent theft, became a commonplace. Protective tariffs raised the price but enabled expanded production of sugar beets in states like Michigan and Cali- fornia. Meanwhile, a reciprocity treaty allowed free entry of raw sugar from the Kingdom of Hawaii, which increased its cultivation of cane for the U.S. market. As a result of lower prices, per capita consump- tion of refined sugar rose from thirty-six pounds in 1877 to fifty-six pounds in 1888. It was at this moment that the United States saw the development of mass-produced candies like the Hershey bar and soft drinks like Coca-Cola.

Middle-class Americans had long worn imported clothes, but styles drew more explicitly upon foreign sources in the 1880s and

1890s. Commerce with China and Japan led designers to incorporate elements of the kimono into their clothes. During the day, American women began eschewing corsets for loose silk tea dresses to entertain guests, a nod to the less confining clothes of East Asia. *Demarest's Family Magazine* published an annual supplement with fashions from abroad, showing readers what their peers were wearing in places such as Switzerland and Russia. Paris remained, of course, the beacon of couture. In the most distant parts of the United States, retailers stressed the fashionable Frenchness of their establishments, giving their stores names such as the "City of Paris," "The Paris," and "The Bon Marché."[9]

The period's cosmopolitan aesthetic condemned tradition. The 1890s were known as the Mauve Decade because connoisseurs wore the lavender shade, enabled by new chemical dyes, as a way of shedding the burdens of Victorianism. American realists like Jack London, Frank Norris, and Stephen Crane embraced the naturalism of Emile Zola, writing fiction in a spare, impressionistic style, skeptical of capitalism, puritanism, and patriotism. The bohemian writers congregated in Antonio Buchignani's Caffe Dell'Opera, eating ravioli, drinking Chianti, and mingling with European musicians. A romantic figure, Buchignani had emigrated from Tuscany and married Jacksonian icon Margaret "Peggy" Eaton, a woman forty years his senior. In 1866, he eloped with Eaton's pregnant granddaughter, fled to Montreal, and dabbled in smuggling. After obtaining a divorce, Buchignani returned to New York and reinvented himself as a host. A charming raconteur, he was described as knowing "everybody who" had "any pretensions towards being anybody."[10]

Opium was another import that challenged bourgeois morality. Since the days of Caesar, westerners had taken poppy-based medicines, which were among the sole effective pain relievers yet invented. Opioids were not only legal in the United States, but also available for sale in pharmacies without a prescription. But opium smoking was initially confined largely to Chinese workers who patronized dens, whose proprietors provided the drug, pipes, lamps, couches, and hot tea. Several municipalities tried to clamp down on such "cribs," but the punishment was seldom more than a fine, and by the 1880s non-Chinese had started experimenting with "daube," or "dope." Examining a resort run by a man named Ay Tung, a reporter discovered a room full of "well dressed Americans" with "glassy eyes and hoarse voices," and learned that "most of the patrons of the place were actors and actresses," some of them "well known and very popular." Rose Eytinge's niece Pearl, an actress some called "the hope of the American stage," spent her free time smoking opium, "lying in a joint in Bleeker Street reading poetry to a pickpocket beside her." The writers Jack London, Frank Norris, and Stephen Crane all wrote about the drug as well. And all three men died by the age of forty, partly on account of their abuse of opiates or alcohol.[11]

The public likewise associated bohemianism with absinthe, a highly alcoholic, purportedly hallucinogenic Swiss spirit containing extracts of wormwood. The drink became popular in the United States in the 1890s, arousing fears similar to those regarding opium. According to the *New York Press*, the consumers of "France's Brain Destroyer" were a dissolute set: "the rich young man" who had "been to Paris and seen the *Moulin Rouge*," the weary "man about town," and all those who lived "artificial lives." Women enjoyed the so-called green fairy too, especially those from the "class of persons not generally alluded to in polite society." All these awoke craving an "absinthe drip" or yearned for "the frip of the frivolous sweet frappe." The article lamented that "the men who laid the foundations of the country" enjoyed "hard cider," "Medford rum," or "Madeira," assuming "they got drunk at all." Now, "the use of absinthe" was "increasing so rapidly" that doctors worried that the nation's "brightest young men" might be lost.[12]

WHILE A DEBAUCHED minority experimented with opium and absinthe, the nation was divided about the more benign products of globalization. Between 1887 and 1897, U.S. trade policy resembled a bitter duel between two evenly matched opponents. The protectionists emerged victorious, but also vulnerable to an electorate increasingly accustomed to buying imports, confident regarding international competition, and interested in constructing a more progressive tax system.

President Cleveland fired the first volley, devoting his entire State of the Union speech in 1887 to tariff reduction. But his party failed to pass a new revenue bill during that Congress. The next year, Republican presidential nominee Benjamin Harrison countered Cleveland with a campaign built around protection. Harrison lost the popular vote by a slender margin, but won the Electoral College, primarily because Cleveland was unable to win his home state of New York. Harrison and the GOP then assigned Rep. William McKinley the task of revising duty schedules, resulting in a bill that increased tariffs overall but eliminated unpopular taxes, such as the imposts on sugar and coffee. Amazingly, the unpopularity of the McKinley Act of 1890 allowed Cleveland to return to the White House in 1892, making him the only president in U.S. history to serve two nonconsecutive terms. Now holding the executive and legislative branches by significant margins, the Democrats expected to move the nation toward free trade.

A series of misfortunes hobbled the restored Cleveland. In March 1892, Joseph S. Moore, the Parsee Merchant, died at the age of seventy-one, of a stroke. His death prompted eulogies from both friends and enemies. The *New York Times* lauded his career. The protectionist *Chicago Tribune* averred that while "he had Hebrew blood in his veins," he "maintained a reputation for the highest integrity." He was a "good fellow who did not believe all men opposed to him in theory were tools or rogues," not to mention an "educator" on matters of finance, languages, art, religion, theater, and music. The death of their premier statistician left the Democrats scrambling. One Republican editor gloated that with the demise of "the Parsee," the party of Jefferson had "no one capable of so arduous and complex a task." They could not do "what they were elected to do simply for a lack of brains."[13]

Still more significant was the Panic of 1893, occurring just ten days before Cleveland's inauguration. The subsequent depression was perhaps the worst the nation had ever suffered, leaving thousands of businesses defunct and between five hundred thousand and three million laborers without work. In the winter of 1893–94, Democrats proposed to alleviate poverty by replacing taxes on consumption with taxes on incomes. The House passed a bill significantly lowering tariffs and imposing a 2 percent levy on earnings over $4,000 per year. But the Senate amended the legislation hundreds of times, effectively eliminating most of its reductions. Sugar refiners, now consolidated in a single trust, lobbied and allegedly bribed Congress to protect their business. Then, in an 1895 decision, a divided United States Supreme Court concluded that a tax on investment income was unconstitutional.[14]

The Revenue Act of 1894 thus did little to appease angry workers and farmers. In the spring, Greenback Party politician Jacob Coxey organized an army of the unemployed to march on Washington and demand that the government provide jobs for starving men. Farmers angered by what they saw as extortionate railroad rates had swelled the ranks of groups like the Grange and People's Party (a.k.a. the Populists) calling for government regulation of transportation. Workers were joining new labor unions, such as the American Railway Union and the American Federation of Labor, which rejected the state's authority to interfere with peaceable protests. And a small number adopted still more radical notions, such as socialism, calling for public control over production and the administration of accident and old-age insurance. The voters were tiring of old-style reformers like Cleveland, who promised minimal government and honest administration, but then used the army to crush railway strikes on behalf of corrupt monopolists.

But a surprising number still saw the old protective tariff as essential to class harmony. Finally breaking its tradition of naming New York reformers and Pennsylvania generals, the Democratic Party nominated young Congressman William Jennings Bryan of Nebraska in 1896. Supported by Populists, Bryan campaigned on silver coinage, tax reduction, and antimonopoly. His opponent, William McKinley, ran on the traditional Republican platform of protective tariffs and the gold standard. Though the campaign centered on the currency, Bryan's free-trade sentiments undermined him among workers, allowing McKinley to cruise in Pennsylvania, New York, and Massachusetts, industrial states where Democrats had competed four years earlier.

SMUGGLING ARRESTS EXPRESSED the nation's anxieties, the foremost of which, in the 1890s, was the emergence of an American aristocracy. The 1889 case against Allard & Sons, the French decorators accused of smuggling "paintings, tapestries, and portieres" under upholstery and behind mirrors, continued over a year after the initial arrest, finally ending in a settlement. The firm paid $10,000 plus costs in return for the merchandise seized. The customs had enormous evidence against the firm, including testimony from two of their employees, but the principals lived abroad in France, making their prosecution impossible. The company rebounded and remained an eminent provider of European antiques and reproductions.[15]

The Treasury assigned a special agent, Colonel Charles H. Traitteur, to investigate art imported along the nation's northern border. Tall, blonde, and handsome, Traitteur had been born in Bavaria, moving to the United States in 1863 at the age of seventeen and enlisting the Union Army. From 1865 to 1871, he claimed to have become a captain in the Second U.S. Cavalry regiment, but no record exists of his commission, much less of a promotion to colonel. Traitteur was, however, a talented linguist, who lived in Germany and Russia for parts of the 1870s and served as an interpreter for the New York Court of Sessions. He was also a womanizer and probably a bigamist.

Newspapers reported his almost simultaneous involvement—in varying states of legality—with three or four different women in New York, Washington, D.C., Marienbad, and Kishinev. All this qualified Traitteur for a berth in the custom house, which he won in 1889.[16]

Traitteur's first great seizure involved Ludovic de Spiridon, a Roman art dealer from a family of painters and authenticators. Customs officials had investigated de Spiridon before. In 1882, an agent had accused him of passing unassessed paintings into the country. De Spiridon settled the matter, but by the late 1880s, he began selling European paintings not only to New Yorkers, but also to magnates in smaller cities, such as St. Paul, Minnesota. When newspapers asked why De Spiridon's prices seemed unaffected by the tariff on paintings, the dealer responded that "his great intimacy with the masters in the old world" allowed him to obtain the art cheaply.[17]

De Spiridon aroused Traitteur's suspicions in 1891 when he discovered that several smuggled paintings had been sold to wealthy brewers in Milwaukee and St. Louis. Traitteur traced these canvases to a well-connected New York art dealer, and the agent seized as contraband two of the broker's pieces, *The Lion in Ambush* by Jean-Léon Gérme and *Aux Armes* by Paul Grolleron. Learning that De Spiridon had imported them, Traitteur arrested the Italian and seized over thirty of his paintings. He then secured testimony from one of the dealer's former partners, who claimed that the Italian had not only smuggled the art into the United States in 1887, but also forged the signature of Catalan painter Marià Fortuny on one canvas. De Spiridon managed to convince the commissioner that any undervaluation had occurred too long before for the government to legally prosecute him. And he wrote an open letter insisting that the charges themselves were slanderous. Nonetheless, the accusations continued to haunt him for several years.[18]

Soon thereafter, Traitteur seized sixty-nine paintings, including works by Da Vinci and Rubens, imported by a character named

Annie Louise Churchill Campbell Cacace. She had wed her first husband, wallpaper millionaire William Campbell, in 1875. But love did not last. Annie horsewhipped William in Central Park before a large crowd, and their vigorous fights forced them to relocate several times. Campbell filed for divorce in 1877, accusing Annie of cavorting with a theatrical manager, but the couple reconciled and the marriage limped on for another decade. Despite receiving $4,000 per year in alimony, she struggled financially. She took to the stage as an actress, and then married Dr. Alfonso Cacace and moved with him to the Hotel Royal in Naples, Italy. When this union failed, she tried to guarantee her security by absconding with Cacace's family art treasures, bringing them into the United States free of duty as household furnishings. Learning that she actually planned to sell the paintings, Traitteur had them confiscated.[19]

Dreading the loss of her nest egg, Annie retaliated against Traitteur. Her attorney made wild accusations against the special agent, claiming he had stolen securities from an elderly woman. When this tactic failed, Annie released letters showing that Traitteur had courted her, seizing her art works only when she refused to be seduced. As a recent widower with a sketchy marital history, Traitteur was vulnerable. But he convinced his superiors that he had corresponded with Annie only to win her trust and uncover her smuggling scheme. Meanwhile, she undermined her credibility by continuing to smuggle paintings. In January 1893, Traitteur seized another forty cases she had imported on the steamship *Stura*, containing "bric-a-brac" and forty-eight canvases. Two years removed from her time in Naples, Annie could hardly insist these items were household goods. Her actions grew more suspicious when she married a well-known racetrack starter whom she had met at Saratoga. In the end, Annie died young of a "swollen glottis" in 1895, and the government sold the paintings at a discount.[20]

The government chased after decorators, but it could not afford to entirely alienate them as it needed their expertise. In 1891, the government prosecuted Duveen Brothers for undervaluation of "Japanese and Chinese goods." But seven years later, the U.S. customs depended upon Henry Duveen's testimony in their litigation with George Gould, the son of financier Jay Gould. And experts could testify for either side. In 1901, Stanford White and Joseph Duveen testified that a bas-relief imported by Henry Havemeyer was statuary under the law and thus subject to lower tariff, a battle the sugar magnate won in court.[21]

Developments in modern art threatened to further weaken the customs officials' authority. Arthur Jerome Eddy was a lawyer, art collector, and author advocating free-trade and corporate consolidation. Entranced by Auguste Rodin's works at the Chicago World's Columbian Exposition of 1893, Eddy steamed to Paris to meet the master. But customs officials were unimpressed when Eddy returned home in 1899, bearing "a bust in bronze" of himself molded by Rodin" but produced in a "factory, from clay or plaster model." Seeing the piece as a manufactured object, little more than a heavy piece of metal, they levied a tariff of 45 percent on the work. A relative of the founder of General Motors and a contributor to Gustav Stickley's magazine, *The Craftsman*, Eddy believed that mass production could be creative. And he naturally wanted to save money. He unsuccessfully sued for a reduction of duties, arguing that the mode of fabrication did not change the fact that the bust was an artistic work, subject to a lower rate of taxation.[22]

By exploiting the subjectivity about art's value, smugglers only exacerbated the protectionists' doubts about imported paintings, sculpture, and antiques. It was not just that the buyers were wealthy, the objects decorative, and their provenance foreign. Their concern was that millions of dollars were flowing out of the United States in return for objects whose value resided solely in the minds of experts. Even the tycoons who paid the bills often had no notion of what their purchases were worth. Art's slipperiness frightened men already convinced that a society once built of stone, brick, and iron was becoming something more ephemeral.

CLASHES BETWEEN TYCOONS and the customs appealed to readers of the society page and the police blotter alike. In 1891, Frederick W. Vanderbilt had purchased the *Conqueror*, a 182-foot-long "pleasure yacht," for $77,750. Vanderbilt had his crew retrieve the Glasgow-built vessel in Hull and then sailed it to Halifax, Nova Scotia, and then to New York City. Decorated with "mahogany . . . old English china . . . a heavy Brussels carpet . . . electric lamps . . . fresh flowers," and "light gold tapestry," the vessel contained "the most finely-furnished rooms on any yacht afloat." Upon the vessel's arrival, the collector of customs insisted that the steamer was a "manufacture wholly or in part of iron or steel not otherwise classified" and seized it, demanding payment of taxes equal to 45 percent of its cost. Vanderbilt's lawyers convinced a federal judge to return the vessel pending litigation over the meaning of the statute. Still referencing the Civil War, the protectionist *American Economist* complained that "Vanderbilt goes to the yard which built the pirates launched to burn our merchant ships and whalers for his yacht," but still insists he is the "highest type" of American. It took six years for Vanderbilt to persuade the U.S. Supreme Court that yachts were not specifically listed in the law and thus not dutiable.[23]

The memoirs of customs officials described the growing suspicion of wealthy travelers, who were seen as hedonistic and un-American. A former dry goods importer, Special Treasury Agent William H. Theobald was responsible for tracking large jewelry purchases in Paris between 1897 and 1902. Over his five years watching tourists, Theobald seized $282,000 in diamonds and pearls, necklaces, earrings, and tiaras (over $7.7 million in current dollars). His targets were listed in the Social Register, their names familiar to the reading public: steel tycoon Charles H. Schwab, Philadelphia gentleman L. Harrison Dulles, and skyscraper builder Harry S. Black. Leopold

Stern, an official with the Diamond Cutters' Association, stated that
Theobald had "done more to break up smuggling of jewels in a few
years than all the rest of the department together."[24]

Theobald's first major bust was superficially no different from
similar seizures thirty years before. The perpetrator was jeweler
Max J. Lasar, a diamond merchant operating first on Fulton Street
and then on Maiden Lane. A Jewish native of Ottoman Romania
who had immigrated to the United States in 1872, Lasar was a well-
known downtown wholesaler, who had coincidentally served on the
1887 jury that convicted Louis Bieral. Dismayed by Lasar's low prices,
diamond merchants tipped off Theobald. In December 1897, Theobald and several U.S. marshals arrested Lasar, his brother, and his
sister-in-law, seizing almost $100,000 in uncut diamonds smuggled
from Europe through Montreal. After a lengthy trial, the diamonds
were condemned and sold. In 1900, Lasar was caught again smuggling, this time in Buffalo. To this charge, he pled guilty, receiving a
sentence of six months in Erie County Jail and a $1,000 fine. Upon
his release, Lasar borrowed money from friends to return to Europe,
where he died in 1904.[25]

In his dogged pursuit of Lasar, Theobald eschewed the anti-
Semitic profiling so common after the Civil War. While Secret Service chief Hiram Whitley had caricatured diamond smugglers as
Yiddish-speaking stage Jews, Theobald never mentioned Lasar's
religion. A Romanian immigrant, Lasar may have in fact spo-
ken with an accent, yet the agent presented his speech in normal
English. Theobald made a point in his memoirs of dismissing two
anonymous letters accusing Jews of smuggling. And perhaps to
squelch all suggestions of prejudice, Theobald dedicated his memoir to a well-known Jewish brewer, calling him "one of God's noble-
men . . . staunch, honest, and true."[26]

Instead, Theobald stressed Lasar's wealth and moral dissolution. His account claimed Lasar had earned $250,000 and owned a
"palatial house in the upper part of Manhattan." In the agent's tell-

ing, Lasar's infidelity led his wife to divorce him. Indeed, Theobald gloated that he could not have caught the "smuggler and free lover" had he "remained faithful to his spouse," for it was Lasar's mistress, Ivy Cruede, whose reluctant testimony had damned him. Theobald claimed government officials had begged Cruede to free herself from her lover, but it was fruitless. "He might just as well have tried to build a dividing wall through the Atlantic," the agent wrote, "as to have parted the foolish woman and her knavish paramour."[27]

By connecting smuggling and sexual immorality, Theobald styled the custom house as the guardian of the traditional family against decadent wealth. His memoir described how in 1898 he met a "stately brunette" with vivacious "black eyes" and a "bewitching Parisian costume" on the decks of the S.S. *Kaiser Wilhelm der Grosse* steaming for France. She called herself Phyllis Dodge, and she was traveling with a "stout and florid faced" young banker, Maurice Wormser, as well as a diamond broker and two women. Wormser was married, but his wife was nowhere to be seen. The friends spent the trip drinking wine in the saloon before disembarking at Cherbourg. In Paris, the banker purchased his lover so much expensive jewelry that word reached Theobald, who grew suspicious and decided to befriend the couple. Perhaps misreading Theobald's intentions, Wormser asked the agent to help import the jewels. Theobald declined, but Dodge chose not to declare the merchandise, essentially challenging the Treasury officer to arrest her.[28]

The Treasury seized the mistress's jewelry, estimated to be worth $65,000, leading to a long and intense legal fight. Theobald bragged of facing down the "millionaire," Wormser, who was "livid with rage" and promised to make him "suffer." Once in court, Dodge's counsel argued that she had not intended to deceive the government. Seeing the necklaces, rings, and pins as gifts, she merely believed that they were not dutiable. But she likely hurt her case when the prosecutors asked whether "Phyllis E. Dodge" was her true name. She admitted it was an alias she had begun using ten years before. Pressed by the government, she refused to reveal anything about herself, not her birthplace or maiden name. The litigation continued until 1904, when an appeals judge upheld the government's seizure of the jewels and the Supreme Court refused to hear the case. Wormser returned to his wife, the lovely Miss Dodge disappeared, and the government sold the jewels at auction for the disappointing price of $25,000.[29]

Once an afterthought, policing obscenity became a core function of the port. Customs inspectors seized prints imported for an English edition of a book of French fables, only reluctantly returning them to their owner. In 1886, the Treasury Department began blocking not only erotic images, but also works of literature such as Marguerite de Navarre's sixteenth-century story collection, *The Heptameron*, Henry Fielding's *Tom Jones,* and Giovanni Boccaccio's *Decameron.* And Boston customs officials decided to exclude more recent works, such as Emile Zola's *Nana*, a novel depicting a teen prostitute's ruin. Though newspapers mocked the confiscation of novels, they endorsed the impounding of explicit images, especially those from Asia. For instance, in 1889, the *San Francisco Daily Evening Bulletin* cheered the seizure of shipments belonging to the "Filthy Chinese" because they contained "obscene articles" that might be seen by "white children."[30]

Likewise, moralists demanded the custom house prevent gambling on foreign sweepstakes. The Comstock Act of 1873 and tariff law restricted the importation of lottery tickets, though these statutes disagreed as to whether the chances were themselves contraband or merely became so for any failure to pay taxes on their value. In 1890, the customs impounded "four large packages" of German tickets worth $20,000 being imported by Sender Jarmulowsky, a banker beloved by Lower East Side Russian Jewish immigrants. When his son came to retrieve the chances, famed censor Anthony Comstock himself entered the room and ordered a detective to place the financier in custody. In 1895, Congress made the importation of foreign lottery tickets a criminal offense, but the smuggling of foreign chances continued into the twentieth century.[31]

IN THE LAST DECADES of the century, no form of smuggling inspired more righteous interest than opium. An immense tariff of $10 per pound made trade in contraband opium irresistible. The act of moving the drug from British Columbia to San Francisco tripled the sale price. As a result, the city of Victoria had nineteen refineries or "cook houses," producing 300,000 pounds of the drug each year for the U.S. market. Legendary Puget Sound smuggler Larry Kelly began his career in 1864 trading in silk, rising to "the front rank of contraband runners" by dint of his "seamanship," "disregard to danger," and "ability to keep his own counsel." By the 1880s, he had switched to carrying opium from Victoria, B.C., to Washington State.[32]

As opium smuggling grew, it fed the broader panic over Chinese immigration that overwhelmed the United States in the 1880s and 1890s. The Exclusion Act of 1882 had strictly limited the immigration of all Chinese workers. Congress's decision to assign customs officials to enforce the ban exacerbated the tendency to call unlawful immigration "smuggling," a construction that defined the Chinese as objects rather than people. Conversely, anxiety about opium prompted new restrictions on the few Chinese allowed to reside in the United States. Connecting the two businesses, Congress barred Chinese merchants from importing opium in 1887.[33]

If the opium trade and unlawful immigration flowed through the same channels, it was because American drug smugglers made money helping Chinese workers circumvent exclusion laws. After opium trafficker Louis Greenwald completed his six-year term in San Quentin, he began a business transporting Chinese immigrants from Victoria, B.C., to Mexico, where he provided them with falsified papers allowing them to enter Arizona and New Mexico. Customs inspector Edward T. McLean was implicated in both opium smuggling and schemes to produce fraudulent consular certificates claiming Chinese workers had previously resided in the United States. Never convicted, McLean continued to serve at the Port of San Francisco, representing a gatekeeper for the movement of Chinese goods and people.

Chinese residents manufactured, sold, and consumed "dope," but they seldom transported it. According to newspaper reports, the leading opium smuggler of the 1880s was Charles Sumner Joslyn of Victoria. Joslyn was a tall man, with a high forehead, prominent nose, hazel eyes, and dark brown hair. In 1860, he left his hometown of Batavia, New York, where his father was a teetotaling Republican politician, to move to New York City. Joslyn worked as a bookkeeper, but when war broke out, he enlisted, eventually becoming a sergeant major in the Second New York Cavalry. After his discharge, he returned to Manhattan, ran a brokerage with his brother, and finally accepted a customs clerkship. Dismissed for some indiscretion, Joslyn obtained a job as a ship's purser for the Pacific Mail Company, whose steamers plied the waters between San Francisco and China, Australia, and Fiji.[34]

By 1880, Joslyn had resurfaced as "Boss Harris," the face of a $5 million syndicate, backed by a Sino-Canadian nicknamed "Opium Pete" and an anonymous California merchant. Initially, Joslyn hired Louis Charles Dugal, a.k.a "La Belle," a.k.a. "Frenchy," an associate from the Pacific Mail Company, to carry opium directly from China into San Francisco, landing it with the aid of customs inspectors like Edward McLean. But when police arrested one gang member, Boss Harris sent Dugal and a Chinese merchant named Bow Yuen north to start their own refinery in Victoria. Frenchy initially shipped the drug by land through Idaho, but shifted his route when officials grew suspicious. Henceforth, Joslyn's gang sent the opium from Victoria to Sarnia, Ontario, by the Canadian Pacific Railway and across the watery border to Port Huron. Once in the United States, the opium traveled by train to dealers in California.[35]

The opium crossed Michigan's St. Clair River on the schooner *Emma*, captained by Harry Durant, and manned by "Handsome Charley" Weizel and his brother George. Despite their colorful names, these men were reportedly temperate, churchgoing farm boys. Officials became aware of Durant's business in the summer of 1888, but the U.S. commissioner released him for lack of evidence. The following winter, Treasury agents chased Durant on horseback from Port Hope into the forest. After eight miles, they ordered him to halt. The dashing young captain turned and shot his pistol at his pursuers, jumped off his mount, and fled into the darkness. The officials returned fire, then searched the area, finding 1,300 packages of opium weighing 650 pounds and worth $6,500 (over $151,000 today). Durant remained at large until the next year, when he overconfidently returned to Michigan, where he was caught, tried, and sentenced to nine months in prison and a $5,000 fine. His confederate, Dugal escaped custody until the end of 1890, when he was captured in Olympia, Washington, driving a laundry wagon under the name Boulanger, and sentenced to eighteen months in prison.[36]

Joslyn continued to traffic in opium for years to come. In January 1894, San Francisco customs officials uncovered a "gigantic smuggling ring" using the sloop *Emerald* to carry opium and Chinese workers from Victoria to California. Though the ship "escaped to sea . . . chased by revenue steamers," officers obtained warrants for five men and arrested three of them. Joslyn was revealed as their supplier, but while three other defendants received six years in San Quentin, he remained in Canada. Later in the year, using the false name "Fred Jamieson," Joslyn personally escorted four trunks containing four hundred pounds of opium into Hawaii, then an independent republic. Hawaiian officials seized the baggage but not the smuggler, who escaped on the S.S. *Warrimoo* back to Victoria. The next year, Joslyn was implicated in transporting 3,730 tins of opium into the islands on the S.S. *Henrietta*. While the government confiscated the ship, Joslyn never served any time for his involvement. He continued to travel to and from the islands, undisturbed by officials.[37]

Opium smuggling aroused not only longstanding concerns about revenue, honesty, and nationalism, but also a new moral panic about the effects of specific foreign products on American society. The press chastised Joslyn, as they did Charley Lawrence, for deceiving the government and depriving it of the funds it needed. But opium transformed the logic of protection itself. If congressmen had long justified higher tariffs on silk, tobacco, and alcohol as necessary to protect American morals, they also defended import duties as necessary to nurture domestic manufacturers of these goods. No legislator bragged of saving opium workers' jobs. Newspaper accounts suggested that Chinese people and products were corrupting the nation. By this logic, the opium trade needed to be curtailed, and Treasury agents were an alternative to a "fleet of gunboats" with which the *Chicago Daily Tribune* proposed "Uncle Sam" roust the "daring lawbreakers of" Victoria.

Joslyn felt the stigma attached to his trade. He asserted his respectability, listing himself in the Victoria city directory as a "capitalist." When a man proposed to open a saloon in his neighborhood, he called it "an outrage and an insult to the people" and promised to "sign a petition every week" to prevent it. His true occupation was still too taboo to be advertised, even in British Columbia. The *Victoria Daily Colonist* slammed the sensationalism of "Chicago press men" who wrote stories about Joslyn and his gang of smugglers. Reporters drew upon "imagination" for "subject matter" that would have been "most interesting to the several characters who are now resident in Victoria." By 1900, Joslyn had returned to San Francisco, the city directory listing him as nothing more than a "purser." His circumspection meant that when he died in 1903, his career went unremembered. The papers published no obituary, and his death notice described him as a mere "native of New York" and a member of the Odd Fellows fraternal society.[38]

EXPANSION

I n the final years of the century, the United States became a world power, and the military began to overshadow the custom house. Congress funded the construction of armored steamers capable of projecting force abroad. American soldiers occupied Cuba and established U.S. sovereignty over the Philippines, Puerto Rico, and the Hawaiian Islands. In 1900, the president sent 5,000 troops to China to help suppress the *Yihetuan* or "Boxer" movement, which demanded the expulsion of foreigners. The soldiers joined an eight-nation alliance that looted property, killed civilians, and forced concessions from the Empress Dowager. These displays of military dominance made the Gilded Age war on smuggling seem quaint and the Treasury less imposing.

Fewer Americans envisioned revenue cutters sheltering the American democracy from the world's inequality. Each day, thousands of European immigrants steamed past the Statue of Liberty to land at New York's new inspection station, Ellis Island. Having streamlined production, manufacturers sought markets in other lands. Middle-class consumers resented taxes that raised the price of imports. Strikes in the nation's mills disrupted the claim that duties preserved peace between capital and labor. Farmers, miners, and some workers called for the taxing of incomes and regulation of corporations. But creating such a new government required disassembling the old one, built upon the principles of protection.

———

THE CONSTRUCTION OF American military power began in 1885, when William C. Whitney moved to Washington, D.C., to become Grover Cleveland's secretary of the navy. At this point, he had just left his position as New York City corporation counsel. He had not yet installed his protégé Hans Beattie in the custom house. He had not hired Stanford White to furnish his mansion. Whitney lacked any military experience, having spent the Civil War at Yale and Harvard. Whitney's qualifications for the job were his vast investments in steamships, his opposition to Tammany Hall, and his financial support of President Cleveland's campaign.

The navy had fallen far since the Civil War. For lack of repair, the cutting-edge armada that had strangled Confederate trade had become a "flotilla of deathtraps and defenseless antiques." The fleet had almost two thousand vessels, but fewer than fifty possessed working artillery. Under Whitney's leadership, the navy oversaw construction of thirty new warships, including the U.S.S. *Maine*. Yet, the continuing concern about smuggling and coastal defense prevented the government from building heavily armed battleships to trade broadsides with European ironclads. Instead, the new ships were light, fast cruisers capable of defending the shore and capturing contraband.

In 1889, control over the navy passed from Whitney to Benjamin Tracy, that is, remarkably, from Robert P. Noah's former boss to one of Charles L. Lawrence's defense attorneys. Tracy supported rearmament. His department produced a report, influenced by seapower advocate Alfred Thayer Mahan, which advised the government to finance a squadron of twenty battleships capable of steaming far from the shores of North America. Though Congress saw the department's recommendations as too costly, they did sponsor the construction of a "New Navy," composed of steel-plated battleships such as the U.S.S. *Massachusetts*, the *Indiana*, and the *Oregon*, as well as the first armored cruisers, the *New York* and the *Brooklyn*.

Tracy was the foremost advocate of territorial expansion in the cabinet of new president Benjamin Harrison. His counterpart at the State Department, James Blaine, saw a different future for the United States. Though known as "Jingo Jim" for his aggressive diplomacy, Blaine's four decades as a legislator made him sensitive to racial and fiscal politics. Blaine fretted that annexing tropical islands meant enfranchising their nonwhite residents. And if the U.S. annexed Cuba, for instance, the island's sugar and tobacco ceased to be imports, duties on which comprised a sizable percentage of federal revenue. Blaine preferred to promote American power through reciprocity treaties that lowered duties in return for concessions. For instance, the 1875 compact between the United States and the independent Kingdom of Hawaii allowed free trade in agricultural goods grown in the archipelago and finished goods produced on the mainland.[1]

MEANWHILE, MERCHANTS SCOURED the world for trade, creating new contexts for expansion. In 1870, David Abinun de Lima steamed from the Dutch colony of Curacao to the United States, bringing with him $17,000 in gold and a line of credit worth £5,000 sterling, not to mention letters to "first class parties" who called him "an honorable straightforward good business man . . . worthy of confidence and credit." Importing sugar, salt, skins, hats, aloe, and coffee, he accrued a staggering $130,000 in three years. From this comfortable position, he lobbied unsuccessfully for the U.S. to annex the Dominican Republic, earning himself a position as the island's consul in New York.

De Lima and Charley Lawrence likely knew one another. They both belonged to the Spanish-rite synagogue, Shearith Israel, and the De Limas were east-side neighbors of Charley's cousin, poet Emma Lazarus. But the reputation of the De Limas was comparatively irreproachable. One merchant attributed David's success to his "reputation of being strictly honest." The family was enrolled in the city's

Social Register and sent the younger generation to Europe and the Ivy League to be educated.[2]

The De Limas put their reputation at risk by engaging in the revolutionary politics of Latin America and the Caribbean. They attended a dinner for a deposed Venezuelan dictator. One of the scions of the family married Gloria de Céspedes, the sister of a leader of the Cuban revolt against Spain. In March 1888, the customs seized a shipment of gunpowder belonging to the De Limas, allegedly destined for Santa Marta, Colombia. Only a month later, David de Lima was chosen as a director of the Panama Railway, the line running through what was then Colombia's northernmost province. The next year, officials investigated the firm's shipment of "a box of revolvers and 500 boxes of cartridges" being carried on the Steamer *Ozama* bound for Hispaniola. The *Ozama* had been running guns to Haitian rebels for some time, but the De Limas insisted that their arms were bound for Puerto Plata, in the Dominican Republic. When the vessel arrived, the Haitian government seized it, prompting a U.S. Navy commander to demand its release. Unwilling to risk destruction, the Haitians freed the steamer and paid the United States a $7,500 indemnity.[3]

At home, the De Limas also called for new policies to increase commerce with Latin America. David argued for the professionalization of the consular force and the removal of "unqualified" officials. He savaged navigation laws that prohibited shippers from Americanizing ships registered under foreign flags. He buoyantly envisioned the U.S. dollar becoming common currency in South America, not to mention replacing "infinite" and "petty" customs regulations with a consistent system of valuation. "Once we have uniformity in the various systems and equitable regulations to govern our exports," De Lima wrote in 1889, "capital will more easily flow into the channel thus broadened and deepened." David even dreamed of the possibility of an "American customs union," that is, free trade between the United States and its neighbors.[4]

Other merchants turned to the Pacific. For most of the nineteenth century, the Kingdom of Hawaii had attracted primarily Yankee missionaries. But the Reciprocity Treaty of 1875 turned the islands into a duty-free port to sell American manufactured goods and buy agricultural products. The cession of Pearl Harbor gave American steamships a port on the way to East Asia. Riding the ensuing prosperity, the children of evangelists turned to business. For instance, Samuel Mills Damon, the son of a missionary, became the kingdom's premier financier, corporate director, and executive. When Damon's estate was distributed to his great-grandchildren in 2005 according to the terms of his will, it was worth over $800 million.[5]

The growth of California also spurred investment in Hawaii. The leading West Coast refiner was Claus Spreckels, a native of Hanover, who had immigrated to the United States in 1846 at the age of eighteen. Wending his way about the country, he eventually settled in San Francisco where he built a sugar refinery in 1867. After the Reciprocity Treaty of 1875, Spreckels hustled to Hawaii and "made contracts for the purchase of more than half the crop of sugar." He purchased plantations himself, acquiring as much as forty thousand acres of land, primarily on Maui, as well as the right to redirect water from the slope of Mt. Haleakala to his farms. By 1880, he held a virtual monopoly on the archipelago's sugar crop, as well as the ownership of its main newspaper and the steamship line connecting the islands to California. Finally, he established close ties to Hawaii's royal family, including King Kalakaua.[6]

Former smuggler Abraham Hoffnung also invested in the Kingdom of Hawaii. In the aftermath of Charley Lawrence's arrest, his fellow silk smugglers scattered around the globe. Brothers Aaron and George Wolf moved to the diamond fields of Kimberly, South Africa. Aaron died there in 1882, but George flourished, eventually winning election to the Cape parliament. Lewis Levey relocated to Bombay, India. Abraham Hoffnung stayed in Liverpool, but turned his attention to the Pacific, where his brother was established. In 1877, Abraham struck a deal to send Portuguese laborers to Hawaii to work the sugar plantations. Over the next decade, mostly under Hoffnung's supervision, 11,057 men, women, and children migrated from the Azores and Madeira. By 1881, his brothers-in-law, Lewis and Samuel Levey, had established an auction house in Honolulu.[7]

Hoffnung and his family became favorites of the Hawaiian royalty. On June 21, 1881, Samuel Levey married a prominent colonist. Attending the celebration were the Queen Dowager Emma, widow of Kamehameha IV, as well as princesses bearing gifts of gold, silver, pearl, and turquoise. In London, Hoffnung met King Kalakaua, who was visiting England on a world tour. The friendship continued when Hoffnung finally came to the islands in 1883. At one dinner dance, the king "proposed the health of Mr. Hoffnung," a toast "received with enthusiasm." The merchant responded by raising his own glass to Kalakaua, stating that "so long as . . . that intelligent and amiable gentleman" ruled the country, "her institutions could not but be safe."[8]

AMERICAN EXPANSION DIVIDED merchants. Naturalized American Claus Spreckels feared annexation of the Hawaiian Islands, which would have ended his control over the archipelago, secured by loaning the king the funds to keep the court running. It also challenged Spreckels's financial empire. Under the Reciprocity Treaty of 1875, Hawaiian agricultural products freely entered the United States, but its manufactured goods were taxed at West Coast custom houses. Spreckels's California sugar mills faced no competition from refineries on the islands. If America absorbed Hawaii, the magnate presumed, this protection would end, for the Constitution explicitly forbade the federal government from imposing any tax or duties "on Articles exported" from one state to another.

Abraham Hoffnung also bet on Hawaii remaining an independent nation. Envisioning a British trading network stretching from England to the Falklands to Hawaii, New Zealand, and Australia, Hoffnung flattered Kalakaua. In 1886, Hoffnung began arranging a $2 million loan in London allowing the king to repay Spreckels and

ABRAHAM HOFFNUNG IN DIPLOMATIC GARB, WEARING PORTUGAL'S STAR
OF THE ORDER OF CHRIST. Courtesy Jesse Thrush and Ancestry.com

feed his own grand ambitions, which included the purchase of the
H.H.M.S. *Kaimiloa*, a $20,000 steam-powered gunboat for pleasure
cruises, chasing smugglers, and establishing a confederacy with
other Polynesian islands. Feeling spurned, Spreckels left Hawaii, and
Hoffnung took his place as the king's enabler. In gratitude, Kalakaua
made Abraham his chargé d'affaires, or diplomatic representative, to
Great Britain, allegedly the first Jewish man to hold such a position at
the Court of St. James.[9]

Many American businessmen on the islands longed for U.S.
annexation. They feared that Hoffnung's loan to Kalakaua would
make the king a British puppet. In January 1887, thirteen Americans
formed the Hawaiian League, an organization dedicated to limiting

the monarchy. They then won the support of the Honolulu Rifles, a white militia group founded in 1884. These merchants bristled at rumors that Chinese merchants had paid bribes as large as $75,000 to Kalakaua for licenses to import opium. After several mass meetings, the Honolulu Rifles took the capital on behalf of the League. With the U.S.S. *Adams* in port to protect Americans and their property, and white riflemen in control of the palace, King Kalakaua disbanded his cabinet and signed a new constitution that shifted power to an elected legislature. But this was no triumph of democracy; the so-called Bayonet Constitution explicitly denied the franchise to Asians, women, and any resident possessing less than $3,000 in property and $600 in annual income, standards that excluded the majority of the indigenous population.[10]

Though Hoffnung had deprecated the possibility of a rebellion and even supplied arms to Royalists, his status somehow rose in both Hawaii and Great Britain. Just days after the cabinet's dismissal, his wife, daughter, and in-laws attended a dance with the U.S. minister on the U.S.S. *Adams*. He retained his position as chargé d'affaires, which allowed him to attend diplomatic functions in London dressed in full regalia: a velvet uniform trimmed with gold braiding, his chest bearing three large medals, his hands protected by white gloves, and his honor guarded by a saber resting on his belt. Newspapers reported his travels alongside those of U.S. minister to England Robert Todd Lincoln and various aristocrats. And members of his family married into England's elite. By 1889, his daughter Caroline was married to the brother of a member of Parliament, while his nephew Sidney had wed the daughter of another MP and peer.[11]

America's changing relationship with the world roiled Hawaiian politics. In 1890, the Republicans tried revising the tariff, handing responsibility for the negotiation to the chair of the Ways and Means Committee, Ohio congressman William McKinley. McKinley was an ardent protectionist, but he hoped to use the new tariff to present himself as an innovator. The resulting bill raised tariffs on many

goods but admitted raw sugar free of duty. To prevent domestic growers in states like Louisiana, Florida, and Michigan from opposing
the bill, he proposed paying them cash bounties. That is, the federal government paid sugar planters money for every acre they had
under cultivation to repay them for the money they lost when the
tariff was removed. The eradication of the tax on raw sugar opened
American markets, effectively granting all nations the privileged
status bestowed on Hawaii by treaty. The islands fell into a deep
depression.[12]

As Americans in Hawaii pushed for annexation, Secretary of State
Blaine preferred that the kingdom become something unprecedented
in U.S. history: a protectorate. Blaine offered Hawaii full reciprocity
and access to the cash bounties received by farmers in sugar states
like Louisiana. In return, he demanded control over the archipelago's diplomacy, free military access, and ownership of Pearl Harbor.
But negotiations faltered in 1891, when Kalakaua died at the age of
fifty-four. The king had no children, so the throne passed to his sister
Lili'uokalani, a supporter of independence. While Blaine pushed forward with the treaty, the Honolulu Rifles schemed to overthrow the
queen. Asked for comment by the newspapers, Hoffnung defended
the royals, deprecated the chance of revolution, and suggested the
islands make a treaty with Australia instead of the United States.
Come September 1891, Hawaii remained autonomous, the queen's
diplomats having added unacceptable provisions to Blaine's treaty.
Ever the Anglophobe, the secretary of state blamed the failure on
Lili'uokalani's friends, in particular "Canadians" keen to hand the
islands to England.[13]

Independence ended on January 17, 1893, when annexationists
deposed the queen. The prior year, they had bristled as she demanded
new measures to raise revenue, such as a lottery or opium-import
licenses. But the final spark was Lili'uokalani's proposal for a new
constitution giving her control over her cabinet and expanding suffrage to more Hawaiians. The Honolulu Rifles hunkered down near

the palace. The U.S. minister to Hawaii ordered marines to disembark the U.S.S. *Boston* to protect the American Embassy, but their effect was to prevent the queen from arming her native supporters. The annexationists declared themselves a committee of safety, asked the queen to abdicate, put the islands under martial law, and sent a commission to the United States to negotiate union with the mainland. Unrepresented were the native residents of Hawaii.[14]

Smuggling served as a trope for both sides of the debate. Opponents claimed that annexation would make the islands a "resort for smugglers," requiring the United States to institute "very costly" surveillance to prevent "millions of dollars" in merchandise from "surreptitiously" passing into the mainland. Annexationists responded that a "couple of Uncle Sam's revenue cutters ... would end the smuggling trade in remarkably short order." Lili'uokalani was a "corrupt and unscrupulous woman," supported "by her paramour and a ring of ... opium smuggling adventurers" seeking "to overthrow the Hawaiian constitution and seize absolute power." They cared little that the queen had actually proposed licensing opium importers to undercut contrabandists.[15]

PRESSURE TO ANNEX Hawaii complicated the American political landscape. In March of 1893, for the first time since before the Civil War, the Democrats took control over the House, Senate, and presidency. Returning to Washington after four years' absence, President Grover Cleveland planned to push for lower tariffs, and an influx of Hawaiian sugar would make the complex negotiations no easier. Moreover, Cleveland was beholden to southern and western Democrats, who feared the addition of tens of thousands of Polynesian, Chinese, and Japanese laborers to the workforce. Finally, the president suspected that the missionary faction had unjustly engineered the overthrow of Queen Lili'uokalani. For all these reasons, Cleveland refused to send the Senate the annexation treaty negotiated by the Harrison administration.

But when Cleveland pushed for tariff reduction, his own caucus prevented any progress. Lower taxes on imports meant less revenue. To make up the difference and balance the budget, Congress had to restore the tariff on raw sugar, as well as end the bounties paid under the McKinley Act. The owner of a 1,600-acre sugar plantation earning him $60,000 (over $1.2 million today) in bounties, Louisiana Democratic senator Edward Douglass White had a personal stake in blocking the bill. Cleveland removed White from the Senate by appointing him to the U.S. Supreme Court. If this neutralized the sugar growers, it strengthened the refiners, who had become by the 1890s one of the most corrosive forces in American politics. A single firm, the American Sugar Refining Company, combining the interests of the Havemeyers, Spreckelses, and several others, controlled 98 percent of the refining market. As a result, the final law—dubbed the Wilson-Gorman Act of 1894—reduced duties less than Cleveland had wanted. The law instituted a landmark 2 percent tax on incomes over $4,000 per year, but it returned refined sugar to the protected list.[16]

Protectionists soon reversed even this modest adjustment. The Supreme Court issued two rulings holding the income tax component of the Wilson-Gorman Act unconstitutional. In 1896, Americans responded to the economic downturn by electing a Republican Congress and William McKinley as president. The new Speaker of the House, Thomas Reed, was an arch-protectionist. The government promptly enacted the Dingley tariff of 1897, raising rates above 50 percent and doubling rates on sugar.[17]

With the depression and taxes decimating American demand for Hawaiian sugar, the islands grew unstable. Stymied in achieving annexation, the Committee of Safety constructed itself as a republican government. But limits on the suffrage undercut any pretense of democracy. Abraham Hoffnung called the elections of 1894 "nothing more than a farce," as the constitution required that all voters swear loyalty to the new government, effectively disfranchising those loyal to the queen. For two weeks in January 1895, monarchists staged an unsuccessful counterrevolution, resulting in the imprisonment of Lili'uokalani and many of her supporters, including Hoffnung's brother-in-law, Lewis Levey. The governor offered to release the auctioneer if he promised to leave the islands. Levey fled to Sydney, but his incarceration "without trial or explanations" in what was described as a "pest hole" left him visibly "old and feeble." He returned to Honolulu the next year, but died soon thereafter of pneumonia.[18]

Meanwhile, the republic tried to demonstrate its potency by chasing smugglers like Charles Joslyn. The legislature appropriated funds for more customs workers, established a special fund for renting revenue cutters, and employed "investigators and informers" in Victoria, Vancouver, and San Francisco. In 1896, this bore fruit when the Hawaiian customs seized the British schooner *Henrietta* containing opium belonging to Joslyn. But similar successes proved elusive, and the Hawaiian republic decided to cease aggressive patrols in 1897.[19]

AT THE SAME MOMENT, islanders in the Caribbean and Pacific stiffened their resistance to Spanish imperial rule. Cubans experienced the same economic hardships as Hawaiians, but they blamed their Habsburg ruler across the Atlantic, Maria Christina, the regent for her not-yet-adult son King Alfonso XIII. By 1897, the island's longstanding independence movement had begun to achieve military success in the field. In the Philippines, a secret society called Katipunan grew and became an effective military insurgency, holding entire provinces of Luzon Island. Puerto Rico experienced not armed rebellion, but rather demands for greater self-rule and democracy.

As the Cuban war of independence intensified, the U.S. consul worried about the safety of American residents, prompting President McKinley to send the U.S.S. *Maine* from Key West to Havana in January 1898. Commissioned in 1886 by Navy secretary William Whitney, the steam-powered cruiser was small by European standards but still an impressive machine of war: almost the length of a football field, armored with nickel-steel plate, possessing long guns capable of firing rounds a distance of eleven miles, and holding a crew of as many as 374 men. This made it all the more shocking when it exploded on February 15, 1898, killing 260 sailors and officers.

Though the sinking of the U.S.S. *Maine* is today considered mysterious, Theodore Roosevelt Jr. had few doubts that Spain had attacked the United States. When the Congress declared war, "Teddy" gathered college friends and cowhands from his time ranching in South Dakota to form a cavalry regiment under his command: the Rough Riders. The son of President Hayes's first choice for collector of the Port of New York, Roosevelt had inherited his place in the reform community. But he adapted the movement to his own obsessions. While the father had been a mild-mannered philanthropist, dedicated to minimal government, the son had an ambitious view of the state and its responsibilities to the people. If his father had declined military service and even deprecated conflict, then Teddy hoped that war with Spain could masculinize American reform, replacing an antiquated government with a new state capable of promoting "Anglo-Saxon" liberty abroad and regulating industry at home.[20]

Roosevelt was not alone in his enthusiasm for the war with Spain. With pale-blue eyes, unsmiling narrow lips, a straight nose, and a square jaw, Emil J. Pepke had an expression that suggested determination. In 1893, twenty-one-year-old Pepke had asked the United States Supreme Court to invalidate North Dakota's prohibition law. Working as an innkeeper and salesman, he hustled to survive fires and the nation's deep depression. On April 29, 1898, nine days after Congress declared war, Pepke went to Wahpeton, North Dakota, and enlisted in the state's first volunteer infantry regiment. By the summer, Pepke was a U.S. Army private, serving on the Philippine island of Luzon under General Arthur MacArthur Jr.[21]

The war with Spain was brief, lasting little more than three months. By the time the Senate had ratified the peace in 1899, the United States owned territory stretching from the port of Manila in the west to Puerto Rico in the east. The U.S. quickly ceded

power over Cuba, giving administration of Puerto Rico and the
Philippines to the army. In the latter case, the conflict with Spain
gave way to a bloody war with advocates of Filipino independence.
Unable to establish American civilian rule, the United States kept
the archipelago under the authority of the military. In 1900, Congress enacted an act establishing the government of Puerto Rico,
giving it the power to raise revenue through taxes on imports, as
well as setting tariffs on goods shipping from the island to the U.S.
The authors of the act were Ohio senator Joseph Foraker and Secretary of War Elihu Root, the lawyer who once defended Horace Claflin against charges of selling contraband silk and prosecuted Edwin
Boyd for smuggling plate glass.

The construction of new governments for the islands raised several basic questions: Were these possessions truly part of the United
States? Did their residents or children born on their soil possess constitutional rights? After the United States had purchased the Louisiana Territory in 1803 and conquered huge swaths of Mexico in
1848, the Congress had chosen to grant citizenship to whites and free
blacks living there. This principle was reaffirmed by the enactment of
the Fourteenth Amendment in 1868, which guaranteed citizenship
to anyone born in the U.S. who was not subject to a foreign power (a
clause intended to exclude members of Native American nations and
diplomats). A simple query neatly summarized the matter: does the
Constitution follow the flag?

The answer directly affected the residents of the islands, but it had
the potential to transform the nation at large. Annexation would add
over eight million persons to the United States, increasing its population by over 10 percent. Many of these claimed Polynesian, Chinese, Malay, African, and other non-European ancestors. Moreover,
full incorporation threatened to eliminate the barriers between the
U.S. and the world's most productive sugar producers, for the Constitution explicitly forbade tariffs between sections of the Union. It thus
also imperiled the nation's finances. One economist estimated that

taxes on imported sugar provided 18 percent of all federal revenue, income that would disappear as the new possessions began to provide the nation's sweetener.[22]

These concerns cut across party lines. Old Republican egalitarians like George Boutwell opposed the entire expansionist project, seeing it as an extension of white supremacy. Other Republicans, such as McKinley, Roosevelt, and Foraker, favored annexation but supported somehow retaining the tariff walls. The *New York Times* derided such thinking as magical, happily predicting that protection could not survive expansion. Southern Democrats, who had opposed conquest on racial grounds, showed surprising principle in favoring the extension of constitutional privileges to the islands. Democratic senator James K. Jones of Arkansas, once a slaveholding Confederate, called legislation taxing Puerto Rican products "monstrous," and promised to "fight it in the Senate," and "before the people from now until the ballots are cast in November."[23]

ON MAY 18, 1900, Chicago customs agents arrested Private Emil Pepke for smuggling fourteen diamond rings, a gold-plated watch, and a German-made Mauser bullet into the United States. The bullet had been taken from a wound in his flank received while marching in the Bulacan province of Luzon. The rings had been bought by the veteran in the Philippines with $1,500 he had won playing poker. Returning with his regiment in July 1899, he first traveled home to North Dakota, heading to Chicago several months later to sell his rings. But as an unknown out-of-towner bearing valuable merchandise, he attracted the attention of detectives, who concluded his diamonds were the spoils of a recent robbery. When Pepke proved his title to the jewels, the police referred the matter to the collector of customs. No criminal charges were filed, but officials impounded his goods. Pepke insisted that the rings could not have been smuggled, as the Philippines were part of the United States, but the court disagreed, forcing him to appeal.[24]

Pepke's suit was one of several dubbed the "Insular Cases," considering the same question: what was the status of the new territories? Caribbean merchant Elias S. A. de Lima had filed a similar complaint the year before. De Lima contended that the collector of the Port of New York, George Bidwell, had unlawfully taxed Puerto Rican sugar in the autumn of 1899, after the United States took possession of the island but before the Foraker Act. Coffee merchant Herman Sielcken, "the most feared and hated man" in the world, filed a protest when customs officers taxed liquor shipped from the U.S. into Hawaii. In November 1900, De Lima recruited a wealthy but nondescript New York commission merchant named Samuel B. Downes who had paid duties on Puerto Rican oranges to complain that the Foraker Act was unconstitutional.[25]

In the Puerto Rico cases, the lead counsel was Frederic R. Coudert Jr., a member of New York's elite bar claiming an unusual background. By dint of his French ancestry, he was treated as a Roman Catholic aristocrat, worthy of invitation to discriminating homes in spite of his faith. His family owned a home next to the Roosevelts in Oyster Bay, New York. Just a few years before, he had married the granddaughter of former Navy Secretary Benjamin Tracy, winning the Republican elder statesman to his law firm as part of the bargain. His firm had offices in New York, Washington, Manila, Havana, and Paris, as well as "half a dozen European governments among its list of clients." For decades, he had represented the De Lima family and served with its patriarch on the corporate board of the Panama Railway.[26]

The Insular Cases were heard by one of the most reviled Supreme Courts in American history. To the modern eye, the court led by Chief Justice Melville Fuller got all the big issues wrong. Its most notorious decision was *Plessy v. Ferguson*, the 1896 ruling upholding a Louisiana law prohibiting African-Americans from sitting with whites on railroads. The court infamously held that the Fourteenth Amendment's guarantee of equal protection under the law did not forbid separate facilities for the races. Only slightly less infamous was its 1905 decision in *Lochner v. New York*, which held a state law setting maximum hours for bakers an unconstitutional intrusion in the individual rights of workers, thus invalidating a range of Progressive Era statutes dedicated to protecting laborers against harsh work conditions.

The court was divided between protectionists and free-traders. Justice Joseph McKenna owed his appointment to the Supreme Court to his assistance constructing the McKinley Tariff of 1890 as a congressman eight years before. Justice George Shiras Jr. was a cousin of James G. Blaine and an attorney for Pittsburgh manufacturing interests. Justice Edward Douglass White was a sugar planter and former senator appointed to the court to stop him from obstructing tariff reduction. On the other side, Justice Rufus Peckham came from a family of New York reform Democrats opposed to both the Conkling machine and Tammany Hall. The author of the *Lochner* decision, Peckham derided government in part because he had experienced corruption first hand. He could recall the time that former Treasury agent Benaiah Jayne purportedly offered his brother $3 million to end his investigation of the Tweed Ring.

The racial implications of the case likewise split the court. A decision holding that the islands were part of the United States had the potential to give millions of nonwhites constitutional rights, including the suffrage. After oral argument, Frederic Coudert complained that Justice White—a former Confederate soldier—was obsessed with the color of the new Americans. These possibilities were no less clear to racial egalitarians on the court, such as justices John Marshall Harlan and David Brewer. Harlan's thundering dissents in the *Civil Rights Cases* and *Plessy* denounced segregation at a moment when the other justices proved deaf to the pleas of African-Americans. Brewer was known as the court's most stalwart defender of the rights of Chinese litigants. To these justices, the failure to offer constitutional rights to the new Americans seemed merely an extension of white supremacy as it was emerging on the mainland.[27]

Over the course of the year 1901, a divided Supreme Court issued what appeared to be a contradictory series of 5-4 decisions with multiple dissents. The De Limas, Pepke, and Sielcken had won, but Downes had somehow lost. Taken as a whole, the rulings upheld American possession of the territories, while giving Congress free rein to govern them. Justice White's concurrence in *Downes* held the new acquisitions to be "foreign in a domestic sense," formally parts of the United States, but alien for legal purposes. Creating what became called "the doctrine of territorial incorporation," he argued that Filipinos, Hawaiians, and Puerto Ricans gained the full slate of constitutional protections given to citizens only when Congress admitted their islands as states. Finally, the court ruled that Congress could impose tariffs on the goods produced in the islands. De Lima and Pepke won their suits only because their goods crossed the border before the Congress had acted. But Downes lost because he had imported his oranges after the passage of the Foraker Act.

The rulings satisfied the nation's political leadership. In November 1900, President McKinley had won a second term, using war nationalism again to defeat pacifist Democrat William Jennings Bryan. Conquest was popular. The war revived the Republican vision of government centered on the custom house, temporarily forestalling the construction of a modern regulatory state. McKinley's running mate, Theodore Roosevelt, who had ridden his service in Cuba to New York's governor's mansion, accentuated the ticket's responsibility for the victory over Spain. The new vice-president, Teddy Roosevelt, declared himself "very much pleased with the decision." Others suggested the justices had merely appeased the public. Popular columnist Finley Peter Dunne's fictional saloonkeeper Mr. Dooley quipped: "Whether th' Constitution follows th' flag or not, th' Supreme Coort follows th' iliction returns."[28]

With the government's power reaffirmed, some criticized the litigants for bringing the cases in the first place. Vice-President Roosevelt upbraided his neighbor Frederic Coudert Jr. as an "enemy of the public weal" blocking America's imperial destiny. One paper granted the importers' right to test the matter, but insisted that they accept the court's ruling in order to be "wise and patriotic citizens." The protectionist *Chicago Tribune* presented wounded ex-serviceman Emil Pepke as a smuggler out of anti-Semitic literature: an "itinerant jewelry peddler," of "thrifty disposition," who had bought his "international fourteen" in "Manila pawnshops," using cash earned through money lending. It did not matter that Pepke was a Methodist born in Wisconsin.[29]

Coudert rejected such criticisms. "Is not the real question" not whether the U.S. would grow, the attorney wrote, but "how should we expand?" If America was to be an empire, would it be "Carthage, Rome, Spain," or England? Coudert argued that "[t]he framers of the Constitution did not believe that a Government was impotent because it could not crucify or confiscate." He believed that American expansion needed to "be a better and different kind of expansion from any that has yet preceded," a continuation of "English expansion," namely "the domination of foreign peoples or possessions with as little absolutism as possible." Coudert then defended the court by contending that the Insular Cases applied only to tariffs, not the "fundamental rights and immunities" enunciated in the Constitution.[30]

The plaintiffs resumed their businesses. Samuel Downes recommenced selling groceries on commission. The De Limas shifted from importing to finance, their ties to Latin America tightening with time. Elias S. A. de Lima moved to Mexico City, where he became a bank president, a director of the National Railway, and a friend to liberal president Francisco Madero. Herman Sielcken concocted a scheme to purchase Brazil's coffee crop, effectively allowing him to set the worldwide price of the commodity. He married the daughter of a Hawaiian sugar planter and retired to his Baden Baden estate, Mariahalden, which included a two-hundred-acre private park.

Never a wealthy man, Emil Pepke returned to North Dakota. Unable to pay his legal fees by selling his jewelry, he unsuccessfully sued the police and customs for $25,000, charging arbitrary arrest and deprivation of property. One local newspaper teased, "Emil always was good at a game of bluff as well as several other games." For several years, the media treated "Diamond Pepke" as a celebrity, reporting him foiling an armed robbery, working at a lumberyard, and marrying. Working as a salesman, he ran for office in 1912 first as a Socialist and as a member of the Nonpartisan League, a populist insurgency that became a force in the northern plains.[31]

Abraham Hoffnung continued to prosper. After the 1893 overthrow of Queen Lili'uokalani, he was removed as chargé d'affaires to the Court of St. James. But he continued arranging the transport of Portuguese laborers to work the sugar plantations. In 1900, Hoffnung visited the islands once again in an effort to purchase the queen's extensive land claims. When he died in 1912, the Polish-born son of a rabbi and former blockade runner left an estate large enough to enable his daughter Caroline to wed the 16th Marquess of Winchester.[32]

Insular Cases fell hardest on the natives of the new American territories. Contrary to the prediction of Frederic Coudert Jr., the 1901 rulings were not limited to the Constitution's tariff clause. They unleashed the full power of the state. Within the next two years, the Supreme Court denied that the Bill of Rights protected criminal defendants in Hawaii, the Philippines, and Puerto Rico. If the military possessed any lingering constitutional inhibitions on its ruthlessness, the rulings removed them. U.S. suppression of the Philippine independence forces resulted in the death and torture of an estimated 250,000 Filipinos.[33]

TRANSFORMATION

ionel E. Lawrence was a libertine. An actor who had performed in London, Paris, Budapest, and all over the United States, "Larry" married eleven women before his death from apoplexy in 1914 at the age of fifty-one. A theatrical paper memorialized him as a "happy-go-lucky character, his own worst enemy, but always with a host of friends." If his "matrimonial adventures" were "grossly exaggerated," Lionel certainly survived several spouses, annulments, and divorces. One wedding he blamed on alcohol, his favorite drink being twelve-year-old whiskey. "I was spificated [sic] I had such a souse on my hair was wet." Perhaps his most famous wife was vaudeville actress Dorothy Drew, who was later connected with boxer Jim Jeffries. When the press asked Lawrence his secret, he replied, "[Y]ou can search me," but guessed, "It is easy to get acquainted with women on the stage."[1]

Lionel was the youngest of Charles L. Lawrence's surviving sons. Freed in 1876, the smuggler had helped the U. S. attorney pursue customs frauds until 1881, when the government abandoned his prosecution entirely. For several years, Charley worked as a stockbroker, then ran a restaurant in the basement underneath Wallack's Theatre. In 1883, newspapers reported that actors had fleeced Charley by purchasing "German champagne and various toothsome delicacies like cheese sandwiches, Welsh rarebits and English hares, together with mineral waters of various brands" and signing Lester Wallack's name. When Lawrence pressed the impresario to pay for the food, Wallack passed the management of the café to another businessman.[2]

Lionel's parents wanted him to become a naval officer like his cousin Uriah Phillips Levy, the nation's first Jewish commodore. They sent him to a military school in South Carolina, where Zipporah had relatives, after which he attended the U.S. Naval Academy. Years later, amid the patriotic afterglow of the Spanish-American War, Lionel claimed that he had graduated third in his Annapolis class, and then served three years on the U.S.S. *Alert* in the Pacific before being blinded by an exploding shell. His experience in the navy, he suggested without sarcasm, had given him the discipline to be an effective stage manager.

At the age of twenty, Lionel was not in Asia, as he later claimed, but rather in New York City, where he worked at a bookstore and lived in a boardinghouse. On October 8, 1883, he was arrested for stealing diamond cuff links worth $150 from a "wealthy Peruvian" and pawning them for $15. Lionel's parents begged for his release, arguing that an abscess in his side required him to take morphine, which made him mentally incompetent. By 1884, Lionel had moved to San Francisco, touring the West as an actor before again attracting the attention of the authorities. Amazingly, under a false name he posed as a "microscopical expert" in a sensational divorce case. Eventually arrested, Lionel was sentenced to three months in a California prison for various frauds.[3]

Charley Lawrence returned to the public consciousness on July 15, 1890, when he died in New York City in his fine brick home on West End Avenue. He was only fifty-seven. The *New York Times* was subdued, mentioning only his theatrical achievements, but papers around the nation recalled his crime, escape, and prosecution. The *New York Sun* gave his story two columns on the front page, calling him "the leading spirit in the most systematic, far-reaching, and successful conspiracy ever organized to defraud Uncle Sam's Custom House." The *Sun* specifically noted that Charley was born "a Jew," with the "surname Lazarus" and wrongly claimed him as a native of London. The *Hartford Courant* declared him "A Famous Conspirator," and the *New Orleans Picayune* detailed "his meteoric career." The *Boston Daily Advertiser* called him the "King of the Smugglers," while the *Waukesha Daily Freeman* downgraded him to a mere "Prince." And nearly all of the papers mentioned his religion and relationship with William M. "Boss" Tweed. With her beloved husband gone, Zipporah died on October 11 of that same year.[4]

Within months of his father's death, Lionel was back in trouble. In Chicago, police had arrested him after an actress named Nellie Atherton claimed he had stolen her jewels. At the same time, his wife of less than one year, Kittie Howard, sued for divorce, accusing Larry of "intimacy with Miss Atherton." For the rest of his life, Lionel appeared regularly in theatrical notices, gossip pages, and police blotters, which reported his adventures with lovers, process servers, infuriated creditors, and out-of-state detectives, not to mention local law enforcement.[5]

But the most dramatic moment in Lionel's disordered life occurred on the evening of June 25, 1906, in the theater atop Madison Square Garden, where he was the manager. Lawrence was prepping a new musical comedy, *Mam'zelle Champagne*, when architect Stanford White walked backstage and asked Lawrence to introduce him to one of the company's starlets. Having designed the building, White expected Lionel to indulge his love of teenaged beauties, but the manager begged the roué to "wait until afterwards." Among the spectators were playboy Harry Thaw and his wife, celebrated model Evelyn Nesbit Thaw. At about 11:05 p.m., the couple decided to leave the show, but Thaw saw White, marched up to him and fired his revolver three times into White's head and shoulder. Lawrence leaped on a table and begged the orchestra to keep playing. When the performers faltered, Larry "shouted for quiet," told "the audience that a serious accident had happened," and asked them to leave quietly. He looked down and saw Evelyn soothe Harry, saying, "I'll stick to you through thick

and thin." Thaw then turned to Lawrence and rationalized, "that —
ruined my wife, and I got him and fixed him for it."[6]

The twentieth century's first "Crime of the Century," White's murder became a national sensation. The victim was the famous architect and decorator of America's mansions. The perpetrator was an
heir to a Pittsburgh railroad fortune, well known in several cities for
lavish expenditure and hedonistic excess. Thaw's outrageous public
behavior had gotten him expelled from Harvard and blackballed at
countless New York City clubs. In private, he reveled in sex, violence,
and drugs. He loved whips and used them to lash prostitutes, male
bellhops, and, later, his wife, Evelyn. His favorite injection was a
mixture of cocaine and morphine. And yet to juries, Thaw presented
himself as defending traditional morality. He twice evaded conviction
by insisting that he shot White to punish him for raping Evelyn back
when she was sixteen years old. Declared not guilty by reason of temporary insanity, Thaw was sent to the Matteawan State Hospital in
1908. Seven years later, he was a free man.[7]

Had the murder occurred in 1876, commentators might have
connected it to smuggling, the tariff, and the custom house. They
would likely have depicted Harry Thaw, whose money came from the
nation's industrial heartland, as the avenging angel of protectionism,
striking out at Stanford White, the purveyor of smuggled luxuries.
But in 1906, no newspapers mentioned that the eyewitness, Lionel
E. Lawrence, was the son of the nineteenth century's greatest contrabandist. And, in any case, Americans had moved beyond isolation-
ism. Their décor, their diet, and their apparel all demonstrated their
newly global sensibility. Nonetheless, for many observers the murder
demonstrated how the nation's wealth and hedonism had destroyed
its virtue, symbolized by the chastity of the pale, slender beauty, Evelyn Nesbit. The rich were running wild, and something had to be
done before the country was destroyed.

———

FOUR DAYS AFTER Stanford White's murder, in an unconnected development, President Theodore Roosevelt signed the Pure Food and Drug Act, initiating a new era in national regulation of the domestic consumer economy. Rather than depending on custom-house assessments to protect consumers, the law empowered the federal government to govern the labeling, preparation, and safety of medicines and foodstuffs. The law required manufacturers to mark their products as "dangerous" if they contained any of ten ingredients, including opium, alcohol, cocaine, and cannabinoids. A reaction to the pressure of corporations desperate for national standards, as well as reformers outraged by factory conditions, fraudulent advertising, and dangerous products, the act broke the tariff's hammerlock on national policy, beginning the era of direct federal regulation of domestic life in the United States.[8]

This new mode of direct federal regulation differed markedly from the tax-based system of the eighteenth and nineteenth centuries. Under the old scheme, the government discouraged citizens from consuming items deemed morally suspect, such as alcohol and tobacco, by making them more expensive. The state protected products made under democratic conditions in the United States by taxing goods manufactured in nations with lower wage rates and less democratic politics. By contrast, newer modes of regulation restricted the sale of specific consumer products in America and controlled particular business practices within the domestic U.S.

Furthermore, direct regulation separated fiscal, economic, diplomatic, and welfare functions of government. At root, the tariff existed to generate revenue for the government. But tariff supporters argued that duties promoted a strong, diverse, independent economy. They contended that taxing imports prevented poverty by benefiting industrial workers. And they saw tariffs as the core of American foreign policy, a means of rewarding friends, punishing enemies, and even annexing territory. Between 1890 and 1920, the push to expand the navy, impose income taxes, and institute direct regulation essentially segregated these various purposes. Each policy goal had a specifically tailored policy solution.

Some laborers found this shift jarring. The tariff surreptitiously benefited manufacturing workers by guarding them against competition with lower-paid personnel abroad. To a puddler at a Pittsburgh steel mill, the tax assessed at the Port of New York was almost invisible. Moreover, protectionist rhetoric celebrated the American worker as superior; a wage earner in the United States required protection because he was not "degraded" like foreign laborers. By contrast, Progressive Era governance put inspectors in the factories themselves and enforced rules binding both employers and workers. A law that restricted the hours a proprietor could demand from an operative also restricted the hours a laborer could choose to toil. Cherishing their virile independence, workers resented the suggestion that they were too weak to negotiate with their bosses.

Progressive Era reformers, like their Gilded Age predecessors, welcomed a move away from the tariff. Ida Tarbell, the journalist who had made her name uncovering the seamy practices of John D. Rockefeller's Standard Oil trust, turned her sights on protectionism in 1911, painting the tariff as a tool of the trusts. Perhaps unsurprisingly, her book celebrated the late Joseph Solomon Moore, the Parsee Merchant, as "a clever German-Hebrew," a "brilliant talker," and the "most effective" free-trade writer in the nation. For other reformers, the custom house offered Americans insufficient defense against the might of capital. National Consumers' League director Florence Kelley had inherited her support for workers from her father, Rep. William "Pig Iron" Kelley, the nation's leading protectionist. In 1883, William had taken Florence on a tour of the factories of England. The poverty they saw affirmed the Radical Republican's faith in protective tariffs. But it sent his daughter on a trajectory from regulation to socialism.[9]

Supporters of direct regulation emphasized the hazards of unfettered markets. At the time of the founding, states and municipalities had exercised power over business, but now corporations such as the railroads were too large to be wrangled by anything but the federal government. Between 1890 and 1920, the U.S. Congress experimented with laws dividing monopolies, enacting rules for fair competition, banning child labor, and setting rates, minimum wages, and maximum hours in the jurisdictions it controlled. And while many businessmen opposed these laws, others actually endorsed them, seeing them as creating a competitive floor in their industries.

But the new regulatory philosophy also excited moralists hoping to enlist the federal government in their crusade against sin. Having pushed for the prohibition of alcoholic beverages at the state level since the 1840s, evangelicals now perceived that the United States could do more than simply tax beer, wine, and liquor. It seemed possible to implement national laws banning these drinks. Nor was booze the only sin reformers could abate. They could do something about the kidnapping and trafficking in prostitutes—what they called "white slavery." They could ban addictive mind-altering drugs like cocaine and opium.

America's new internationalism helped inspire efforts to abolish the opium trade. In particular, sovereignty over the Philippines made the United States responsible for thousands of opium smokers. Before 1898, the Spanish had, like the Hawaiian monarchy, sold exclusive licenses to merchants who imported the drug for the seven hundred thousand Chinese living on the archipelago. But progressives like President Roosevelt viewed the islands as a testing ground for their governing principles. In 1902, Congress enacted a resolution to bar the sale of opium and alcohol to all "aboriginal tribes and uncivilized races," a category that included not only Filipinos, but also Hawaiians, Indians, and Alaskans. By the end of Roosevelt's term, the United States had committed itself to prohibition of the drug. Between 1909 and 1914, the United States outlawed the importation of smoking opium, required the registration of all those selling opium and cocaine, and raised tariffs on both products. A nation that had indicted smugglers for lying to the government now prosecuted them for importing illegal commodities.[10]

EVEN AS ITS AMBIT CHANGED, the custom house continued to pursue revenue frauds. When William Howard Taft succeeded Theodore Roosevelt as president of the United States in 1909, he rewarded his predecessor by appointing his closest confidant, William Loeb Jr., as collector of the Port of New York. To catch smugglers, Loeb built a new federal force consisting of 275 men led by the former chief of police for Puerto Rico. During his four-year tenure, Loeb vigorously prosecuted affluent travelers who hid valuables in sleeper trunks. He likewise investigated the sugar refiners, pushing for the termination and prosecution of corrupt customs workers and obtaining over $3 million in duties from the trust.

Loeb likewise revived the war on art smuggling. On October 18, 1910, Treasury officials invaded the Fifth Avenue store of the Duveen brothers and seized millions of dollars in paintings and antiquities. Serving as the purveyors of high visual culture for America's upper classes, the Duveens had escaped their humble beginnings in Hull and Holland to become the world's preeminent art dealers. Loeb's men had successfully obtained testimony from a former employee of the firm, who accused the Duveens not only of lying about the worth of their merchandise, but of smuggling valuable paintings inside furniture, an intentional act making them subject to criminal indictment and arrest. The government also sued the brothers for $10 million. In the end, the Duveens escaped with fines totaling $35,000 plus a settlement of $1.2 million, but only because of the strenuous lobbying of their most avid client, banker J. P. Morgan.[11]

Loeb's diligence infuriated New York's wealthy. One woman fresh from a European tour purportedly raged that "the appropriate death for him would be choking with Irish lace—and I'd like to contribute some lace for the purpose." Others punished the collector by calling him a Jew and using his religion as justification for blackballing him from the Union League Club of New York. Loeb protested that his father was a Lutheran, his mother a Catholic. "If I were of Jewish blood I would be proud of it," he responded, "But I am not—I am of pure German blood, and I am proud of that too." Nonetheless, he was never admitted to the Union League.[12]

The middle classes also seemed frustrated with the custom house. The humor magazine *Puck* defended Loeb, saying that many smugglers who complained about abuse were hypocrites, who belonged "to that class whom the High Protective Tariff . . . has made rich at the expense of the masses." Yet the satirical magazine also published a series of cartoons depicting inspectors as menacing and intrusive, tearing apart both the private property and respectability of their victims. They represented the protective tariff as a whip and described a trip through the port as an "ordeal." Perhaps the ultimate such cartoon appeared in 1906, showing a customs officer roughly handling sacks belonging to a red-faced Santa Claus. For many Americans, modern consumer desires had made the custom house a source of irritation rather than pride.[13]

As more Americans traveled abroad, a wider swath of the population experienced government scrutiny. In 1912, Jack Johnson, the world's first African-American heavyweight boxing champ, sailed to England to attend the coronation of King George V. Johnson's dominance in the ring made him heroic to blacks. Segregationists hated him not only for disproving white supremacy, but for his love of fine clothes, fast cars, and white women. Upon his return, Johnson appeared in Chicago with his white wife, Etta, who was wearing a $6,000 diamond necklace. Treasury officials checked their records, concluded he had not declared the jewels at the New York Custom House, seized the contraband, and indicted the couple for smuggling. The boxer shrugged off the charges, crushed his next opponent, and then paid a $1,000 fine. But the prosecution weighed on his wife

AS THE AMERICAN PUBLIC GREW ACCUSTOMED TO BUYING INDULGENCES LIKE
TOYS, CANDY, AND CLOTHES, HUMORISTS BEGAN CRITIQUING THE EFFECTS OF CUS-
TOMS INSPECTION ON CONSUMERS. Courtesy The Beinecke Library, Yale University, New Haven,
Connecticut

Etta. Victimized by social disapproval, as well as her husband's abuse
and infidelity, she killed herself in September 1912.[14]

BETWEEN 1913 AND 1921, a new American government crystalized.
First, a coalition of Democrats, Progressives, and reform Republicans
enacted the Sixteenth Amendment, establishing the constitutionality
of the income tax. President Woodrow Wilson then begged, bribed,
and cajoled legislators to enact tariff reduction, surmounting the
obstacles that had humbled Grover Cleveland. The Revenue Act of
1913 assessed a 1 percent tax on individuals making more than $3,000
per year and married couples making $4,000, with a surtax of 1 to 6
percent on incomes over $20,000. Furthermore, the law expanded
the list of items that could be imported free of duty while dramati-

cally lowering rates overall. High tariffs returned briefly in the 1920s and 1930s, but the Revenue Act established the fiscal framework still in place one hundred years later.[15]

Society had changed. The argument that tariffs enabled a male laborer to support a wife and children seemed dated. By 1910, nearly a quarter of all American females over the age of ten were gainfully employed. Industrial investigators reported they could not find "the so-called normal family—father with wife and children dependent upon him for support." Four decades before, humorist Thomas Bangs Thorpe had painted women as natural smugglers, predicting that they would remove all tariffs if given the suffrage. When Wilson took office, nine states had already given over two million women the vote. And the states that had already established sexual equality at the ballot box—such as Oregon, Washington, and California—were the ones most open to Wilson's vision, which rejected the tariff in favor of a government offering direct protection to citizens, paid for by a tax on high incomes.[16]

The promise of new labor legislation allayed workers' fears about tariff reduction. When tariff supporters tried to turn workers against the Revenue Bill in 1913, American Federation of Labor secretary Frank Morrison publicly questioned the beneficial effects of tariffs while AFL president Samuel Gompers condemned employers for trying to pressure employees into opposing it. In the ensuing four years, labor received in return a series of legislative victories: an exemption from antitrust prosecutions, a law guaranteeing merchant seamen fair wages, an eight-hour day for railroad workers, and worker's compensation for federal employees. In 1916, Wilson appointed Louis Brandeis to the U.S. Supreme Court. An activist attorney tied to organized labor, Brandeis became the leading defender of the constitutionality of the progressive state, as well as a right to privacy based upon the court's 1886 decision in *Boyd v. United States*.[17]

By the end of the decade, the United States had cemented its place as one of the world's great powers. Wilson campaigned in 1912 against the imperialism of prior administrations, yet once in power, the president and Congress could not bring themselves to relinquish sovereignty over the Philippines. The United States was somewhat more generous to Puerto Rico, giving citizenship and civil rights to residents, but neither self-rule nor voting representation in Congress. And whatever Wilson's objections to empire, he believed that America needed to be economically, diplomatically, and militarily engaged with the rest of the globe.

United States involvement in World War One permanently transformed the meaning of smuggling. Never again would America's custom houses exceed the navy in size and might, as they had in the 1790s and 1880s. When Congress expanded the Department of Justice's Bureau of Investigation to prevent espionage, the Treasury Department's Secret Service ceased being the primary federal police force. And while Republicans revived the tariff in the 1920s, the labor policies established in the Great War predominated through the twentieth century. Most importantly, with the prohibition of alcoholic beverages in late 1918, liquor became the dominant form of contraband crossing the border. Even after the Great Experiment was over, the United States committed itself to the abolition of drugs such as heroin, cocaine, and marijuana. Anxiety about narcotics overwhelmed the fear of revenue fraud, making the latter seem somehow romantic, comical, or perhaps quaint.

Memory of these smugglers and their pursuers faded, their families disappearing from the front pages. Charley Lawrence's other sons, Walter and Percy, became known not for their father's crimes, but for their own exploits on Broadway and Wall Street. His niece, Florence Noah, made news in 1912, when she was murdered by her husband, actor Junius Brutus Booth III, the nephew of Lincoln's assassin. Charley's only granddaughter married the respectable heir to a wholesale drug empire. The Hoffnungs became British aristocrats. Treasury agents Hiram C. Whitley and Benaiah G. Jayne moved to towns in Kansas and Iowa respectively. Rose Eytinge continued her stage career, eventually dying in penury at a sanitarium. Louis Bieral's relations thrilled to rediscover his career. Benjamin F. Butler's heirs obtained the status he so jealously resented during his life, becoming fixtures in America's northeastern elite, his most famous descendant being the brilliant dabbler George Plimpton.[18]

These themes remained more resonant in the American South. In 1953, Ward Moore, the grandson of the Parsee Merchant, wrote a popular novel titled *Bring the Jubilee*, which speculated about a world where the Confederacy won the Civil War. In his alternative history, the South abolished slavery, and became a global empire, while the North became depressed, racist, and corrupt. Likewise, Louisianans memorialized Jean Lafitte. First, in the 1950s, the city of Lake Charles began celebrating a "Contraband Days" festival every May. And in the 1970s, the federal government designated a portion of the Gulf the Jean Lafitte National Historical Park and Preserve. Keen to honor a Franco-American war hero, and enthralled by the romance of piracy, they looked past Lafitte's slave trading.[19]

But if Charley Lawrence and other smugglers are now forgotten, traces of their America remain. Travelers must still submit to bodily inspection. The profiling of passengers is unlawful but informally practiced. Americans buy foreign merchandise, but feel more embarrassed than angry if anyone questions their patriotism for doing so. Pundits complain about effete cosmopolitan urban elites who betray heartland workers when they buy imports. The United States is fully in the world, but many Americans still long for the unifying nationalism of the past.

ACKNOWLEDGMENTS

Historians generally write alone, but few produce anything without the contributions of other scholars, friends, archivists, and funders. I have received fruitful counsel from George Chauncey, Alan Brinkley, Rebecca Plant, Eric Rauchway, Tony Horwitz, Michael Willrich, Nelson Lichtenstein, Elizabeth Shermer, Ari Kelman, Paul Kramer, Carol Faulkner, Geri Thoma, and Alane Salierno Mason. I will always owe a debt to my undergraduate advisor Richard Bulliet. I was fortunate to have the help of two assistants, Tyler Goodspeed and Diana Siu. To complete the book, I depended upon the generosity of the Radcliffe Institute for Advanced Study, the American Council of Learned Societies, Syracuse University's Maxwell School of Citizenship and Public Affairs, James Steinberg, Michael Wasylenko, Jeffrey Scruggs, and Robbin Mitchell. I enjoyed the assistance of specialists at the Library of Congress, New York University, the New York Public Library, the New York Historical Society, and National Archives. I must thank Tom Tryniski of the Fulton Post Cards site, as well as the unknown digitizers employed by Proquest, Ancestry, EBSCO, Cengage, NewspaperArchive, and the Library of Congress. Finally, I must express my love for my father Robert Baer Cohen, brother Randolph Baer Cohen, sister Sheryl Cohen Fine, my late mother Marilyn Wender Cohen, and my aunts Elaine S. Wender and Lois Feldstein. My wonderful daughter Mae keeps me entertained.

This book is dedicated to my dearest, Carol Faulkner.

NOTES

Anglo-American Times	AAT	*Frank Leslie's Popular Monthly Magazine*	FLPM
American Historical Review	AHR	*Grand Forks Herald*	GFH
American National Biography	ANB	*Hartford Daily Courant*	HC
Boston Daily Atlas	BA	*Journal of American History*	JAH
Boston Daily Advertiser	BAD	*Jewish Messenger*	JM
Brooklyn Eagle	BE	*Los Angeles Times*	LAT
Boston Daily Globe	BG	*London Daily News*	LDN
Baltimore Sun	BS	*Library of Congress*	LOC
Bangor Daily Whig & Courier	BWC	*London Week's News*	LWN
		Milwaukee Sentinel	MS
Chicago Daily Tribune	CT	*Mississippi Valley Historical Review*	MVHR
Daily Alta California	DAC		
Daily Graphic	DG	*National Archives and Records Administration*	NARA
Frank Leslie's Illustrated Newspaper	FLIN	*Newport Daily News*	NDN

Daily National Intelligencer	NI	New York Tribune	NYTrib
New Orleans Picayune	NOP	New York World	NYW
National Police Gazette	NPG	Pomeroy's Democrat	PD
National Republican (Washington, D.C.)	NR	Philadephia Inquirer	PI
		Philadelphia North American	PNA
New York Commercial Advertiser	NYCA	San Francisco Daily Evening Bulletin	SFB
New York Evening Express	NYE	Spirit of the Times	ST
New York Herald	NYH	Sunday Times and Noah's Weekly Messenger	STNWM
New York Post	NYP		
New York Press	NYPrs	Times of London	TL
New York Sun	NYS	Trow's New York City Directory	Trow's
New York Times	NYT		
New York Telegram	NYTel	Washington Post	WP

CHAPTER I: THE PRINCE

1   "Smugglers," *NYTrib*, 9/17/1875, 1; "Smuggling," *AAT*, 10/1/1875, 8–9; "Arrivals," *NYH*, 1/8/1875, 10; "Smugglers," *NYT*, 5/14/1875, 12; Robin Winks, *The Civil War Years* (Johns Hopkins, 1960), 141; Wesley Miller, *The Rebel and the Rose* (Cumberland, 2007), 211; "Absconding," *NYTrib*, 3/10/1875, 2; "Lawrence," *NYS*, 5/14/1875, 1; "Credit," *NYH*, 5/15/1875, 3; "Local Miscellany," *NYTrib*, 5/15/1875, 12; "Smugglers," *NYTel*, 5/13/1875, 1; "Requisition," *NYS*, 1/9/1876, 1; "Dead," *NYS*, 7/20/1890, 1; "Customhouse," *NYTrib*, 4/13/1870, 5; "Correspondence Respecting Extradition," in House of Commons, *Accounts and Papers*, v. 41 (Harrison & Sons, 1876), 1; Charles L. Lazarus passport, 10/27/1859.

2   "Smugglers," *NYT*, 5/14/1875, 12; "Credit," *NYH*, 5/14/1875, 3; "Smugglers," *NYTel*, 5/13/1875, 1; "Dead," *NYS*, 7/20/1890, 1; Harold Pinkett, "Efforts to Annex Santo Domingo," *Journal of Negro History* 26, no. 1 (Jan. 1941): 26.

3   "Smugglers," *NYT*, 5/14/1875, 12; "Dead," *NYS*, 7/20/1890, 1; "Married," *NYT*, 11/14/1856, 8; "Change of Name," *NYH*, 12/15/1864, 6; Letter, Charles L. Lawrence to George Bliss, 5/29/1876, v. 114, Fish Papers, LOC; "Gordon,"

NYT, 4/24/1872, 8; "Gordon," *NYT*, 8/5/1874, 3; John Bulloch, ed., *The House of Gordon*, v. 1 (Aberdeen, 1903), lxviii; Percy Colson, *The Strange History of Lord George Gordon* (Robert Hale & Co., 1937), 228; "Officer," *NYT*, 1/5/1875, 5; "Smith," *NYT*, 8/10/1875, 8; "Correspondence," *Accounts and Papers*, 1; "Telegraph," *St. Albans Messenger*, 3/31/1875, 3; "New York," *BAD*, 4/1/1875, 1; "Credit," *NYH*, 5/14/1875, 3; "Smugglers," *NYTel*, 5/13/1875, 1; Thomas Bartlett, *Ireland* (Cambridge, 2010), 304–5; Henry Mayhew and John Binny, *The Criminal Prisons of London* (Griffin, Bohn, 1862), 611–23; "Lawrence," *PD*, 5/29/1875, 4.

4   Letter, Charles L. Lawrence to George Bliss, 5/29/1876, Fish Papers, v. 114; Letter, Lawrence to Sidney Webster, 6/15/1876, Fish Papers, v. 114; Richard Davenport-Hines, "Lewis, Sir George Henry, first baronet (1833–1911)," *Oxford Dictionary of National Biography* (Oxford, 2004), online ed., May 2010. "At Bow Street," *TL*, 4/16/1875, 1; "Latest," *NYT*, 5/3/1875, 1; "Correspondence," *Accounts and Papers*, 1–5; "Smugglers," *NYT*, 5/14/1875, 12; "Dead," *NYS*, 7/20/1890, 1; "Ludlow St.," *NYTel*, 5/13/1875, 1; Leo Hershkowitz, *Tweed's New York* (Anchor, 1978), 282–83.

5   "Credit," *NYH*, 5/14/1875, 3; "Prince," *NYTel*, 5/18/1875, 4; "Effect," *DG*, 5/3/1875, 1.

6   William Wyckoff, *Silk Goods of America* (Van Nostrand, 1880), 88; "Ludlow," *NYTel*, 5/13/1875, 1; "Smugglers," *NYTel*, 5/13/1875, 1; "Smugglers," *NYT*, 5/14/1875, 12; "Frauds," *New Hampshire Patriot*, 3/8/1876, 4; John Simon ed., *The Papers of Ulysses S. Grant*, v. 27, January 1–October 31, 1876 (SIU, 2005), 150–52; Allan Nevins, *Hamilton Fish* (Dodd, Mead, 1936).

CHAPTER 2: REPUBLIC

1   "Wells," *NYW*, 8/24/1875, n.p.; "Wells," *MS*, 8/24/1875, n.p.; Peter Andreas, *Smuggler's Nation* (Oxford, 2013).

2   John Phillip Reid, *In a Rebellious Spirit* (Penn State, 1979); Frank McLynn, *Crime and Punishment in Eighteenth-Century England* (Routledge, 1989), 188; Paul Monod, "Dangerous Merchandise," *Journal of British Studies* 30, no. 2 (Apr. 1991): 150–82; Steven Pincus, *1688* (Yale, 2009).

3   William Fowler, "John Hancock," *ANB*; Reid, *Spirit*, 7, 37–38, 104–6; Oliver Dickerson, *The Navigation Acts and the American Revolution* (University of Pennsylvania, 1974); Timothy Breen, *Marketplace of Revolution* (Oxford, 2005), 195–293, 299–302.

4   Gautham Rao, "The Creation of the American State: Customhouses, Law, and Commerce in the Age of Revolution," PhD diss., University of Chicago, 2008, 52–74; William A. Williams, "The Age of Mercantilism," *William and Mary Quarterly*, 3d ser., 15, no. 4 (Oct. 1958): 420–37; Burton Spivak, *Jefferson's English Crisis* (University of Virginia, 1979), 2–4; Max Edling, *A Revolution in Favor of Government* (Oxford, 2003); Richard John, *Spreading the News*

(Harvard, 1998); Daniel Walker Howe, *What Hath God Wrought* (Oxford, 2007), 271.

5   Gary Kornblith, "Cementing the Mechanic Interest . . . ," in *New Perspectives on the Early Republic*, eds. Ralph D. Gray and Michael A. Morrison (University of Illinois, 1994), 125; "Extract," *Connecticut Gazette*, 9/17/1790, 3; John Kaminski, *George Clinton* (Rowman & Littlefield, 1993), 90; Joshua Smith, *Borderland Smuggling* (University of Florida, 2006), 17–27, 43–45.

6   "Report," *Pennsylvania Packet*, 1/27/1790, 3; Rao, "Creation," 111–12, 121–23.

7   Joanna Nicholls, "United States Revenue Cutter Service," *FLPM* 42, no. 4 (1896): 18; Harold Syrett, *The Papers of Alexander Hamilton*, v. 7 (University of Virginia, 2011), 75, 123, 150–52; Terry Bouton, *Taming Democracy* (Oxford, 2007), 197–243; Robert Ayer, "Shifty Seafarers, Shifting Winds," PhD diss., Tufts University, 1993; Smith, *Borderland*, 34; Syrett, *Papers of Hamilton*, v. 7, 152.

8   William Davis, *The Pirates Lafitte* (Harcourt, 2005), 51–52.

9   Robert Lee, *Blackbeard the Pirate* (Blair, 1974); Marcus Rediker, *Villains of All Nations* (Verso, 2004), 16, 32; Douglas Burgess, "A Crisis of Charter and Right," *Journal of Social History* 45, no. 3 (Spring 2012): 605–22; Virginia Lunsford, *Piracy and Privateering in the Golden Age Netherlands* (Palgrave Macmillan, 2005), 120; Brian Lavery, *Nelson's Navy* (Naval Institute, 1989), 116; Alexander DeConde, *The Quasi War* (Scribner's, 1966), 125–26.

10 Charles Gayarre, "Historical Sketch of Pierre and Jean Lafitte," *Magazine of American History* 10, no. 6 (Nov. 1883): 392; Davis, *Pirates*, 65–66.

11 *Imperial Gazetteer*, quoted in R. P. Hampton Roberts, "Barataria," *Notes and Queries*, 5th ser., 7 (Jan.–June, 1877): 115; Davis, *Pirates*, 26–28, 31, 45, 58.

12 Davis, *Pirates*, 53–59, 68–69, 99–101; Washington Irving, *Biographies and Miscellanies* (Putnam, 1869), 95; Charles Gayarre, "Historical Sketch of Pierre and Jean Lafitte," *Magazine of American History* 10, no. 5 (Oct. 1883): 285.

13 "Latour's Historical Memoir," *Analectic Magazine* 6 (Dec. 1815): 472–75.

14 United States Bureau of the Census, *Fifteenth Census of the United States: 1930, Population*, v. 1 (G.P.O., 1930), 455, 471, 511, 743, 1109; Samuel Eliot Morison, *Harrison Gray Otis, 1765–1848* (Houghton Mifflin, 1969); John Lowell, *The New-England Patriot* (Russell and Cutler, 1810), 147–48.

15 Jane Kamensky, *The Exchange Artist* (Penguin, 2008), 120–22; Robert Winthrop, *Memoir of the Hon. Nathan Appleton, LL.D.* (J. Wilson and Son, 1861), 8, 15–17; Smith, *Borderland*, 13–16, 72; "Congress," *NI*, 12/03/1812, 2; Alan Taylor, *William Cooper's Town* (Knopf, 1996), 325, 344; Lewis Tappan, *The Life of Arthur Tappan* (Hurd & Houghton, 1870), 44–59; "Died," *NYCA*, 10/7/1807, 3.

16 Wayne Franklin, *James Fenimore Cooper* (Yale, 2007), 118; James Fenimore Cooper, *The Water-witch* (Houghton Mifflin, 1884), xv, xx, 296; L. L. Dutcher, "St. Albans," *Vermont Historical Gazetteer*, v. 2, ed. Abby Maria Hemenway (Hemenway, 1871), 245, 344–47; Karen Campbell and John Lovejoy, "Black Snake Affair," *Vermont Encyclopedia*, eds. John Duffy, Samuel Hand, and Ralph Orth (University Press of New England, 2003), 58.

17 Donald Hickey, "American Trade Restrictions during the War of 1812" *JAH* 68, no. 77; Rao, "Creation," 317; "Message," *Maryland Gazette*, 11/7/1811, n.p.

18 "Reflections," *Vermont Washingtonian*, reprinted in *The Tickler*, 12/11/1811, 2; Donald Hickey, "Federalist Party Unity and the War of 1812," *Journal of American Studies* 12, no. 1 (Apr., 1978): 26; La Fayette Wilbur, *Early History of Vermont*, v. 4 (Roscoe, 1903), 372.

19 Stephen Budiansky, *Perilous Fight* (Vintage, 2012), 162–63.

20 Morison, *Otis*, 336–38, 367; Alan Taylor, *The Civil War of 1812* (Knopf, 2010), 277, 415–416; Hickey, "Restrictions," 530; Smith, *Borderland*, 81–82, 109–10.

21 "The Morality of Boston," from the *Boston Patriot*, reprinted in the *NI*, 9/11/1813, n.p.

22 Tappan, *Life*, 44, 56–57; Spivak, *Crisis*, 200–201; Hickey, "Restrictions," 530–31, 534; "Song," *Green-Mountain Farmer*, 8/21/1815, 1.

23 Taylor, *Civil War*, 243–45, 402–3, 413, 416–17, 420–421; Davis, *Pirates*, 121–23; Arsene Latour, *Historical Memoir of the War in West Florida and Louisiana in 1814–15* (Florida, 1999), 26.

24 Davis, *Pirates*, 77–79, 107–226; Gayarre, "Historical Sketch, I," 290, 297; Gayarre, "Historical Sketch, II," 392–95; Robert Remini, *The Battle of New Orleans* (Penguin, 1999), 48, 101.

25 Davis, *Pirates*, 224–25; "Suppression of Piratical Establishments," American State Papers: Foreign Relations 4, no. 290 (Gale and Seaton, 1834), 134; *Report of Mr. Kennedy . . . May, 1842* (Gale & Seaton, 1843), 244–45; "Notice," *National Messenger*, 7/29/1818, 3; "Latour's," *National Register*, 5/11/1816, 161; Carolyn DeLatte, *Antebellum Louisiana*, v. 2 (Center for Louisiana Studies, 2004), 85.

26 Howe, *Wrought*, 132–33; Samuel Hadley and Mabel Hill, "Lowell: A Character Sketch of the City," *New England Magazine* 19, no. 5 (Jan. 1899): 628–30; Linda Kistler, "The Middlesex Canal," *Accounting Historians Journal* 7, no. 1 (Spring 1980), esp. 47; Joseph Davis, *Essays in the Earlier History of American Corporations* (Harvard, 1917), 173; Robert Remini, *Henry Clay* (Norton, 1993), 78–79, 135–39; Maurice Baxter, *Henry Clay and the American System* (University of Kentucky, 2004), 17–20; Robert Dalzell, *Enterprising Elite* (Harvard, 1987), 33–34, 36, 47; Douglas Irwin and Peter Temin, "The Antebellum Tariff on Cotton Textiles Revisited," *Journal of Economic History* 61, no. 3 (Sep., 2001): 779; Henry Clay, speech, Sept. 1842, quoted in Jonathan Glickstein, *American Exceptionalism, American Anxiety* (University of Virginia, 2002), 192.

27 Kamensky, *Artist*, 120–22; Winthrop, *Memoir*, 28, 33; Donald Radcliffe, "The Nullification Crisis," *American Nineteenth-Century History* 1, no. 2 (2000): 12–13; Howe, *Wrought*, 401, 544–45; Sean Wilentz, *The Rise of American Democracy* (Norton, 2006), 312–29.

28 Howe, *Wrought*, 272–73; Radcliffe, "The Nullification Crisis," 4–5; Michael Tadman, *Speculators and Slaves* (University of Wisconsin, 1996), 238–39; Adam Rothman, *Slave Country*, 26, 83–91, 195–96; John Conger, "South

Carolina and the Early Tariffs," *MVHR* 5, no. 4 (Mar., 1919): 415–33; Sven Beckert, "Emancipation and Empire," *AHR* 109, no. 5 (Dec. 2004): 1405–38; Elizabeth Fox-Genovese and Eugene Genovese, *The Mind of the Master Class* (Cambridge, 2005), 135–36, 305–60; "Coalitions," *United States Telegraph*, 1/9/1833, n.p.

29 "Lafitte," *Niles National Register*, 4/27/1816, 130; Richard Penn Smith, *Lafitte or The Baratarian Chief, a Tale. Founded on Facts* (Providence, 1826); Morton McMichael, ed., *The Miscellaneous Works of the Late Richard Penn Smith* (H. W. Smith, 1856), 8; David Copeland, *The Antebellum Era* (Greenwood, 2003), 59, 64; Harold Watson, *Coasts of Treasure Island* (Naylor, 1969), 111; Davis, *Pirates*, 463–64, 468.

30 Davis, *Pirates*, 472; Joseph Holt Ingraham, *Lafitte: the Pirate of the Gulf* (Harper & Brothers, 1836); Joseph Holt Ingraham, *The Sunny South* (G. G. Evans, 1860); Robert Weathersby, *Joseph Holt Ingraham: A Critical Introduction to the Man and His Work* (University of Tennessee, 1974); Joseph Cobb, *The Creole: A Story of the Siege of New Orleans* (Hart, 1850); George Buckley, "Joseph B. Cobb: Mississippi Essayist and Critic," *American Literature* 10, no. 2 (May 1938), 169; Joseph Holt Ingraham, "The Life and Times of Lafitte," *DeBow's Review* 1, no. 4 (Oct. 1851): 372–73, 376; Alexander Walker, *Jackson and New Orleans* (J. C. Derby, 1856), 48.

31 Edgar Allan Poe, *Southern Literary Messenger*, August 1836; Charles Ellms, *The Pirates Own Book* (Sanborn & Carter, 1837); Boyd Childress, "Ellmes, Charles," *Encyclopedia of American Literature of the Sea and Great Lakes*, ed. Jill Gidmark (Greenwood, 2001), 129–30; Davis, *Pirates*, 472, 645 n. 29; "Lafitte," *PNA*, 11/20/1851, 1; "Believed," *BA*, 11/27/1851, 1; W. B., "Lafitte," *Littell's* 32, no. 407 (3/6/1852): 1; "Smugglers," *FLIN*, 11/8/1856, 349.

CHAPTER 3: LAZARUS

1 "Obituary," *NYT*, 7/17/1890, 5; Isaac Goldberg, *Major Noah* (Jewish Publication Society, 1938), 288; William White, *History . . . Directory of Nottinghamshire* (William White, 1832), 255.

2 "Married," *Bristol Mercury*, 1/12/1830, n.p.; "Israel Lazarus," 1851 British Census, Kingston-upon-Hull; Lewis Hyman, *The Jews of Ireland* (Irish, 1972), 108; Israel Finestein, *Scenes and Personalities in Anglo-Jewry* (Vallentine Mitchell, 2002), 114–61, esp. 121–22; V. D. Lipman, *Social History of the Jews in England* (Watts, 1954), 5; Michael Jacobs, *Ghost Train through the Andes* (John Murray, 2006), xix–xx, 2–8.

3 Tony Kushner, "A Tale of Two Port Jewish Communities," in *Port Jews*, ed. David Cesarani (Frank Cass, 2002), 98; "Pawnbrokering," *Hampshire Telegraph*, 7/17/1817, n.p.; "Furniture," *Hampshire Telegraph*, 8/3/1829, n.p.; Hyman, *Jews*, 108; Finestein, *Scenes*, 121–22; "Promenade," *Freeman's Journal*, 12/23/1842, n.p.

4   "Smugglers," *NYTel*, 5/13/1875, 1; Thomas Perry, *Perry's Bankrupt and Insol-vent Gazette* (William Myers, 1829), 271; "Married," *Bristol Mercury*, 1/12/1830, n.p.; "Legal," *Hull Packet*, 12/4/1840, n.p.; White, *History*, 255; "J. L. Lazarus," 1841 British Census, Kingston-upon-Hull.

5   "Southhampton," *Hampshire Telegraph*, 8/1/1831, n.p.; "Brussels," *Satirist*, 9/29/1829, n.p.; "Driving," *Bell's Life*, 11/11/1832, n.p.

6   *The Circular to Bankers* 689 (7/9/1841): 295; "Bankruptcy," *TL*, 4/12/1848, 7; Perry, *Perry's Bankrupt and Insolvent Gazette* 27 (1852): 548; George Elwick, *The Bankrupt Directory* (Simpkin, Marshall, 1843), 251; "Insolvents," *Bell's Life*, 12/12/1847, 8; *Cunliffe and Others v. Booth*, 3 Bingham's N.C. 821 (1837); *The Queen v. Kenrick*, 1 Cox Cr. Cas. 146 (1845); "Bankruptcy," *London Era*, 4/9/1848, 14; Proceedings of the Central Criminal Court, 1/29/1849, 5, Old Bailey Online Project; Proceedings of the Central Criminal Court, 1/7/1850, 5, Old Bailey Online Project.

7   "Bills of Exchange," *The Era*, 4/4/1841, 7; "Abridged Police Intelligence," *Observer*, 4/14/1844, n.p.; "Bankruptcy Court," *TL*, 1/8/1850, 7; Andrew Lang, *The Life and Letters of John Gibson Lockhart*, v. 2 (Scribner's, 1897), 291, 293–94, 302, 312, 314–16.

8   "J. B. Cary [sic] & Co.," *Broadway Journal*, 7/26/1845, 47; "J. B. Carey & Co.," *Scientific American* 1, no. 4 (9/18/1845): 4; "Requested," *Broadway Journal*, 7/26/1845, 47; "Arrivals," *New London Morning News*, 10/10/1845, 3; Renée Susan Jackson, "Use of Noninvasive Methods to Document the Characteris-tics of Sewing Thread Used in U.S. Women's Dress Ensembles from 1880 to 1909," master's thesis, Virginia Polytechnic Institute, December 1997, 18; "Editor," *Broadway Journal*, 6/14/1845, 384; Roger Tilley, *A History of Playing Cards* (C. N. Potter, 1973), 157; Malcolm Stern, *First American Jewish Families*, 3rd ed. (Genealogical Pub., 1991), 33, 147; Frederic Lazarus, 1841 British Cen-sus, Edmonton, London, Middlesex, England, 25.

9   *United States v. Lawrence*, Case No. 15,573, 26 F. Cas. 879 (1876); Richard Stott, *Workers in the Metropolis* (Cornell, 1990), 8–11; Joseph Ferrie, *Yankeys Now* (Oxford, 1999), 50.

10 M. C. N. Salbstein, *The Emancipation of the Jews in Britain* (Fairleigh Dickin-son, 1982); "Sabbath," *Cottager's Monthly Visitor* 8 (Jan. 1828): 9–10.

11 Kushner, "A Tale," 96; Frederick Marryat, *The Complete Works of Captain F. Marryatt*, vol. 1 (Charles Lane, 1840), 5, 20, 21, 46, 312, 385, 386, 387, 388, 389, 391, 403, 480; Edmund Hodgson Yates, *My Haunts and Their Frequenters* (David Bogue, 1854), 5.

12 "Commission," *Freeman's Journal*, 4/16/1842, n.p.; Arnold Sorsby, "John Zachariah Laurence," *British Journal of Ophthalmology* 16, no. 11 (Nov. 1932): 727–40.

13 George Orwell, *The Lion and the Unicorn* (Secker and Warburg, 1941), 33; "Bankruptcy," *TL*, 1/8/1850, 7; "Brussels," *Satirist*, 9/29/1829, n.p.; "Rogue," *Punch* 38 (11/10/1860): 183.

14   Jacob Rader Marcus, ed., *The Jew in the American World* (Wayne State, 1996), 101; "Question," *NYT*, 5/11/1867, 2; Simon Wolf and Lewis Levy, *The American Jew as Patriot, Soldier and Citizen* (Levytype, 1895), 57; Stephen Birmingham, *"Our Crowd"* (Harper & Row, 1967), 74–75, 127; Jacob Rader Marcus, *United States Jewry, 1776–1985*, v. 2 (Wayne State, 1989), 242; Stern, *Families*, 150; Walter Barrett, *The Old Merchants of New York City*, v. 1 (Knox, 1885), 184; Bette Young, *Emma Lazarus in Her World* (Jewish Publication Society, 1995), 6, 43–44, 48–49; Lance Sussman, *Isaac Leeser and the Making of American Judaism* (Wayne State, 1995), 55; Stephen Birmingham, *The Grandees* (Harper & Row, 1971), 266–67; Jonathan Sarna, *Jacksonian Jew* (Holmes & Meyer, 1981), 16–33.

15   Beaumont Newhall, *The Daguerreotype in America* (Dover, 1975), 19–20; "Charles L. Lazarus," *NDN*, 7/11/1850, 23; *Supplement to Doggett's New York City Directory* (John Doggett, Jr., 1845), 215; *Doggett's New York City Directory for 1848–9* ((John Doggett, Jr., 1848), 243; *Rode's New York City Directory for 1850–1* (Rode, 1850), 300; Clare Phillips, *Bejewelled by Tiffany, 1837–1987* (Yale, 2006), 296.

16   Newhall, *Daguerreotype*, 55–60; "Lazarus," *NDN*, 7/11/1850, 23; "Daguerreotypes," *NDN*, 7/22/1850, 66; "Daguerreotype," *NDN*, 7/24/1850, 74; "Notice," *NDN*, 7/29/50, 94.

17   Jacobs, *Ghost*, 5, 8; Robert Grau, *The Business Man in the Amusement World* (Broadway, 1910), 335; "Dodworth," *NYT*, 11/20/1852, 5; Vera Lawrence, *Reverberations, 1850–1856* (University of Chicago, 1995), 311; "Home," *Harper's Weekly*, 3/28/1868, 203; "Larceny," *NYT*, 8/5/1853, 8; "Obituary," *NYT*, 1/25/1891, 3.

18   "Chief," *NYT*, 1/14/1885, 1; Tyler Anbinder, *Five Points* (Plume, 2002), 166; Herbert Asbury, *The Gangs of New York* (Thunder's Mouth, 1928), 40–41.

19   "Dodworth," *NYT*, 1/25/1891, 3; "Complimentary," *NYTrib*, 2/25/1853, 1; William Upton, *William Henry Fry* (Crowell, 1974); "Congratulate," *ST*, 8/27/1853, 336; "King," *BE*, 4/4/1880, 4.

20   Frank Franklin, "The Legislative History of Naturalization in the United States from the Revolutionary War to 1861," PhD diss., University of Chicago, 1905, 278–300; Hyman, *Jews*, 108; Finestein, *Scenes*, 115; Lucy Salyer, "The Reconstruction of American Citizenship: Fenians and the Expatriation Crisis of the 1860s," unpublished paper, American Society for Legal History Annual Meeting, 2006.

21   "Dissolution," *NYT*, 6/10/1854, 7; *Graduating Song, Class of 1855: West Point* (C. L. Lazarus, 1855); T. B. Thorpe, "The New York Custom-House," *Harper's New Monthly Magazine* 43 (1871): 21–23; "Hopper," *Church's Musical Visitor* 11, no. 15 (Dec. 1882): 413.

22   Goldberg, *Noah*, 290; Alfred Trumble, "Jews," *FLPM* 4, no. 2 (Aug. 1877): 135; "Passengers, *NYT*, 10/1856; "Wedding," *Wisconsin Pinery*, 12/4/1856, 2.

23   "Ladies," *NYTrib*, 12/22/1856, 6; *Trow's*, 1856, 619; "Capitalists," *NYH*, 1/30/1857, 3; "Let," *NYH*, 6/10/1857, 3.

24 James Huston, *The Panic of 1857 and the Coming of the Civil War* (LSU, 1987), 14–15, 20; James McPherson, *Battle Cry of Freedom* (Oxford, 1988), 189; Iver Bernstein, *The New York City Draft Riots* (Oxford, 1990), 138–40.

25 "Marine," *NYT*, 9/22/1858, 8; "Marine," *Boston Courier*, 11/25/1858, 4; "Health," *NYH*, 10/5/1856, 8; "Express," *Philadelphia Press*, 9/7/1857, 1; "Landing," *NYH*, 4/11/1858, 8; "Outrage," *Ohio Statesman*, 5/20/1859, 2; "Another," *NDN*, 8/21/1860, 2; "Steamer," *Richmond Dispatch*, 9/17/1861, n.p.; "Pirates," *NYTrib*, 4/8/1861, 8; House of Commons, *Accounts and Papers*, v. 33 (Harrison & Sons, 1862), 118.

26 "Personal," *NYT*, 3/23/1858, 1; "Passengers," *NYT*, 3/29/1858, 8; Charles L. Lazarus passport, 10/27/1859; "Empire City," 2/16/1860, *Passenger Lists of Vessels Arriving at New Orleans, Louisiana, 1820–1902*, NARA, microfilm publication accessed via Ancestry.com; "Notaries," *NYT*, 2/3/1859, 5.

27 "Marriages," *TL*, 5/4/1858, 1; "Lawrence," *STNWM*, 1/16/1859, 3; "Case," *NYT*, 8/30/1859, 5; "A Correction," *NYTrib*, 8/31/1859, 7; "Alleged," *NYT*, 8/31/1859, 5; "Safes," *NYH*, 10/25/1859, 11.

28 Bernstein, *Riots*, 137, 142–43; Bertram Korn, *Eventful Years and Experiences* (American Jewish Archives, 1954), 12, 74–76; Sarna, *Jacksonian Jew*, 48–52; Thorpe, "Customhouse," 16; *Poillon v. Lawrence et al.*, 77 N.Y. 207 (1879).

29 "Died," *NYTrib*, 8/12/1860, n.p.; "Smugglers," *NYTel*, 5/13/1875, 1; "Freedom," *TL*, 2/15/1859, 15; *London Blue Book* (1860), 734; *Boyle's Court Guide for January 1860*, 35; George H. Davis household, Census of 1860, East Ward, City of Petersburg, State of Virginia.

CHAPTER 4: SLAVES

1 *Letter from the Secretary of the Treasury relative to Secret Inspectors of Customs* (G.P.O., 1847), 3, 7, 9, 11–12; Frank Taussig, *Tariff History of the United States* (Putnam's, 1892), 140; *Report of the Secretary of the Treasury . . . to Prevent Frauds upon the Revenue since the Passage of the Act of 1846* (G.P.O., 1850); *Letter from the Secretary of the Treasury . . . Receipts and Expenditures of the Government* (G.P.O., 1847), 424; *Letter from the Secretary of the Treasury . . . Receipts and Expenditures of the Government* (G.P.O., 1848), 362; *Report of the Acting Secretary of the Treasury . . . Seizure and Forfeiture of Goods under the Tariff Act of 1846* (G.P.O., 1852), 2–5.

2 James Winston, "The Mississippi Whigs and the Tariff 1834–1844," *MVHR* 22, no. 4 (Mar., 1936): 505–24; Antoinette Lee, *Architects to the Nation* (Oxford, 2000), 40–43, 77; James D. B. DeBow, *The Industrial Resources, etc., of the Southern and Western States*, v. 2 (DeBow's Review, 1852), 435; Letter, Alexander S. Brownlow to Col. L. C. Haynes, *Jonesborough* (Tenn.) *Sentinel*, quoted in "Premonitory," *Weekly Ohio Statesman*, 8/28/1844, n.p.; "Congress," *BE*, 5/22/1844, 4; "Brooks," *NI*, 7/31/1851, n.p.

3 "Court," *Placer Times Transcript*, 3/23/1855, 2; "Law," *DAC*, 10/31/1855, n.p.;

"Levy," *DAC*, 11/6/1855, n.p.; "Levy," *SFB*, 11/17/1855, 2; David Frederick, *Rugged Justice* (University of California, 1994), 11–12; James D. B. DeBow, *The Industrial Resources, etc., of the Southern and Western States*, v. 1 (DeBow's Review, 1852), 11; *United States v. Sixty-Seven Packages*, 58 U.S. 85 (1855); Michael Ross, "Obstructing Reconstruction," *Civil War History* 49 (Sept. 2003): 235–53.

4   Hiram Whitley, *In It* (Riverside, 1894), 20; Joseph Ferrie, *Yankeys Now* (Oxford, 1999), 161; Christopher Tomlins, *Law, Labor, and Ideology in the Early American Republic* (Cambridge, 1993), 303, 344–82; Richard West, *Lincoln's Scapegoat General* (Houghton Mifflin, 1965), 26.

5   West, *Scapegoat*, 35, 51; Mark Schmeller, "Eating Fire: Journalistic Combat in Antebellum America," unpublished manuscript in author's possession, 16, 38–42; Levi Reese, *Funeral Oration . . . of Hon. Jonathan Cilley* (Wiley & Putnam, 1838); Hans Trefousse, *Ben Butler* (Twayne, 1957), 41, 34–46; David Grimsted, *American Mobbing, 1828–1861* (Oxford, 1998), 22, 26–27, 35–38, 42, 46–47, 53–54; Bruce Laurie, *Beyond Garrison* (Cambridge, 2005), 12–13, 136–68; Iver Bernstein, *The New York City Draft Riots* (Oxford, 1990), 5, 24; George Thompson, *Venus in Boston and Other Tales of Nineteenth-Century City Life*, eds. David Reynolds and Kimberly Gladman (University of Massachusetts, 2002), 4–104, esp., 103–4.

6   Charles Francis Adams, *Richard Henry Dana: A Biography*, v. 1 (Houghton Mifflin, 1891), 1–70, 128–29; Richard Henry Dana, *Two Years before the Mast and Other Voyages* (Library of America, 2005).

7   Adams, *Richard Henry Dana*, v. 1, 121–201; Louis Menand, *The Metaphysical Club* (Farrar, Straus & Giroux, 2002), 11–13; Trefousse, *Butler*, 208; George Boutwell, *Reminiscences of Sixty Years in Public Affairs*, v. 1 (McClure, Phillips, 1902), 227; Edward Waldo Emerson, *The Early Years of the Saturday Club, 1855–1870* (Houghton Mifflin Company, 1918), 39–45, esp. 44; John Mulkern, *The Know-Nothing Party in Massachusetts* (Northeastern, 1990), 32, 47–48; Richard Henry Dana, *The Journal*, v. 2, ed. Robert Lucid (Belknap, 1968), 599, 622.

8   Menand, *Metaphysical*, 11; Albert J. von Frank, *The Trials of Anthony Burns* (Harvard, 1999), 68, 84–88, 91–96; "Butler," *Lowell Citizen*, 9/5/1856, n.p.; "The Man," *BA*, 5/29/1854, n.p.; Von Frank, *Trials*, 68; "Deaths Registered in the City of Charlestown for the year 1854, Charles Poole, City Clerk," 40, 61; Benjamin Franklin Butler, *Autobiography* (A. M. Thayer, 1892), 41.

9   Richard Henry Dana, Jr., "Against the Rendition of Anthony Burns to Slavery," in *Speeches in Stirring Times and Letters to a Son*, ed. Richard Henry Dana III (Houghton Mifflin, 1910), 210–11; "Rehearing in the Case of Judge Loring," *Liberator*, 4/13/1855, 59.

10 Adams, *Richard Henry Dana*, v. 1, 328; "Bieral," *BG*, 11/2/1886, 1; "Career," *Long Island City Star*, 11/2/1886, 1; "Boston," *NYT*, 11/5/1886, 5; "Beattie," *NYS*, 11/2/1886, 1; David Long, *Gold Braid and Foreign Relations* (Naval Insti-

tute, 1988), 256–57; "Police," *Boston Courier*, 12/16/1841, 1; "Mary," *NYH*, 12/13/1841, 1; "Louis," *DAC*, 8/10/1850, 2; "Court," *DAC*, 8/15/1850, 1; "Commonwealth," *BA*, 5/14/1850, 1; David Reynolds, *Mightier than the Sword* (Norton, 2011), 108.

11   "Assault," *HC*, 6/5/1854, 2; "Arrest," *NOP*, 7/6/1854, 1; "Sullivan," *NOP*, 7/31/1854, 1; Von Frank, *Trials*, 224–25; Adams, *Richard Henry Dana*, v. 1, 282–85, 303–4, 310–30.

12   "Third," *BA*, 10/24/1856, n.p.; "Fifth," *BA*, 10/27/1856, n.p.; "Commonwealth," *BA*, 3/30/1857, 1; "Talked," *Boston Gazette*, 11/21/1857, 4; "Boxer," *NYT*, 2/7/1907, 15; "Domestic," *Harper's Weekly*, 10/30/1858, 694; "The Fight," *NYT*, 10/22/1858, 5; "Affairs," *BA*, 10/27/1856, n.p.; "Trotting," *ST*, 6/16/1860, n.p.; "Reorganization," *NYT*, 9/1/1859, 5; "Pronouncements," *NYT*, 7/2/1860, 9.

13   Eric Foner, *Free Soil, Free Labor, Free Men* (Oxford, 1971); David Montgomery, *Beyond Equality* (Knopf, 1967).

14   Manisha Sinha, *The Counterrevolution of Slavery* (UNC, 2000), 139, 150, 151–62, esp. 161; Eric Walther, *William Lowndes Yancey and the Coming of the Civil War* (UNC, 2006), 214; Ronald Takaki, *A Pro-Slavery Crusade* (Free Press, 1971); "Miscellaneous: 1. African Labor Supply Association," *DeBow's Review* 27, no. 2 (Aug. 1859): 231–35; "Courier," *Charleston Mercury*, 9/9/1858, n.p.

15   W.E.B. DuBois, *The Suppression of the African Slave-trade to the United States of America, 1638–1870* (Longmans, 1904), 178–79, 180–93; Ernest Obadele-Starks, *Freebooters and Smugglers* (University of Arkansas, 2007), 8; Michael Tadman, "Slave Trading in the Ante-Bellum South," *Journal of American Studies* 13, no. 2 (Aug. 1979): 195–220; Reynolds Farley, "The Demographic Rates and Social Institutions of the Nineteenth Century Negro Population," *Demography* 2 (1965), 386–98; P. D. Curtin, *The Atlantic Slave Trade: A Census* (University of Wisconsin, 1969), 72–75; Alan Singer, "Nineteenth-Century New York City's Complicity with Slavery . . . ," in *Redress for Historical Injustices in the United States*, eds. Michael Martin and Marilyn Yaquinto (Duke, 2007), 283–84.

16   "Slave," *NYT*, 4/20/1859, 4; West, *Scapegoat*, 44–46; Trefousse, *Butler*, 56; "Boxer," *WP*, 2/7/1907, 15.

17   West, *Scapegoat*, 20, 36, 42, 44–46, 76–86; Trefousse, *Butler*, 55–61, 62–64, 78–79; "Contraband," *OED*, 2nd ed., (1989), online ed.; Kate Masur, " 'Contraband' and the Meanings of Emancipation," *JAH* 93, no. 4 (Mar. 2007): 1050–84.

18   John Carter, "Abraham Lincoln and the California Patronage," *AHR* 48, no. 3 (Apr. 1943): 495–506; Gary Lash, *"Duty Well Done"* (Butternut and Blue, 2001); Paul Fatout, "The California Regiment, Colonel Baker, and Ball's Bluff," *California Historical Society Quarterly* 31, no. 3 (Sept. 1952): 229–40; "Letter," *Sacramento Union*, 5/28/1861, 1; "Accession," *NYH*, 5/27/1861, 8.

19   Fatout, "California," 234–35; Elijah Kennedy, *The Contest for California in 1861* (Houghton Mifflin Company, 1912), 275; "The War," *NYTrib*, 10/25/1861, 5;

"Important," *NYT*, 10/27/1861, 1; "Battle," *NI*, 10/28/1861, n.p.; "Military," *NYS*, 10/30/1861, 1; "Fight," *Saturday Evening Post*, 11/2/1861, 3; Robert Tomes and Benjamin Smith, *The War with the South . . .* , v. 1 (Virtue & Yorston, 1862), 582.

20 "Obituary," *NYT*, 4/13/1878, 4; James Rowley, "Gordon," *Civil War History* 39, no. 3 (Sept. 1993): 216–24; Obadele-Starks, *Freebooters*, 185–191.

CHAPTER 5: BLOCKADE

1 Hans Trefousse, *Ben Butler* (Twayne, 1957), 107; James Parton, *General Butler in New Orleans* (Mason Bros., 1864), 71–74; T. Harry Williams, *P.G.T. Beauregard* (LSU, 1955), 40; Walter Johnson, *Soul by Soul* (Harvard, 1999), 1–2.

2 Richard Hofstadter, "The Tariff Issue on the Eve of the Civil War," *AHR* 44, no. 1 (Oct. 1938): 54–55; Reinhard Luthin, "Abraham Lincoln and the Tariff," *AHR* 49, no. 4 (Jul. 1944): 627–28; Ludwell Johnson, "Commerce between Northeastern Ports and the Confederacy," *JAH* 54, no. 1 (June 1967): 21; Frank Merli, *The Alabama, British Neutrality, and the American Civil War* (Indiana University, 2004), 3–10; James McPherson, *Battle Cry of Freedom* (Oxford, 1988), 384–87; David Surdam, *Northern Naval Superiority and the Economics of the American Civil War* (University of South Carolina, 2001), 33–34; Stephen Wise, *Lifeline of the Confederacy* (University of South Carolina, 1991), 11; John Majewski and Jay Carlander, "Virginia and the Possibilities of a Confederate Tariff," *Civil War History* 49, no. 4 (Dec. 2003): 334.

3 Brian McGinty, *Lincoln and the Court* (Harvard, 2009), 120–24; Abraham Lincoln, "Proclamation of Blockade," *Speeches and Writings 1859–1865* (Library of America, 1989), 233–34; *Prize Cases*, 67 U.S. 635 (1863); McGinty, *Lincoln*, 125–30; Union Defence Committee, *Minutes, Reports, and Correspondence; with an Historical Introduction* (Union Defence Committee, 1885), 131, 144–45; U.S. Congress, House of Representatives, 64th Congress, 1st Session, *Claims of the City of New York, Report No. 966* (G.P.O., 1916), 8; Charles Francis Adams, *Richard Henry Dana: A Biography*, v. 2 (Houghton Mifflin, 1891), 134–35, 153, 172–73, 256–57, 266–71.

4 Surdam, *Northern*, 154–59; Robert Browning, *From Cape Charles to Cape Fear* (University of Alabama, 1993), 1–3; Wise, *Lifeline*, 7; Mountague Bernard, *A Historical Account of the Neutrality of Great Britain During the American Civil War* (Longmans, 1870), 299–307; "Commerce," 34.

5 Wise, *Lifeline*, 99–100, 139; Browning, *Cape Charles*, 255, 259; Dave Horner, *Blockade Runners* (Dodd, Mead, 1968), 6, 140; John Wilkinson, *The Narrative of a Blockade-Runner* (Sheldon, 1877), 251; John Scharf, *History of the Confederate States Navy* (Rogers & Sherwood, 1886), 462–63; Jesse Wilkinson household, Norfolk, Virginia, 1860 Census, 172.

6 Michael Kauffman, *American Brutus* (Random House, 2004), 131; Andrew Bell, *Mosquito Soldiers* (LSU, 2010), 109–10; Catherine Clinton, *Mrs. Lin-*

coln (HarperCollins, 2010), 214–15; John Bennett, *The London Confederates* (McFarland, 2008), 161–63; Wise, *Lifeline*, 46, 116; "Fulton's," *NYH*, 11/09/1863, 4; *Official Records of the Union and Confederate Navies in the War of the Rebellion*, series I, v. 6 (G.P.O., 1897), 407.

7   Richard Bensel, *Yankee Leviathan* (Cambridge, 1990); Mark Wilson, *The Business of Civil War* (Johns Hopkins, 2006); Surdam, *Northern*, 3–4, 58–59, 170–71, 194; Wise, *Lifeline*, 74–89; Stanley Lebergott, "Through the Blockade: The Profitability and Extent of Cotton Smuggling," *Journal of Economic History* 41, no. 4 (Dec. 1981): 867–88; Marcus Price, "Ships that Tested the Blockade of the Carolina Ports, 1861–1865," *American Neptune* 8 (1948): 196–241; "Ships that Tested the Blockade of the Gulf Ports, 1861–1865," *American Neptune* 11 (1951): 262–90; "Ships that Tested the Blockade of the Georgia and East Florida Ports, 1861–1865," *American Neptune* 15 (1955): 97–132.

8   Allan Pinkerton, *Spy of the Rebellion* (Dillingham, 1883), 583–84; Lafayette Baker, *History of the United States Secret Service* (L. C. Baker, 1867), 45–46, 671: "Drolleries," *SFB*, 9/8/1859, 2; "Baker," *SFB*, 8/2/1864, 2; "History," *SFB*, 7/6/1867, 1; "California," *DAC*, 11/5/1859, n.p.

9   Baker, *History*, 18–20, 45–46, 671; Jacob Mogelever, *Death to Traitors* (Doubleday, 1960), 46–47.

10   Baker, *History*, 71–84; "Local," *PI*, 9/24/1861, 8; "Arrests," *BS*, 9/25/1861, 1; "Government Police," *CT*, 9/26/1861, 1; A Prisoner [William Gilchrist], *Two Months in Fort La Fayette* (Printed for the Author, 1862); "Sent," *BS*, 10/30/1861, 2; United States House of Representatives, 55th Congress, 3rd Session, *The War of the Rebellion*, Document No. 66, Series II, v. 2 (G.P.O., 1897), 821–54, 857; "Released," *BAD*, 4/16/1862, 4; "Affairs," *BS*, 4/19/1862, 4; Frank Howard, *Fourteen Months in American Bastiles* (Kelly, Hedian & Piet, 1863), 52; "Distressing," *BS*, 11/21/1849, 2.

11   Lonnie Speer, *Portals to Hell* (University of Nebraska, 2005), 35–38; *Appleton's Annual Cyclopaedia* (Appleton, 1864), 361; Baker, *History*, 335–69; John Marshall, *American Bastille* (T. W. Hartley, 1869), 139–52, 642–711.

12   Baker, *History*, 112–40, 181–92, 335–69.

13   Bertram Korn, *American Jewry and the Civil War* (Jewish Publication Society, 2001), 201; Deborah Dash Moore, *B'nai B'rith and the Challenge of Ethnic Leadership* (SUNY, 1981), 26; Esther Panitz, *Simon Wolf* (Fairleigh Dickinson, 1987), 27; Baker, *History*, 40, 72; James Morris Haig, U.S. Passport Application, 5/7/1851; James M. Haig, 1860 U.S. Census, 10th Ward, City of Baltimore, County of Baltimore, State of Maryland, 40; James M. Haig, 1880 U.S. Census, County of Baltimore, State of Maryland, Supervisor's District 1, Enumeration District 227, 54; "Robbery," *BS*, 5/26/1849, 1.

14   Baker, *History*, 65, 81–84; *Israelite*, 9, no. 34 (2/27/1863): 268; "Confederacy," *CT*, 3/24/1864, 3; "Grant," *CT*, 6/30/1868, 1; Korn, *Jewry*, 154–56, 188–93; Bertram Korn, *Eventful Years and Experiences* (American Jewish Archives, 1954), 143; Eli Evans, "Jewish Brothers," in *Jews and the Civil War*, eds. Jona-

than Sarna and Adam Mendelsohn (NYU, 2010), 42; Jonathan Sarna, *When General Grant Expelled the Jews* (Random House, 2012).

15   Eli Evans, "Overview: The War between Jewish Brothers in America," in *Jews and the Civil War*, 28–29; "Letter," *NYP*, 11/23/1864, reprinted in "A Defense," *The Israelite* 11, no. 25 (12/16/1864): 196–97; "Case," *NYW*, 12/16/1862, 4.

16   "Custom," *NYTrib*, 6/16/1864, 4; "Customhouse," *NYT*, 11/6/1863, 8; Arthur Rice, "Henry B. Stanton as a Political Abolitionist," quoted in Faye Dudden, *Fighting Chance* (Oxford, 2011), 56, 221; Lori Ginzberg, *Elizabeth Cady Stanton* (Hill and Wang, 2009), 111–14; Mark Neely, *The Union Divided* (Harvard, 2002), 28–30.

17   "Blockade," *NYT*, 1/3/1864, 4; "Blockade," *NYTrib*, 1/4/1864, 1; "Blockade," *NYT*, 1/4/1864, 8; "Blockade," *NYH*, 1/4/1864, 5; "Customhouse," *NYW*, 1/5/1864, 5.

18   Gerald Tulchinsky, *Taking Root* (Brandeis, 1993), 64–65, 67; "Abraham Hoffnung," *Canadian Jewish Times* 11, no. 11 (4/15/1908), in *A Biographical Dictionary of Canadian Jewry, 1897–1909*; "Victoria," *FLIN*, 8/11/1860, 179–80.

19   Albert Riddle, *Recollections of War Times* (G. P. Putnam, 1895), 240.

20   Benjamin Household, 1860 U.S. Census, 2nd District, 5th Ward, City of New York, County of New York, State of New York, 228; Malcolm Stern, *First American Jewish Families*, 3rd ed. (Genealogical Pub., 1991), 19, 243; "Naphtali," *NYT*, 11/4/1870, 5; "Financial," *NYH*, 8/10/1860, 6; Jonathan Sarna, *Jacksonian Jew* (Holmes & Meyer, 1981), 35.

21   John Niven, *Salmon P. Chase* (Oxford, 1995), 351–53; "Blockade," *NYT*, 1/3/1864, 4; *Customhouse Hearings*, 1864, 69–70.

22   "Extraordinary," *Glasgow Herald*, 7/19/1864, n.p.; Horner, *Blockade*, 9; Wise, *Lifeline*, 278; "Blockade," *NYT*, 1/8/1864, 5; *Papers Relating to Foreign Affairs accompanying the Annual Message of the President, Part II* (G.P.O., 1865), 553–54.

23   "Blockade," *NYT*, 1/8/1864, 5; "Law," *NYTrib*, 8/2/1864, 8; "Palmer," *NYT*, 10/17/1865, 8.

24   "Passengers," *BAD*, 1/19/1864, n.p.; "Blockade," *NYT*, 1/23/1864, 8; "Charges," *NYTrib*, 6/8/1864, 6; "Arbitrary," *NYH*, 6/3/1864, 8; "News," *Kingston News*, 6/9/1864, 2; "Arrest," *NYH*, 7/6/1864, 8; "Extraordinary," *Glasgow Herald*, 7/19/1864, n.p.

25   *Customhouse Hearings*, 1864, 62, 87, 136, 173, 179; "Blockade," *NYT*, 1/8/1864, 5; "Blockade," *NYT*, 1/23/1864, 8.

26   Editorial from *NYW*, quoted in "Arrests," *Newark Advocate*, 1/22/1864, 1; "Abolition," *BE*, 1/7/1864, n.p.; "Reign," *Albany Atlas*, reprinted in *Philadelphia Age*, 1/12/1864, 1.

27   Jacob Schuckers, *The Life and Public Services of Salmon Portland Chase* (Appleton, 1874), 477–79; Michael Burlingame, ed., *With Lincoln in the White House* (SIU, 2006), 132–33; Niven, *Salmon P. Chase*, 371; "Collector," *NYT*, 9/7/1864, 4.

28   West, *Scapegoat*, 127; Trefousse, *Butler*, 105.

29 West, *Scapegoat*, 19–24; Trefousse, *Butler*, 23–24.

30 West, *Scapegoat*, 127, 129–43, 149–53; Crystal Feimster, *Southern Horrors* (Harvard, 2009), 17–19; Judith Schafer, *Brothels, Depravity, and Abandoned Women* (LSU, 2009), 155.

31 Jacob Rader Marcus, *Memoirs of American Jews, 1775–1865*, v. 2 (Jewish Publication Society of America, 1955), 187; Stephanie McCurry, *Confederate Reckoning* (Harvard, 2011), 113–14; Robert Rosen, *The Jewish Confederates* (University of South Carolina, 2000), 282–94; P. Philips [*sic*] Household, 1860, U. S. Census, Slave Schedule, District of Columbia, City of Washington, First Ward, 31.

32 Michael Pierson, "Benjamin F. Butler and Class Politics in Lowell and New Orleans," *Massachusetts Historical Review* 7 (2005): 36–68.

33 "Drolleries," *SFB*, 9/8/1859, 2; "Miscellaneous," *SFB*, 3/25/1861, 3; "Will," *BS*, 6/2/1864, 1; West, *Scapegoat*, 189–90, 200, 202.

34 Trefousse, *Butler*, 124–27; West, *Scapegoat*, 194–98.

35 *Appleton's Annual Cyclopaedia* (Appleton, 1871), 737–38; William Cooper, *Jefferson Davis, American* (Vintage, 2001), 244.

36 Browning, *Cape Charles*, 72, 288.

37 West, *Scapegoat*, 315; Surdam, *Northern*, 58.

38 "Butler's," *Janesville Weekly Gazette*, 4/17/1863, 1; "Three," *Israelite*, 3/11/1864, 292; Korn, *Eventful*, 146; Korn, *Jewry*, 194–97; "Philip," *NYT*, 1/7/1890, 5; Simon Wolf and Lewis Levy, *The American Jew as Patriot, Soldier and Citizen* (Levytype, 1895), 199, 201–9, 236–301, esp. 263.

39 Browning, *Cape Charles*, 129–32; Ludwell Johnson, "Contraband Trade during the Last Year of the Civil War," *MVHR* 49, no. 4 (Mar. 1963): 635–36.

CHAPTER 6: EXPATRIATE

1 Jonathan Sarna, *Jacksonian Jew* (Holmes & Meyer, 1981), 110–13; George H. Davis household, 1860 U.S. Census, East Ward, City of Petersburg, State of Virginia, 138; William Henderson, *12th Virginia Infantry* (H. E. Howard, 1984), 177; George Davis, Slave Owner, East Ward, City of Petersburg, State of Virginia, 1860 Slave Census, 41.

2 Charles Flandreau, "The Bench and Bar of Ramsey County, Minnesota. II.," *Magazine of Western History* 8, no. 1 (May 1888): 61; Gerald Horne, *The Deepest South* (NYU, 2007), 160; "Robert," *Sacramento Union*, 10/1/1861, 3; "Major," *NYT*, 5/20/1901, 7.

3 Mark Schmeller, "Eating Fire: Journalistic Combat in Antebellum America," unpublished manuscript in author's possession, 36–37; James Crouthamel, *James Watson Webb* (Wesleyan, 1969), 5–6, 11, 30, 70–79; Sarna, *Jacksonian Jew*, 85–86, 95–96.

4 "Funeral," *NYT*, 10/23/1861, 1; Crouthamel, *Webb*, 148, 156; Lawrence Hill, *Diplomatic Relations between the United States and Brazil* (Duke, 1932); "Brazil," *NYT*, 3/15/1862, 3.

5   Crouthamel, *Webb*, 132–33, 48–149, 164–65; D. P. Kidder and J. C. Fletcher, *Brazil and the Brazilians* (Childs and Peterson, 1857); Christopher Benfey, *A Summer of Hummingbirds* (Penguin, 2009), 9, 88–95; John Simon, ed., *The Papers of Ulysses S. Grant*, v. 23, *February 1–December 31, 1872* (SIU, 2000), 343–45.

6   Crouthamel, *Webb*, 153; "Brazil," *NYT*, 3/15/1862, 3; "Brazil," *NYT*, 7/11/1862, 6; "Contractos Commerciaes," *Rio de Janeiro Constitucional*, 8/5/1862, 4; Letter, Charles L. Lazarus to James Watson Webb, 5/23/1862, Series I, Box 8, Folder 99, in James Watson Webb Papers, Sterling Library Special Collections, Yale University.

7   John Marshall, *American Bastille* (T. W. Hartley, 1869), 583–85; "Despotism," *Old Guard* 1, no. 9 (Sept. 1863): 271–72; "Arbitrary," *DAC*, 2/7/1863, 1.

8   Letter, A. N. Tolentino to James Watson Webb, 11/3/1862, Box 9, Folder 108, Webb Papers; Letter, James Watson Webb to A. N. Tolentino, 11/5/1862, Box 9, Folder 108, Webb Papers; Letter, A. N. Tolentino to James Watson Webb, 11/7/1862, Box 9, Folder 109, Webb Papers.

9   Crouthamel, *Webb*, 74–75, 86, 156, 191–93; Edward Balleisen, *Navigating Failure* (UNC, 2001), 63–64.

10 Letter, James Watson Webb to A. N. Tolentino, 11/4/1862, Box 9, Folder 108, Webb Papers.

11 "City," *BA*, 12/15/1853, n.p; *Boston Directory for the Year 1858* (George Adams, 1858), 419; George Jaquith and Georgetta Walker, *Jaquith Family in America* (New England Gen. Soc., 1982), 124; *National Cyclopaedia of American Biography*, v. 11 (J. T. White, 1901), 176; "Insolvency," *BAD*, 4/4/1859, n.p.; Letter, James Watson Webb to A. N. Tolentino, 11/4/1862, Box 9, Folder 108, Webb Papers; Letter, George N. Davis to James Watson Webb, 11/13/1862, Box 9, Folder 110, Webb Papers.

12 Letter, George N. Davis to James Watson Webb, 11/15/1862, Box 9, Folder 110, Webb Papers; Letter, George N. Davis to James Watson Webb, 11/17/1862, Box 9, Folder 110, Webb Papers; Horne, *Deepest*, 309; James Watson Webb to C. L. Lazarus, 2/23/1863, Box 10, Folder 111, Webb Papers; "Prints," *Zion's Herald*, 10/31/1878, 348; "Obituary," *BAD*, 10/24/1878, 1.

13 "Gatto," *LDN*, 12/22/1864, 6; "Court," *TL*, 12/22/1864, 10; "Gatto," *TL* 7/9/1864, 1; "Advances," *TL*, 8/9/1864, 11; "Gatto," *TL*, 9/17/1864, 2; "Advances," *TL*, 10/6/1864, 3.

14 "Brazil," *NYT*, 3/5/1862, 3; Isaac Goldberg, *Major Noah* (Jewish Publication Society, 1938), 288; "Dead," *NYT*, 5/20/1901, 7; "Alhambra," *TL*, 6/29/1863, 3; "Declarations," *TL*, 7/30/1864, 6; "Sales," *LDN*, 10/21/1863, n.p.; "Brandon," *TL*, 5/13/1864, 11; "Noah," *TL*, 4/9/1864, 13; "Noah," *LDN*, 11/20/1863, 6; "Brandon," *LDN*, 10/1/1863, 7; "Brandon," *TL*, 10/1/1863, 9; C., J., and E. Weatherby, *The Racing Calendar, for the year 1863* (C. W. Reynell, 1863), xv.

15 "Bankruptcy," *TL*, 10/18/1864, 11; "Undersigned," *TL*, 11/28/1863, 3; "Gatto," *LDN*, 12/22/1864, 6; "Court," *TL*, 12/22/1864, 10.

16 "Change," *NYH*, 12/15/1864, 6; Manifest, S.S. *City of Cork*, 2/1/1865; Kenneth

Scott, *Petitions for Name Changes in New York City, 1848–1899* (National Gen. Soc., 1984), 53; *Poillon v. Lawrence*, 43 Super. 385 (1879); *Poillon v. Lawrence*, 77 NY 207 (1879); "Academy," *NYT*, 7/17/1865, 7; P. T. Barnum, *Struggles and Triumphs* (Courier, 1889), 245; *Statutes at Large of the State of New York*, v. 6 (Weed, Parsons, 1868), 668.

CHAPTER 7: THE PARSEE

1   Ida Tarbell, *The Tariff in Our Times* (Macmillan, 1911), 91–92.

2   "More," *NYW*, 11/26/1869, 8; "Parsee," *NYW*, 11/9/1869, 4; "Parsee," *NYW*, 11/10/1872, 6; "Gas," *NYW*, 7/1/1872, 5; "Currency," *NYW*, 10/23/1874, 8.

3   "Obituary," *NYT*, 3/6/1892, 13; Ida Tarbell, "Tariff in Our Times," *American Magazine* 64, no. 2 (June 1907): 177; Tarbell, *Tariff*, 157; Mark Summers, *The Press Gang* (UNC, 1994), 14.

4   E. L. Godkin, *Unforeseen Tendencies of Democracy* (Houghton, Mifflin, 1898), 188.

5   "Obituary," *NYT*, 3/6/1892, 13; Benjamin P. Moore Household, UK Census of 1851, Parish of Birmingham, Ecc. Dist. of Christ Church, Borough of Birmingham, Household 158, 41–42; *The Edinburgh Gazetteer* (Constable, 1822), 798; "San Francisco," *Galveston News*, 4/5/1875, 2; "Destructive," *Weekly Pacific News*, 12/31/1849, 2; "Appalling," *DAC*, 12/31/1849, n.p.

6   *History, Gazetteer, and Directory of Warwickshire* (Francis White, 1850), 215; *Corporation General and Trades Directory of Birmingham* (William Cornish, 1861), 235; Aubrey Newman, "A Portrait of Birmingham Jewry in 1851," unpublished paper, University College, London, 7/6/1975; Harold Pollins, *Economic History of the Jews in England* (Fairleigh Dickinson, 1982), 107; Lewis Hyman, *The Jews of Ireland* (Irish, 1972), 99–100, 107–8; Isaac Markens, *The Hebrews in America* (Markens, 1888), 232–33; "Obituary," *NYT*, 3/6/1892, 13; "Moore" *Birmingham Post*, 3/16/1865, n.p.; "Moore," *Birmingham Post*, 3/17/1865, 4; "Moore," *Birmingham Post*, 3/30/1865, 7; "Law," *LDN*, 7/20/1866, 6; *Moore v. United States*, 91 U.S. 270 (1876); "Notice," *NYTrib*, 8/2/1867, 6; "Bankruptcy," *Birmingham Post*, 9/10/1867, 3.

7   Markens, *Hebrews*, 232–33; Kathryn Jacob, *King of the Lobby* (Johns Hopkins, 2010), 73–74; *Treasury Register* (G.P.O., 1873), 115; Tarbell, "Tariff," 177.

8   Joseph S. Moore, *Report of the Chief of the Bureau of Statistics on Customs—Tariff Legislation, Appendix B* (G.P.O., 1872), 99–127, esp. 108; E. J. Edwards, "Origin," *NYT*, 10/28/1904, 8.

9   "Salty," *NYTrib*, 1/21/1871, 4; Horace Greeley, *The Great Industries of the United States* (J. B. Burr & Hyde, 1872), 778–83.

10 Hans Trefousse, *Ben Butler* (Twayne, 1957), 178–208, 231; Richard West, *Lincoln's Scapegoat General* (Houghton Mifflin, 1965), 320–33, 334–36; David Montgomery, *Beyond Equality* (Knopf, 1967), 74–76, 90, 114–21, 373; Mark Summers, *The Era of Good Stealings* (Oxford, 1993), 174–77.

11   Irwin Unger, *The Greenback Era* (Princeton, 1965), 15–17; David Camp, ed., *The American Year-book . . . for 1869* (Case, 1869), 240; Edward Kirkland, *A History of American Economic Life* (Appleton, 1951), 345, 392.

12   Eric Foner, *Free Soil, Free Labor, Free Men* (Oxford, 1971), 16–17; Montgomery, *Beyond*, 14–15, 223–25; David Montgomery, "William Sylvis," in *Labor Leaders in America*, eds. Melvyn Dubofsky and Warren Van Tine (University of Illinois, 1987), 3–29; Michele Dauber, "Judicial Review and the Power of the Purse," *Law and History Review* 23, no. 2 (Summer 2005): 451–58; Robert Reeder, "The Constitutionality of Protective Tariffs," *University of Pennsylvania Law Review* 76, no. 8 (June 1928): 974–79; Andrew Wender Cohen, "Unions, Modernity, and the Decline of American Economic Nationalism," *American Right and U.S. Labor*, eds. Nelson Lichtenstein and Elizabeth Tandy Shermer (University of Pennsylvania, 2011), 20; William Sylvis, *The Life, Speeches, Labors and Essays of William H. Sylvis* (Claxton, Remsen & Haffelfinger, 1872), 292–93; John Jarrett, "The Story of the Iron Workers," in *The Labor Movement*, ed. George McNeill (Bridgman, 1886), 275; E. Benjamin Andrews, "A History of the Last Quarter Century in the United States," *Scribner's* 18 (July 1895): 86.

13   Frank Taussig, *The History of the Present Tariff, 1860–1883* (G.P. Putnam, 1885), 60; "Parsee," *BE*, 1/10/1870, n.p.

14   Henry Carey, *The Harmony of Interests* (Henry Carey Baird, 1872), 54, 201; Montgomery, *Beyond*, 86; Rebecca Edwards, *Angels in the Machinery* (Oxford, 1997), 75–81; Kathryn Kish Sklar, *Florence Kelley and the Nation's Work* (Yale, 1995), 37.

15   "Savans," *NYH*, 8/25/1870, 7; Joshua Greenberg, "The Panic of 1837 as an Opportunity for Radical Economic Ideas," unpublished paper, 10/12/2007, 19–28; *Love, Marriage, and Divorce, and the Sovereignty of the Individual* (M & S, 1975), 36, 48; John Humphrey Noyes, *History of American Socialisms* (Lippincott, 1870), 634–35; J. M. W. Yerrinton, *Proceedings of the Free Convention held at Rutland, VT, June 25th, 26th, 27th, 1858* (J. B. Yerrinton, 1858), 10, 128; "Freedom," *NYTel*, 4/8/1872, 2; "Official . . . ," *Woodhull and Claflin's Weekly*, 5/25/1872, n.p.

16   William Dean Howells, *Their Wedding Journey* (Houghton Mifflin, 1895), 273, 277–78, 346.

17   *Testimonials to Henry C. Carey Esq. Dinner at the LaPierre House. Philadelphia, April 27, 1859* (Collins Printer, 1859), 50–51; Joanne Reitano, *The Tariff Question in the Gilded Age* (Penn State, 1994), 74–86; Horace Greeley, *Essays Designed to Elucidate the Science of Political Economy while Serving to Explain and Defend the Policy of Protection to Home Industry as a System of National Cooperation for the Elevation of Labor* (Porter & Coates, 1869), 160–61; Brian Balogh, *A Government Out of Sight* (Cambridge, 2009), 177.

18   Roland Ringwalt, "Greeley," *Protectionist* 22, no. 262 (Feb. 1911): 517; Montgomery, *Beyond*, 202–5, 246–47; Greeley, *Political Economy*, 166–67.

19 *Miscellaneous Works of Henry C. Carey*, 10, 16, 17, 22.

20 Montgomery, *Beyond*, 82–85; Carey, *Harmony*, 202–9; Greeley, *Political Economy*, 166–67.

21 William Kelley, *Speech of Hon. William D. Kelley, of Pennsylvania, on Protection to American Labor* (Congressional Globe Office, 1866), 11, 15–17, 27; Carey, *Miscellaneous*, 5; "Gold," *NYTrib*, 5/24/1869, 1; "Free," *NYTrib*, 11/8/1869, 2; "Gold," *Free-Trader* 4, no. 10 (Jan. 1871): 190; Marc-William Palen, "Foreign Relations in the Gilded Age," *Diplomatic History* 37, no. 2 (2013): 217–47.

22 Samuel Daddow and Benjamin Bannan, *Coal, Iron, and Oil* (Bannan, 1866), 596; Carey, *Harmony*, 75; "Taxers," *NYP*, 9/6/1881, 1.

23 Ari Hoogenboom, *Outlawing the Spoils* (University of Illinois, 1961), 21, 191–94; Anthony Howe, *Free Trade and Liberal England, 1846–1946* (Oxford, 1997); John Sproat, *The Best Men* (Oxford, 1968), 39–44, 172–203, 257–71.

24 "Wells," *NYT*, 11/6/1898, 6; Stephen Meardon, "Postbellum Protection and Commissioner Wells's Conversion to Free Trade," *History of Political Economy* 39, no. 4 (2007): 571–604.

25 William McFeely, *Grant* (Norton, 2002), 298; Tarbell, *Tariff*, 91; David Tucker, *Mugwumps* (University of Missouri, 1998), 26–37.

26 "Butler," *Nation* 10, no. 241 (2/10/1870): 84; "Butler," *Nation* 23, no. 590 (10/19/1876): 236; "Butler," *NYTrib*, 1/27/1868, 4; "Debate," *NYTrib*, 3/10/1876, 4; Charles Francis Adams, *Studies Military and Diplomatic, 1775–1865* (Macmillan, 1911), 279–80; Heather Richardson, *The Death of Reconstruction* (Harvard, 2004), 117.

27 Ernest Samuels, *Henry Adams* (Harvard, 1989), 104; E. L. Godkin, *The Gilded Age Letters of E. L. Godkin*, ed. William Armstrong (SUNY, 1974), 144–45; Sproat, *Best Men*, 250–54; "Writer," *CT*, 3/13/1892, 25; "Obituary," *NYP*, 3/7/1892, 12; "Writer," *BE*, 3/7/1892, 4; Sarna, *Jacksonian Jew*, 10; Thomas White, "A Voyage," *Southern Literary Messenger* 5, no. 1 (Jan. 1839): 32; Tom Reiss, *The Orientalist* (Random House, 2005), xx, xxi.

28 "Week," *Nation* 23, no. 597 (12/7/1876): 333; "White," *ST*, 10/2/1869, 112; "Writer," *BE*, 3/7/1892, 4.

29 Joseph Solomon Moore, *The Parsee Letters* (American Free Trade League, 1869), 2, 10.

30 Moore, *Parsee*, 5.

31 Moore, *Parsee*, 6–7; Leonard Swann, *John Roach* (Ayer, 1980), 32–33.

32 Moore, *Parsee*, 27; "No. 56," *NYW*, 11/9/1869, 5.

33 Moore, *Parsee*, 30–31; Edwards, *Angels*, 68–82.

34 Moore, *Parsee*, 2, 9–10, 18–19, 19–20.

35 Henry Adams, "Art II. The Session," *North American Review* 111, no. 228 (July 1870): 45.

36 Tucker, *Mugwumps*, 57; Andrew Slap, *The Doom of Reconstruction* (Fordham, 2006), 1–24, 26–34; Hans Trefousse, *Carl Schurz, a Biography* (Fordham, 1998).

CHAPTER 8: LEVIATHAN

1   "Frauds," *NYT*, 7/31/1869, 2; "Customs," *BWC*, 11/29/1869, 1; "Weighers,"
    NYTrib, 12/2/1869, 5.

2   "Antecedents," *NYTrib*, 3/7/1874, 1; "Moiety," *NYT* 3/12/1874, 5; John Leon-
    ard, *Who's Who in New York City and State* (Hamersly, 1904), 329; "Freshet,"
    FLIN, 7/18/1857, 106; *Clerks in Departments* (G.P.O., 1866), 21; "Green," *CT*,
    12/15/1901, 36; "Jayne," *SFB*, 3/19/1874, 1; *Treasury Register*, 1872, 144.

3   *Annual Report of the Secretary of the Treasury on the State of the Finances for
    the year 1885*, v. 2, Collection of Duties (G.P.O., 1885), 551; "Moiety," *NYT*,
    3/12/1874, 5; Phelps, Dodge & Co. [David A. Wells], *Our Revenue System:
    History of the Proceedings in the Case of Phelps, Dodge & Co.* (Martin's, 1873);
    Benjamin Butler, *The Necessity of Rewards for the Detection of Crime* (G.P.O.,
    1874); David A. Wells, *Congress and Phelps, Dodge & Co.* (1875), 8–9; House
    of Representatives, 43rd Congress, 1st Session, *Evidence before the Committee
    on Ways and Means Relative to Moieties and Customs-Revenue Laws* (G.P.O.,
    1874), 17–24.

4   *U.S. IRS Tax Assessment Lists, 1862–1918* (2008), Ancestry.com; Sven Beck-
    ert and Seth Rockman, "Partners in Iniquity," *NYT*, 4/2/2011; "House," *PNA*,
    3/2/1865, 1.

5   Nicholas Parrillo, *Against the Profit Motive* (Yale, 2013), 232–41; Richard Ben-
    sel, *Yankee Leviathan* (Cambridge, 1990), 251; Albert Bolles, *Financial History
    of the United States from 1861 to 1885* (Appleton, 1886), 306.

6   Richard Wheatley, "The New York Customhouse," *Harper's Monthly* 69 (1884):
    38–61, esp. 39–40, 44.

7   Philip Melanson with Peter Stevens, *The Secret Service* (Carroll & Graf, 2002),
    11; Curtis Davis, "The Craftiest of Men," *Maryland Historical Magazine* 83, no.
    2 (Summer 1988): 111–26; "News," *NYS*, 7/22/1865, 1; "Counterfeiters," *NYH*,
    8/16/1865, 5; "Baker," *MS*, 7/9/1868, n.p.

8   *Congressional Globe*, 39th Congress, 1st Session (March 7, 1866), 1250; George
    Sanger, ed., *The Statutes at Large* (Little, Brown, 1868), 178; Uriah Barnes, ed.,
    Barnes Federal Code (Bobbs-Merrill, 1919), 1201–2; *Congressional Globe*, 39th
    Congress, 1st Session (May 15, 1866), 2564.

9   *Congressional Globe*, 39th Congress, 1st Session (June 27, 1866), 3440–3; *Con-
    gressional Globe*, 39th Congress, 1st Session (May 15, 1866), 2564–6; "Cus-
    toms Law," *Suffolk Transnational Law Journal* 13 (1989–1990): 444; Herman
    Belz, *Abraham Lincoln, Constitutionalism, and Equal Rights in the Civil War
    Era* (Fordham, 1998), 109.

10 Chester Jones, *The Consular Service* (University of Pennsylvania, 1906), 8,
    79–82; S. G. W. Benjamin, "Ocean Steam–Ships," *Century* 24, no. 5 (Sept.
    1882): 670–72; R. A. Fletcher, *Steam-ships* (J. B. Lippincott, 1910), 241; Henry
    James, *The American* (Macmillan, 1879), 62.

11 T. B. Thorpe, "The New York Custom-House," *Harper's New Monthly Maga-*

zine 43 (1871), 22–24; "American Honesty," *Scribner's Monthly* 11, no. 1 (Nov. 1875): 126; Joanna Nicholls, "United States Revenue Cutter Service," *FLPM* 42, no. 4 (1896): 18–32; Worth Ross, "Our Coast Guard," *Harper's Monthly* 73, no. 438 (1886): 911; Walter LaFeber, *The New Empire* (Cornell, 1963), 58–60; H. D. Smith, "Trip," *FLPM* 11, no. 5 (1881): 621–25; "Contraband," *LAT*, 3/20/1894, 3; "Retreat," *San Francisco Chronicle*, 10/25/1882, 1.

12 Charles Edwards, *A Story of Niagara* (International, 1871), 328.

13 Ava Kahn, *Jewish Voices of the California Gold Rush* (Wayne State, 2002), 325; Eric Monkkonen, *The Dangerous Class* (Harvard, 1975).

14 Thorpe, "Custom-House," 23–24.

15 Hiram C. Whitley with George P. Burnham, *Three Years with Counterfeiters, Smugglers, and Boodle Carriers* (John P. Dale, 1875), 382–84.

16 George Sanger, ed., *Statutes at Large from December 1865 to March 1867* (Little, Brown, 1868), 178; *Stockwell et al. v. United States*, 23 F. Cas. 116 (1870); *Stockwell et al. v. United States*, 80 U.S. 531 (1871); *U.S. v. Two Trunks*, 28 F. Cas. 320 (1872); *In re Platt et al.*, 19 F. Cas. 815 (1874).

17 Whitley, *Three Years*, 268; Edwards, *Niagara*, 304–6.

18 "Women," *St. Louis Globe-Democrat*, 3/14/1880, 11.

19 Thorpe, "Custom-House," 23.

20 Leonard White, *The Republican Era, 1869–1901* (Macmillan, 1958), 123–25; Thorpe, "Custom-House," 12, 16–18, 21–23.

21 Patricia Cohen, Timothy Gilfoyle, and Helen Horowitz, *The Flash Press* (University of Chicago, 2008), 90; "Stereoscopic," *NYH*, 10/20/1859, 10; "Stereoscopic," *NYH*, 10/27/1859, 8; "Chow-Chow," *NYT*, 7/22/1878, 1; "Comical," *PI*, 9/13/1882, 3; "Seized," *WP*, 10/17/1883, 2.

22 "Hopper," *Church's Musical Visitor* 11, no. 15 (Dec. 1882): 413; Thorpe, "Custom-House," 22.

23 *Treasury Register*, 1873, 72–143; Thorpe, "Custom-House," 11; Edwin Burrows and Mike Wallace, *Gotham* (Oxford, 2000), 681; Iver Bernstein, *The New York City Draft Riots* (Oxford, 1990), 124, 277.

24 Thomas Reeves, *Gentleman Boss* (Knopf, 1975), 84; John Goss, *The History of Tariff Administration in the United States* (Columbia University, 1897), 64; "Service," *NYT*, 3/9/1871, 8; Louis Bagger, "The 'Secret Service' of the United States," *Appleton's Journal* 10, no. 235 (9/20/1873): 360–65; "Inquiry," *NYT*, 2/8/1872, 5; "Counterfeiters," *Chicago Inter-Ocean*, 4/18/1874, 5.

25 "Brackett," *NYT*, 3/27/1888, 2; *Investigation of the Customs Service* (G.P.O., 1877), 16–19; "Obituary," *NYT*, 9/12/1877, 4; *Treasury Register*, 1873, 109; Thorpe, "Custom-House," 20.

26 Herman Melville, *Redburn: His First Voyage* (Harper Brothers, 1850), 175; "Poets," *BE*, 7/16/1893, 9; "Following," *Lowell Courier*, 9/20/1870, n.p.

27 "Poets," *BE*, 7/16/1893, 9; Thorpe, "Custom-House," 19, 26; "Briggs," *NYT*, 7/22/1877, 5; Richard Grant White, "The Business of Office-Seeking," *North American Review* 135, no. 138 (Jul. 1882): 29; Francis Church, "Richard Grant

White," *Atlantic Monthly* 67, no. 401 (Mar. 1891): 303–14; "White," *NYT*, 8/9/1885, 5.

28   Stanton Garner, "Herman Melville and the Customs Service," in *Melville's Evermoving Dawn*, ed. Robert Milder (Kent State, 1997), 277–80; "Thorpe," *NYT*, 9/21/1878, 2.

29   "Crutchley," *BE*, 1/21/1894, 1; "Lee," *NYT*, 3/4/1890, 2.

30   "Celebrities," *NYS*, 4/30/1876, 7; *Treasury Register*, 1873, 112, 113, 115, 117, 121; Mary Dearing, *Veterans in Politics* (LSU, 1952); Stuart McConnell, *Glorious Contentment* (UNC, 1997); Theda Skocpol, *Protecting Soldiers and Mothers* (Harvard, 1995), 17–19, 46.

31   *Treasury Register*, 1873, 108–26, 139; "Editorial," *Flake's Bulletin*, 10/27/1869, 4; "Unjust," *NYT*, 8/12/1878, 5; Eric Foner, *Freedom's Lawmakers* (Oxford, 1993), 55, 187.

32   "Downing," *BG*, 7/23/1903, 6; "Downing," *San Francisco Elevator*, 6/25/1869, n.p.; "Downing," *NYS*, 4/2/1916, 9; "Downing," *Buffalo Courier*, 4/14/1866, 4; "Leader," *BG*, 7/22/1903, 4.

33   "Beginning," *Syracuse Union*, 6/22/1861, n.p.; "Customhouse," *BE*, 6/19/1861, 2; *Treasury Register*, 1873, 110, 114.

34   "Methods," *NYT*, 4/3/1879, 2; "Demise," *Colored American*, 4/4/1903, 3; "Letter," *New York Globe*, 1/27/1883, 1; Frank Mather, ed., *Who's Who of the Colored Race*, v. 1 (n.p., 1915), 222; William Powell household, U.S. Census, 1860, Dwelling 18, 2nd District, 4th Ward, City of Brooklyn, County of Kings, 811.

35   Julia Powell household (listed as Jane A. Power), U.S. 1880 census, Household 71, City of Brooklyn, County of Kings, State of New York, Sup. Dist. 2, E.D. 25, 11; Alexander Powell household, U.S. 1920 census, Household 150, 12th Ward, City of Jersey City, County of Hudson, Sup. Dist. 9, E.D. 259, 6B; "Veteran," *Amsterdam News*, 6/13/1923, 11; "Death," *Philadelphia Tribune*, 1/21/1920, 1; "Saunders," *NYS*, 8/16/1872, 1; "Colored," *NYTel*, 4/21/1873, 1; "Real," *NYS*, 4/21/1873, 1.

36   "Powell's," *WP*, 8/22/1884, 2; "Munificent," *Frederick Weekly Herald*, 12/27/1883, 7.

37   "Meeting," *NYP*, 9/22/1830, n.p.; "Obituary," *Emancipator*, 5/30/1839, 20; "Married," *New York Spectator*, 1/17/1839, 1; New York Board of Education, *Manual of the Board of Education* (Wm. C. Bryant, 1850), 105; "Died," *New York Freeman*, 6/27/1885, n.p.; "Vogelsang," *New York Freeman*, 4/9/1887, 3; Patricia Click, *Time Full of Trial* (UNC, 2001), 86; Donald Yacovone, ed., *A Voice of Thunder* (University of Illinois, 1998), 247; Craig Townsend, *Faith in Their Own Color* (Columbia, 2005), 153; Julie Winch, *A Gentleman of Color* (Oxford, 2002), 277; Craig Wilder, *A Covenant with Color* (Columbia, 2000), 76, 103, 110.

38   "Axe," *NYH*, 6/11/1886, 8; "Stanch," *NYPrs*, 8/5/1888, n.p.

39   "Gold," *Iowa State Register*, 4/28/1869, 4; "Men," *Crisis* 4, no. 3 (July 1912): 118–19; "Weather," *NYT*, 4/4/1871, 1; Stacy Sewell, "Remond, Charles Lenox,"

American National Biography Online (Feb. 2000); "A Colored Official in the Customhouse," *NYT*, 4/4/1871, 1; "Republicans," *New York Age*, 7/28/1888, n.p.; "Mr. Cleveland," *BWC*, 4/11/1887, n.p.

40 "Wedding, *NYT*, 1/17/1879, 8; "Hearts," *NYH*, 1/17/1879, 8.

41 Thorpe, "Custom-House," 20–21; "Carl Schurz Contradicted," *NYS*, 11/28/1871, 1; "Mysterious," *BE*, 1/29/1883, 4; "Various," *NYP*, 1/29/1883, n.p.; "Brother," *NYT*, 4/13/1892, 10.

42 "Laudanum," *NYH*, 8/5/1863, 4; "Ladies," *NYH*, 2/22/1860, 5; "Hair," *Boston Evening Transcript*, 1/23/1856, 3; "Wadham," *NYTrib*, 2/15/1860, 7; "Female," *Oswego Commercial Advertiser*, 12/5/1865, n.p.; "Smugglers," *NYS*, 9/12/1887, 3; Lillian Foster, *Way-side Glimpses, North and South* (Rudd and Carlton, 1860), iii; "Literary Notices," *Knickerbocker* 55, no. 1 (Jan. 1860): 84; "Notices," *NYH*, 10/30/1859, 5; Lillian Foster, *Andrew Johnson, President of the United States* (Richardson, 1866); *New York Customhouse Investigation*, v. 3 (1872), 120.

43 *Gideon Hawley and James King, appellants, vs. William James and others, respondents* (Packard and Van Benthuysen, 1836), 14; "Kossuth," *Evening Auburnian*, 6/12/1878, 1; "Washington," *Oneida Herald*, 3/9/1850, n.p.; "Tourists," *NYH*, 9/11/1887, 17; "Steele," *NYT*, 7/29/1890, 5; "Steele," *Cleveland Plain Dealer*, 7/30/1890, n.p.; "Steele," *Utica Morning Herald*, 7/29/1890, 4; John Van Wyhe, *Phrenology and the Origins of Victorian Scientific Naturalism* (Ashgate, 2004), 190; "Steele," *New York Observer*, 1/16/1879, 18; "Dead," *NYS*, 1/7/1879, n.p.; Albert Steele Household, 1870 census, Brooklyn Ward 2, Kings, New York, Roll M593_946, Page 192B, Image 390.

44 *NYH*, 11/17/1861, 5; *Trow's*, 1860, 281; Frederick Phisterer, ed., *New York in the War of the Rebellion, 1861–1865* (Weed, Parsons, 1890), 129; "Searching," *St. Louis Globe-Democrat*, 3/14/1880, 11; Skocpol, *Protecting*, 1, 65–66.

45 Whitley, *Three Years*, 286–89; *Report of the Joint Select Committee on Retrenchment inquiring into the Expenditures of all the Branches of the Service of the United States* (G.P.O., 1870), 47; Wheatley, "New York Customhouse," 49; "Grief," *NYH*, 4/21/1870, 6; Israelites of San Francisco, *John T. McLean and the Israelites: Unfounded and Gross Slander* (1870), reprinted in Robert J. Chandler, "That Lurking Prejudice, 1869–1870," *Western States Jewish History* 27 (July 1995): 205–9.

46 Israelites, *McLean*, 205–9; "Special Treasury Agent," *DAC*, 1/25/1871, 1.

47 Otis Gibson, *The Chinese in America* (Hitchcock and Walden, 1877), 46–48; W. W. Bode, "Searching Chinese Immigrants for Opium," *Harpers Weekly* 26, no. 1307 (1/7/1882): 5, 11.

48 "Trade," *New York Courier and Enquirer*, 4/21/1830, n.p.; Fanny Howell, "Woman as Smuggler, and Woman as Detective," *Scribner's* 4, no. 3 (July 1872): 354–58; Thorpe, "Custom-House," 23; "Women," *WP*, 11/4/1888, 9; *Niagara*, 294–95, 303, 325; "Luggage," *NYT*, 9/7/1877, 2; article from *Detroit Free Press*, 10/22/1872, reprinted in "Comedy," *Titusville Morning Herald*,

11/2/1872, 1; Rebecca Edwards, *Angels in the Machinery* (Oxford, 1997), 69–90.

49   Ari Hoogenboom, *Outlawing the Spoils* (University of Illinois, 1961), 17.

50   Lester Dorman, "Some New York Customhouse Investigations," *New Englander*, 36, no. 4 (Oct. 1877): 792–95; Thomas Barbour, *Appraisers, Spies and Informers* (Chamber of Commerce, 1874); Butler, *Rewards*, 9; Shelbourne Eaton, *Seizing Books and Records under the Revenue Law* (Chamber of Commerce, 1874), 51–52.

51   Thorpe, "Custom-House," 14, 26.

CHAPTER 9: DECEIVERS

1   Rose Eytinge, *The Memories of Rose Eytinge* (Frederick A. Stokes, 1905), 94–100; William Winter, *Vagrant Memories* (George H. Doran, 1915), 121; "Passengers Arrived," *NYT*, 8/5/1868, 8; "Rose Eytinge Dead at 76," *NYT*, 12/21/1911, 11.

2   Robert Swierenga, *The Forerunners* (Wayne State, 1994), 100, 124, 127, 136–37, 148, 155, 194, 196, 198, 200, 336, 369; Eytinge, *Memories*, 40, 149, 151, 153–54, 224, 298, 300; "Fisticuffs," *NYTrib*, 8/13/1896, 13; John Niven, *Gideon Welles* (Oxford, 1973), 569; Charles Kennedy, *American Consul* (Greenwood, 1990), 170–71; "Wife," *Atlanta Constitution*, 11/21/1872, 2; John Simon, ed., *The Papers of Ulysses S. Grant*, v. 22, *June 1, 1871–January 31, 1872* (SIU, 1998), 192; "Poisoning," *NYS*, 6/20/1876, 1.

3   U.S. Treasury, *Annual Report of the Secretary of the Treasury on the State of the Finances for the Year 1870* (G.P.O., 1870), 59–60; U.S. Treasury, *Report of the Secretary of the Treasury on the State of the Finances for the Year 1871* (G.P.O., 1871), 105–6; U.S. Treasury, *Annual Report of the Secretary of the Treasury on the State of the Finances for the Year 1872* (G.P.O., 1872), 145; U.S. Treasury, *Report of the Secretary of the Treasury on the State of the Finances for the Year 1873* (G.P.O., 1873), 173–74; U.S. Treasury, *Annual Report of the Secretary of the Treasury on the State of the Finances for the Year 1874* (G.P.O., 1874), 221–27.

4   "Smuggling," *BWC*, 11/26/1874, n.p.; "Revenue," *NYTrib*, 5/22/1877, 2; William Lyman Fawcett, *Gold and Debt* (S. C. Griggs, 1877), 157–58; Charles Rebello, *The Pith of the Sugar Question* (Magowan & Slipper, 1879), 9.

5   "Brandy," *NYH*, 10/21/1870, 9.

6   Rachel St. John, *Line in the Sand: A History of the Western U.S.-Mexico Border* (Princeton, 2011), 97–98; Samuel Bell, "The Mexican *Zona Libre*: 1858–1905," master's thesis, Texas Tech University, 1969; "Mexico," *NYH*, 5/22/1869, 10; "Mexico," *NYH*, 1/22/1872, 6; "Report," *NYH*, 11/30/1872, 6.

7   James McCurdy, "Criss-Cross over the Boundary: the Romance of Smuggling across the Northwest Frontier," *Pacific Monthly* 23, no. 2 (Feb. 1910), 190; Elizabeth Gibson, *Outlaw Tales of Washington* (Globe Pequot, 2001), 1–2.

8   "Commissioner," *NYH*, 8/23/1871, 8; "Married," *NYTel*, 3/11/1870, 4; "Attempted,"

NYH, 6/10/1870, 7; "Court Notes," *NYT*, 4/5/1877, 8; "Smuggling," *DG*, 10/15/1877, 730; "Smuggling," *NYTrib*, 4/4/1877, 2; "Smuggling," *NYT*, 10/16/1877; "Notes," *NYTrib*, 4/2/1879, 2; "Boatman," *NYT*, 2/21/1885, 8; Criminal Docket, U.S. Circuit Court, Southern District of New York, v. 3, p. 236, in NARA-NYC; Criminal Docket, U.S. Circuit Court, Southern District of New York, v. 4, 163, 442, in NARA-NYC; "Conviction," *NYT*, 12/10/1886, 8; "Wanted," *NYTrib*, 7/8/1889, 2; "Bets," *NYH*, 3/19/1897, 4.

9   "Resisting," *NYP*, 6/19/1871, n.p.; "New York," *NOP*, 3/31/1872, 8; "New York," *PD*, 3/31/1872, 1; "Unearthing," *NYS*, 8/23/1883, n.p.; "Talbot," *Montreal Herald*, 4/4/1887, 6; Thomas Byrnes, *Professional Criminals of America* (Cassell, 1886), 136.

10 "Smuggler," *NYT*, 3/12/1880, 3; "Courts," *NYH*, 3/12/1880, 2; "Boots," *NYS*, 1/10/1885, n.p.

11 "Smuggling," *NYTrib*, 2/3/1872, 2; *New York Customhouse Investigation*, v. 2 (1872), 403; "Metropolis," *Utica Observer*, 4/22/1872, n.p.; Hiram C. Whitley with George P. Burnham, *Three Years with Counterfeiters, Smugglers, and Boodle Carriers* (John P. Dale, 1875), 381.

12 "Smuggling," *Salt Lake Tribune*, 10/8/1874, 2; Hiram Whitley, *In It* (Riverside, 1894), 268.

13 "Smuggling," *NYE*, 10/2/1879, n.p.; "City," *NYT*, 10/3/1879, 8; "New York," *NYT*, 10/2/1879, 8; "Boatman," *NYT*, 2/21/1885, 8.

14 "Items," *Ogdensville Journal*, 4/16/1866, n.p.; "Hoboken," *NYH*, 7/19/1869, 8; "Murder," *NYTrib*, 7/19/1869, 8; "Murder," *NYH*, 7/21/1869, 8; "Murder," *NYH*, 7/23/1869, 8; "Hoboken," *NYH*, 7/25/1869, 9; "Mystery," *NYTrib*, 8/6/1869, 5; "Mystery," *NYT*, 8/11/1869, 5.

15 Whitley, *Three Years*, 237–40.

16 "Passengers," *NYE*, 8/5/1870, n.p.; Passenger Manifest, S.S. *Java*, 10/5/1870; "Smuggling," *NYT*, 1/28/1871, 2; "Who Got the $4,500?," *NYS*, 5/8/1871, 1; "Smuggling," *NYH*, 5/17/1871, 4; "Smuggling," *NYH*, 5/19/1871, 4; "Smuggling," *NYH*, 5/21/1871, 10; "Smuggling," *NYH*, 5/27/1871, 5; Whitley, *In It*, 268–69; "White v. Herrick," *The Weekly Reporter* 21 (3/22/1873): 454–55; "Dividends," *The Patriot* (London), 7/13/1846, 8; "Who," *NYS*, 5/8/1871, 1; "Vicinity," *Geneva Gazette*, 3/31/1876, n.p.; "Vicinity," *Geneva Gazette*, 1/12/1877, n.p.; James Fell, *Ores to Metals* (University of Colorado, 2009), 17–25, 280.

17 "Smuggling," *Boston Journal*, 11/27/1869, 2; "Smuggling," *NYH*, 12/16/1874, 8; United States Circuit Court, *NYH*, 10/8/1875, 9; "Smugglers," *NYH*, 1/14/1875, 11; "Customs," *NYS*, 3/12/1874, 1; "Smuggling," *Philadelphia Public Ledger*, 8/13/1870, 1; "Violating," *PI*, 8/5/1870, 2; "Case," *PNA*, 8/5/1870, 4; *U.S. v. Kimmett*, Case #10, United States District Court, Eastern District of Pennsylvania, Criminal Docket, v. 5, p. 206, in NARA-PHL (1870); *United States v. The Stadacona*, 8 Phil. 155 (1870); "Smuggling," *NYH*, 10/11/1870, 4; "Smuggling," *NYH*, 6/18/1871, 5.

18 "Customs," *NYS*, 3/12/1874, 1.

19   Charles Edwards, *A Story of Niagara* (International, 1871), 295–96, 301–2

20   Edwards, *Niagara*, 323; "Smuggling," *NYT*, 5/19/1870, 2.

21   "Smuggling," *St. Lawrence Plaindealer*, 8/29/1878, n.p.; "Smuggling," *NYTel*, 3/6/1871, n.p.; "Customs," *NYTrib*, 5/19/1875, 2.

22   "Smuggling," *NYT*, 5/20/1870, 8; "Trousseau," *PI*, 5/21/1870, 7.

23   "Government," *NYS*, 6/4/1874, 1; "Items," *BWC*, 3/26/1870, 3; "Crimes," *Syracuse Journal*, 3/26/1870, n.p.; "Smuggling," *NYTrib*, 4/2/1870, 4; "Notes," *Burlington Free Press*, 7/30/1875, 1; "Smuggling," *NYTrib*, 6/14/1875, 12.

24   "Corruption," *NYH*, 8/19/1873, 8; "Paez," *NYH*, 8/20/1873, 10; Michael Cavanagh, ed., *Memoirs of Gen. Thomas Francis Meagher* (Messenger, 1892), 347.

25   "Smuggler," *NYT*, 12/6/1874, 7; "Smuggler," *NYT*, 12/8/1874, 12; "Clandestine," *NYTrib*, 1/16/1875, 5.

26   "Sensation," *DG*, 8/15/1873, 318; "Smuggling," *NYT*, 5/19/1870, 2; "Officer," *NYH*, 7/14/1873, 4.

27   Andrew Wender Cohen, "Smuggling, Globalization, and America's Outward State, 1870–1909," *JAH* 97, no. 2 (2010): 371; "News," *NYT*, 5/18/1870, 4; "Diamonds," *BE*, 5/18/1870, 4; "Smuggling," *NYH*, 5/17/1870, 5; "Smuggling," *NYT*, 5/18/1870, 2; Guimarães household, 1870 U.S. Census, New York, New York, Ward 21, District 18 (2nd Enum), sheet 39, dwelling 344, Ancestry.com; George Boutwell, *Letter of the Secretary of the Treasury, Communicating, in Compliance with the Resolution of the Senate of December 14, 1870, Certain Statements Relative to the Collection and Distribution of Fines and Forfeitures under the Customs Laws* (G.P.O., 1871), 88; *Suits, etc. for Violation of the Revenue Laws* (G.P.O., 1874), 42.

28   *United States v. Tilton*, 28 F. Cas. 190 (1874); "Frauds," *NYT*, 2/27/1870, 8; "Smuggling," *NYT*, 5/27/1870, 2; "Smuggling," *NYH*, 6/14/1870, 8; "Case," *NYH*, 6/22/1870, 10; "Local," *NYT*, 6/16/1870, 8; "Moore," *NYT*, 7/30/1871, 8; "Seizure," *NYT*, 9/24/1871, 8; "Seizure," *NYTrib*, 9/25/1871, 2.

29   "Artistic," *DG*, 5/13/1874, 549; "Frauds," *DG*, 6/17/1874, 819.

30   Stephen Birmingham, *"Our Crowd"* (Harper & Row, 1967), 101; Boutwell, *Fines and Forfeitures*, 47; "Frauds," *NYTel*, 12/21/1868, 1; "Frauds," *NYT*, 1/13/1869, 2; "Smuggling," *NYT*, 1/22/1869, 2; "Smuggling," *NYTrib*, 1/25/1869, n.p.; "Smuggling," *NYT*, 1/30/1869, 5.

31   *History of the Chemical Bank: 1823–1913* (Privately printed, 1913), 112; "Yachting," *ST*, 5/14/1881, 378; "Trade," *NYE*, 3/11/1875, n.p.; "Fate," *NYS*, 7/1/1885, 1; "Green," *BE*, 7/2/1885, n.p.

32   "Frauds," *DG*, 7/2/1874, 1; "Bribery," *DG*, 6/18/1875, 835; "Shaking," *NYS*, 8/15/1873, 1.

33   Paul Vogt, *The Sugar Refining Industry in the United States* (University of Pennsylvania, 1908), 30.

34   "Frauds," *NYT*, 7/6/1869, 3; "Frauds," *NYT*, 7/11/1869, 3; "Frauds," *NYT*, 11/27/1869, 3; "Frauds," *NYT*, 7/31/1869, 2; "Customs," *BWC*, 11/29/1869, 1; "Pacific," *NYT*, 12/10/1869, 5; "Frauds, *NYT*, 12/17/1869, 5; "Investigation,"

NYT, 9/17/1878, 8; "Sugar," *NYT,* 9/18/1878, 2; "Fraud," *NYT,* 9/19/1878, 2; Donald Dozer, "The Opposition to Hawaiian Reciprocity," *Pacific Historical Review* 14, no. 2 (June 1945): 157–83.

35   "Frauds," *NYT,* 11/27/1869, 3; "Frauds," *NYT,* 7/6/1869, 3; "Frauds," *NYT,* 12/17/1869, 5; "Fraud," *SFB,* 1/29/1873, n.p.; "Sugar," *St. Louis Globe-Democrat,* 5/15/1876, 2; "Fraud," *NYT,* 8/2/1877, 8.

36   "Washington," *NYTrib,* 7/13/1869, 1; "Stabbed," *NYT,* 10/12/1870, 5; *Bradley's Case,* 104 U.S.R. 442 (1882); Select Committee, *Federal Offices in Louisiana* (G.P.O., 1876), 248–51, 323–26.

37   David A. Wells, *Congress and Phelps, Dodge & Co.* (1875), 195; "'Old Cockeye' on the Warpath," *DG,* 7/2/1874, 1.

38   "Millionaire Importer Imprisoned," *NYS,* 12/30/1874, 1; "Conspiracy," *NYTrib,* 5/16/1871, 2; "Failures," *NYT,* 7/10/1857, 8; "Camels," *NYTrib,* 1/14/1859, 3; Earl Fornell, *The Galveston Era* (University of Texas, 2009), 255–60.

39   Whitley, *In It,* 267–68; "History," *DG,* 5/19/1877, 554; "Smuggling," *St. Lawrence Plain Dealer,* 8/29/1878, n.p.; "Smuggling" *NYTel,* 3/6/1871, n.p.

40   "Smuggling," *FLPM* 6, no. 1 (July 1878): 2–12; "Smuggling," *NYH,* 2/16/1877, 8; "Cheating," *DG,* 6/5/1875, 729; "Swindling," *DG,* 5/13/1874, 549; T. B. Thorpe, "The New York Custom-House," *Harper's New Monthly Magazine* 43 (1871), 23.

41   "Smuggler," *Decatur Local Review,* 10/1/1874, 3; "Seizure," *NYT,* 8/19/1871, 3; "Smuggling," *BE,* 9/20/1872, 1; "Rogues," *BE,* 7/25/1873, 1; "Smuggling," *NPG,* 6/28/1879, 2, 16.

42   "Smuggling," *FLPM* 6, no. 1 (July 1878): 5; "Smugglers," *NYTel,* 12/10/1874, 2; "Comedy," *Titusville Morning Herald,* 11/2/1872, 1.

43   "Smuggling," *New York Illustrated News,* 9/19/1863, 333; "Smuggling," *NPG,* 6/28/1879, 16; "Female," *FLIN,* 2/25/1888, 28.

44   "Wife," *Auburn Morning News,* 12/23/1873, 1; "News," *BE,* 1/5/1874, n.p.; Thorpe, "Custom-House," 23; "Parsee Letters," *The Revolution,* 10/21/1869, 253.

45   "Smuggled," *NYTrib,* 5/17/1871, 2; "Smuggling," *NYE,* 9/21/1867, n.p.; "Victims," *NYTrib,* 2/28/1874, 1; *Suits, etc. for Violation of the Revenue Laws* (G.P.O., 1874), 4, 5, 12, 14, 20, 22, 26, 28, 34, 36, 38, 42, 44, 48, 52, 54, 56, 58, 62, 64, 68, 70, 74, 76, 78, 82, 84, 86; Boutwell, *Fines and Forfeitures* (G.P.O., 1871), 21, 38, 40, 46, 47, 52, 75, 88.

46   "Massachusetts," *Ft. Wayne Gazette,* 1/13/1871, 1; "Court," *Lowell Citizen,* 1/18/1872, n.p.; "Smuggling," *NYH,* 12/16/1874, 8; "Court," *NYH,* 10/8/1875, 9; "Smugglers," *NYH,* 1/14/1875, 11; "Pistols," *NYS,* 3/12/1874, 1; "Watches," *NYH,* 2/12/1872, 9; "Smuggling," *NYH,* 6/12/1872, 4; "Courts," *NYH,* 6/21/1872, 8.

47   "Smuggling Cigars," *NYTel,* 1/27/1874, 4; "Sentences in the Federal Courts," *NYTrib,* 1/31/1874, 5; "Secreted," *NYS,* 10/10/1872, 2; "Smuggling," *NYTrib,* 6/3/1870, 8; *New York Customhouse Investigation,* v. 2 (1872), 405–6.

48 "Moiety," *NYT*, 3/12/1874, 5; "Victims," *NYTrib*, 2/28/1874, 1; "Secret Service," *NYT*, 3/9/1871, 8; "Smuggling," *NYH*, 4/3/1870, 3; "Secreted," *NYS*, 10/10/1872; Whitley, *In It*, 267–69; *New York Customhouse Investigation*, v. 2 (1872), 610–19.

49 David A. Wells, *Congress and Phelps, Dodge & Co.: An Extraordinary History* (n.p., 1875), 9–11, 25–26, 130, 162.

50 "Antecedents," *NYTrib*, 3/7/1874, 1; "Frauds," *BE*, 2/9/1872, 4; *New York Customhouse Investigation* (1872), 97.

CHAPTER 10: GILDING

1 "Drama," *NYE*, 10/3/1867, n.p.; Lately Thomas, *Delmonico's* (Houghton Mifflin, 1967), 116; "Drama," *NYTrib*, 10/4/1867, 4; "Waifs," *NYE*, 10/15/1867, 4; "Amusements," *NYT*, 10/24/1867, 4; "Auction," *Evening Leavenworth Bulletin*, 10/12/1867, 3; Barbara Barker, "The Case of Augusta Sohlke vs. John DePol," *Educational Theatre Journal* 30, no. 2 (May 1978): 232–39.

2 John Hanners, *Acting in the Nineteenth-Century American Popular Theatre* (Bowling Green State, 1993), 71–77; Thomas Brown, *A History of the New York Stage from the First Performance in 1732 to 1901*, v. 2 (Dodd, Mead, 1903), 522–23; Henry Morais, *The Jews of their History* (Levytype, 1894), 376.

3 "Amusements," *NYT*, 10/4/1867, 4; "Drama," *NYTrib*, 10/4/1867, 4; Barker, "The Case of Augusta Sohlke," 233–36.

4 "Passengers," *NYT*, 1/23/1866, 8; "Passengers," *NYT*, 2/11/1866, 8; "Died," *NYCA*, 6/7/1866, 3; "Passengers," *NYT*, 3/18/1867, 8; "Robbery," *NYT*, 2/4/1868, 2; "Robbery," *NYT*, 2/8/1868, 2; "Dickens," *NYTrib*, 12/18/1904, 9; "Official Catalogue of the Paris Exposition of 1867," *NYH*, 12/9/1866, 1; "Official Catalogue of the Paris Exposition of 1867," *Alta California*, 2/4/1867, 4; Robert Grau, *The Business Man in the Amusement World* (Broadway, 1910), 335; Dixie Hines and Harry Prescott Hanaford, eds., *Who's Who in Music and Drama* (H. P. Hanaford, 1914), 231; James Morrissey, "Noted," *NYTrib*, 11/27/1904, SM3.

5 Malcolm Stern, *First American Jewish Families*, 3rd ed. (Genealogical Pub., 1991), 232; "Supreme Court," *NYTrib*, 9/21/1867, 7; "Americus," *NYS*, 5/26/1876, n.p.

6 Quote from Gideon Welles, cited in Ruth Randall, *Mary Lincoln* (Little, Brown, 1953), 47; Thomas Smith, *Political Parties and Their Places of Meeting in New York City* (Printed for the author, 1893), 19; "Obituary," *NYT*, 3/6/1892, 3.

7 U.S. Register, 1867, 109; U.S. Dept. of the Interior, *Register of Officers and Agents, Civil, Military, and Naval, in the Service of the United States, on the Thirtieth September, 1867* (G.P.O., 1868), 104–16; *Treasury Register*, 1873, 119; Document, Francis G. Young to Abraham Lincoln, December 7, 1861 (American Memory); Gary Lash, *"Duty Well Done"* (Butternut and Blue, 2001), 148–49, 165; "Bieral, Louis, Capt. [January 1862]," Military Discipline during the Civil

War: Courts-Martial Case Files from the Records of the Judge Advocate General, Case #0314, Reel 9, File #105; "Personal," *NYTrib*, 4/15/1862, 7; *Manual of the Corporation of New York*, 1863, 69; *Proceedings of the Board of Supervisors of the County of New York from January 1 to June 30, 1863* (Wm. L. S. Harrison, 1863), 838; "Police," *NYH*, 11/21/1863, 10; "City," *NYP*, 11/19/1863, 10; Thomas Byrnes, *Professional Criminals of America* (Cassell, 1886), 161–62; New York Board of Assistant Aldermen, *Documents of the Board of Councilmen of the City of New York*, v. 8 (Edmund Jones, 1862), 31; "Diversions," *NYT*, 1/12/1865, 8; "Jefferson," *NYH*, 1/19/1865, 4; "Third," *ST*, 11/19/1864, 189; D. T. Valentine, *Manual of the Corporation of the City of New York* (Harper, 1865), 78.

8   "Registrars," *NYTrib*, 10/17/1859, 6; "Surveyor," *NYH*, 3/9/1867, 10; "Frauds," *NYTrib*, 3/7/1867, 5; *Journal of the House of Representatives, 3/21–22/1867, 40th Congress, 1st session* (G.P.O., 1867), 80, 89.

9   "Frauds," *NYTrib*, 3/4/1867, 1; *Letter from the Secretary of the Treasury Relative to the Amount of Money Paid . . . for the Violation of the Revenue-Laws at the Boston and New York Customhouses, etc.* (G.P.O., 1874), 4–5, 18–19, 28–29, 32–33; George Boutwell, *Letter of the Secretary of the Treasury, Communicating, in Compliance with the Resolution of the Senate of December 14, 1870, Certain Statements Relative to the Collection and Distribution of Fines and Forfeitures under the Customs Laws* (G.P.O., 1871), 45–47, 63.

10   "Arrival," *NYH*, 9/30/1868, 7; "Frauds," *NYTrib*, 3/4/1867, 1; "Changes," *NYTrib*, 7/7/1869, 8; "Customhouse," *NYTrib*, 4/13/1870, 5; "Grief," *NYH*, 4/21/1870, 6; "Brigade," *NYS*, 2/3/1872, n.p.; *NYT*, 4/29/1869, 3; *Poillon v. Lawrence et al.*, 77 N.Y. 207 (1879); "Appointments," *NYTrib*, 8/14/1869, 1; "Ring," *NYH*, 4/23/1870, 8; *New York Customhouse Investigation*, v. 2 (G.P.O., 1872), 396–97; T. B. Thorpe, "The New York Custom-House," *Harper's New Monthly Magazine* 43 (1871), 15.

11   "Frauds," *NYT*, 1/13/1869, 2; "Court," *NYTel*, 12/21/1868, 1; "Office," *NYT*, 1/22/1869, 2; "Smuggling," *NYTrib*, 1/25/1869, n.p.; "Custom House," *NYS*, 9/28/1878, n.p.; "Smuggling," *NYTrib*, 4/2/1870, 4.

12   *Report of the Joint Committee on Retrenchment* (G.P.O., 1871), 122; *New York Customhouse Investigation*, v. 2 (G.P.O., 1872), 396; "Customhouse Matters," *NYTrib*, 4/13/1870, 5; "Smuggling," *NYH*, 4/14/1870, 5; "Smuggling," *NYH*, 4/15/1870, 8; "Smuggling," *NYH*, 4/16/1870, 5; "Curtis," *NYT*, 1/9/1910, 9; John Haddock, *The Growth of a Century* (Sherman & Co., 1894), 47–48.

13   "Smuggling," *PI*, 4/14/1870, 1; "Telegrams," *WS*, 4/14/1870, 3; "Condensed," *BAD*, 4/14/1870, 1; "Telegraphic," *BS*, 4/14/1870, 1; "Grief," *NYH*, 4/21/1870, 6.

14   "Ring," *NYH*, 4/23/1870, 5; "Smuggling," *NYTrib*, 5/4/1870, 2; "Smuggling," *NYH*, 5/4/1870, 2; "New York," *Cleveland Herald*, 5/7/1870, 1.

15   "Tweed," *Albany Evening Journal*, 1/6/1871, n.p.; M. R. Werner, *Tammany Hall* (Doubleday, 1928), 166.

16   "Americans," *NYT*, 2/19/1871, 4; *London Gazette*, 2/10/1871, 503; Robert and Harriett Swedberg, *American Clocks and Clockmakers* (Wallace-Homestead,

1989), 21; *Annual Report of the Commissioner of Patents for the Year 1871*, v. 2 (G.P.O., 1872), 438; "Eighth," *NYTrib*, 11/25/1871, 4; "City," *NYTrib*, 3/8/1872, 3; Graff Passport, 6/5/1872; "Died," *NYH*, 1/16/1872, 9.

17 "Americus," *Sunday Mercury*, 6/11/1871, 4; "Lawrence," *NYS*, 5/14/1875, 1; "Revenue," *Manchester Times*, 5/29/1875, n.p.; "Americus," *NYH*, 8/10/1873, 5; "Americus," *NYT*, 8/6/1873, 1; Werner, *Tammany*, 196; Oliver Allen, *The Tiger* (Addison-Wesley, 1993), 83, 114–15.

18 Thomas Reeves, *Gentleman Boss* (Knopf, 1975), 55–56; Stephen Skowronek, *Building a New American State* (Cambridge, 1982), 57, 308.

19 "Irrepressible," *NYW*, 4/8/1873, 6; "Usurpation," *NYW*, 5/20/1873, 6; "Election," reprinted from the *Savannah Advertiser* in *NYH*, 10/7/1872, 10.

20 Transcript, *U.S. v. Stockwell*, 20; United States Brief, *U.S. v. Stockwell*, 3, 11–12.

21 Reeves, *Gentleman*, 59; Ari Hoogenboom, *Outlawing the Spoils* (University of Illinois, 1961), 86–87; Skowronek, *Building*, 56–58.

22 "Message," *BWC*, 12/5/1871, 1; "Boutwell," *Internal Revenue Record* 14, no. 24 (12/9/1871): 190.

23 Seymour Mandelbaum, *Boss Tweed's New York* (Wiley, 1965), 81.

24 Reeves, *Gentleman*, 57–59, 71; Hoogenboom, *Outlawing*, 90, 132; Skowronek, *Building*, 58; "Board of Audit," *NYT*, June 7, 1872, 2; "Fun," *Utica Observer*, 8/31/1869, n.p.; "Narragansett," *ST*, 9/30/1871; Gordon, *The Scarlet Woman of Wall Street* (Grove, 1988), 216, 302, 304–5, 327–31, 340–56; Gerald McFarland, "Dorman B. Eaton and the Genteel Reform Tradition," *JAH* 54, no. 4 (Mar. 1968): 811; "Commission," *NYP*, 5/31/1872, n.p.; "Correspondence," *AAT*, 6/22/1872, 12; "Fisk," *NYS*, 1/8/1872, 1; "Tragedy," *NYE*, 1/8/1872, n.p.; "Stokes," *NYS*, 12/24/1872, n.p.; "Stokes," *NYS*, 11/3/1901, 8; "Stokes," *NYS*, 1/8/1872, 1; "Stokes," *NYS*, 12/24/1872, n.p.; John Townsend and Benjamin Phelps, *Error Book: Edward S. Stokes. Plaintiff in Error, against the People of the State of New York, Defendants in Error* (George G. Nesbit, 1873); "Sam," *NYS*, 3/29/1872, 1; "Queer," *NYTel*, 3/29/1872, 4; "Sporting," *NYCA*, 3/28/1872, 4; "Quarrel," *NYP*, 3/28/1872, n.p.; "Beattie," *NYT*, 11/2/1886, 1.

25 "Parsee," *NYW*, 10/7/1872, 5; "Parsee Letters," *NYW*, 12/5/1872, 2; Ida Tarbell, "Tariff in Our Times," *American Magazine* 64, no. 2 (June 1907), 74–75, 157; Joanne Reitano, *The Tariff Question in the Gilded Age* (Penn State, 1994), 4; Earle Ross, *The Liberal Republican Movement* (Holt, 1919), 86–105; *Proceedings of the Liberal Republican Convention in Cincinnati, May 1st, 2d, and 3d, 1872* (Baker & Godwin, 1872); "Political," *Decatur Republican*, 3/30/1871, n.p.; Walter Houghton, *Early Life and Public Career of Hon. James G. Blaine* (Cincinnati Book and Bible House, 1884), 527; Hans Trefousse, *Carl Schurz, a Biography* (Fordham, 1998), 206; John Sproat, *The Best Men* (Oxford, 1968), 82–83; Mark W. Summers, *Party Games* (UNC, 2004), 187; William McFeely, *Grant* (Norton, 2002), 381–82; Eric Foner, *Reconstruction* (Harper & Row, 1988), 442–44, 508–9; "Saunders," *NYS*, 8/16/1872, 1.

26 Hoogenboom, *Outlawing*, 122–126; Leo Hershkowitz, *Tweed's New York* (Anchor, 1978), 209, 217, 220–23, 231–32.

27 "510," *London Gazette*, 2/21/1873, 747; "Supreme Court," *Chicago Legal News* 5 (4/19/1873): 355; "Howard," *BG*, 5/3/1873, 1; "Horseflesh," *NYTel*, 7/25/1873, 4; "Out-Door," *NYTrib*, 7/8/1873, 5; "Modocs," *New York Clipper*, 5/10/1873, 47; "Noah's," *NYS*, 4/16/1873, 1; "Arrest," *NYH*, 4/16/1873, 9; Eric Ferrara, *The Bowery* (History Press, 2011), 99; A. W. Bates, "Dr Kahn's Museum: Obscene Anatomy in Victorian London," *Journal of the Royal Society of Medicine* 99 (Dec. 2006), 619–24.

28 "Americus," *NYH*, 8/10/1873, 5; "Funeral," *NYS*, 6/16/1873, 1; "Died," *NYH*, 3/30/1873, 7.

29 "Corruption," *NYH*, 8/19/1873, 8; "Paez," *NYH*, 8/20/1873, 10; Michael Cavanagh, ed., *Memoirs of Gen. Thomas Francis Meagher* (The Messenger, 1892), 347.

30 "Tweed," *NYH*, 11/20/1873, 5; Hershkowitz, *Tweed's*, 4, 256, 266; "Dead," *NYS*, 7/20/1890, 1.

31 "'Relations'," *NYS*, 1/18/1873, 1.

32 "Seizures," *DG*, 7/22/1873, 1; "Miscellany," *NYTrib*, 8/15/1873, 8; *Stockwell v. U.S.*, 23 F. Cas. 116 (1870); John Hopper, *Examine!!! All Who are Interested, and Who is Not? Administration of Customs Collection* (National Revenue Reform Association, 1873).

33 *Annual Report of the Secretary of the Treasury on the State of the Finances for the year 1885*, v. 2, *Collection of Duties* (G.P.O., 1885), 551; "Moiety," *NYT* 3/12/1874, 5; David A. Wells, *Congress and Phelps, Dodge & Co.* (1875), 145, 287; Dodge noted in Benjamin Butler, *The Necessity of Rewards for the Detection of Crime* (G.P.O., 1874), 9.

34 Phelps, Dodge & Co. [David A. Wells], *Our Revenue System: History of the Proceedings in the Case of Phelps, Dodge & Co.* (Martin's, 1873), passim; Wells, *Congress*, passim; Lester Dorman, "Some New York Customhouse Investigations," *New Englander*, 36, no. 4 (Oct. 1877) 792–93; Shelbourne Eaton, *Seizing Books and Records under the Revenue Law* (Chamber of Commerce, 1874), 24, 29–30.

35 *Evidence before the Committee on Ways and Means relative to Moieties and Customs Revenue Laws, May 2,1874* (G.P.O., 1874), 6–7, 9, 12.

36 "House," *PNA*, 3/2/1865, 1; Butler, *Necessity*, 4–5, 7, 11.

37 "New York," *Janesville Gazette*, 4/9/1874, 1; *Evidence . . . Moieties* (1874), 131; John Goss, *The History of Tariff Administration in the United States* (Columbia University, 1897), 69–70; Nicholas Parrillo, *Against the Profit Motive* (Yale, 2013), 345–51; *In re Platt et al.*, 19 F. Cas. 815 (1874).

CHAPTER II: SILK

1 "Chevalier," *NYH*, 2/29/1873, 1; "For Sale," *NYH*, 3/22/1873, 1; "Trust," *NYH*, 1/26/1873, 5; "238," *NYH*, 9/22/1872, 14.

2 "Personalities," *DG*, 6/20/1873, 6; "Married," *NYE*, 4/21/1865, n.p.; "Died,"
   NYTrib, 3/23/1867, 5; "Trial," *NYS*, 8/6/1872, n.p.; "Funeral," *DG*, 1/30/1885,
   656; "Roberts," *NYS*, 9/12/1880, 1; William Stoddard, *Men of Business* (Scribner's, 1897), 229–45; "Collector," *NYT*, 3/20/1873, 8.

3 Linus Brockett, *The Silk Industry in America* (Silk Association of America,
   1876), 15–16, 18; Dieter Kuhn, "Tracing a Chinese Legend: In Search of the
   Identity of the 'First Sericulturalist'," *T'oung Pao*, 2nd ser., 70, no. 4/5 (1984),
   213–45; Gaines K. C. Liu, "The Silkworm and Chinese Culture," *Osiris* 10
   (1952): 129–47; Catharine Edwards, *The Politics of Immorality in Ancient Rome*
   (Cambridge, 2002), 68; Lucius Annaeus Seneca, *On Benefits*, trans. Miriam
   Griffin and Brad Inwood (University of Chicago), 174.

4 J. Thorley, "Trade between the Roman Empire and the East under Augustus,"
   Greece & Rome, 2nd ser., 16, no. 2 (Oct., 1969), 216–17; Grant Parker, "Indian
   Commodities and Roman Experience," *Journal of the Economic and Social His-
   tory of the Orient* 45, no. 1 (2002): 61; Brockett, *Silk Industry*, 18–19, 26–28.

5 Brockett, *Silk Industry*, 61, 114.

6 "Prince," *NYTel*, 5/17/1875, 1; "Charley," *NYTel*, 5/18/1875, 1; Joshua Chamber-
   lain, ed., *Universities and their Sons*, v. 5 (Herndon, 1900), 360; *Trow's*, 1874,
   745, 973; "Local," *JM*, 2/21/1873, 2; "Prospectus," *NR*, 2/12/1874, n.p.; "Inven-
   tion," *NR*, 2/5/1874, n.p.; Donald Ritchie, *Gallery* (Harvard, 1992), 80.

7 "Internal," *NYT*, 9/10/1869, 2; "Washington," *NYE*, 11/13/1868, 1; "Alabama,"
   NYTrib, 11/21/1874, 3.

8 "Home," *NYTrib*, 5/9/1874, 12; *McMicken v. Lawrence*, 39 N.Y. Super. Ct. 540
   (1875); "Recorded," *NYT*, 10/3/1874, 8; "Real," *DG*, 10/20/1874, 800; "Real,"
   NYT, 10/21/1874, 10.

9 *Trow's*, 1872, 658; "Smugglers," *NYTel*, 5/13/1875, 1; "Lawrence," *NYS*, 5/14/1875,
   1; Herbert Asbury, *Sucker's Progress* (Dodd, Mead, 1938), 20–35.

10 "Bahamas," *Memphis Appeal*, 1/7/1864, n.p.; "Messrs. Benjamin," *NYTrib*,
   1/22/1864, 4; "Outrages," *Liverpool Mercury*, 7/19/1864, 7; *New York Custom-
   house* (1864), 69–70.

11 *Recopilacion de Leyes, Decretos y Providencias de los Poderes Legislativo y Ejecu-
   tivo de la Union*, Tomo 24 (Imprenta del Gobierno, en Palacio, 1876), 291–94;
   Trow's, 1872, 672, 1249; "Fashionable," *NYTel*, 3/3/1871, 2; "Lawrence," *NYS*,
   5/14/1875, 1; "Smugglers," *NYTel*, 5/13/1875, 1.

12 "Married," *JM*, 11/25/1859, 158; George Wolf household, U.S. 1870 Census,
   Household 483, 11th Election District, 22nd Ward, City of New York, County
   of New York, State of New York, 62; "Married," *NYH*, 11/3/1871, 8.

13 "Smugglers," *NYTel*, 5/13/1875, 1; Matilda Wolf, 1861 U.K. Census; "Boarding,"
   JM, 5/6/1864, 133; *Palgrave Dictionary of Anglo-Jewish History*, eds. William
   Rubinstein, Michael Jolles, and Hilary Rubenstein (Palgrave–Macmillan,
   2011), 852–53; Isaac Goldberg, *Major Noah* (Jewish Publication Society, 1938),
   263, 288–90, 293.

14 "Auctioneer," *NYH*, 4/3/1872, 2; "Compositions," *London Commercial Gazette*, 7/15/1872, 512.

15 George Boutwell, *Letter of the Secretary of the Treasury, Communicating, in Compliance with the Resolution of the Senate of December 14, 1870, Certain Statements Relative to the Collection and Distribution of Fines and Forfeitures under the Customs Laws* (G.P.O., 1871), 47; "Frauds," *NYTel*, 12/21/1868, 1; "Frauds," *NYT*, 1/13/1869, 2; "Arrest," *NYT*, 1/22/1869, 2; "Smuggling," *NYTrib*, 1/25/1869, n.p.; "Smuggling," *NYT*, 1/30/1869, 5; "Smuggling," *NYTrib*, 1/27/1869, 2.

16 Letter, Sidney Webster to Edwards Pierrepont, 5/18/1876, v. 114, Hamilton Fish Papers, LOC.

17 "City," *NYTrib*, 4/28/1869, 8; "Collectorship," *NYTel*, 7/19/1870, 1; "Washington," *NYTrib*, 5/24/1871, 5; "New York," *BE*, 7/14/1871, 1; "Tourist," *NYW*, 10/24/1871, 3; "Nomination," *NYW*, 10/25/1872, 5; "Miscellany," *NYTrib*, 1/11/1873, 8; "Tweed," *NYTrib*, 1/14/1873, 2; "Tweed," *NYH*, 2/2/1873, 10; Henry M. Williams, United States Passport Application, 7/30/1874; "Died," *NYW*, 9/5/1879, 5.

18 "Personal," *NYW*, 12/3/1869, 4; "Notes," *Troy Whig*, 9/10/1870, n.p.; "Death," *NYT*, 4/4/1873, n.p.; "Statesman," *Hamilton Telegraph*, 7/11/1854, n.p.; Phineas Headley, *Massachusetts in the Rebellion* (Walker, Fuller, 1866), 603; "Swisshelm," *Janesville Gazette*, 5/27/1863, n.p.; "Arrests," *NYTrib*, 1/24/1877, 8.

19 *New York Customhouse Investigation*, v. 2 (G.P.O., 1872), 396–97; "Courts," *NYH*, 11/10/1875, 3; "Late," *SFB*, 11/6/1860, 3; Thomas Perry, ed., *Perry's Bankrupt and Insolvent Gazette* (Griffiths, 1840), 144; Joany Hichberger, "The Victoria Cross Paintings of Louis Desanges," *Oxford Art Journal* 7, no. 2 (1984): 42–51, esp. 43; Desanges household, Parish of Marylebone, Town of London, County of London, Country of England, Page 13, Household 36, *Census Returns of England and Wales, 1871*, Kew, Surrey, England: The National Archives of the UK (TNA): Public Record Office (PRO), 1871; Warren Scoville, *The Persecution of Huguenots and French Economic Development 1680–1720* (University of California, 1960), 325; William Ashworth, *Customs and Excise* (Oxford, 2003), 168; "Death," *London Morning Chronicle*, 9/24/1860, n.p.; Arnold Sorsby, "John Zachariah Laurence: A Belated Tribute," *British Journal of Ophthalmology* 16, no. 11 (Nov. 1932): 737.

20 George Collen, *Debrett's Baronage of England* (William Pickering, 1840), 622; "Credit," *NYH*, 5/14/1875, 3; "Smugglers," *NR*, 11/11/1875, 1; "Robert William Desanges," London Metropolitan Archives, Saint Marylebone, Day Book of baptisms, 1834 May–1837 Apr., P89/MRY1/101; Joany Hichberger, "Democratising Glory? The Victoria Cross Paintings of Louis Desanges," *Oxford Art Journal* 7, no. 2 (1985): 43; "Printing," *BAD*, 10/3/1866; "Deputy Collector," *NYT*, 3/20/1873, 8; *New York Customhouse Investigation* (G.P.O., 1872), 468; I. S. Bangs, "The Ullman Brigade," in *War Papers Read before the Commandery*

of the State of Maine, Military Order of the Loyal Legion of the United States, v. 2 (Lefavor-Tower, 1902), 298; "Trick," *NYS*, 10/5/1872, n.p.

21 "Desanges v. Gregory," *TL*, 12/19/1835, 3; "Bagley," *The Farmer's Magazine* 7 (1837): 125; "List," *Mechanic's Magazine* 36 (1842): 270; *Re Loughborough*, Cases in Chancery (1857), 439; "Death," *London Morning Chronicle*, 9/24/1860, n.p.; "Death," *TL*, 9/25/1860, 10; "Stray," *NYE*, 10/11/1860, 1; *Desanges v. Desanges and Griffiths*, Divorce Court file, Item reference J 77/14/D60, The National Archives, Kew.; Edward Barnard Household, 1851 U.K. Census; Robert Desanges Household, 1861 U.K. census; Alice Jenkins, *Michael Faraday's Mental Exercises* (Liverpool, 2008), 10; "Credit," *NYH*, 5/14/1875, 3; "Naval," *LDN*, 9/3/1862, n.p.; "Thieves," *PD*, 11/13/1875, 1; "Law," *NYT*, 6/22/1875, 5; "Lawrence," *NYT*, 2/8/1879, 3.

22 "Smugglers," *NYTel*, 5/13/1875, 1; "Johnston," *NYH*, 4/3/1872, 2; Letter, Sidney Webster to Edwards Pierrepont, 5/18/1876, Fish Papers, v. 114.

23 Lafayette Graff passport, No. 12196, May 29, 1871, Passport Applications, 1795–1905, ARC Identifier 566612, MLR Number A1 508, NARA Series M1372, Roll #83, NARA-D.C.; Malcolm Stern, *First American Jewish Families*, 3rd ed. (Genealogical Pub., 1991), 46, 244; "Indiana," *JM*, 10/5/1866, n.p.; "Local," *JM*, 4/17/1868, n.p.; "Des Anges," *NYH*, 11/4/1875, 5; "Mills," *NYTrib*, 4/12/1867, 3.

24 William Wyckoff, *Silk Goods of America* (Van Nostrand, 1880), 28–32, 90–93; Brockett, *Silk Industry*, 82–87, 128–32.

25 Stoddard, *Men of Business*, 211–28; "Horace B. Claflin," *Phrenological Journal* 52, no. 1 (Jan. 1871): 16–20.

26 Barbara Goldsmith, *Other Powers* (Harper, 1999), 211–12, 332, 366–68; "Beecher," *BE*, 6/26/1873, n.p.; "Tappan," *Brooklyn Union*, 6/24/1873, n.p.; Marion Marberry, *Vicky* (Funk & Wagnalls, 1967), 145.

27 Stoddard, *Men of Business*, 225–26.

28 "Smugglers," *NYTrib*, 9/17/1875, 1; "Lawyers," *NYS*, 6/5/1871, n.p.; "Lagrave," *NYS*, 10/29/1872, 1; "Duty," *NYH*, 10/19/1873, 9; "Secret," *NPG*, 12/13/1879, 6; "Heart," *NYS*, 10/4/1872, n.p.; "New Orleans," *NYS*, 4/21/1874, 1; "Dead," *Shenandoah Evening Herald*, 3/10/1892, n.p.; "Dead," *Crawford County Democrat*, 3/17/1892, 1; "Items," *Virginia State Journal*, 9/2/1871, 1; J. M. Mayorga, "Ryan," *NYH*, 10/20/1872, 12; "Washington," *NYH*, 10/18/1872, 7; "Antecedents," *NYS*, 8/17/1872, n.p.; "Criminal," *NYTrib*, 10/6/1873, 12; "Virginius," *NYW*, 11/11/1873, 3.

29 "Smugglers," *NYTrib*, 9/17/1875, 1; "Lawrence," *NYS*, 5/14/1875, 1.

30 "Victims," *NYTrib*, 2/28/1874, 1; Hamilton Fish Diary, 11/22/1875, Fish Papers, v. 4, 373, 278; Thomas Reeves, *Gentleman Boss* (Knopf, 1975), 67–136.

31 William McFeely, *Grant* (Norton, 2002), 396–98; "Burglary," *AAT*, 12/19/1874, 7–8; Philip Melanson with Peter Stevens, *The Secret Service* (Carroll & Graf, 2002), 21; Alan Lessoff, *The Nation and its City* (Johns Hopkins, 1994), 95–96; Mark Summers, *The Era of Good Stealings* (Oxford, 1993), 144; "Silica," *NR*, 2/12/1874, n.p.

32 *Official Proceedings of the National Republican Conventions of 1868, 1872, 1876, and 1880* (Johnson, 1903), 141, 196, 208; McFeely, *Grant*, 253, 282, 291–95.

33 *Treasury Register*, 1873, 113, 115; "Smugglers," *NYTrib*, 9/17/1875, 1; "Custom-house," *NYT*, 2/20/1874, 2; *Edward S. Stokes, Plaintiff in Error, Against the People of the State of New York* (Nesbitt, 1873); "Career Ended," *NYT*, 12/31/1880, 5.

34 "Arrivals," *NYH*, 1/8/1875, 10; "Smugglers," *NYTrib*, 9/17/1875, 1.

35 "Topics," *DG*, 1/11/1875, 508; "Cold," *NYP*, 2/6/1895, 1; "Smugglers," *NYTrib*, 9/17/1875, 1.

36 "Smugglers," *NYTrib*, 9/17/1875, 1; "Autograph," *DG*, 5/18/1875, 596.

37 "Tybee," *NYTrib*, 6/3/1870, 8; *U.S. v. Harris*, Docket, v. 78, p. 3 (1874); "Smuggling," *NYH*, 12/29/1874, 11; "Circuit Court," *NYH*, 10/8/1875, 9; *Treasury Register*, 1873, 117; "Punished," *NYTrib*, 1/25/1875, 7; "Notes," *NYT*, 1/27/1875, 5; "Cigars," *NYT*, 2/26/1875, 2; "Cigars," *NYS*, 2/26/1875, n.p.

38 "Seizure," *NYH*, 1/18/1875, 8; "Smuggling," *NYH*, 1/20/1875, 3; "Custom," *NYTel*, 1/27/1875, 1; "Reforms," *NYTrib*, 1/27/1875, 2.

39 "Goods," *NYTrib*, 1/29/1875, 2.

40 *Wilson's New York City Copartnership Directory* (Trow, 1874), 108; "Smuggling," *NYT*, 2/5/1875, 10; "Frauds," *NYS*, 2/5/1875, 1; "Courts," *NYT*, 2/6/1875, 3.

41 "Frauds," *NYS*, 2/5/1875, 1; "Frauds," *DG*, 2/6/1875, 701.

CHAPTER 12: FLIGHT

1 "Smugglers," *NYT*, 3/10/1875, 5; "Married," *NYH*, 6/27/1873, 8; Jonathan Plaut, *The Jews of Windsor, 1790–1990* (Dundurn, 2007), 34; Malcolm Stern, *First American Jewish Families*, 3rd ed. (Genealogical Pub., 1991), 46.

2 E. D. Adams, "Lord Ashburton and the Treaty of Washington," *AHR* 17, no. 4 (July 1912): 764–82; Jacques Semmelman, "The Doctrine of Specialty in the Federal Courts: Making Sense of *United States v. Rauscher*," *Virginia Journal of International Law* 34 (Fall 1993): 81–83, 92–93; Bradley Miller, "International Law, Imperial Power, and Extradition in Canada, 1865–1883," *Canadian Historical Review* 90, no. 4 (Dec. 2009): 639–69.

3 Adam Mayers, *Dixie & the Dominion* (Dundurn, 2003), esp. 242; William Davis, *An Honourable Defeat* (Harcourt, 2001).

4 "Curiosities," *NYS*, 10/3/1871, 1; "News," *DG*, 2/12/1874, 695; "Escape," *NYE*, 5/10/1875, n.p.; "Breakers," *NYTrib*, 5/11/1875, 12; "News," *DG*, 7/31/1875, 228; "Tired," *NYS*, 6/11/1879, n.p.; "Cashier," *NYTrib*, 4/1/1872, 8; "Bank," *NYTrib*, 4/12/1872, 1.

5 "Abduction," *NYE*, 3/7/1868, 1; *Adriance v. Lagrave*, 59 N.Y. 110 (1874); Semmelman, "Specialty," 101–4.

6 "Smugglers," *NYT*, 3/10/1875, 5; "Absconding," *NYTrib*, 3/10/1875, 2; "Lawrence," *NYS*, 5/14/1875, 1; "Smugglers," *NYT*, 5/14/1875, 12; "Credit," *NYH*, 5/15/1875, 3; "Miscellany," *NYTrib*, 5/15/1875, 12; "Requisition," *NYS*, 1/9/1876, 1.

7   David Pottinger, "Canada-Intercolonial Railway," in *Americana*, v. 4 (Scientific American, 1912).

8   "Absconding," *NYTrib*, 3/10/1875, 2; "Lawrence," *NYS*, 5/14/1875, 1; "Smugglers," *NYT*, 5/14/1875, 12; "Credit," *NYH*, 5/15/1875, 3; "Miscellany," *NYTrib*, 5/15/1875, 12; "Requisition," *NYS*, 1/9/1876, 1; "Dead," *NYS*, 7/20/1890, 1; "'Gordon," *NYT*, 8/5/1874, 3.

9   "Attachment," *NYTrib*, 2/16/1875, 2; "New York," *NYT*, 2/17/1875, 10; "Arrested," *NYT*, 2/19/1875, 7; "Smugglers," *DG*, 5/29/1875, 681.

10   "Absconding," *NYTrib*, 3/10/1875, 2; "Extradition," *Quebec Mercury*, 3/10/1875, 2; "Smugglers," *NYT*, 3/10/1875, 5; "Smugglers," *NYT*, 5/14/1875, 12; "Lawrence," *NYS*, 5/14/1875, 1; "Credit," *NYH*, 5/15/1875, 3; "Smuggling," *NYS*, 5/26/1875, 1.

11   "Removed," *NYT*, 8/10/1875, 8; Mark Hirsch, *William C. Whitney* (Dodd, Mead, 1948); Michael McGerr, *The Decline of Popular Politics* (Oxford, 1986), 97; *Noah v. Noah*, Divorce Court file, Case #2437, 7/13/1872, The National Archives, Kew, Ancestry.com.

12   John Simon, ed., *The Papers of Ulysses S. Grant*, v. 27, *January 1–October 31, 1876* (SIU, 2005), 151; "Smugglers," *NYT*, 5/14/1875, 12; "Absconding," *NYTrib*, 3/10/1875, 2; "Smuggler," *NYS*, 3/10/1875, 1; "Fugitive," *NYT*, 3/10/1875, 5; "Lawrence," *PD*, 5/29/1875, 4; "Lawrence," *AAT*, 6/12/1875, 13; "Bow-street," *TL*, 3/24/1875, 11; "Bow-street," *TL*, 4/16/1875, 1.

13   Letter, Charles L. Lawrence to George Bliss, 5/29/1876, Hamilton Fish Papers, LOC, v. 114; Richard Davenport-Hines, "Lewis, Sir George Henry, first baronet (1833–1911)," *Oxford Dictionary of National Biography* (Oxford, 2004), online ed.

14   "Smugglers," *NYT*, 5/14/1875, 12; Letter, Charles L. Lawrence to George Bliss, 5/29/1876, Fish Papers, v. 114; *Report of the Commissioners Appointed to Inquire Into the Present Position of the Royal Academy in Relation to the Fine Arts* (Eyre and Spottiswoode, 1863), 62.

15   Letter, Charles L. Lawrence to Sidney Webster, 6/15/1876, Fish Papers, v. 114; Letter, Charles L. Lawrence to George Bliss, 5/29/1876, Fish Papers, v. 114; Edward Clarke, *A Treatise Upon the Law of Extradition*, 2nd ed. (Stevens and Haynes, 1874).

16   "Bow-street," *TL*, 3/24/1875, 11; "Bow-street," *TL*, 4/16/1875, 1; "Lawrence," *NYT*, 4/16/1875, 10; "Frauds," *LWN*, 4/17/1875, 492; "Extradition," *Pump Court* 7, no. 95 (Aug. 11, 1888): 244; *Extradition Treaty with Great Britain, Message from the President* (G.P.O., 1876), 60; Semmelman, "Specialty," 80 n. 59.

17   "Position," *NYTrib*, 6/2/1875, 7; "Smuggling," *NYS*, 5/25/1875, 1; "Lawrence," *NYS*, 5/14/1875, 1; "Frauds," *NYTrib*, 5/14/1875, 12; "Smugglers," *NYT*, 5/14/1875, 12; "Smugglers," *NYTrib*, 9/17/1875, 1; "Latest," *NYT*, 5/3/1875, 1.

18   "Smugglers," *NYTel*, 5/11/1875, 1; "Smugglers," *NYTel*, 5/12/1875, 1; "Lawrence," *NYW*, 5/13/1875, 5; "Lawrence," *DG*, 5/13/1875, 558; "Smugglers," *NYT*, 5/14/1875, 12; "Ludlow," *NYTel*, 5/14/1875, 4; "Lawrence," *NYW*, 5/14/1875,

5; "Lawrence," *NYS*, 5/14/1875, 1; "Credit," *NYH*, 5/14/1875, 3; "Smuggling," *Indianapolis Sentinel*, 5/18/1875, 7.

19   "Smuggling," *AAT*, 6/5/1875, 9; "Ireland," *LWN*, 3/13/1875, 324; "Ireland," *Madras Mail*, 4/7/1875, 1; "Prince," *NYTel*, 5/18/1875, 4; "Credit," *NYH*, 5/14/1875, 3; "Lawrence," *NYS*, 5/14/1875, 1; "Frauds," *NYTrib*, 5/14/1875, 12; "Smugglers," *NYT*, 5/14/1875, 12.

20   "Absconding," *NYTrib*, 3/10/1875, 2; "Smuggler," *NYS*, 3/10/1875, 1; "Silk," *NYT*, 6/15/1875, 9; "Frauds," *NYS*, 2/6/1875, 1; "Frauds," *DG*, 2/6/1875, 701; "Lawrence," *NYS*, 5/14/1875, 1; "Lawrence," *NYW*, 5/14/1875, 5; "Smugglers," *NYTel*, 5/14/1875, 4; "General," *BAD*, 6/7/1875, 1; "Personalities," *New York Independent*, 5/27/1875, 6; Joe Joggs, "Letter," *Bucks County Gazette*, 5/20/1875, 3.

21   "Ireland," *LWN*, 3/13/1875, 324; "Ireland," *Madras Mail*, 4/7/1875, 1; "By Telegraph," *St. Albans Messenger*, 3/31/1875, 3; "Charles L. Lawrence," *AAT*, 6/12/1875, 13; "The Silk Smugglers, *NYS*, 2/9/1875, n.p.; "Charles L. Lawrence," *New York Sabbath Recorder*, 4/29/1875, n.p.

22   "Frauds," *NYTrib*, 5/22/1875, 2; "Smuggling," *AAT*, 6/5/1875, 9; "Frauds," *NYS*, 2/6/1875, 1; "Moieties," *NYW*, 2/10/1875, 4; "Congress," *DG*, 5/17/1875, 586; "There," *DG*, 2/26/1875, 862.

23   Allan Nevins, *Hamilton Fish* (Dodd, Mead, 1936), 771–73; "Another," *DG*, 8/18/1874, 336; Austin Abbott, *Official Report of the Trial of Henry Ward Beecher* (George W. Smith, 1875), 514–15; "Washington," *Albany Evening Journal*, 4/28/1875, 3; "Pardoning," *NYE*, 5/20/1875, 1; "Customhouse," *NYT*, 1/24/1875, 12.

24   Diary, 5/22/1875, Fish Papers, v. 5, 243–47; Simon, ed., Grant Papers, v. 27, 151; "Developments," *NYTrib*, 5/24/1875, 5.

25   "Developments," *NYTrib*, 5/24/1875, 5; "Trial," *NYH*, 11/4/1875, 5.

26   "Developments," *NYTrib*, 5/24/1875, 5; "Unmasking," *DG*, 5/29/1875, 681; "Lafayette," *NYT*, 6/3/1875, 5; "Informer," *NYTrib*, 6/4/1875, 12; "Proverbial," *NYTrib*, 6/4/1875, 6; Supreme Court, City and County of New York, *Appeal from Order denying Motion to Vacate Attachment* (Evening Post Steames, 1875); *U.S. v. Graff*, 67 Barb. 304 (1875); *U.S. v. Graff*, 4 Hun 634 (1875).

27   "Claflin," *DG*, 6/10/1875, 775; "Developments," *NYTrib*, 5/24/1875, 5; "Smuggling," *BE*, 6/7/1875, n.p.; "Smugglers," *Brooklyn Union*, 6/7/1875, n.p.; "Local," *NYT*, 6/11/1875, 10; "Smuggling," *Brooklyn Union*, 6/11/1875, n.p.

28   "Smugglers," *NYT*, 6/15/1875, 9; "The Smuggling Cases," *NYT*, 6/17/1875, 3.

29   "Imprisonment," *NYH*, 12/30/1880, n.p.; Leo Hershkowitz, *Tweed's New York* (Anchor, 1978), 282, 286.

30   Hershkowitz, *Tweed's*, 216–18; "Gunboats," *NYTrib*, 12/10/1869, 1; "The New York Bar Association," *The Green Bag* 8 (1896): 450–58, esp. 456; Kathryn Greenthal, *Augustus Saint-Gaudens* (Metropolitan Museum of Art, 1985), 72–75; "Personal," *NYP*, 7/5/1901, n.p.; "Know," *New York Whole Truth*, 11/30/1880, n.p.

31 "Frauds," *NYTrib*, 5/25/1875, n.p.; "Courts," *NYTrib*, 5/26/1875, 5; "Rights," *NYTrib*, 5/27/1875, 3.

32 "Correspondence Respecting Extradition," House of Commons, *Accounts and Papers* (Harrison & Sons, 1876), v. 40, 24–29; Simon, ed., Grant Papers, v. 27, 151; *Extradition Treaty with Great Britain, Message from the President* (G.P.O., 1876), 58–66.

33 Simon, ed., Grant Papers, v. 27, 151–52; Diary, Fish Papers, v. 5, 331–32, 377.

34 "Correspondence," *Accounts and Papers*, 11–17, esp. 12; Letter, Robert P. Noah to Sir Fred Perkins, 8/2/1875, v. 108, Fish Papers; Letter, Robert P. Noah to Sir James Ferguson, 8/3/1875, v. 108, Fish Papers; Unsigned note to Stephen Clarke, 8/5/1875, v. 108, Fish Papers; Letter, Robert Noah (signed Bob) to Zipporah Lawrence, undated, v. 108, Fish Papers; Letter, Charles L. Lawrence to George Bliss, 5/29/1876, v. 114, Fish Papers; T. H. Sanderson, "Thornton, Sir Edward (1817–1906)," rev. H. C. G. Matthew, *Oxford Dictionary of National Biography* (Oxford, 2004), online ed.; Caleb Cushing, *The Treaty of Washington* (Harper & Brother, 1873), 11.

35 Diary entry, 8/21/1875, Fish Papers, 309–10; Nevins, *Fish*, 15; Letter, Charles L. Lawrence to George Bliss, 5/29/1876, v. 114, Fish Papers; William McFeely, *Grant* (Norton, 2002), 296–98.

36 Ivan Kalmar, "Benjamin Disraeli: Romantic Orientalist," *Comparative Studies in History and Society* 47, no. 2 (2005): 348–71; Adam Kirsch, *Benjamin Disraeli* (Random House, 2008), 211; Robert Blake, *Disraeli* (St. Martin's, 1967), 581–87.

37 "Wells," *NYW*, 8/24/1875, n.p.; "Wells," *MS*, 8/24/1875, n.p.

38 Letter, Zipporah Lawrence to Charles L. Lawrence, 8/24/1875, v. 108, Fish Papers; "Liquidations," *Manchester Guardian*, 12/27/1875, 8; Letter, Thornton to Robert P. Noah, 9/2/1875, v. 109, Fish Papers; Note, Clarke, 9/23/1875, v. 109, Fish Papers; Letter, J. J. Noah to Zipporah, 9/28/1875, v. 109, Fish Papers; "Correspondence," *Accounts and Papers*, 30; Letter, W. Stoughton to S. G. Clark, 10/29/1875, v. 110, Fish Papers.

39 "Convicted," *NYT*, 11/10/1875, 8; "Convicted," *NYH*, 11/10/1875, 3; "Smugglers," *NR*, 11/11/1875, 1; "Thieves," *PD*, 11/13/1875, 1; "Case," *NYT*, 11/14/1875, 10; "Sentenced," *NYTel*, 11/27/1875, 4; "Des Anges," *NYT*, 11/28/1875, 7; "Prisoner," *Hudson Register*, 11/30/1875, n.p.; "Penitentiary," *NYT*, 12/9/1875, 5.

40 Hershkowitz, *Tweed's*, 280–84; "Gone," *NYH*, 12/5/1875, 5.

41 "Imprisonment," *NYT*, 12/5/1875, 1; "Fugitive," *NYT*, 12/6/1875, 1.

42 "Smuggling," *NYT*, 12/9/1875, 3; "Arraignment," *NYH*, 12/14/1875, 8; "Postponement," *DG*, 12/15/1875, 350; "Preliminaries," *NYS*, 12/17/1875, 1; "Lawrence," *NYT*, 12/22/1875, 2; "Respite," *NYS*, 12/23/1875, 1; McFeely, *Grant*, 429–30; Simon, ed., Grant Papers, v. 27, 116–21; "Lawrence," *NYTrib*, 7/3/1875, 4; "Extradition," *NYT*, 7/3/1875, 5; "Emma," *TL*, 1/15/1876, 7; "Railway," *TL*, 2/7/1876, 7; "Intelligence," *TL*, 2/8/1876, 5; "United States," *TL*, 2/9/1876, 12.

43 Margaret Thompson, "Ben Butler versus the Brahmins: Patronage and Pol-

itics in Early Gilded Age Massachusetts," *New England Quarterly* 55, no. 2 (June 1982): 163–86, esp. 168–71.

44 McFeely, *Grant* 429–30, 439; Simon, ed., Grant Papers, v. 27, 120; *Edwin Wilson et al. v. Cecilia Kerr*, New York Supreme Court General Term (1872).

45 "Lawrence," *NYTrib*, 1/8/1876, 3; "Lawrence's," *NYTrib*, 1/11/1876, 2; "Extradition," *Saturday Review* 41, no. 1078 (7/24/1876): 792–93; "Correspondence," *Accounts and Papers*, 38–48; Semmelman, "Specialty," 115–21; Blake, *Disraeli*, 539.

46 "Custom House," *NYH*, 10/22/1875, 7; "Scrambling," *NYS*, 11/22/1875, 1; "Custom House," *NYH*, 1/19/1876, 8; "Moiety," *NYT*, 1/27/1876, 8.

47 Michael DeGruccio, "Unmade: American Manhood in the Civil War Era," PhD diss., University of Notre Dame, 2007, 88–239, esp. 232; "Courts," *NYTrib*, 5/24/1875, 5; "Des Anges," *NYH*, 11/4/1875, 5; Sympathy notes, Benjamin F. Butler Papers, Box 87, Folder 4; Letter, Sidney Webster to Benjamin Butler, 5/1/1876, Butler Papers, Box 88, Folder 1; Letter, Sidney Webster to Benjamin Butler, 5/4/1876, Butler Papers, Box 88, Folder 1; Letter, B. G. Jayne to Butler, 5/5/1876, Butler Papers, Box 88, Folder 1; Letter, Sidney Webster to Benjamin Butler, 5/5/1876, Butler Papers, Box 88, Folder 1; Letter, Sidney Webster to Benjamin Butler, 5/6/1876, Butler Papers, Box 88, Folder 1; Letter, Sidney Webster to Edwards Pierrepont, 5/18/1876, Fish Papers, v. 114; Letter, Lawrence to Sidney Webster, 6/15/1876, Fish Papers, v. 114; Letter, Sidney Webster to Hamilton Fish, 5/17/1876, Fish Papers, v. 113.

48 "Lawrence," *NYTrib*, 5/26/1876, 1; *United States v. Lawrence et al.*, CR A-1, NARA-NYC.

49 "Independence," *NYT*, 7/5/1876, 5; "Centennial," *NYT*, 7/4/1876, 5.

50 "Cases," *NYH*, 6/22/1876, 11; "Morning," *NYTrib*, 6/23/1876, 4; "Lawrence," *Utica Herald*, 6/24/1876, 1; "So Long As," *HC*, 6/27/1876, 3; "Preparing," *NYTrib*, 7/1/1876, 5; Nevins, *Fish*, 822–23.

51 *United States v. Claflin et al.*, 25 F. Cas. 433 (1875); "Summary," *NYH*, 4/1/1876, 2; "Claflin," *Brooklyn Union*, 12/1/1876, n.p.; "Government," *NYTrib*, 2/23/1877, 4; "Disallowing," *NYTel*, 12/1/1880, 1; *United States v. Claflin*, 97 U.S. 546 (1878); "Business," *NYP*, 9/16/1881, n.p.; "Death," *NYTrib*, 11/15/1885, 7.

52 "Parts," *NYS*, 6/4/1876, n.p.

53 David A. Wells, "Extradition," *NYTrib*, 8/5/1876, 3–4; "Extradition," *Nation* 23, no. 581 (8/17/1876): 101–2; George Bliss, "Extradition," *Nation* 23, no. 583 (8/31/1876): 131–32; George Bliss, "Reply," *Nation* 23, no. 584 (9/7/1876): 151–52; George Bliss, "Republican," *Nation* 23, no. 585 (9/14/1876): 164–65.

54 Mark W. Summers, *Party Games* (UNC, 2004), 21–22; Rebecca Edwards, *Angels in the Machinery* (Oxford, 1997), 59–61.

55 Mark W. Summers, *The Era of Good Stealings* (Oxford, 1993), 296; "Pardoned," *NYT*, 8/4/1877, 8; "Pardoned," *NYS*, 8/4/1877, 1, 8–9; *List of Pardons by the President* (G.P.O., 1878), 8–9; *Trow's*, 1880, 370; *Radges' Topeka Directory*, 1883, 73.

CHAPTER 13: PRIDE

1   "Shots," *NYH*, 11/2/1886, 3; "Beattie," *NYT*, 11/2/1886, 1; "Beattie," *NYS*, 11/2/1886, 1; "Beattie," *NYTrib*, 11/2/1886, 1.

2   "Broom," *NYH*, 9/9/1886, 9; "Beattie," *NYT*, 11/2/1886, 1; "Beattie," *NYS*, 11/2/1886, 1.

3   "Nominations," *DG*, 6/28/1885, n.p.; "Beattie," *Chicago Inter-Ocean*, 11/14/1886, 18; "Joshua Wray, a novel," *Art Amateur*, 12/1892, 35; "Beattie," *NYS*, 2/24/1919, 7; "Voice," *WP*, 3/15/1908, 11.

4   "Beattie," *NYS*, 11/2/1886, 1.

5   "Guiteaued," *NPG*, 11/2/1886, 7; "Guiteau," *NPG*, 11/2/1886, 4.

6   Robert Bruce, *1877: Year of Violence* (Quadrangle, 1959), 19; Alexander Keyssar, *Out of Work* (Cambridge, 1986), 133; Samuel Rezneck, "Depression of 1873–78," *Journal of Political Economy* 58, no. 6 (Dec. 1950): 496; Samuel Bernstein, "American Labor in the Long Depression, 1873–1878," *Science & Society* 20, no. 1 (Winter, 1956): 77.

7   Bruce, *1877*, 35–37, 90–92, 310–11; Ari Hoogenboom, *Rutherford B. Hayes* (University of Kansas, 1995), 333–34; Eric Foner, *Reconstruction* (Harper & Row, 1988), 585–86.

8   "Protection," *NYTrib*, 2/11/1878, 8; "Demonstration," *NYW*, 4/16/1880, 1.

9   "Seizures," *NYTrib*, 9/6/1877, 8; "Sentenced," *NYT*, 1/26/1878, 3; "Miscellany," *NYTrib*, 7/13/1878, 10; "Vessels," *NYE*, 7/18/1878, n.p.; "Telegraph," *NYP*, 11/4/1878, n.p.

10 *Treasury Register* (G.P.O., 1874), 121; "Frauds," *NYTrib*, 7/10/1877, 5; "Fracas," *NYTrib*, 7/21/1877, 2;

11 "Sharpe," *DG*, 9/21/1877, 570; "Law," *NYT*, 9/22/1877, 3; "Broil," *NYH*, 9/25/1877, 5; "Miscellany," *NYTrib*, 9/25/1877, 2; "Tombs," *NYE*, 10/1/1877, 1.

12 "Surveyor," *NYTrib*, 11/29/1877, 8; "Ex-Inspector," *NYT*, 12/19/1877, 8; "Fraud," *NYT*, 8/2/1877, 8; "Washington," *NYTrib*, 9/8/1877, 5; "Frauds," *NYTrib*, 9/15/1877, 3; "Artificial," *NYTrib*, 9/21/1877, 2; "Stopping," *NYTrib*, 9/30/1877, n.p.; "Miscellaneous," *NYT*, 4/13/1878, 8.

13 "Fraud," *NYT*, 9/19/1878, 2; David A. Wells, *The Sugar Industry of the United States, and the Tariff* (Evening Post, 1878); Henry Brown, *Sugar Frauds and the Tariff* (1879); "A Workingman" Robert Howe [pseud.], *The Labor Side of the Great Sugar Question* (1878); William Grace, *Grace's Exposure! Or: Unsweetened Sugars* (Randel & Bruno, 1879); "Quarrel," *NYT*, 1/7/1879, 5; "Sugar," *NYT*, 5/24/1878, 2.

14 *Commissions to Examine Certain Customhouses of the United States* (G.P.O., 1877); George Howe, "The New York Customhouse Controversy, 1877–1879," *MVHR* 18, no. 3 (Dec. 1931): 353–54; Thomas Reeves, *Gentleman Boss* (Knopf, 1975), 114–24.

15 Reeves, *Gentleman*, 42–43; Frederick Douglass, *The Life and Times of Frederick Douglass* (Dover, 2003), 393, 406.

16 Reeves, *Gentleman*, 94, 125, 126–31; Edmund Morris, *The Rise of Theodore Roosevelt* (Random House, 2001), 8–10, 69–70; H. W. Brands, *T.R.* (Basic, 1998), 12–13, 16–17, 79–83.

17 Reeves, *Gentleman*, 130; Edwin Merritt, *Recollections, 1828–1911* (Lyon, 1911), 1–3, 109–12; "Rules," *NYT*, 2/16/1878, 8; "Uproar," *NYS*, 2/16/1878, 3.

18 "Arthur," *Auburn Morning News*, 2/8/1879, n.p.; Ari Hoogenboom, *Outlawing the Spoils* (University of Illinois, 1961), 171; George Howe, *Chester A. Arthur* (Dodd, Mead, 1934), 91; "Ended," *NYT*, 2/4/1879, 1; Reeves, *Gentleman*, 146–147.

19 "Tariff," *NYT*, 2/3/1878, 10; "Bill," *NYH*, 6/12/1880, 4; "Bill," *WP*, 6/12/1880, 1; "Two Horse," *WP*, 10/22/1880, 2; "Garfield," *WP*, 10/22/1880, 2; "'Cobden,'" *WP*, 10/25/1880, 1.

20 David Jordan, *Winfield Scott Hancock* (Indiana University, 1995), 301.

21 Hoogenboom, *Outlawing*, 206–7; "Dead," *NYTrib*, 12/7/1898, 7.

22 John Howe household, 1850 U.S. Census, Wisconsin, Washington County, Grafton District No. 15, 228; "Dead," *Janesville Democratic Standard*, 2/28/1855, n.p.; "Guiteau," *NYT*, 7/12/1881, 3; Lawrence Foster, *Religion and Sexuality* (University of Illinois, 1984); Charles Rosenberg, *The Trial of the Assassin Guiteau: Psychiatry and the Law in the Gilded Age* (University of Chicago, 1968), 24; "City," *Syracuse Times*, 9/23/1877, n.p.; "Free," *Utica Morning Herald*, 9/28/1877, n.p.; "Literature," *Chicago Inter-Ocean*, 12/6/1879, 10; "Announcements," *Chicago Inter-Ocean*, 1/17/1877, 8; "Jefferson," *NYH*, 12/12/1874, 8; "Court," *Chicago Inter-Ocean*, 7/20/1877, 3; "Civil," *NYTrib*, 4/21/1874, 2; "Civil," *NYTrib*, 3/17/1874, 2; "Civil," *NYTrib*, 7/16/1874, 2.

23 "Guiteau," *NYT*, 7/12/1881, 3; Lawrence Friedman, *Crime and Punishment in American History* (Basic Books, 1994), 252; Rosenberg, *Guiteau*, 36; Kenneth Ackerman, *Dark Horse* (Carroll & Graf, 2004); Letter, Guiteau to Garfield, 5/16/1881, in H. G. Hayes and C. J. Hayes, *A Complete History of the Life and Trial of Charles Julius Guiteau* (Hubbard Bros., 1882), 206–7.

24 Rosenberg, *Guiteau*, 40; Reeves, *Gentleman*, 236–37.

25 Reeves, *Gentleman*, 319, 322–24; Hoogenboom, *Hayes*, 482; "Conversion," *Hudson Evening Register*, 12/23/1882, n.p.

26 Reeves, *Gentleman*, 331–35; Frank Taussig, *Tariff History of the United States* (Putnam's, 1892), 231–36.

27 Gerald McFarland, "Dorman B. Eaton and the Genteel Reform Tradition," *JAH* 54, no. 4 (Mar. 1968), 815–22; Hoogenboom, *Outlawing*, 123, 254–55; Stephen Skowronek, *Building a New American State* (Cambridge, 1982), 64–68; Reeves, *Gentleman*, 323–24.

28 "Millionaire," *NYS*, 7/1/1885, 1; Allan Nevins, *Hamilton Fish* (Dodd, Mead, 1936), 771–73; "Bribery," *DG*, 6/18/1875, 835; "Courts," *NYH*, 9/21/1879, 13; "Departments," *Washington Critic*, 11/23/1882, 1; "Washington," *NYTrib*, 2/21/1882, 1; "Washington," *NYT*, 12/3/1882, 1; "Plate," *NYT*, 7/25/1884, 1; "Verdict," *NYT*, 11/27/1884, 8.

29   Philip Jessup, *Elihu Root*, v. 1, *1845–1909* (Dodd & Mead, 1938), 15, 48, 114–32, 136–37; "Trial," *NYT*, 5/2/1885, 2; "Father," *NYT*, 7/1/1885, 8.

30   "Father," *NYW*, 7/1/1885, 10; "Father," *NYT*, 7/1/1885, 8; "Prostrated," *NYT*, 7/3/1885, 8; "Jail," *NYT*, 7/4/1885, 8; "Penitentiary," *NYT*, 7/5/1885, 3; "Boyd," *NYT*, 7/7/1885, 3; "Charms," *NYTrib*, 7/26/1885, n.p.

31   "Court," *NYT*, 12/12/1885, 3; Hoogenboom, *Hayes*, 251, 482, 505.

32   William Wiecek, *The Lost World of Classical Legal Thought* (Oxford, 2001).

33   John Witt, "The Constitutionalization of American Self-Incrimination Doctrine, 1791–1903," 77 *Tex. L. Rev.* 825 (Mar. 1999); Katharine Hazlett, "The Nineteenth Century Origins of the Fifth Amendment Privilege against Self-Incrimination," *American Journal of Legal History* 42, no. 3 (July 1998): 235–60; Ken Kersch, "The Reconstruction of Constitutional Privacy Rights and the New American State," *Studies in American Political Development* 16 (Spring 2002): 63, 65–68, 70–72.

34   *Boyd v. United States*, 116 U.S. 630 (1886).

35   *Boyd v. United States*, 116 U.S. 623 (1886); Nicholas Parrillo, *Against the Profit Motive* (Yale, 2013), 353.

36   *Spies v. Illinois*, 123 U.S. 131 (1887); "Anarchists," *Buffalo Courier*, 11/3/1887, 1.

37   *Olmstead v. United States*, 277 U.S. 438 (1928); *Mapp v. Ohio*, 367 U.S. 643 (1961); Samuel A. Alito Jr., "Documents and the Privilege against Self-Incrimination," 48 *U. Pitt. L. Rev.* 27 (Fall 1986); Samuel Dash, *The Intruders* (Rutgers, 2004), 46–56; *Griswold v. Connecticut*, 381 U.S. 479 (1965).

38   "Washington," *NYT*, 4/10/1886, 3; "Brooklyn," *NYT*, 4/11/1886, 7; "Prison," *NYT*, 4/12/1886, 2; "Boyd," *NYT*, 7/13/1886; "Trouble," *NYT*, 12/25/1890, 8.

39   "Quaker," *New York Globe*, 10/18/1884, 4; "Bolt," *PI*, 9/25/1886, 8; "Home," *New York Freeman*, 2/14/1885, n.p.; "Restaurant," *NYP*, 7/11/1885, 1; "Axe," *NYH*, 6/11/1886, 8; "Stanch," *NYPrs*, 8/5/1888, n.p.; "Mr. Cleveland," *BWC*, 4/11/1887, n.p.

40   "Indicted," *NYH*, 3/11/1885, 5; "Summary," *NYH*, 4/28/1885, 6; "Brackett," *NYT*, 3/27/1888, 2; "Chalker," *HC*, 7/21/1890, 5; "Appointments," *BWC*, 1/21/1887, 3.

41   "Bieral," *NYT*, 1/25/1887, 2; "Insanity," *NYT*, 1/26/1887, 8; "Bieral," *NYT*, 1/27/1887, 8; "Fate," *NYW*, 1/28/1887, 6; "Insanity," *NYT*, 1/26/1887, 8; Elliot Gorn, *The Manly Art* (Cornell, 1986), 83–94, 109, 123, 135–37.

42   "Bieral," *NYT*, 1/29/1887, 8; "Bieral," *NYT*, 3/11/1887, 8; "Bieral," *NYT*, 10/10/1890, 2; "Beiral," *NYTrib*, 10/26/1890, 10; "Bugle," *NYTrib*, 3/27/1893, n.p.; *Report of the Board of Managers of the National Home for Disabled Volunteer Soldiers* (G.P.O., 1893), 715; "Poverty," *NYT*, 6/6/1887, 2; "City," *NYT*, 6/7/1887, 2; "Bieral," *NYW*, 10/1/1900, 5.

CHAPTER 14: LUXURY

1   Wayne Craven, *Stanford White* (Columbia, 2005), 76.

2   "White," *ST*, 10/2/1869, 112; Francis Church, "Richard Grant White," *Atlan-*

tic Monthly 67, no. 401 (Mar. 1891): 303–14; Mosette Broderick, *Triumvirate* (Knopf, 2010), 61–68.

3   "Confessed," *NYT* 4/5/1889, 1; "Smuggling," *NYH*, 4/6/1889, 7.

4   Robert May, "Culture Wars: The U.S. Art Lobby and Congressional Tariff Legislation," *Journal of the Gilded Age and Progressive Era* 9, no. 1 (Jan. 2010): 45, 58.

5   Raymond Cohn, "The Transition from Sail to Steam in Immigration to the United States," *Journal of Economic History* 65, no. 2 (June 2005): 475; Mark Twain, *Tom Sawyer Abroad* (Webster, 1894), 97–98; Paul Varg, *Missionaries, Chinese, and Diplomats* (Octagon Books, 1977), 13, 52–67.

6   Christopher Benfey, *The Great Wave* (Random House, 2004), 87; Broderick, *Triumvirate*, 416, 426–28.

7   Israel Finestein, *Scenes and Personalities in Anglo-Jewry* (Vallentine Mitchell, 2002), 115, 120; Meryle Secrest, *Duveen* (University of Chicago, 2005), 6–12, 18–19; *Trow's*, 1880, 427; "Worker," *NYH*, 2/7/1880, 4.

8   Kristin Hoganson, *Consumers' Imperium* (UNC, 2007), 13–20.

9   Hoganson, *Imperium*, 110, 67–68.

10 Thomas Beer, *The Mauve Decade* (Knopf, 1926); Simon Garfield, *Mauve* (Norton, 2002); "Marriage," *BWC*, 6/23/1866, 1; "Buchignani," *CT*, 11/12/1869, 4; "Academy," *NYT*, 7/8/1887, 5; "Goers," *Denver News*, 12/16/1888, 32; "Queer," *NYS*, reprinted in *Current Literature* 6, no. 1 (Jan.–Apr. 1891): 83; "Buchignani," *NYT*, 12/23/1891, 9; John Marszalek, *The Petticoat Affair* (Free Press, 1997), 228–33.

11 Timothy Gilfoyle, *A Pickpocket's Tale* (Norton, 2006), 80–91; 153–56; David Courtwright, *Dark Paradise* (Harvard, 2001), 69–79; Beer, *Mauve*, 106–7; James Ford, *Forty-odd Years in the Literary Shop* (E. P. Dutton, 1921), 203–5, 208, 213–14; "Opium," *NYTrib*, 1/30/1882, n.p.

12 "Paris," *NYPrs*, 1/25/1896, n.p.

13 "Obituary," *NYT*, 3/6/1892, 3; "Moore," *NYT*, 3/7/1892, 4; "Writer," *BE*, 3/7/1892, 4; "Death," *JM*, 3/11/1892, 4; "Obituary," *NYP*, 3/7/1892, 12; "Dead," *CT*, 3/13/1892, 25; "Brains," *Middletown Times*, 8/24/1892, 2.

14 Douglas Steeples and David Whitten, *Democracy in Desperation* (Greenwood, 1998), 50; *Pollock v. Farmers' Loan*, 157 U.S. 429 (1895).

15 "Compromises," *NYT*, 6/6/1890, 8.

16 "Russia," *St. Paul Globe*, 3/3/1878, 2; "Divorced," *WS*, 10/1/1878, 4; Charles H. Traitteur, Passport Application, 8/30/1876; "Police," *NYH*, 11/25/1879, 5.

17 'Pictures," *St. Paul Globe*, 9/12/1887, 3.

18 "Gross," *NYS*, 12/18/1891, 8; "Notes," *The Collector* 3, no. 5 (1/1/1892): 66; "Gallery," *NYS*, 1/21/1892, 6; "Spiridon," *NYS*, 1/28/1892, 5; "Fortuny," *NYS*, 1/30/1892, 6; "Spiridon," *NYS*, 2/25/1893, 2; "Spiridon," *NYS*, 3/6/1892, 3; "Kentish's," *NYS*, 3/13/1892, 13; "Buffalo," *NYH*, 4/24/1900, 5.

19 "Campbell," *NYT*, 4/28/1877, 6; "Matron," *Oswego Times*, 4/13/1877, n.p.; "Park," *NYH*, 4/2/1877, 3; "Alimony," *NYS*, 2/26/1885, n.p.; "Horses," *NYS*,

7/29/1886, n.p.; "History," *DG*, 4/27/1887, 463; "Poor," *NYW*, 1/21/1892, 9; "New York," *NYTrib*, 12/21/1892, 12; "Annie," *NYW*, 1/30/1892, 10; "Doings," *NYTel*, 2/1/1890, 5; "Pictures," *NYW*, 10/29/1895, 5; "Queer," *NYPrs*, 4/6/1893, 4; "Campbell," *NYH*, 10/7/1892, 10.

20   "Campbell," *NYH*, 10/7/1892, 10; "Lou," *NYS*, 10/8/1892, 7; Traitteur, *NYP*, 12/1/1892, 12; "Seized," *NYTrib*, 1/21/1893, 1; "Court," *NYH*, 10/29/1895, 15; "Starter," *NYW*, 4/4/1893, 6; "Auction," *NYS*, 10/14/1892, 5; "Paintings," *NYPrs*, 11/3/1895, II, 4.

21   "Agents," *NYT*, 12/29/1891, 3; "Antiquities," *NYT*, 4/15/1898, 9; "Havemeyer," *NYH*, 11/22/1901, 11.

22   Arthur J. Eddy, *A Plain Talk to Farmers about the Tariff* (A. J. Eddy, 1884); "Contempt," *Chicago-Inter Ocean*, 8/3/1893, 7; "Eddy," *NYH*, 7/22/1920, 9; Lee Sorensen, "Eddy, Arthur Jerome," *Dictionary of Art Historians* (online); *U.S. v. Eddy*, USDC, ND, E. IL., Case #25917 in NARA-GL (1899); "Rodin," *CT*, 6/2/1899, 5.

23   "Yacht," *Illustrated American* 8, no. 83 (9/19/1891): 202; "Conqueror," *NYH*, 10/9/1891, 8; "Yacht," *NYT*, 10/10/1892, 2; "Telegrams," *American Economist* 11, no. 23 (6/9/1893): 223; *The Conqueror*, 166 U.S. 110 (1896).

24   "Theobald," *NYH*, 11/27/1902, 5.

25   Manifest, S.S. *Holsatia*, 11/7/1872; "Failures," *NYT*, 10/11/1889, 5; William Theobald, *Defrauding the Government* (Myrtle, 1908), 200, 214–28; "Flashes," *LAT*, 3/31/1904, 11.

26   Theobald, *Defrauding*, ii, 496, 497, 504.

27   Theobald, *Defrauding*, 1, 5, 14, 212; "Choate," *NYS*, 6/30/1897, 9; "Diamond," *NYH*, 12/4/1897, 5; "Diamonds," *NYS*, 12/4/1897, 5; "Lasar," *NYH*, 11/18/1898, 4.

28   Theobald, *Defrauding*, 264–72; "Seizure," *NYT*, 6/27/1899, 1; "Seizure," *NYT*, 6/25/1899, 1.

29   Theobald, *Defrauding*, 264–301; "Shayne," *Nation* 69, no. 1778 (7/27/1899): 62–63; "Dodge," *NYW*, 6/15/1900, 2; *Dodge v. United States*, 131 F. 849 (1904); "Dodge," *NYT*, 1/6/1905, 7.

30   "Bonaventure's," *NYP*, 4/12/1884, 1; "Washington, *NYT*, 10/21/1886, 5; "Starting," *NYTel*, 10/21/1886, 2; "Chinese," *SFB*, 10/9/1889, 3; "Chinese," *SFB*, 11/28/1889, 2; "Seized," *WP*, 9/12/1890, 1; "Comstock," *CT*, 7/21/1894, 7.

31   "Lottery," *NYT*, 10/30/1890, 8; "Lottery," *NYT*, 11/19/1890, 8; "Lottery," *NYP*, 6/29/1891, 8; "Lottery," *NYP*, 10/14/1891, 9; "Lottery," *NYT*, 3/2/1895, 1; Elizabeth Dale, "Criminal Justice in the United States, 1790–1920," in *Cambridge History of Law in America*, v. 2, eds. Michael Grossberg and Christopher Tomlins (Cambridge, 2011), 138.

32   James McCurdy, "Romance of Smuggling across the Northwest Frontier," *Pacific Monthly* 23, no. 2 (Feb. 1910), 190; Elizabeth Gibson, *Outlaw Tales of Washington* (Globe Pequot, 2001), 1–2.

33   "Smuggling," *NYTrib*, 10/10/1883, 2; "Murdering," *NYTrib*, 12/31/1885, 1;

Erika Lee, *At America's Gates* (UNC, 2003), 24, 41, 172; Mae Ngai, *Impossible Subjects* (Princeton, 2003), 58–59; Lucy Salyer, *Laws Harsh as Tigers* (UNC, 1995), 15–32; *United States v. Kee Ho* et al., 33 F. 333 (1887); Sarah Griffith, "Race, Class, and Smuggling in Pacific Coast Chinese Immigrant Society," *Western Historical Quarterly* 35, no. 4 (Winter 2004): 473–92.

34 "Officers," *San Francisco Call*, 6/14/1904, 4; "Excise," *Batavia Spirit of the Times*, 5/22/1844, 3; Charles S. Joslyn, U.S. Passport Application, 7/25/1860; Charles S. Joslyn Household, 1860 U.S. Census, Town of Lenox, County of Madison, State of New York, 88; *Annual Report of the Adjutant-General of the State of New York for the Year 1898*, Serial No. 17 (Wynkoop, 1899), 885; *Annual Report of the Adjutant-General of the State of New York for the Year 1893*, v. 2 (Lyon, 1894), 499; "Copartnerships," *NYE*, 1/11/1866, n.p.; "Death," *NYT*, 3/19/1903, 9; "Litigation," *Buffalo Courier and Enquirer*, 3/11/1869, 1; "Clerks" [sic], *NYH*, 1/7/1871, 8; *Lang's City Directory of San Francisco*, 1875, 409; "Arrival," *New Zealand Herald*, 7/29/1876, 6.

35 "Bold," *CT*, 12/21/1888, 1; "Opium," *CT*, 2/6/1889, 1; "Opium," *SFB*, 2/14/1889, 3.

36 "Smuggling," *LAT*, 9/1/1888, 4; "Opium," *LAT*, 12/16/1888, 4; "Opium," *CT*, 12/16/1888, 15; "Opium," *CT*, 11/1/1889, 1; "Durant," *NYT*, 11/28/1889, 2; "Slope," *LAT*, 12/30/1890, 5; "Smuggling," *NOP*, 1/21/1891, 1.

37 "Smuggling," *Springfield Idaho Republican*, 1/10/1894, 5; "Smuggling," *Hawaiian Star*, 9/4/1894, 3; "Fooled," *Hawaiian Gazette*, 9/7/1894, 7; "Smuggling," *Hawaiian Gazette*, 10/9/1894, 4; "Wilder," *San Francisco Call*, 12/20/1895, 8; "Henrietta," *Hawaiian Gazette*, 1/10/1896, 1; "Before," *Hawaiian Star*, 1/10/1896, 3; *In re Schooner Henrietta*, 10 Haw. 241 (Haw. Rep. 1896); "Alameda," *Honolulu Evening Bulletin*, 1/3/1898, 1.

38 *British Columbia Directory* (Mallandaine and Williams, 1887), 51; "Liquor," *Victoria Colonist*, 6/20/1888, 1; "Opium," *Victoria Colonist*, 2/16/1889, 1; *Crocker-Langley San Francisco Directory* (Crocker, 1901), 964; "Died," *San Francisco Call*, 12/16/1903, 15.

CHAPTER 15: EXPANSION

1 Walter LaFeber, *The New Empire* (Cornell, 1963), 58–60; Franklin Cooling. "Tracy, Benjamin Franklin," *American National Biography Online* (Feb. 2000); Robert Seager, "Mahan, Alfred Thayer," *American National Biography Online* (Feb. 2000); "Benjamin F. Tracy Dead at Age of 85," *NYS*, 8/7/1915, n.p.; Eric Love, *Race over Empire* (UNC, 2004), 91–93.

2 "Personal," *Syracuse Journal*, 12/27/1870, n.p.; "Miscellaneous," *NYH*, 9/2/1871, 2; Josette Capriles Goldish, "The De Limas of New York," unpublished manuscript, 6–9; Abram Wakeman, *History and Reminiscences of Lower Wall Street* (Spice Mill Publishing, 1914), 116; *Social Register, New York, 1898* (Social Register Association, 1897), 104.

3   "Blanco," *NYT*, 6/13/1884, 5; "World," *NYT*, 5/4/1896, 8; "Flamborough," *NYPrs*, 3/2/1888, 4; "Newton," *NYT*, 4/3/1888, 1; "City," *NYT*, 3/1/1889, 3; "Compensation," *NYTrib*, 8/10/1889, 3.

4   "Trade," *NYT*, 8/8/1889, 8; "Stupid," *NYH*, 8/15/1889, 5; Thomas Paterson, "American Businessmen and Consular Service Reform, 1890's to 1906," *Business History Review* 40, no. 1 (Spring 1966): 77–97.

5   Rick Daysog, "Damon Heiresses," *Honolulu Advertiser*, 6/19/2005, online.

6   Ralph Kuykendall, *The Hawaiian Kingdom*, v. 3, *1874–1893* (University of Hawaii, 1967), 59–61.

7   Robert Turrell, *Capital and Labour on the Kimberley Diamond Fields, 1871–1890* (Cambridge, 1987), 190; "Imperial," *Times of India*, 5/17/1881, 3; Kuykendall, *Kingdom*, 124–125.

8   "Tuesday," *Pacific Commercial Advertiser*, 6/25/1881, 3; "Letter No. 53," *Pacific Commercial Advertiser*, 9/3/1881, 1; "Hoffnung," *Pacific Commercial Advertiser*, 11/10/1883, 1.

9   "Sheep," *Colonies and India*, 10/30/1885, 10; Gerald Horne, *White Pacific* (University of Hawaii, 2007), 122; Kuykendall, *Kingdom*, 334–37, 354.

10 Kuykendall, *Kingdom*, 350–67; Lily Lim Chong and Harry Ball, "Opium and the Law: Hawaii, 1856–1900," *Chinese America* (2010): 65–66.

11 "Hoffnung," *Honolulu Herald*, 6/29/1887, n.p.; "Yankees," *MS*, 7/11/1887, n.p.; "Dancing," *Hawaiian Gazette*, 7/5/1887, 5; "Minister," *NYH*, 10/16/1892, 16; "Goldsmid," *Gentlewoman*, 8/16/1913, 195.

12 Kathleen Mapes, *Sweet Tyranny* (University of Illinois, 2009); Ida Tarbell, *The Tariff in Our Times* (Macmillan, 1911), 195–99, 222–27; F. W. Taussig, "The McKinley Tariff Act," *The Economic Journal* 1, no. 2 (June 1891), 344.

13 Kuykendall, *Kingdom*, 486–87, 492; LaFeber, *Empire*, 142–43; "Faith," *CT*, 3/7/1891, 8.

14 Kuykendall, *Kingdom*, 582–623.

15 "Annexation," *NYH*, 4/29/1893, 9; "Many," *WS*, 11/14/1893, 4; "Instructions," *WS*, 11/16/1893, 1; "Seekers," *WS*, 5/31/1894, 4; "Renunciation," *Hawaiian Star*, 2/7/1895, 6; "Correspondent," *Hawaiian Star*, 5/13/1893, 2.

16 Louisiana Historical Records Survey, *Inventory of the Parish Archives of Louisiana* (Service Division Work Projects Administration, 1942), 8; Robert Highsaw, *Edward Douglass White* (LSU, 1981), 16–17, 50–51; Henry Abraham, *Justices, Presidents, and Senators* (Rowman & Littlefield, 1999), 109; Tarbell, *Tariff*, 222–27, esp. 226–27.

17 *Pollock v. Farmers' Loan*, 157 U.S. 429 (1895); F. W. Taussig "The Tariff Act of 1897," *Quarterly Journal of Economics* 12, no. 1 (Oct. 1897), 60–64; Tarbell, *Tariff*, 240–45.

18 "Hawaii," *BS*, 1/22/1895, 6; "Levey," *Honolulu Bulletin*, 8/25/1896, 8; "Return," *Hawaiian Gazette*, 3/15/1895, 5; "Death," *Hawaiian Independent*, 8/24/1896, 2; "Levey," *Hawaiian Gazette*, 8/25/1896, 2.

19 "Smuggling," *Victoria Colonist*, 1/11/1896, 6; "Before," *Hawaiian Star*,

1/10/1896, 3; "Taking," *Hawaiian Star,* 1/10/1896, 3; "Henrietta," *Hawaiian Gazette,* 1/10/1896, 1; Ronald DeLorme, "Revenuers in Paradise," *Hawaiian Journal of History* 15 (1981): 72–73.

20 Walter LaFeber, "The Constitution and United States Foreign Policy: An Interpretation," *JAH* 74, no. 3 (Dec. 1987): 695–717; William Leuchtenburg, "Progressivism and Imperialism: The Progressive Movement and American Foreign Policy, 1898–1916," *MVHR* 39, no. 3. (Dec., 1952): 483–504; Paul Kramer, "The Spoils of Empire: Debating Corruption, State-Building and Colonialism in the Early 20th Century," unpublished essay, 2005.

21 "Around," *GFH,* 1/15/1893, 3; "Upheld," *GFH* 10/30/1894, 1; "Pepke," *Minneapolis Journal,* 6/15/1901, 20; *Pepke v. Cronan,* 155 U.S. 100 (1895); Transcript of Record, *Fourteen Diamond Rings, Emil J. Pepke, Claimant, Plaintiff in-error v. United States,* Supreme Court of the United States, October Term 1900, 5.

22 Frank McVey, "Sugar Importations and Revenues," *Journal of Political Economy* 7, no. 1 (Dec. 1898), 98–99.

23 "Expansion," *NYT,* 11/23/1899, 6; "Porto Rico," *CT,* 3/3/1900, 1; "Jones," *CT,* 6/2/1908, 7.

24 "Pepke," *Minneapolis Journal,* 6/15/1901, 20.

25 Bartholomew Sparrow, *The Insular Cases and the Emergence of American Empire* (University of Kansas, 2006), 55; "Penniless," *NYT,* 11/2/1913, SM12; *De Lima v. Bidwell,* 182 U.S. 1 (1901); *Goetze v. United States,* 182 U.S. 221(1901); *Dooley v. United States,* 182 U.S. 222 (1901); *Armstrong v. United States,* 182 U.S. 243 (1901); *Downes v. Bidwell,* 182 U.S. 244 (1901).

26 Sparrow, *Insular,* 76–77; "Coudert," *NYT,* 12/21/1903, 1; "Bliss," *NYT,* 9/3/1897, 7.

27 William Wiecek, *The Lost World of Classical Legal Thought* (Oxford, 2001), 152–54; Charles McCurdy, "Peckham, Rufus Wheeler," *American National Biography Online* (Feb. 2000); "Jayne," *NYT,* 2/24/1875, 2; "Nominated," *NYT,* 2/12/1892, 5; Henry Abraham, *Justices, Presidents, and Senators* (Rowman & Littlefield, 1999), 113–16; Gerald Neuman, "Whose Constitution," *Yale Law Journal* 100, no. 4 (Jan. 1991): 960–62; Mark Weiner, "Teutonic Constitutionalism: The Role of Ethno-Juridical Discourse in the Spanish-American War," *Foreign in a Domestic Sense,* ed. Burnett and Marshall (Duke, 2001), 80 n.74.

28 *Fourteen Diamond Rings v. United States,* 183 U.S. 176 (1901); Transcript of Record, *Fourteen Diamond Rings;* "North Line," *Bismarck Tribune,* 10/4/1899, 3; "Pleased," *Titusville Herald,* 5/29/1901, n.p.; Finley Peter Dunne, quoted in Martin Nolan, "Mr. Dooley," *BG,* 11/30/2000, n.p.

29 "Coudert," *NYT,* 7/3/1901, 6; "Coudert," *Rochester Democrat and Chronicle,* 7/5/1901, 6; "Soldier Peddler," *CT,* 2/2/1902, 2.

30 "Coudert," *NYT,* 7/3/1901, 6.

31 "Elias S. A. de Lima," *Bankers* 80, no. 4 (Apr. 1910): 661–62; "Dies," *NYT,* 11/24/1928, 11; "Penniless," *NYT,* 11/2/1913, SM12; Robert Sloss, "Coffee,"

World's Work 24, no. 2 (June 1912): 194–205; "Pepke," *Bismarck Tribune*, 5/22/1902, 2; "North Dakota," *GFH*, 5/24/1902, 3; "Correspondence," *GFH*, 8/8/1902, 3; "Correspondence," *GFH*, 2/10/1905, 2; "Pepke," *GFH*, 7/7/1905, 1; "Medicine Men," *GFH*, 6/5/1910, 8; "Socialists," *GFH*, 9/28/1912, 4; "Leaguers," *Bismarck Tribune*, 11/13/1924, 1; Robert Morlan, *Political Prairie Fire* (University of Minnesota, 1955).

32 "Mr. Hoffnung," *Hawaii Holomua*, 10/12/1893, 2; "Portuguese," *Hawaiian Gazette*, 11/11/1898, 7; "Portuguese," *Hawaiian Star*, 1/20/1899, 1; "Syndicate," *Hawaiian Gazette* 7/3/1900, 3; "Hoffnung," *TL*, 4/9/1912, 9; "Winchester," *TL*, 6/30/1962, 10; "Dowager," *TL*, 9/7/1995, 19.

33 *Territory of Hawaii v. Mankichi*, 190 U.S. 197 (1903); *Kepner v. United States*, 195 U.S. 100 (1904); *Dorr v. United States*, 195 U.S. 138 (1904); Sparrow, *Insular*, 200–202; Paul Kramer, *The Blood of Government* (UNC, 2006), 140, 157.

CHAPTER 16: TRANSFORMATION

1   "Lawrence," *NYT*, 1/31/1914, 11; "Lawrence," *NYC*, 2/14/1914, 8; "Manager," *NYW*, 10/3/1901, n.p.; "Lionel," *NYW*, 4/7/1903, 2.

2   "Prosecutions," 9/16/1881, 3; "Swearing," *New York Whole Truth*, 9/29/1882, n.p.; "Unsettled," *NYH*, 12/31/1882, 11; "Departure," *NYH*, 1/14/1883, 12; "Died," *NYH*, 8/1/1883, 9; "Jokers," *NYH*, 12/17/1884, 9; "Consumed," *NYTrib*, 12/18/1884, 8.

3   "Back," *Columbia State*, 9/17/1909, 10; "Manager," *NYW*, 10/3/1901, n.p.; "Excuses," *NYT*, 10/8/1883, 5; "Theft," *NYH*, 10/8/1883, 5; "Accused," *NYS*, 10/8/1883, 1; "City," *NYT*, 10/9/1883, 8; "Lionel," *NYH*, 10/9/1883, 10; "Embezzlement," *SFB*, 8/25/1884, 1; "Lionel," *SFB*, 8/26/1884, 2; "Lionel," *SFB*, 8/27/1884, 2; "Items," *Sacramento Record-Union*, 8/29/1884, 2.

4   "Obituary," *NYT*, 7/17/1890, 5; "Dead," *NYS*, 7/20/1890, 1; "Smuggler," *NYPrs*, 7/21/1890, 6; "Conspirator," *HC*, 7/21/1890, 1; "Smugglers," *BAD*, 7/21/1890, n.p.; "Smugglers," *Waukesha Freeman*, 7/28/1890, 1; "Gotham," *NOP*, 7/25/1890, 6; "Died," *NYH*, 10/13/1890, S1; "Deaths," *JM*, 10/17/1890, 6.

5   "Divorce," *NYS*, 9/5/1890, 2; "Lawrence," *NYH*, 5/20/1892, 5; "Arrest," *NYTel*, 5/27/1897, 3; "Theatre," *NYTel*, 7/23/1901, 1; "Police," *NYH*, 4/1/1902, 11; "Roof," *NYPrs*, 4/1/1902, n.p.

6   "Thaw," *NYT*, 6/26/1906, n.p.; "Stanford," *NYS*, 6/26/1906, 1; "Tragic," *San Francisco Call*, 6/29/1906, 1–2; "Thaw," *Syracuse Herald*, 6/28/1906, 1; Harry Thaw, *The Traitor* (Dorrance & Co., 1926), 141–45; Paul Baker, *Stanny* (Free Press, 1989), 372–74; Mosette Broderick, *Triumvirate* (Knopf, 2010), 494–96.

7   Baker, *Stanny*, 331–33, 385–93; Broderick, *Triumvirate*, 477–79, 502–4.

8   Donna Wood, "Business Support for the 1906 Food and Drug Act," *Business History Review* 59, no. 3 (Autumn 1985): 403–32.

9   Andrew Wender Cohen, "Unions, Modernity, and the Decline of American

Economic Nationalism," *and U.S. Labor*, eds. Nelson Lichtenstein and Elizabeth Tandy Shermer (University of Pennsylvania, 2011), 20; Ida Tarbell, "Tariff in Our Times," *American Magazine* 64, no. 2 (June 1907), 91–92, 98–99, 143–44, 157; Dana Frank, *Buy American* (Beacon, 1999), 45, 49–51; Joanne Reitano, *The Tariff Question in the Gilded Age* (Penn State, 1994), 86; Kathryn Kish Sklar, *Florence Kelley and the Nation's Work* (Yale, 1995), 37–38, 82, 86–87, 111.

10   David Courtwright, *Dark Paradise* (Harvard, 2001), 100–4; Thomas Dormandy, *Opium* (Yale, 2012), 200–211; Peter Andreas, *Smuggler's Nation* (Oxford, 2013), 257–60.

11   "Loeb's," *Auburn Weekly Bulletin*, 8/28/1909, 3; "Loeb," *NYS*, 11/19/1909, 5; "Sugar?," *NYS*, 11/19/1909, 5; "Loeb," *NYT*, 9/20/1937, 23; "Employes," *NYH*, 10/15/1910, 5; "Duveen," *NYS*, 10/15/1910, 5; "Duveen," *NYH*, 10/18/1910, 6; Meryle Secrest, *Duveen* (University of Chicago, 2005), 95–99.

12   "Culprit," *CD*, 8/12/1911, 3; "Loeb," *NYPrs*, 12/28/1910, 3; "Loeb," *LAT*, 12/29/1910, 14; "Fight," *Albany Journal*, 12/29/1910, 1.

13   "Fools," *Puck* 66, no. 1702 (10/13/1909): 2; "Ordeal," *Puck* 50, no. 1282 (9/25/1901): 8; "Customs-Inspector," *Puck* 70, no. 1811 (11/15/1911): 5; "Animal," *Puck*, 74, no. 1917 (11/26/1913): 4; Frank Nankwell, "Bagdad," *Puck* 66, no. 1697 (9/8/1909): 5; L. M. Glackens, "Customhouse," *Puck* 67, no. 1734 (5/25/1910): 3; Nuttall, "Santa," *Puck* 60, no. 1553 (12/5/1906): 37.

14   "Johnson," *CD*, 4/6/1912, 5; "Suit," *CT*, 6/11/1912, 8; "Championships," *NYH*, 7/5/1912, 13; "M'Cartney," *CT*, 7/12/1912, 15; "Johnson," *CD*, 7/13/1912, 7; "Kills," *CD*, 9/14/1912, 1; "Smuggling," *Oakland Tribune*, 4/23/1913, 1; Geoffrey Ward, *Unforgivable Blackness* (Random House, 2004), 278, 287–89, 327–31.

15   Ajay Mehrotra, *Making the Modern American Fiscal State* (Cambridge, 2013), 278.

16   William Hunt, *Thirteenth Census of the United States taken in the year 1910*, v. 4, *Population 1910: Occupation Statistics* (G.P.O., 1914), 26; Alice Kessler-Harris, *Out to Work* (Oxford, 2003), 122; T. B. Thorpe, "The New York Custom-House," *Harper's New Monthly Magazine* 43 (1871), 23; Ida Harper, ed., *The History of Woman Suffrage*, v. 5, *1900–1920* (NAWSA, 1922), 432; Howard Allen, "Geography and Politics: Voting on Reform Issues in the United States Senate, 1911–1916," *Journal of Southern History* 27, no. 2 (1961): 216–28; Robert Johnston, *The Radical Middle Class* (Princeton, 2003), 33.

17   Samuel Gompers, editorial, *American Federationist* 20, no. 7 (July 1913): 530; Lyle Cooper, "The Tariff and Organized Labor," *American Economic Review* 20, no. 2 (June 1930): 210–25; Daniel Mitchell, *Essays on Labor and International Trade* (Institute of Industrial Relations, 1970), 49; "Wilson," *NYT*, 5/16/1913, 2; Cohen, "Unions," 22–23.

18   "Lawrence," *NYTrib*, 6/10/1913, 7; "Suicide," *NYS*, 12/8/1912, 1; "Winchester,"

TL, 6/30/1962, 10; "Whitley," *Emporia Weekly Gazette*, 10/23/1919, 5; "Duffy,"
NYT, 7/28/1894, 8; "Lone," *Iowa City Citizen*, 1/7/1922, 4; "Eytinge," *NYT*,
12/21/1911, 11; Letter to the author, 7/2006; Nelson Aldrich, ed., *George, Being
George* (Random House, 2008), 12.

19 Ward Moore, *Bring the Jubilee* (Ballantine, 1953); Janet Allured et al., *Lake
Charles* (Arcadia 2012), 85; Craig Colten, *An Unnatural Metropolis* (LSU,
2005), 177.

INDEX

Page numbers in *italics* refer to illustrations.